Modern Witchcraft

by Lorraine Monteagut, PhD

for dummies®
A Wiley Brand

Modern Witchcraft For Dummies®

Published by: **John Wiley & Sons, Inc.**, 111 River Street, Hoboken, NJ 07030-5774, www.wiley.com

Published simultaneously in Canada

For general information on our other products and services, please contact our Customer Care Department within the U.S. at 877-762-2974, outside the U.S. at 317-572-3993, or fax 317-572-4002. For technical support, please visit https://hub.wiley.com/community/support/dummies.

Wiley publishes in a variety of print and electronic formats and by print-on-demand. Some material included with standard print versions of this book may not be included in e-books or in print-on-demand. If this book refers to media that is not included in the version you purchased, you may download this material at http://booksupport.wiley.com. For more information about Wiley products, visit www.wiley.com.

Library of Congress Control Number: 2025933220

ISBN 978-1-394-30363-2 (pbk); ISBN 978-1-394-30365-6 (ebk); 978-1-394-30366-3 (ebk)

SKY10099376_030425

Modern Witchcraft

for dummies®
A Wiley Brand

Contents at a Glance

Table of Contents

Introduction

Modern witches stand at the intersection of countless roads. Paths of magical practice have proliferated in recent decades, connecting diverse histories and traditions. Old paths fork into unknown territories and new footpaths are constantly treaded. Some roads are dead ends. Some lead to private drives with access codes. And some are downright dangerous. If you're just now stepping onto this crossroads, it's challenging to get your bearings. Where exactly have you come from, and where are you going?

Magical practice has no universal roadmap, so new witches are increasingly walking the crooked path, blending different influences and beliefs together as they go along. The crooked path is nothing new; witchcraft has always been for those who walk their own way. This book will guide you through the tangle of information about witchcraft and light your way as a modern witch when you're ready to plot your own course.

About This Book

This book is about *modern* witchcraft. It's not a history book. The concept of witchcraft has existed for as long as humans have, and you could fall into thousands of rabbit holes trying to find the universal witch. Although I always encourage research and nuance, I'll save you some time and let you know that nobody has ever agreed on the definition of the witch. The witch is constantly being defined.

In this book, you'll learn about modern witchcraft beyond Wicca and the neopagan traditions that arose in Europe. These traditions have dominated the witchcraft discourse for decades, and Wicca has erroneously been considered synonymous with witchcraft. Although these strong and well-documented traditions are important, they're just one territory in a larger world. This book widens the scope of witchcraft to encompass folk magic across the world, inspiring modern witches from all walks of life.

What you *will* find in this book is a guide that will help you orient yourself to what witchcraft means today. What inspires real contemporary witches? What are some common practices that you can start right now? What opportunities and challenges should you be aware of as you grow into your own practice?

To make it easy, I've organized the content of this book into seven parts:

Part 1: Opening to Modern Witchcraft. The first part of the book outlines common terms and introduces pagan pantheons and regional folk magic practices that inspire modern practice. I outline the first steps of dedicating yourself to "the Craft," including setting up your space, selecting tools, casting spells, and choosing common paths of practice. I touch on ethical topics like cultural appropriation and hexing.

Part 2: Dabbling in Witchy Mythologies. What stories do you keep turning to? This part explores the witch folklore that has made it into the modern lexicon, revolving around the triple goddess: the maiden, the mother, and the crone. This mythological framework has expanded to encompass more diverse cultures that are destigmatizing the witch of the past. Throughout this part of the book, I offer spells and rituals to begin wielding energy like the witches you're learning about.

Part 3: Practicing Your Craft. What do witches do? This part gets really hands-on. You'll learn how to initiate into your practice and start your own grimoire (often referred to as a book of shadows). You'll learn how to clear and protect your space and how to set up a home altar. You'll learn spell work basics and how to choose and consecrate your tools and symbols. I present more complex spells and specific rituals, particularly candle magic.

Part 4: Exploring Paths of the Modern Witch. What type of witch are you? Each chapter in this part dives deeper into specific paths of witchcraft. I start with the divination chapter, which explores intuition, psychic magic, and different modalities like tarot reading and scrying. Next is the chapter on green witchcraft, which focuses on honoring the land and herbal magic. Then comes the chapter about cosmic witchcraft, astrology, and planetary magic. The last chapter deals with energy, focusing on the body's energy and different states of consciousness.

Part 5: Expanding Beyond Personal Practice. This part of the book introduces the coven, offering a guide to practice with others and perform ceremonies. I cover buzz terms like *gatekeeping*, *holding space*, and *spiritual activism*. I offer some of the wisdom I've gathered from my own practice to help you avoid common pitfalls and align your work with your ethics.

Part 6: The Part of Tens. Here, you'll find ten foundational spells you can use immediately and ten days of observance in modern witchcraft.

The Appendix. The appendix provides common associations and correspondences for symbols and materials you'd use in specific paths of practice, including tarot meanings for divination, herbal properties for green witchcraft, astrology associations for cosmic witchcraft, and crystal properties to work with energy.

I've written this book to help you orient yourself to witchcraft and explore your individual path in a way that's as informed, safe, and fun as possible. This book isn't an encyclopedia or a complete compendium. Instead, it's a starting point for further exploration. I hope that it helps you understand what kind of witch you'd like to be and inspires you to learn more, serving as a handy reference to return to again and again.

Foolish Assumptions

I imagine that if you picked up this book, you're either curious about witchcraft, or you're a witch somewhere in the beginning or middle of your practice who is looking for an inclusive education about the new wave of witchcraft. You're not looking for a history book or a book about a particular religion or practice, though this book touches on many histories and religions.

I assume that you're coming to this book with no previous knowledge of witchcraft, but I also considered more advanced witches as I wrote. If you're anything like me, you'll always find value in the foundational topics. I intend for this book to appeal to those who forever retain a "beginner's mind" and would benefit from my perspective as a synthesist of worldwide practices and contemporary trends.

Icons Used in This Book

Throughout this book, icons in the margins highlight certain types of valuable information that call out for your attention. Following are the icons you'll encounter and a brief description of each.

TIP

Marks tips and shortcuts that you can use to make your magical practice easier.

REMEMBER

Highlights information that's especially important for you to know.

FUN FACT

Denotes bits of information that are simply interesting to know or that can deepen your understanding of a topic.

WARNING

Tells you to watch out! It marks important information that may save you headaches down the road.

Beyond the Book

In addition to the abundance of information and guidance related to modern witchcraft that I provide in this book, you can find even more help and information online at Dummies.com. Check out this book's online Cheat Sheet: Just go to www.dummies.com and search for "Modern Witchcraft For Dummies Cheat Sheet."

1 Opening to Modern Witchcraft

IN THIS PART . . .

Orient to common concepts and terms in modern witchcraft. Get acquainted with neopaganism and the traditions and pantheons that inform modern witches. Understand "reclaiming" movements and how you might fit into them.

Learn about ancestral and regional folk practices. Find information on indigenous wisdom and the ways it has inspired modern spiritualities. Incorporate folk magic and folklore into your practices.

Identify your personal entry points into witchcraft practice. Understand the difference between dedication and initiation. Learn the basics of starting your practice. Explore different paths of the modern witch.

Find information about cultural appropriation. Develop your own ethics for your personal practice. Discover ways to engage in spiritual activism.

IN THIS CHAPTER

» Introducing concepts of modern witchcraft

» Clarifying common terms, including neopaganism

» Considering witchcraft outside of Wicca and European traditions

Chapter 1
Reclaiming Witchcraft

Witch is a bad word, historically speaking. It has carried negative connotations and been associated with evil practices. Modern witchcraft turns the witch into something new. *Reclaiming* movements have embraced the witch as a symbol of healing, empowerment, and resistance. Today's witch defies neat definitions and shakes off the stigma of the past, constantly shifting to reflect the ideologies and challenges of the times. To call yourself a witch is to call back the power that was taken from all those who were cast to the margins or branded as dangerous "others." Even now, identifying as a witch can be an act of courage. The shadow of the evil witch is still there.

This chapter serves as an introduction to modern witchcraft, in contrast to the historical record of oppression and persecution that witches and those accused of witchcraft have endured over the centuries. I cover key terms and introduce the myriad neopagan practices out there. The chapter ends with some context to consider if you're looking to come out of the broom closet yourself.

Before Wicca, Beyond Wicca

First things first. Yes, witches are real. I am one, and if you're reading this, you might be one too. Or maybe you've heard that people are walking around calling themselves witches, and you're interested in learning what that's all about. All are welcome here.

Take a moment to picture a witch.

Whatever you've imagined, it's probably not what most witches look like. Maybe you've pictured what you imagine a Wiccan to look like; Wicca and witchcraft are often confused. Or maybe you've conjured an image that resembles something like what's shown in Figure 1-1. While I do love a good broom, most witches don't look like the stereotype unless they're in costume.

FIGURE 1-1: A pretty cool illustration of a witch.

Dugald Stewart Walker/The New York Public Library/Public domain

TIP

Anyone can be a witch, and they can look like anything. If you want to avoid being cursed (only half joking), I suggest accepting the way everyone likes to self-identify, as long as it's not harming anyone.

In fact, acceptance and individuality are core tenets of modern witchcraft. The modern witch, like its predecessors, resists classification. Most books on witchcraft grapple with definitions and histories in their first chapters. As a scholar of witchcraft, I consider this an important though sometimes frustrating task. Seeing how witches and authors of vastly different perspectives define the witch has helped me expand my views and refine my own identity as a modern witch.

TIP

Think of a few words that you associate with the term *witch*. This will reveal a lot about your underlying assumptions.

In the past, the label *witch* was hurled at those who didn't fit neatly in society. These individuals may not have even identified as witches, but simply lived life differently. It's no coincidence that most people who were called witches were female, elderly, disabled, or (gasp!) single hermits with penchants for gardening. Often, these "witches" challenged the status quo and were deemed a threat.

REMEMBER

Understanding modern witchcraft is a matter of perspective. Knowing where you stand is more important than perfect definitions and histories. Your own beliefs, backgrounds, and desires are valid and probably compatible with today's forms of witchcraft unless you follow a religion that explicitly forbids any kind of magic. There are even a good many Christian witches these days! Modern witchcraft is the confluence of many perspectives and beliefs.

The number of people worldwide who identify as witches isn't precisely documented; it varies depending on cultural, religious, and individual interpretations of witchcraft. Modern witchcraft and related practices related to paganism and folk magic have seen significant growth, particularly in the United States and Europe. Some surveys suggest that hundreds of thousands to a few million people in the world identify as Wiccan or other kinds of neopagans.

WARNING

Don't mistake witchcraft for Wicca — they're not the same thing. *Witchcraft* is a broad term that encompasses many different magical traditions and practices, whereas Wicca is a specific religion. In other words, all Wiccans are witches, but not all witches are Wiccans.

Coming to terms

When I was growing up, my understanding of witches was shaped greatly by Wicca because it was the main form of witchcraft portrayed on television, and the only witches I encountered in real life were Wiccans.

REMEMBER

Although Wicca comes in many forms, including Gardnerian, Dianic, and Alexandrian, it's generally a modern, nature-centered religion that celebrates the cycles of Earth, honors a dual divinity often represented as the goddess and the god, and incorporates rituals, magic, and seasonal festivals. Wicca is an eclectic religion that synthesizes elements from a variety of sources, including ancient pagan traditions, Western esotericism, and folklore. Find out more in *Wicca & Witchcraft For Dummies* by Diane Smith (Wiley).

As a child, I was especially drawn to Wiccan reimaginings of Greek mythology, a common gateway for many witch-curious folk! But I encountered the opposing beliefs of some of my Latin American family members, who viewed witches as inherently bad. They associated witches with monsters lurking in folk stories or the elusive "devil worshippers."

FUN FACT

Speak of the devil: Despite common misconceptions, many modern Satanists are nice, normal people. Most don't even worship the devil. Members of the Church of Satan and the Satanic Temple typically reject the concept of a literal Satan, instead focusing on self-empowerment, individualism, and the rejection of oppressive systems.

Satanists who do worship the devil see their work as a reclamation of the horned gods of nature-based pagan traditions. Satanism is philosophically distinct from witchcraft, though the two are often conflated due to shared outsider status in mainstream culture.

These conflicting images fueled my curiosity and created a tension that I still wrestle with to this day. The cultural perceptions of witches are vast and often contradictory, ranging from empowered healers and wise figures to villains in folklore. These differing views reflect societal attitudes about power, gender, and spirituality.

To complicate things further, you might hear the term *witch* used interchangeably with other terms, though each carries its own unique context. These include the following:

- **Sorcerer:** A practitioner of magic who often uses their power for personal gain, associated with manipulating energy to their will.
- **Warlock:** Originally meaning "oath-breaker," this term was historically used pejoratively to refer to diabolical practitioners. In modern contexts, some male witches have reclaimed the term, but others avoid it due to its negative connotations.
- **Magician:** A broader term for someone who performs magical acts, ranging from ritualistic magic to stage illusions.
- **Wizard:** Often linked to fantasy and literature, the wizard is typically depicted as a scholarly figure who studies and practices magic.

Pop culture further confuses the understandings of these terms. Fictional representations vary greatly and influence understandings of modern witchcraft.

REMEMBER

The word *witchcraft* is also wrought to the whims of the moment. It's often associated with feminine power due to its association with healing, midwifery, and nature worship, which are roles that women often fulfill.

However, witchcraft today is a gender-inclusive practice. Men, nonbinary individuals, and those of diverse gender identities also claim the title of witch, reflecting the universal appeal of its principles. Additionally, modern witchcraft challenges traditional gender norms, embracing fluidity and inclusivity in its rituals and communities.

Just as the idea of a witch is fluid and ever-changing, so too is the concept of magic. It's the word people use when they don't fully understand something. In witchcraft, magic operates on the belief that the cosmos is interconnected, a unified whole where energy can be moved and directed with intention. You might come across *magic* used interchangeably with many other terms, including these:

- **The Occult:** *Occult* means hidden. That's how I use it — magic as something subtle, concealed, and full of potential — but it's also tied to specific traditions of magical practice, including Thelema, the Hermetic Order of the Golden Dawn, and the Rosicrucians. (See Chapter 9, where I cover initiation into different kinds of occult traditions.)
- **Animism:** *Animism* is the belief that all things — living and nonliving — possess a spirit or consciousness. This includes animals, plants, stones, rivers, mountains, and even human-made objects. For witches, working with animism means recognizing and interacting with the spiritual essence of the natural world and the objects within it.
- **Esotericism:** *Esotericism* refers to a body of knowledge or practices that are meant to be understood by a select, initiated group, often focusing on hidden, symbolic, or spiritual truths beyond the ordinary. It encompasses traditions like alchemy and ceremonial magic that explore the deeper nature of reality.
- **Mysticism:** *Mysticism* is the pursuit of direct, personal experience of the divine or ultimate reality, often through practices like meditation, prayer, or ecstatic states, aiming to transcend ordinary perception and achieve spiritual union or enlightenment.

Many of the terms used in modern witchcraft today come from European traditions and *Europaganism*, including many pre-Christian, polytheistic, and nature-centered spiritual traditions and practices that were historically prevalent across Europe. These include the religious systems of the Celts, Norse, Slavs, Greeks, Romans, and other ancient European cultures. They were characterized by polytheism, connection to nature, oral traditions, and rituals and festivals.

"Re-"volutionizing the Craft

The *Craft* is a term often used to refer to the practice of modern witchcraft, encompassing a wide range of magical, spiritual, and ritual practices. (Not to be mistaken for the 1990s cult classic film that I reference many times in this book!) A lot of "re"s are at play in the Craft, including reviving, reconstructing, and reclaiming older traditions.

FUN FACT

I was called to my scholarly work in witchcraft because I noticed that most books centered only on European pagan histories, without mentioning histories and traditions across the Global South, including Africa, Latin America, and Asia. That realization inspired me to write my first book, *Brujas: The Magic and Power of Witches of Color* (Chicago Review Press), to trace the ways modern witches reclaim their ancestral traditions, particularly *brujería*, the Spanish word for witchcraft. Like witchcraft, *brujería* is an umbrella term that encompasses magical practices throughout the indigenous Americas and the Afro-Caribbean diaspora. A modern *bruja* is a witch who reclaims these practices.

Reclaiming literally means taking back. You might hear that word thrown around by modern witches because a consensus purports that witches are recovering practices that were once stigmatized or oppressed. Although this is true, that consensus sometimes carries a false expectation that what modern witches do must be rooted in ancient paganism, particularly from Europe.

FUN FACT

The word *pagan* originates from the Latin term *pāgānus*, which initially meant "villager," "rustic," or "country dweller."

During the rise of Christianity in the Roman Empire, the term *pagan* came to be used pejoratively to describe those who continued practicing polytheistic or traditional local religions, often in rural areas, because Christianity was more quickly adopted in urban centers. Today *pagan* refers to practitioners of pre-Christian, polytheistic, or earth-centered spiritual traditions. Although paganism isn't inherently synonymous with magic, many pagans integrate rituals and spiritual practices that naturally overlap with witchcraft and other magical systems.

REMEMBER

Neopaganism is a modern spiritual movement that seeks to revive, reinterpret, or draw inspiration from pre-Christian, polytheistic, or nature-based religions. It's also characterized by a focus on earth-centered spirituality and reverence for the cycles of nature, and it usually involves the worship of multiple deities from various traditions across the world.

For instance, Wicca is a modern neopagan tradition, though its founders might have conceived of it as an ancient practice. Witches today still disagree about Wicca's origins. Among religious studies scholars, it's generally assumed that Wicca, along with other European neopagan traditions, blends elements of pagan religion and folklore with modern interpretations of magic — including Christian theology, as it was the dominant religion that neopaganism arose under.

RECLAIMING THE WITCH

When Gerald Gardner introduced Wicca to the public in the mid-20th century, he claimed it was the survival of an ancient, pre-Christian witchcraft tradition. Gardner based much of his assertion on the work of Margaret Murray, whose witch-cult hypothesis suggested that a hidden, pagan fertility cult had persisted throughout European history under the guise of witchcraft. However, Murray's theory, presented in *The Witch-Cult in Western Europe* (1921), has been largely discredited by historians due to a lack of reliable evidence and overinterpretation of trial records.

Gardner's Wicca, while deeply influenced by Murray's ideas, was more accurately a synthesis of older folk practices, ceremonial magic, and esotericism, combined with Gardner's own innovations. Despite this, Gardner insisted on its ancient lineage, giving Wicca an air of historical authenticity that helped it gain credibility and attract followers during the mid-century pagan revival. Doreen Valiente, known as the "Mother of Modern Witchcraft," played a pivotal role in extending Gerald Gardner's legacy. As Gardner's High Priestess in the early 1950s, Valiente revised and expanded the foundational rituals and texts of Wicca, including the *Book of Shadows*, bringing poetic elegance and coherence to its structure.

Valiente's understanding of folklore and her vision of Wicca as a nature-based, inclusive spiritual path helped establish it as a structured and appealing modern religion. Her influence ensured that Wicca moved beyond Gardner's initial framework, becoming a tradition with broader spiritual and cultural resonance. While Gardner is credited as the founder of Wicca, Valiente's work ensured its survival and growth into the widespread spiritual movement it is today.

Alexandrian Wicca emerged in the 1960s as an offshoot of Gardnerian Wicca, founded by Alex and Maxine Sanders in the United Kingdom. While it drew heavily on Gerald Gardner's teachings and the framework of Gardnerian Wicca, Alexandrian Wicca incorporated additional elements and practices, distinguishing it as a separate tradition. Generally more open to adaptation and experimentation, it reflects Alex Sanders' theatrical personality and innovative approach.

Though the idea of Wicca as an unbroken ancient tradition has been debunked, this does not diminish its cultural or spiritual significance. Wicca and other modern pagan traditions have embraced their creative roots, reclaiming and reimagining rituals to suit contemporary needs. One specific movement, called Reclaiming, emerged in the late 1970s through the work of feminist activist and author Starhawk. The Reclaiming tradition blends modern paganism with feminist ideals, eco-consciousness, and social justice activism, emphasizing collective rituals and empowerment.

This reclamation of tradition highlights the evolving nature of witchcraft and paganism — not as static relics of the past, but as living, breathing practices that adapt and grow with the people who embrace them. Rather than being bound by the need for historical continuity, these traditions celebrate their dynamic essence.

REMEMBER

Traditional witchcraft is distinct from Wicca and includes a much broader range of practices tied to specific regions and cultures. For example, British traditional witchcraft draws deeply from the folk magic and cultural heritage of the British Isles, but you'll also find rich traditions in the Americas, Africa, and beyond.

Reclaiming in the context of neopaganism is more of a creative act than an act of pure historical accuracy. This is referred to as *pagan reconstruction.* Most neopagan traditions arose in the 200 years between the Enlightenment and the early 21st century. There's no neat, unbroken history of witchcraft or paganism; witches invent and adapt these practices for modern times. That doesn't mean the original traditions lack value. In fact, many threads of pagan reconstructionism remain deeply faithful to their roots.

But the idea that something must be ancient to be meaningful or valid? That's outdated.

On a deeper level, reclaiming is about redefining who gets to say what it means to be a witch. It's no longer up to the religious authorities, or even the historians, to define witchcraft. That power belongs to the witches.

Besides pagan traditions, current trends offer major inspirations for witchcraft that can't be discounted, including these:

- **Pop culture:** Contemporary portrayals of witches, such as in *Wicked* or *Agatha All Along,* reflect modern attitudes and perspectives that reframe the witch as a complex, empowered figure. Literary retellings of mythologies exploded following Madeline Miller's *Circe*. You'd be hard-pressed to find a modern book on witchcraft that doesn't include 1996's *The Craft,* a masterclass in modern witch aesthetics. I'm partial to *Practical Magic* and *Buffy the Vampire Slayer*.
- **Tarot and astrology:** The demand for "witchy" services like tarot readings and astrological consultations has skyrocketed, with these tools serving as gateways for self-reflection and spiritual exploration.
- **Science:** Magic often acts as a placeholder for the mysteries that haven't been explained scientifically. The recognition that unseen forces — like energy or connection — can exist and be influenced might be "magical thinking," but it's a tool that's often used in thought experiments in experimental sciences such as quantum physics.
- **Psychology trends:** Concepts like "holding space" have gained popularity (especially following the viral holding space moment on the recent *Wicked* movie press tour). Therapeutic language and methods are increasingly mixed

with spiritual practices. These terms often take on new dimensions in cultural phenomena, and there's a risk that they can be misconstrued. When in doubt, consult a licensed therapist.

- **Other spiritualities:** Witchcraft frequently draws from diverse traditions, including energy healing, meditation, and indigenous spiritual practices. This often rides the line of cultural appropriation (see Chapter 4).
- **Folk tales:** Stories and symbols from folklore express collective unconscious ideas and continue to inspire magical practices by connecting to cultural and psychological themes.

Modern witches embrace creativity and new inspirations as part of their magical practices. As a modern witch, you aren't just connecting to the past. You're building traditions for the future.

TIP

If you want to begin identifying as a witch and need a little boost of confidence, I offer this template: I'm ________, a modern witch with interests in ________ and roots in ________. Example: I'm Lorraine, a modern witch with interests in tarot and astrology and roots in brujería.

In the next chapter, I explore folk magic and folklore that might provide further entry points and inspirations into the Craft.

Getting Out of the Broom Closet

Neopaganism isn't a single, unified belief system but an umbrella term that encompasses a variety of practices and traditions that brought occult practices into the mainstream. Many neopagan traditions are eclectic, blending diverse influences into meaningful, personalized, or community-based spiritual practices. An example is the *Feri* tradition (sometimes spelled "Faery" or "Fairy"), which is an initiatory, ecstatic, and nature-based spiritual path that focuses on personal empowerment, connection to divine forces, and working with energy.

In contrast to eclectic traditions, *reconstruction* in neopaganism refers to the process of reviving and practicing ancient, pre-Christian spiritual traditions in a modern context. Reconstructionists aim to authentically reconnect with the beliefs, rituals, and cultural practices of specific historical pagan religions by relying on historical, archaeological, and literary sources. Most reconstructionist approaches strive for fidelity to the original practices while adapting them to contemporary life.

Neopagan traditions largely emerged in the 19th and 20th centuries, founded on specific sects of ancient *pantheons*, or groups of deities, including Celtic, Greco-Roman, Egyptian, Slavic, and Norse mythologies:

- **Druidry:** Rooted in ancient Celtic practices, modern Druidry honors nature, sacred groves, and the interconnectedness of life. Key deities often include Brigid (goddess of poetry, healing, and smithcraft) and Cernunnos (the horned god of the forest and fertility).
- **Hellenistic polytheism:** Inspired by ancient Greek religion, Hellenistic polytheism involves the worship of gods like Zeus (king of the gods), Athena (goddess of wisdom and war), and Apollo (god of the sun, music, and healing). It also includes participation in festivals such as the Panathenaea and Dionysia, which celebrate these deities and ancient traditions.
- **Kemeticism:** A revival of ancient Egyptian religious practices, Kemeticism focuses on maintaining *ma'at* (cosmic balance) through the veneration of deities such as Ra (the sun god), Isis (goddess of magic and motherhood), Osiris (god of the afterlife), and Anubis (god of mummification and protector of the dead).
- **Rodnovery:** A Slavic neopagan revival that celebrates pre-Christian Slavic traditions, Rodnovery venerates gods like Perun (god of thunder and war), Mokosh (goddess of fertility and the earth), and Veles (god of cattle, commerce, and the underworld). Seasonal rituals, such as Kupala Night and Maslenitsa, are central to the practice.
- **Heathenry:** Inspired by ancient Norse traditions, Heathenry centers on the worship of gods such as Odin (god of wisdom, magic, and war), Thor (protector and god of thunder), and Freyja (goddess of love, fertility, and battle). Practices often include ancestor veneration and rituals like *blót* (sacrificial offerings). A notable subset, *Ásatrú*, is particularly concentrated in Iceland and emphasizes the Norse pantheon.

Just as neopaganism faithfully borrows from pagan traditions, modern witches are beginning to reconstruct and reclaim other traditions, particularly practices from the Afro-Caribbean diaspora, the indigenous Americas, Asia, and Oceania, which have largely been left out of the neopagan chat until now. Similarly, although the literature about traditional witchcraft has been mostly based in Europaganism, modern witchcraft is diversifying its sources.

WARNING

Despite how exciting this diversification is, it creates new sets of challenges as the scope of neopaganism continues to widen. For one thing, many original practitioners of indigenous and pagan traditions would never consider themselves witches because many of their traditions were formed against witchcraft. And then there's the problem of *cultural appropriation*, the adoption of elements from one culture by members of another, often without understanding, respect, or permission, and typically involving a power imbalance.

For instance, *neoshamanism*, inspired by indigenous shamanic traditions, explores spiritual journeys, communication with spirit guides, and working with the energy of the natural world. Unfortunately, neoshamanism has led to a glut of new "shamans" that are appropriating indigenous resources with little to no real connection to the lands they're extracting from. I touch on cultural appropriation and the line between appreciating and appropriating throughout the book and explore it in more detail in Chapter 4.

WARNING

In recent years, Norse and Slavic spiritual traditions have been misappropriated by nationalist and white supremacist groups, who distort these ancient belief systems to serve exclusionary and extremist ideologies. Symbols like the Norse *Mjölnir* (Thor's hammer) and the *Othala* and *Algiz* runes, which hold rich cultural and spiritual meanings, have been co-opted as emblems of racial purity or ethnonationalism. This misuse not only misrepresents the inclusive and diverse historical contexts of these traditions but also alienates practitioners who approach them with respect and authenticity. Efforts within pagan and reconstructionist communities have sought to reclaim these symbols and traditions from hate groups, emphasizing their true spiritual and cultural heritage.

I'm not usually an alarmist, and I tend to encourage exploration, but dangers abound in appropriative practices devoid of a true faithfulness and respect to reconstruction. Practices that are taken up purely for trend or profit tend to water down traditions, exclude historically marginalized groups, and ignore the long history of persecution that many original and indigenous practitioners have faced — and continue to face.

Defying persecution

Although this book isn't a historical treatment of witchcraft, it's impossible to write about modern witchcraft without at least touching on the witch hunts of the Renaissance, Reformation, and 17th century. These remain harrowing periods in history for the witch. Most of those persecuted had little to do with the practices associated with witchcraft today, but the witch hunts and trials have certainly become intertwined with the mythos of the modern witch.

REMEMBER

Between the mid-1400s and mid-1700s, tens of thousands of people — predominantly women — were executed under accusations of witchcraft. This period saw widespread panic and persecution fueled by religious, political, and social upheaval. The infamous *Malleus Maleficarum*, a 15th-century treatise on witch-hunting, provided a blueprint for identifying, trying, and executing so-called witches. This text portrayed witchcraft as a satanic conspiracy, embedding the association of witches with devil worship into Western consciousness.

The *Salem Witch Trials* of 1692 (depicted in Figure 1-2) in colonial Massachusetts became one of the most infamous episodes of this hysteria, resulting in the execution of around 20 individuals and the imprisonment of many more. Though these trials occurred later and on a smaller scale than the European hunts, they highlight how fear of the "other" could spiral into communal paranoia.

FIGURE 1-2: An accused witch stands trial in Salem.

Joseph E/Library of Congress/Public domain

Although accounts of the witch hunts tend to center on Europe, witches were hunted all over the world, particularly in heavily colonized regions. During the Spanish and Portuguese colonization of Latin America, European ideas about witchcraft and heresy were imported, often through the Inquisition. Indigenous and African spiritual practices were labeled as witchcraft or sorcery, leading to persecution. In Asia, European colonizers also imposed their views of witchcraft, often demonizing local spiritual leaders, shamans, or practitioners of traditional medicine. For example, in the Philippines, *babaylan* (indigenous priestesses) were marginalized under Spanish rule, with some accused of witchcraft.

REMEMBER

A key distinction between high magic and low magic was often made during this era. *High magic,* associated with divination, astrology, and deity communication, was often sanctioned by authorities and practiced by educated men of the upper classes. In contrast, *low magic* — practical applications like healing, protection, and fertility rituals — was dismissed as superstition and typically linked to rural women or the lower classes.

This divide wasn't just about practice; it reflected deep social and gender inequalities. High magic's association with elites offered it a level of legitimacy, whereas low magic — seen as the domain of midwives, healers, and folk practitioners — was vilified. Accusations of witchcraft frequently targeted these low magic practitioners, further marginalizing the powerless.

For this reason, many modern witches are wary of the high magic occult orders that were largely founded by men who appropriated indigenous practices without reparations or repercussion, including the Hermetic Order of the Golden Dawn and Thelema, the latter founded by Aleister Crowley, an interesting but problematic figure.

FUN FACT

The foundation of Thelema is based on the reception of *The Book of the Law*, which Crowley claimed was dictated to him by a supernatural entity named Aiwass in 1904 while he was in Cairo, Egypt. That's highly suspect, if I do say!

The hysteria of the Renaissance witch hunts echoes in more recent moral panics, such as the *Satanic Panic* of the 1980s, when unfounded fears of widespread devil worship swept through Western societies. Although modern witches have reclaimed much of the narrative surrounding their identity, these dark historical events are a reminder of how societal fears can spiral into devastating consequences.

Today's modern witch carries the weight of this history as both a cautionary tale and a source of empowerment. The persecution of the past informs the witch's contemporary role as a symbol of rebellion, resilience, and transformation in the face of oppression.

Empowering witchcraft

The witch is always political, no matter your definition, because the witch walks on the margins. The witch has long been a symbol of feminism, often vilified by patriarchal systems. Reclaiming movements, closely tied to feminist ideologies, celebrate the witch as a figure of resilience and defiance.

FUN FACT

Witchcraft has mirrored the waves of feminism, serving as a symbol of resistance and empowerment for women reclaiming autonomy and power. During the second wave of feminism in the 1960s and 70s, the witch became a potent figure for challenging patriarchal structures, using witchcraft imagery in protests. In the 1990s, the witch in pop culture offered a punk aesthetic that endures to this day. In the current wave of intersectional feminism, witchcraft continues to evolve, embracing inclusivity and diversity while aligning with broader social justice movements and eco-conscious activism.

At their core, witches are figures who work to heal, to help, and to challenge the status quo. Their power lies in their ability to embody revolutionary and often uncomfortable truths. This inherently political role places them on the edge of what society deems acceptable, always pushing boundaries and redefining norms.

The witch is forever moving the needle on what's considered transgressive, asking others to reevaluate their definitions of what's right, beautiful, or possible. Yet this evolution comes with challenges. In the age of social media, practices are reduced to what looks good on a quick reel or what gets attention. The proliferation of practitioners highlights the tension between witchcraft as a serious practice and a passing trend. Such moments underscore how witchcraft can sometimes lose its depth and meaning when reduced to aesthetic or viral moments.

This dynamic has sparked frequent debates about what it means to be a "real" witch, with disagreements over proper practices and authenticity often dominating conversations. But these debates miss the point: The witch has never conformed to a single definition. The witch never fits neatly into the norms of the time. Ever an outsider and a provocateur, the witch is a reminder to question the systems and assumptions that are often taken for granted.

By constantly challenging what's acceptable, witchcraft remains a vibrant and evolving tradition. It thrives on diversity, innovation, and the willingness to embrace both its seriousness and its playfulness. In this way, the witch continues to lead all toward new possibilities, asking society to engage more thoughtfully.

IN THIS CHAPTER

» Integrating ancestral and regional practices

» Getting acquainted with folk magic traditions

» Tuning into folklore across the world

Chapter 2 Rooting in Folk Magic

Folk magic has experienced a revival as modern spiritualists incorporate ancestral traditions and regional lore into their practices. It's an umbrella term encompassing thousands of hyper-local traditions across the world. No two folk practitioners are the same. Practices evolve over generations, shared directly within families and communities, often through oral stories. Folk rituals and spells tend to be practical and results-focused, addressing immediate needs like protection and healing.

Although folk magic is distinct from witchcraft, it's impossible to understand modern witchcraft without it because witches are increasingly inspired by local cultural practices. Folk practitioners don't necessarily believe in deities or consider themselves religious, appealing to secular witches. Conversely, many *magico-religious* traditions (which blend magical rituals and religious beliefs) have their own specific folklore. Folk magic is always evolving to fit the needs of practitioners and their communities. In this chapter, I explore some universal folk practices and the ways you can connect to ancestral traditions and lore to inspire your own magic.

Finding Power in the Roots

Modern witchcraft is so diverse because of the proliferation of folk wisdom and practices in recent years.

FUN FACT

The word *folk* originates from the Old English word *folc*, which means "people" or "a group of people." (And it's one of my favorite words!)

At its core, *folk magic* is the magic of the people. In contrast to institutional religions and prescribed practices, folk magic shifts to reflect the customs and traditions of a cultural region. Although it's always specific to each group or location, most kinds of folk magic share the following characteristics:

- **Practical outcomes:** Folk magic addresses concerns like healing, protection, fertility, love, and prosperity. It employs rituals, charms, and spells designed to achieve specific, tangible results, such as curing an illness or averting misfortune.
- **Common materials:** Folk magic relies on easily accessible items such as herbs, household tools, candles, and natural elements like water or dirt.
- **Oral transmission:** Practices are often shared orally or through demonstrations within families or communities. They evolve with each generation, adapting to cultural and environmental changes.
- **Local environments:** Practices are tailored to the local landscape, incorporating native plants, animals, and spirits.
- **Cultural fusion:** Folk magic frequently incorporates elements from multiple spiritual or religious systems of an area.
- **Integration with folklore and myth:** Folk magic is informed by local myths, legends, and superstitions.

I consider myself a folk practitioner because I pull my practices from the intersecting traditions in my life. I call on symbols of Catholicism, Latin American ancestral rituals, resources from the U.S. south, and family folk stories. This blending of different religious, cultural, or philosophical traditions is called *syncretism*. Syncretism typically combines elements from distinct traditions, creating a hybrid system that incorporates aspects of each. For example, the integration of African deities with Catholic saints in Afro-Caribbean religions like Santería and Vodou is considered a kind of syncretism. Often, syncretism arises as a survival strategy, allowing marginalized or suppressed traditions to continue by blending with the dominant culture. This helps groups maintain their traditions under oppressive conditions.

WARNING

Folk magic isn't necessarily synonymous with witchcraft, and many practitioners of folk magic wouldn't call themselves witches because the word still carries a stigma in some cultures.

Modern witches are increasingly using folk magic in their practices. They might consider themselves *eclectic witches*, drawing inspiration from multiple magical systems across the world (as I outline in Chapter 1). Folk magic often blends different kinds of practices, but it's more tied to heritages and communities than are eclectic practices. The power of folk magic rests in the roots — that is, the strength of its connection to ancestral knowledge and to the land.

TIP

Although it's possible to practice folk magic outside of your own culture or geographic region, your work will be more effective and respectful if you have an authentic connection to the folk practices you're employing. Your own ancestry is a great place to start.

Calling on the ancestors

Ancestral reclamation has emerged as a vital component of modern folk magic and witchcraft. As I introduce in Chapter 1, to *reclaim* literally means "to take back." You can seek to honor your lineage by calling to ancestors and traditions that may have been suppressed or forgotten due to colonization, migration, or systemic oppression.

REMEMBER

Ancestral reclamation involves exploring family stories, cultural heritage, and spiritual practices that connect you to your ancestors, creating a sense of continuity and belonging. You may incorporate rituals that honor ancestral spirits, use tools or symbols tied to your heritage, and draw on historical folklore to enrich your practice.

By integrating ancestral wisdom, you can resist cultural erasure and diversify your practices to reflect your own cultures. Ancestral communion, whether with living or deceased ancestors, can personalize spiritual practices that might otherwise feel unrelatable. This includes learning about and from your ancestors, making offerings at your ancestral altars, and studying your lineage's histories and practices.

FUN FACT

My maternal grandmother used folk healing remedies from Colombia and passed magical folk stories down to her grandchildren. My great-grandmother on my dad's side was a spirit medium in Cuba, and she practiced a syncretic form of spiritism that blends Catholicism, Afro-diasporic traditions, and indigenous Caribbean spiritualities. On my path, I have connected with their stories, which they passed to me directly, and which I further researched after they'd died.

This ancestral connection influenced my relationship with magic. Learning about my ancestry on both sides of my family has led me to identify as a *bruja*, the Spanish word for witch. In my definition, *bruja* is a form of reclamation encompassing both modern witchcraft and the ancestral traditions of folk magic that my grandmothers called on (though they would never have called themselves witches).

It's important to know your family histories, but you don't necessarily need to have blood ties or be a hereditary practitioner to use folk magic. Many other kinds of connections can be considered "ancestral," such as these:

- **Cultural forebears:** Figures who represent your cultural background, such as historical or artistic icons from your heritage, although they may not be direct relatives.
- **Spiritual teachers:** Individuals tied to the spiritual practices or traditions you follow, such as mentors or trailblazers in your magical path.
- **Craft ancestors:** Pioneers or influential figures within your profession, art, or magical practice who inspire and guide your work.
- **Mythical inspirations:** Characters from folklore, mythology, or even literature who embody traits or stories that resonate with your spiritual or personal journey.
- **Adoptive ancestors:** People you admire and have chosen to honor as part of your personal spiritual or emotional lineage, regardless of blood ties.
- **Stewards of the land:** Those who historically lived on, cultivated, or protected the land where you now reside, often including indigenous communities.

WARNING

Although folk magic is generally open to everyone, some hereditary traditions will certainly require you to be related or have undergone a formal initiation. As a modern witch exploring folk magic, you'll have to learn which practices aren't open to you. See Chapter 4 for more.

TIP

No matter where you're coming from, knowledge is power. Do your research and choose your ancestors wisely. In Chapter 9, I expand on ways you can trace your ancestry.

Choosing the ancestors you want to call on is an empowering creative exercise. You can't choose where you're born or who you're born to, but you can make your own ancestral stories, which form the roots of your practice. In Chapter 10, I cover how to create a home altar so you can make offerings to your ancestors and call on them for help. Figure 2-1 shows an example of a Day of the Dead altar.

Honoring indigenous ways of knowing

Many folk magic practices are based in indigenous wisdom and the roots of the land. *Indigeneity* refers to the qualities, cultural practices, and identities of indigenous peoples — those who are the original inhabitants of a specific land or region and who maintain distinct cultural, spiritual, linguistic, and social traditions tied to their ancestral territories.

FIGURE 2-1: *Ofrendas*, or offerings, on a Day of the Dead altar at Mission Marquee Plaza in San Antonio, Texas.

National Park Service/Public domain

Indigeneity emphasizes the interdependence of humans, nature, and the spiritual realm. Indigenous wisdom is shaped by long-standing relationships with the land, community, and cosmos and is often passed down orally or through lived experience. Some indigenous cosmologies and beliefs have inspired many folk magic practices, including these:

- **Multiple realms:** Many indigenous traditions conceptualize the universe as consisting of interconnected realms. Often, three realms exist, including Earth (the everyday material world, or "middle world"), Sky (divine celestial realms, or "upper world"), and Underworld (ancestral and elemental realms, or "lower world").
- **Animism and spirit work:** Most indigenous traditions view all elements of nature — the land, animals, plants, rivers, and even celestial bodies — as having spirits or energies. Magic often involves honoring and working with these spirits to achieve harmony, guidance, or transformation.
- **Sacred directions:** In many tribes, cosmology is tied to the four cardinal directions (North, South, East, West), each associated with specific energies, seasons, and spiritual forces.

FUN FACT

Indigenous cultures offer many of the stories and even words used to explain the creation of the world. The word *hurricane*, for example, comes from the Taíno word *hurakán*, referring to their storm deity.

REMEMBERING THE TAÍNO

The Taíno people were the indigenous inhabitants of the Caribbean, primarily living in the Greater Antilles, including modern-day Cuba, Puerto Rico, the Dominican Republic, Haiti, and Jamaica. Their rich culture left an indelible mark on the spiritual and cultural practices of the Caribbean, even after colonization devastated their population and disrupted their way of life.

The Taíno believed in a cyclical and interconnected universe, where everything — humans, nature, and spirits — was inextricably linked. They worshipped a pantheon of spirits called *zemi* (or cemi), which represented natural forces, ancestors, and deities. These zemi were honored in rituals and ceremonies designed to ensure balance, fertility, and protection. Although the Taíno people were largely displaced or absorbed into the colonial populations, their influence survives in the Caribbean's cultural and spiritual practices, including Espiritismo and Santería.

In recent decades, efforts have been made to revive Taíno identity and spirituality. Descendants in Puerto Rico, the Dominican Republic, and Cuba have sought to reclaim their heritage, emphasizing the enduring presence of Taíno culture in language, food, and spiritual practices. Through this reclamation, the Taíno continue to inspire modern practitioners seeking to honor the land, the ancestors, and the interconnectedness of life.

TIP

You don't have to be indigenous to practice folk magic, but the most conscientious folk magic practitioners honor and respect indigenous wisdom. One good way to do this is to learn about the original stewards of the land that you're practicing on. You can also protect native flora and fauna or honor the land spirits during your rituals. (See Chapter 7 for a libation to the land ritual.)

Conjuring Resistance

Colonization is the greatest threat to indigenous wisdom, and folk magic represents resistance to indigenous erasure. As I introduce in Chapter 1, indigenous traditions have been impacted greatly by empire building projects and religious crusades throughout history. Witch hunts are popularly understood to have taken place in Europe and the United States, but over the centuries, they've targeted pagan and folk practices across the world.

Colonization isn't a thing of the past. To this day, colonizing powers seek to "civilize" indigenous peoples by erasing or replacing their spiritual traditions, usually with Abrahamic religions or Western secularism. Folk practices are often marginalized as "superstitions" or "primitive," forcing practitioners to adapt or go underground. Although the popularity of folk magic has gone a long way toward destigmatizing these practices, many indigenous and pagan traditions continue to be criminalized and persecuted.

REMEMBER

An *ethno-religion* is one that's closely tied to a specific ethnic or cultural group, with its beliefs, practices, and identity deeply intertwined with the group's cultural and social practices. Ethno-religions often don't actively seek converts because they're rooted in the history, traditions, and ancestral heritage of a particular people or region. For example, the Yoruba religion is practiced predominantly by the Yoruba people of West Africa.

WORKING CONJURE

Rootwork, also known as *Hoodoo* or *Conjure*, is a spiritual and magical tradition of African American culture. Emerging from the blending of African spiritual practices with Native American knowledge and European influences, it developed as a tool of empowerment and survival during the era of slavery in the United States. Rootwork stems from the spiritual practices of enslaved Africans brought to the Americas. These traditions merged with Native American knowledge, as indigenous peoples shared their understanding of local plants and herbs. Rootwork also borrowed from and *occulted*, or hid, itself with Christianity. Enslaved Africans incorporated Christian elements (Psalms and biblical references), creating a unique syncretic practice.

The term *rootwork* emphasizes the use of roots, herbs, minerals, and other natural materials as sources of power. Ancestor veneration is a central component, with practitioners seeking wisdom and protection from those who came before. Hoodoo often involves calling upon divine or spiritual forces, blending African cosmology with Christian prayers.

In Hoodoo, a *working* refers to a magical or spiritual operation performed to achieve a specific outcome. It involves the intentional use of spiritual energy, natural materials, and symbolic actions to focus on a goal, whether it's for love, protection, prosperity, healing, or justice.

Rootwork continues to be a vibrant practice within African American communities, preserving cultural heritage and serving as a powerful spiritual tool. Although its techniques are widely studied and practiced, it remains tied to the experiences and resilience of Black culture, emphasizing personal empowerment and connection to ancestry.

Preserving regional folk magic

Modern folk practices draw from magico-religious traditions across the world, many of which were targets of oppression and colonization at one point or another. They have survived persecution and continue to inspire modern witches looking to reclaim their ancestral traditions.

In Europe, the witch trials of the 15th and 18th centuries targeted local healers and folk magic practitioners, including each of these:

- **Cunning folk of England, Scotland, and Ireland:** These traditions, including herbal healing, divination, and charms, influenced modern witchcraft and Wicca. (See the sidebar in Chapter 14 about cunning folk.)
- **Hexerei of Germany:** Derived from the German word *Hexe*, meaning witch, *Hexerei* is a form of folk magic that reflects a mix of ancient pagan beliefs, Christian influences, and local folk customs.
- **Stregheria of Italy**: *Stregheria* is a modern revival and adaptation of Italian folk magic and witchcraft, rooted in ancient pre-Christian traditions of Italy. Sometimes referred to as the "Old Religion," it blends elements of traditional Italian peasant magic, spirituality, and neo-pagan practices.
- **Sámi Shamanism of the Nordic regions**: *Sámi noaidi* (shamans) were persecuted as witches during Scandinavian witch trials. Their practices, including drum divination and spirit communication, influence modern Nordic paganism.

The Transatlantic Slave trade spread African cosmologies throughout the Caribbean and the Americas. They resisted persecution by becoming syncretized, or blended, with Christianity and indigenous traditions to form new ethno-religions and regional practices. These include Santería (Lucumí) and Palo Mayombe in Cuba; Candomblé in Brazil; Hoodoo (Rootwork or Conjure) in the U.S.; Vodou in Haiti; the 21 Divisions in the Dominican Republic; and Obeah in Jamaica.

The *African traditional religions* (ATRs) that form the roots of these newer religions encompass diverse spiritual systems centering on ancestors, nature spirits, and deities. They include but aren't limited to the following:

- **Yoruba of southwestern Nigeria, Benin, and Togo:** Yoruba involves the worship of deities known as orishas, each representing natural forces and aspects of human life. Yoruba religion became the foundation for syncretic traditions like Santería, Candomblé, and Vodou in the Americas.
- **Vodun of present-day Benin, Togo, and parts of Ghana:** Vodun involves worship of spirits that govern nature and human affairs. Vodun influenced Haitian Vodou, New Orleans Voodoo, and other Afro-diasporic traditions.

- **Akan of Ghana and the Ivory Coast:** Akan spiritual practices influenced Obeah in the Caribbean and folk traditions in Suriname and Jamaica.
- **Igbo of Southeastern Nigeria:** Igbo spiritual concepts contributed to Hoodoo in the Americas.
- **Bantu of Congo, Angola, and Zambia:** Bantu spiritual practices influenced Palo Mayombe and Kongo-derived traditions in the Americas.

In the Americas, indigenous spiritualities have informed nature and healing-based folk magic. Many have survived colonization and continue to inspire modern spiritual practices. Some examples include these:

- **Shamanic practices of North and South America:** Indigenous healers, often referred to as "medicine people" or shamans, were targeted during the European colonization of the Americas. Practices such as smoke cleansing and working with spirits were suppressed but have been revived and integrated into neo-shamanism and modern spiritualities.
- **Curanderismo of Mesoamerica:** Indigenous Mexican healers (curanderos) blended Aztec and Maya magical traditions with Catholicism to survive persecution. This syncretic system, which includes herbalism, rituals, and spiritual cleansings, continues to influence modern folk magic.
- **Brujería of Latin America and the Caribbean:** Practiced primarily in Puerto Rico and across Latin America, *brujería* incorporates indigenous spiritual traditions, Catholicism, and African influences. It's a blanket term that means "witchcraft" in Spanish and includes magical practices, healing rituals, and veneration of saints and spirits, often focusing on personal empowerment.

Asia's folk magic traditions reflect the rich spiritual and cultural diversity of the continent, blending animistic beliefs, ancient philosophies, and religious practices like Hinduism, Buddhism, and Islam. These systems often center on ancestral reverence, nature spirits, and rituals for healing and protection. They include, but are not limited, to:

- **Babaylan practices of the Philippines:** The *Babaylan*, spiritual leaders of pre-colonial Philippines, were labeled witches or heretics during Spanish colonization. Elements of their practices, such as working with ancestors and spirit guides, persist in modern Filipino magic and healing.
- **Balinese and Javanese Mysticism of Indonesia:** These magical practices are tied to animism and Hindu-Buddhist traditions and were suppressed during Islamic and colonial rule. Modern Balinese magic, including working with spirits and sacred objects, retains these ancient roots.

- **Adivasi Shamanism in India:** Indigenous tribes in India faced persecution during witch hunts. Their animistic practices, including healing rituals and spirit invocation, survive in modern folk magic.
- **Bektashism in Turkey:** The Bektashi order, an Islamic mystic sect of Sufi origin, incorporated folk magic, symbolism, and rituals into their practices, which were suppressed by the Ottoman authorities.
- **Sri Lankan Yakadura Practices:** *Yakadura*, indigenous Sri Lankan exorcists, were suppressed under colonial rule, but their magical and healing rituals persist in modern spiritual practices.

Working the roots at home

Despite cultural diversity, many folk magic practices share common themes, techniques, and tools across regions and traditions. These similarities arise from universal human experiences and shared connections to nature, community, and spirituality. The following section presents common practices that transcend cultures and are acceptable starting points to develop your own folk magic.

Cleansing magic

In Chapter 1, I introduce the concept of energy in witchcraft. Many folk magic practices deal with energy in some way, and cleansing magic is foundational to most traditions. Cleansing rituals clear negative energy and restore energetic balance. I cover cleansing and protection in more depth in Chapter 10, which walks you through setting up your sacred space and clearing energy.

Following are three common cleansing rituals:

- **Smoke clearing:** Burning herbs or incense is one of the most frequently used methods for clearing energies in people, places, or things. (See Chapters 10 and 14 for more applications.)
- **Ritually washing:** Ritual baths or herbal washes remove negativity and prime you for magical work. (See the sidebar in Chapter 10 about *limpias* in Latin America and Chapter 14 for a Florida Water recipe.)
- **Using a broom:** Sweeping is both a physical and a spiritual act of clearing energy. (See Chapter 11 for more on ritual tools.)

FUN FACT

Holy water predates Christianity and can be traced back to ancient pagan practices. The Egyptians, Greeks, and Romans used *consecrated*, or blessed, water in their rituals to purify spaces and ward off evil. Ancient Romans, for example, used water from sacred springs to bless people and objects.

Protection magic

Protection magic is a cornerstone of many folk traditions, focusing on shielding individuals, homes, and objects from harm or negativity. Across different regions, these practices take unique forms. Protective symbols are frequently placed near entrances. In some traditions, iron horseshoes are used for protection and red strings are used to ward against the evil eye. Other protective rituals include the following:

- **Wearing charms:** Amulets or talismans are commonly used to protect against negative energies. (See Chapter 12 for more about ritually crafted objects, including the *gris-gris* or mojo bags of Hoodoo.)
- **Making a barrier:** Salt is sprinkled around doors or windows to create a barrier against negativity. Some traditions hang onions at thresholds to keep evil away. (See Chapter 10 for more protection tips.)
- **Uncrossing:** *Uncrossing* refers to the process of removing negative energy, hexes, curses, or spiritual blockages that may be affecting a person, space, or object. An example ritual for uncrossing is turning your clothes inside out to undo energetic ties.

Healing and herbal magic

Healing practices in folk magic frequently blend the medicinal and the magical, using herbs, roots, and plants for their physical and spiritual properties. Remedies are prepared as teas, poultices, or infusions to address ailments, with prayers, spells, or chants enhancing their efficacy. See the appendix for herbal healing associations.

TIP

Folk practitioners use local resources and household objects when possible. Across Latin America, salves made from camphor, eucalyptus oil, and menthol are used for healing all kinds of ailments. In modern times, it's common to use what you have laying around. For example, instead of gathering her own ingredients, my grandmother used Vicks VapoRub as a healing fix-it-all, as do many Latin American grandmothers to this day. She rubbed it on my chest when I was sick, no matter the ailment, and it truly did the trick every time. Folk magic can be mundane, and remedies don't necessarily have to be very involved or glamorous.

Attraction and love magic

Time for some real talk: Maybe you're into magic for what it can offer you. Love spells are one of the most popularly sought forms of magic, and across cultures, people turn to folk practitioners for help attracting their heart's deepest desires. Attraction magic is used to manifest fertility, abundance, and love, drawing on symbols and rituals that resonate with the cycles of growth and prosperity. Fertility rituals often use eggs, seeds, or planting crops as symbolic acts to attract abundance and ensure the health of both land and people.

WARNING

Be careful when engaging in any kind of love magic. Never perform a love spell on another lightly, especially as a beginner. Instead, focus on self-love and attracting authentic and sustainable love to your life in all the potential forms that might take.

Some go-to attraction rituals include these:

- **Knot magic:** Based on Celtic folk magic, this ritual involves focusing on your intention while tying knots into a cord, string, ribbon, or thread.
- **Honey jars:** Inspired by Hoodoo, honey jars have become popular spells for sweetening relationships.
- **Candle magic:** Candles are one of the most accessible ways to attract specific things into your life.

Divination and spirit magic

Divination, the practice of seeking knowledge or guidance from unseen forces, is a universal feature of folk magic traditions. It can involve interpreting natural signs and omens, such as the behavior of animals and weather patterns, or working with specific tools like tarot cards, runes, pendulums, and scrying mirrors. Casting lots, bones, or shells is another widespread method for divination, connecting the practitioner with spirits or ancestors. Check out Chapter 13, which is all about divination.

Honoring spirits and ancestors is a fundamental part of folk magic, fostering connections with the past and seeking guidance for the present. Practitioners often create altars adorned with offerings, candles, and prayers to venerate their ancestors and seek their protection. Family stories and traditions play a crucial role in these practices, reinforcing the link between generations. Regional approaches to ancestor veneration vary widely, but ancestral altars are common across regions. I cover altars in Chapter 10.

Evolving Through Folklore

As I explore in Chapter 1, the tales that inform your views of witches shape you more profoundly than you might realize. Contemporary reinterpretations often subvert age-old tropes, reframing villains as nuanced, relatable figures. Modern examples like *Wicked* and *Agatha All Along* highlight this evolution, presenting the witch as a multifaceted character while challenging ingrained stereotypes. By offering alternative perspectives, these stories transform perceptions, fostering empathy and dismantling stigma surrounding the witch.

In popular culture, depictions of witches have long been dominated by Europagan and Wiccan goddess traditions, which draw heavily from Hellenistic and European mythologies. The triple goddess — encompassing the maiden, mother, and crone — has become a central symbol in Western paganism and witchcraft lore. These archetypes gained strength through repeated retellings, spreading across the globe via European colonization. In recent decades, modern retellings of the triple goddess have proliferated through new books and media.

In contrast, folk magic traditions are primarily preserved through oral storytelling. Only in recent decades have many of these *occult*, or hidden, stories been written down, allowing for their preservation and broader dissemination. In Part 2, I explore folk mythologies using the structure of the maiden, mother, and crone, drawing parallels between these archetypes and the witches and magical figures found in diverse traditions. This framework highlights how modern witches are reinterpreting or departing from the triple goddess, bridging the gap between diverse ancestral traditions and contemporary mythologies of the witch.

Telling old stories

Certain tropes in folk magic lore transcend cultural boundaries, appearing in diverse traditions worldwide. These recurring elements reflect universal human concerns, convey moral lessons, and offer warnings about the boundaries between the mundane and the mystical. These recurring motifs underline shared cultural values and existential questions, offering a mirror into the human psyche and its relationship with the unseen world. Recurrent themes in common folklore include these:

- **Liminal spaces:** Locations like crossroads, graveyards, doorways, and bridges are considered powerful in folklore. These transitional spaces are believed to connect the physical and spiritual realms, creating opportunities for transformation but also posing significant danger due to their volatile energy.
- **Spirit allies and familiars:** Animals or spirits often serve as guides, protectors, and intermediaries in magical practices. Familiars — such as cats, toads, snakes, owls, bats, and crows — are thought to enhance a practitioner's abilities and offer insight from other realms.
- **Hidden worlds:** Dark forests, wild, untamed landscapes, and mystical figures like crones and fairies represent the unknown and the magical. These settings and beings often challenge characters to confront their fears or embrace their intuition and resourcefulness.

- **The forbidden or taboo:** Themes of curiosity and consequence appear prominently, such as warnings against opening locked doors, breaking vows, and trespassing sacred spaces. These stories teach caution, self-restraint, and respect for boundaries.
- **Bewitching and curses:** Folklore often includes figures like the *femme fatale*, a seductive and dangerous woman, or the concept of the "evil eye," representing jealousy or malice that causes misfortune. These tropes explore power, desire, and the consequences of envy.
- **Shapeshifters and tricksters:** Characters that can change form, like werewolves and *skinwalkers*, symbolize transformation and duality. Tricksters, such as Anansi the Spider and Loki, use their cleverness to outwit others, often teaching morality lessons through their antics.
- **Demons, ghosts, and cryptids:** Supernatural beings like demons, restless spirits, and mysterious creatures embody humanity's fears of the unknown. They serve as cautionary figures or symbols of unresolved issues, urging individuals to confront hidden truths or moral lapses. (Figure 2-2 features one such being called *Sankchinni*, a Bengali ghost.)

FIGURE 2-2: A *Sankchinni* ghost from *Folk-Tales of Bengal* (1912).

Warwick Goble/University of Toronto/Public domain

Redefining monsters

Throughout the world, monsters and *cryptids* — mythical creatures whose existence is claimed but not proven — occupy a powerful place in folk magic lore, bridging the gap between myth and reality. These creatures symbolize societal fears, misunderstood natural phenomena, or the demonization of marginalized individuals. They serve not only as warnings but as cultural mirrors, reflecting what a society fears, reveres, or struggles to understand.

REMEMBER

Some of the most iconic mythological witches in modern witchcraft started as monsters and were redefined to fit the modern witchcraft cannon. For example, in ancient Greek mythology, Medusa was one of the Gorgons, three sisters with snakes for hair and a gaze that turned people to stone. Modern reinterpretations of Medusa emphasize her feminine power and defiance. These associations are more representative of contemporary cultural shifts rather than classical mythology.

As witchcraft evolves and diversifies, new monsters are being reinterpreted. An increasing segment of witches who don't see themselves in Europagan myths are turning to their own cultural folk monsters for lessons about power.

Although many of these entities inspire terror, they also transmit lessons, protecting cultural traditions and offering explanations for the unexplainable. Recent reinterpretations, often from feminist or decolonial perspectives, have reclaimed these figures, challenging their demonization and exploring how they reflect societal biases and oppression. Some such creatures across the world include these:

- **Aswangs of the Philippines:** *Aswangs* are often depicted as beautiful women by day and predatory witches or vampires by night. The *Manananggal* is a specific type of aswang that separates its body to hunt pregnant women. Modern reimaginings frame the Manananggal as a feminist figure assisting women with agency over their bodies.
- **The Mona Bruja of Central America:** The "Monkey Witch" is typically depicted as a shape-shifter that can transform into a monkey or a half-monkey, half-human creature. The *Mona Bruja* is known for her mischievous and sometimes malevolent behavior. Recently, new reports of her sightings have circulated around Nicaragua.
- **La Chupacabra of Latin American and the U.S.:** This is a modern cryptid said to prey on livestock, leaving behind unexplained deaths and drained blood. It represents rural anxieties over environmental instability and modern threats to traditional livelihoods. (I grew up hearing about *La Chupacabra* sightings in the Everglades near my home!)

- **Wendigo of the Algonquin:** The *wendigo* is a spirit or creature associated with insatiable greed and cannibalism, often tied to themes of environmental depletion and social imbalance. In modern times, it can serve as a cautionary figure about the dangers of overconsumption and moral decay.
- **Kappa of Japan:** *Kappa* are water-dwelling creatures known for their mischievous or dangerous behavior, including drowning people or livestock. They're also revered as protectors of water sources when appeased through offerings.
- **Pontianak of Malaysia and Indonesia:** The *Pontianak* is a vengeful female spirit believed to arise from women who died during childbirth. It's associated with societal fears surrounding women's reproductive health and the supernatural consequences of maternal death.
- **Kelpie of Scotland:** This is a shape-shifting water spirit, often appearing as a horse to lure victims to their doom in lakes or rivers.

As I explore in Chapter 5, monsters and cryptids in folklore often symbolize what societies demonize or fail to understand. Many of these figures represent marginalized groups, societal taboos, or anxieties about transformation and power. These creatures enrich folk practices by offering society a chance to confront its fears, challenge its stigmas, and reclaim its cultural narratives. As modern retellings give them new life, some are elevated to the status of folk heroes or even gods. In Part 2, I further explore the evolving nature of occult mythologies within modern witchcraft.

IN THIS CHAPTER

» Finding entry points into witchcraft

» Setting up your practice

» Choosing a magical path

Chapter 3
Making Modern Magic

Modern witchcraft sits at the intersection of countless traditional and cultural paths of magic. Today's witchcraft isn't static or uniform; as more and more practitioners take up magic, new collective practices and beliefs emerge. Artistic interpretations of the witch inform modern practices, and vice versa. Traditional paths of magic are constantly revived, reclaimed, and altered to reflect contemporary spiritualities and representations of the witch.

As a modern witch, you stand at the crossroads of these varied paths, and you have the exciting task of choosing which ones you'll follow and which ones you'll pave for yourself. In this chapter, I outline common entry points to magic, tried and true paths of practice, and the basics of modern spellwork and rituals.

A Witch at the Crossroads

Being a witch in the modern world can be tricky. Even now that I'm comfortable in my practice and trust my own process, I'm sensitive to conflicting information about witchcraft, especially in online spaces. Having so much information available is a blessing and a curse. Each time I learn something that challenges what I think I know, I spend some time in research and reflection to decide if I should adjust my beliefs or practices.

REMEMBER

Your path is your own, and you're in control of your practice. You'll always find incompatible information out there. You might even read something in this book that doesn't jibe with something you learn elsewhere. It can feel overwhelming or discouraging to have to constantly discern what to trust, especially if you witness in-fighting in the witch community, which happens quite a lot.

Conflicting information often provides an opportunity to grow and deepen your studies. Many traditions have established rules and rituals. When a practitioner of such a tradition disagrees with something you hold to be true, it presents a chance to learn more about how your beliefs and practices differ. For instance, some witches believe that covens require a high priestess or priest, whereas others have a more decentralized organization.

TIP

Setting out on your path is like becoming a forever student of witchcraft. As you learn different things, maybe you'll find that you prefer someone else's way or are inspired to follow their path. Or maybe it just strengthens the unique way you've chosen to practice your craft. If you remain respectfully curious, you'll find your own inner compass in time — and hopefully have fun in the process!

Identifying your entry points

To begin to walk your own path, it helps to make an inventory of the things that led you to your interest in magic. Think about the histories, memories, beliefs, and art forms that intersect at the spot where you stand now. You might review Chapter 1, which covers pop culture inspirations, traditional witchcraft religions, and *pantheons* — or systems of deities — that inform modern magic; or Chapter 2, which dives into folk magic, ethno-religions, and regional lore. In gathering all this information, a story will start to emerge about what led you to magic.

I'll use myself as an example. My families are from Colombia and Cuba. My mother's side practiced a kind of decentralized folk Catholicism, heavy on saint veneration, altars, and offerings. My great-grandmother on my father's side was a spirit medium; she spoke to the dead and accessed spirit guides in her work. I'm highly influenced by this history and my own memories of my childhood in churches and Catholic after-school programs. I didn't like the rigidity of institutions and had a difficult time reconciling what I was taught with what I knew about science and history.

Over time, I rejected church in favor of a personal practice of study, and I longed to pierce the veil that I perceived was obscuring the roots of my family's magical practices.

FUN FACT

As I came of age, I was inspired by monster lore from my culture and popular media portrayals of the witch. Like so many people of my generation, a now cult-classic movie called *The Craft* captivated my imagination, and I was moved by TV representations of the modern witch, like Willow and Tara in *Buffy the Vampire Slayer*. These stories centered on female empowerment and personal journeys.

In processing all the paths that led to my interest in witchcraft, I started to develop my own beliefs and practices through a combination of study and creativity. Because I didn't have a formal teacher or program, what emerged was an *eclectic witchcraft* that brought together pagan rituals, spiritual practices indigenous to my ancestral homelands, and the styles that I saw and loved on TV. All of these are valid inspirations and entry points into magical practice.

REMEMBER

The abundance of traditions at your disposal offers you the freedom to create a personal path. There's no single "right way" to practice, no universal handbook or prescribed set of beliefs you must follow. Instead, explore, experiment, and choose what resonates with your own history, values, and intuition.

It's ultimately up to you to decide each of these:

- **What you believe:** Will your practice center on reverence for deities, spirits, nature, ancestral wisdom, cosmic forces, or something else?
- **How you practice:** Will you craft intricate rituals, meditate in quiet solitude, or embrace spontaneous acts of magic in your daily life?
- **What tools you use:** Will you work with candles and crystals, tarot and runes, or no tools at all, relying instead on the power of your intentions?
- **Who you work with:** Will you practice alone or in community?

WARNING

Although you're free to explore, not everything is up for grabs. To be a witch at the crossroads is to embrace both the boundless possibilities and the responsibility of shaping your own magical path. It means learning the origins of the practices you adopt, honoring the cultures and communities that shaped them, and ensuring your craft aligns with your own ethical principles.

The path ahead is yours alone, but you should respect its limitations, which I cover in Chapter 4.

Embodying intersectionality

In Chapter 1, I trace how witchcraft trends tend to crest along with waves of feminism. Today's witchcraft mirrors much of the tenets of modern intersectional feminism. Just as you stand at a unique crossroads, so do others, and every crossroads is different.

REMEMBER

Intersectionality is a term that describes how different social identities — such as race, gender, class, sexuality, ability, and others — intersect and overlap, creating interconnected systems of discrimination and privilege.

Power is central to witchcraft practice, and embracing intersectionality is the key to wielding your own power. You can certainly choose to disregard intersectionality, along with the different positions of power you inhabit in this world. But closing your eyes to these differences will limit the level of empowerment you can personally achieve while potentially hurting others with your practice. (More on this in Chapter 4.)

REMEMBER

Historically, witchcraft has been associated with individuals — often women and queer people — who were marginalized, persecuted, or deemed subversive. Modern witches reclaim this narrative, celebrating personal power and resistance to oppression. Intersectional witches recognize and honor the diverse identities, experiences, and belief systems that make up modern witchcraft.

You can embody intersectionality in several ways:

- **Honoring the roots of diverse practices:** Acknowledge the origins of magical traditions, tools, and rituals, and give credit to the cultures that shaped them. Avoid appropriating sacred practices without understanding their context or seeking permission, especially from marginalized communities. (See Chapter 4.)
- **Challenging dominant systems:** Defy patriarchy, white supremacism, colonialism, exploitative capitalism, heteronormativity, and organized religious dogma by reclaiming spiritual autonomy and celebrating alternative worldviews. Choose to engage in different kinds of spiritual activism. (See Chapter 19.)
- **Empowering marginalized voices:** Seek out teachers, authors, and practitioners from diverse backgrounds to expand your understanding of witchcraft and its intersection with social justice. Amplify and support witches of color, LGBTQ+ witches, disabled witches, and others whose perspectives are often overlooked. At the same time, don't expect them to do all the work of educating you and others.
- **Focusing on collective transformation:** Balance personal growth (for example, healing and self-empowerment) with collective goals like environmental justice and community building. Use witchcraft to build bridges between communities.

TIP

Identify the power dynamic that feels out of balance in your life. Restoring a power balance can serve as a kind of motivation for your spiritual work as you seek to empower yourself and others.

Becoming your own witch

Coming out of the broom closet is a big deal. Maybe you've been reading about witchcraft and finding things you'd like to start practicing. Now it's time to get a little more serious.

Dedication and initiation, two ways to step into your identity as a witch, are different. Although they may seem similar, they represent different approaches to embracing and deepening your craft.

Dedicating yourself to "the Craft"

REMEMBER

"The Craft" is an appropriate shorthand for witchcraft because it's something that's cultivated, developed, and honed over time. *Practice* is another term you'll encounter over and over in witchcraft studies, referring to the active, ongoing engagement with the rituals, skills, and beliefs that make up the Craft. These terms suggest a long-term dedication.

Dedication is an act of devotion. It's an inward-facing process in which you commit to your magical practice, your spiritual growth, or your chosen path. It's about forging a personal bond with your craft and the forces you work with.

Dedication is entirely self-directed. It's your choice to declare yourself a witch and to outline the terms of that relationship. It's not bound by external rules.

Dedication can center on any of the following:

- Deities
- Ancestors or spirit guides
- Nature or science
- A spiritual goal
- Activism and community work
- A specific path of practice

And the list goes on. You can dedicate your magical journey to anything. Many witches see dedication as the starting point of their practice. Some witches choose to keep their dedication private, whereas others may share their commitment with trusted friends or fellow practitioners.

TIP

Don't feel pressured to publicly identify as a witch or talk about your practice. Share only what you feel like sharing, only when you feel like sharing it. In turn, respect the privacy of other practitioners and abide by any rules of confidentiality that you've agreed to.

Initiating into your path

Initiation, in contrast to dedication, is often a more formal process that connects you to a specific tradition, coven, or spiritual lineage. It signifies entry into a community or a deeper level of practice, and it typically follows a structured set of rituals or requirements.

Initiation can be characterized by the following features:

- **External structure:** Initiation usually involves an established group or tradition, with its own rules, symbols, and ceremonies.
- **Symbolic threshold:** The process is designed to mark a transformation — a crossing of a threshold into a new phase of understanding, power, or responsibility.
- **Connection to others:** Through initiation, you may gain access to a shared body of knowledge, rituals, or magical techniques that are passed down through the group or tradition.
- **Selective and exclusive:** Unlike dedication, initiation isn't always open to everyone. It often requires training, preparation, and meeting specific criteria set by the tradition or group.

I cover the different types of initiation in Chapter 9.

TIP

You can dedicate yourself to magic or undergo initiation more than once in your life.

Initiations don't necessarily require an audience. I've flown solo as a witch most of my life, so I've performed my initiations alone and in private. My first initiation into witchcraft took place in middle school, and I barely knew what I was doing, as it was the '90s and I didn't have *Modern Witchcraft For Dummies*!

Walking Your Path

Once you've committed to your practice, you can begin your studies and home in on your magical path.

REMEMBER

Magic generally refers to the intentional use of energy, will, and ritual to influence, align with, or transform aspects of reality.

Want to start exploring your abilities and open yourself to the kinds of magical paths you might be compatible with? Try these on for size:

- **Reading and studying:** Explore books, articles, and historical texts on various forms of magic, witchcraft traditions, and metaphysical systems. Chapter 9 lays out the basics of starting your occult studies.
- **Honing intuition through practical magic:** *Practical magic* involves using simple, everyday actions to manifest intentions. Starting small can help you build confidence and experience in your craft. Examples include lighting candles with intention and practicing kitchen witchery by infusing meals with love.
- **Trying out different modalities:** Try out magical tools and techniques like tarot, runes, crystals, and herbs to hone your intuition.
- **Joining a group or program:** Find a community that can provide support, guidance, and shared wisdom as you grow in your magical practice. (See Chapter 17 for information about joining a coven.)

PUTTING THE "K" IN "MAGICK"?

Most modern witches use the word *magic* interchangeably with *witchcraft*. It's a generalized term that encompasses all kinds of practice. Some witches spell the word with a final *k* to differentiate their esoteric practices from the theatrical connotations of stage magic and to signify its roots in mystical traditions.

The term *magick* was popularized by Aleister Crowley, a 20th century occultist and founder of Thelema, an esoteric philosophy inspired by ancient Egyptian cosmology, filtered through the lens of ceremonial magic. Crowley defined *magick* as "the science and art of causing change to occur in conformity with will." Magick emphasizes personal and spiritual growth, transformation, and the alignment of will with universal forces.

Equipping your journey

As you set out to learn your craft, acquiring some basic skills and tools will help you jump into your practice with confidence.

Energizing space through circle casting

In most forms of witchcraft, the circle is one of the fundamental symbols and tools used for ritual work. It's a sacred space, both metaphorically and energetically, that serves as a boundary between the mundane world and the spiritual or magical realms. By creating a circle, you're able to raise, focus, and direct energy in a protected and intentional way.

REMEMBER

The circle is considered a "sphere of energy" that creates a safe container for magical work. It serves multiple purposes, including protection, as it keeps out unwanted energies, and containment, as it holds the energies invoked or raised.

TIP

Casting a circle is a foundational ritual used to create sacred space, and it's one of the first spells you should learn as a witch. You can find step-by-step instructions for casting a circle in Chapter 21. It often goes hand in hand with "calling the quarters," a ritual for calling on the four directions, which I outline in Chapter 16.

In Chapter 10, I go over setting up a sacred space in more detail, including clearing energy and creating an *altar*, the focal point for magical work, which usually contains your main tools of practice, as shown in Figure 3-1.

FIGURE 3-1: A simple altar with candles and a journal.

Selecting tools that speak to you

Tools are wonderful ways to connect to magic in a material way and develop your personal preferences. Witches feel strongly about their tools. I love using the broom, whereas some feel it stereotypically ties witchcraft to domesticity.

FUN FACT

The broom reminds me of my maternal grandmother. She was a cleaning lady, and I remember her always sweeping. When I use the broom to clear energy in my home, I feel I'm honoring her in a small way. The broom reminds me to be humble and that even the greatest transformations begin with simple actions and intentions.

Don't dismiss the tools in popular media portrayals of the witch as simple clichés. Tools and symbols trigger the unconscious mind because these seemingly mundane objects correspond to magical intentions. A lot of power lies within the objects you've integrated into your perceptions of the witch, such as the ones illustrated in Figure 3-2.

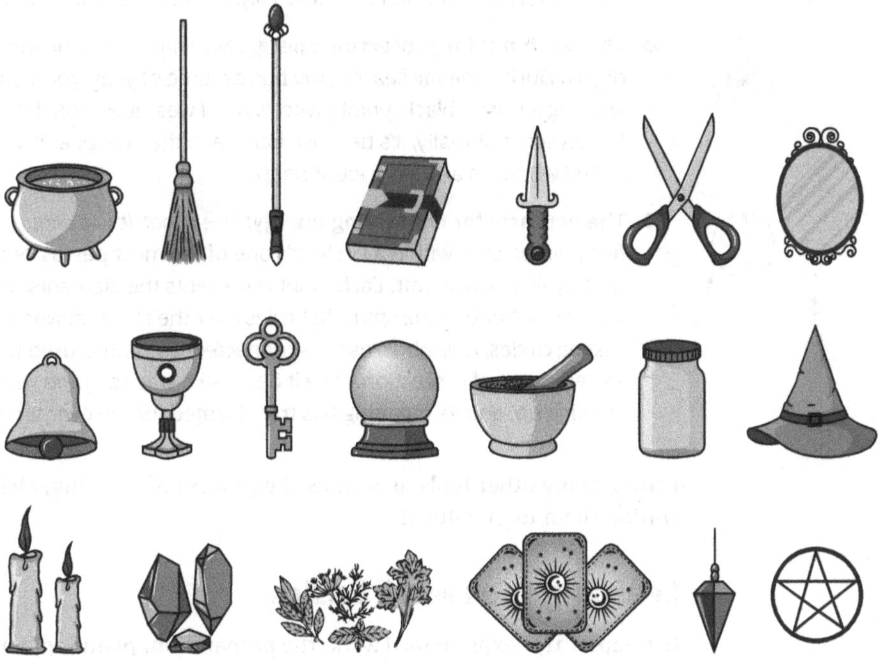

FIGURE 3-2: Common tools associated with witchcraft practice.

Here are a few of my favorites and the ways they inspire me to manipulate energy:

» **The cauldron for transforming energy:** I always think of the first two lines of *The Song of the Witches* in Shakespeare's *Macbeth*: "Double, double toil and trouble; fire burn and caldron bubble." The *cauldron* is a large pot that transforms ingredients (eye of newt, toe of frog!) into something else entirely.

- **The wand for evoking energy:** The *wand* is an iconic tool. It might feel silly to use one, as though you're just playing at being a witch, but the trick is to find or make a wand that helps you connect to the energy of the world. I didn't have access to Harry Potter's Ollivanders wand shop, but I did find mine in an oddities boutique. It's a gnarled branch that the 11-year-old daughter of the shopkeeper found and encrusted with crystals. As soon as I picked it up, I knew it was for me.

- **The athame for directing energy:** *Athame* is a fancy word for a ceremonial dagger or knife. I've always had a healthy fear of sharp weapons, and to be honest, the athame still unsettles me a little. I like how it challenges me to overcome my insecurities and take control. It's used to cast circles, call in energy, or cut off energy, depending on the occasion.

- **The crystal ball for reading energy:** The crystal ball might be the most cliché object related to witches, but I just love the aesthetic, and scrying is one of my favorite forms of divination, personally. (More on that in Chapter 13.)

- **The witch hat for protecting energy:** No, wait. *This* is the most cliché witchy object. During the fall season, my busiest time of year, you'll often catch me wearing a classic black, pointy witch's hat. I wear it to look the part around Halloween, but really, it's because hats keep the energy at my crown protected when I'm around a lot of people.

- **The pentacle for containing energy:** The *pentacle* is a *pentagram*, or five-pointed star, within a circle. It's one of the most pervasive symbols in portrayals of witchcraft. Each point represents the elements, with the top point representing the spirit that rules over the material world. Often used in casting circles, it symbolizes interconnectedness and is used to create a sacred space of protection. I like it because it was so taboo when I was growing up, and its meaning has transformed for me over time.

I cover many other tools as well as the process of cleaning, charging, and consecrating them in Chapter 11.

Learning spell work basics

In Chapter 11, I explore *spell work*, the preparation, planning, and actions involved in casting spells. A few different aspects of spell work are often used interchangeably but are distinct, including these:

- **Spell:** A *spell* is a focused act of intention and energy that seeks to bring about a desired outcome. Spells can raise, direct, attract, release, or transform energy. Popular ones include love and protection spells.

- **Spellcasting:** *Spellcasting* is simply the act of performing a spell.
- **Ritual:** Spell work and rituals are closely related and can be considered synonymous in many cases. *Rituals* are a series of prescribed actions, sometimes performed routinely or repetitively. Although spellcasting and spell work can be considered rituals, rituals don't necessarily have to involve spells, or they can include multiple spells.

See Chapter 11, where I cover these terms in depth and outline the basics of casting, including setting intentions, gathering tools and ingredients, developing incantations, and choosing proper timing. In Chapter 21, I offer ten kinds of spells you can start practicing.

Ritually timing your practice

Whereas rituals are routine or repetitive actions, a *rite* is a formal, structured, and often ceremonial act that marks a significant event, transition, or milestone in a person's spiritual path. The forms of initiation I mention earlier in this chapter are considered rites.

REMEMBER

Rituals and rites in witchcraft are connected to the natural cycles of time, making proper timing a key consideration for magical work. The moon phases and the four seasons provide a consistent and intuitive calendar to guide modern practitioners in aligning their magic with nature's rhythms. For beginners, two primary types of ritual occasions serve as an excellent foundation: Esbats and Sabbats.

Esbats are lunar celebrations that honor the energy of the moon. These rituals often occur during the full moon, a time of heightened energy and illumination, making them ideal for manifestation, divination, and spell work. A key practice during an esbat is "drawing down the moon," a ritual in which the witch channels the moon's power for guidance, empowerment, or transformation.

The new moon is also observed as a time for setting intentions, new beginnings, and quiet reflection. Each phase of the moon — waxing, waning, full, and dark — carries its unique energy, allowing you to tailor your rituals to growth, release, or renewal.

Sabbats, on the other hand, are solar celebrations that mark the changing seasons and key points on the Wheel of the Year. (See the appendix.) They correspond to the equinoxes, the solstices, and the midpoints between them, reflecting the cyclical nature of life, death, and rebirth. The eight sabbats are rooted in ancient agricultural and pagan traditions and are celebrated as times to honor Earth, the changing energies of the sun, and the cycles of life.

Chapter 12 offers rituals you can try, including candle magic.

Exploring common paths of practice

You can dive into more magical paths than I can cover in the span of this book. In the previous chapters, I covered some of the general pantheons and folk practices that inspire modern witchcraft. And in Chapter 9, I outline a few more of the esoteric and occult traditions you can explore to lay the foundation for your studies and narrow your path of practice.

Established traditions, whether they're official religions like Wicca or regional folk practices, can offer helpful structures to guide you in developing your beliefs, cosmologies, methods, and tools.

REMEMBER

As I mention in Chapter 1, *witchcraft* is an umbrella term that encompasses many kinds of beliefs and generalized practices. You don't necessarily have to renounce your religion to practice witchcraft. And if you're non-religious, you can practice *secular witchcraft*, focusing on the practical, personal, and symbolic aspects of magic without considering supernatural or spiritual beings.

For example, some Christians practice divination, and some tarot readers are atheists. Anything is possible!

That said, most witches believe that everything is energetically interconnected and that witches can connect to this energy. Witches come in all different types. Some identify strongly with the methods and tools they use, as in crystal witches, sigil witches, potion witches, and even tech witches.

Although the paths of witchcraft could fill a whole book on its own, I've found that most magical practices fall into four major categories:

- **Divination witchcraft:** Divination witches "read" energy through various modalities, like astrology, dreams, cards, or bones. They interpret the subtle patterns of energy to gain insights, guidance, and clarity about the past, present, or future. Some can connect to angels or spirit guides.
- **Green witchcraft:** Green witches channel the energy of the natural world, working closely with plants, herbs, and the cycles of life. They harness this energy for healing, growth, and balance, often aligning their work with the elements or seasons.
- **Cosmic witchcraft:** Cosmic witches align with celestial energies, including planets, stars, and lunar phases. They tap into the power of astrological events and cosmic forces to enhance their rituals, spells, and intentions.
- **Energy witchcraft:** Energy witches work directly with unseen forces, sensing, channeling, and manipulating energy for healing, protection, and transformation. They can traverse different states of consciousness and communicate with the spirit world.

REMEMBER

I've simplified these categories to help you get started, but keep in mind that most witches work with all four of these modalities regularly. The chapters in Part 4 cover each of these paths of practice in greater detail. Although they're not exhaustive, they're a great place to start to find the beliefs, methods, and tools that call to you.

Divination witchcraft

Divination witches "read" energy, focusing on interpretation to gain insight, guidance, and clarity. They're skilled in recognizing patterns within the subtle currents of the universe, and they use their intuition and chosen tools to connect with higher energies that reveal truths about the past, present, or future. Their work centers on translating these insights into meaningful knowledge for themselves or others.

Following are a few types of divination witches:

- **Augurs:** Interpreting signs and omens in nature
- **Readers:** Using specific modalities for divination, like astrology, tarot, runes, pendulums, palms, and tea leaves
- **Psychics:** Channeling spirit messages or using heightened extrasensory perception (ESP) to intuitively sense messages

Common divination *modalities*, or methods, include using cards like tarot or oracle decks (*cartomancy*), dreams (*oneiromancy*), and bones (*osteomancy*), to name a few. Others divine through altered states of consciousness, receiving messages from their subconscious, spirit guides, ancestors, or higher energies like deities or angels.

I cover forms of divination and many other "mancies" in more detail in Chapter 13.

Green witchcraft

Green witches are connected to the energy of the natural world, working in harmony with plants, elements, and cycles of the earth. They channel energy for healing, growth, and balance, often grounding their magic in sustainable and practical methods. Green witches nurture their connection to the environment, treating the land and its resources as sacred and living forces. They can also operate on the shadow side of the cycle of life, working with baneful energies and death.

Green witchcraft encompasses a wide range of types, including these:

- **Elemental witches:** Encompassing sea witches, who work with oceanic energies; earth witches, who connect with the land; as well as witches who work with natural disasters like hurricanes and wildfires
- **Kitchen witches:** Infusing meals with intention and energy (for example, cooking for healing, love, or prosperity); using herbs, spices, and garden ingredients as magical tools; and treating the kitchen as a sacred space where everyday tasks become acts of magic
- **Hearth witches:** Creating sacred, harmonious energy throughout the entire home, especially the hearth or central gathering place; using fire and the hearth as a symbol of warmth, protection, and community; and engaging in rituals for home protection, family well-being, and balance within the household
- **Forest witches:** Connecting with forest ecosystems; working with trees, plants, animals, and the energy of wild, untamed spaces to channel magic; and honoring the interconnectedness of all life

Green witches may also incorporate psychic abilities to sense the energetic properties of plants, landscapes, or natural forces. Common methods include working with elements, cooking and homesteading, creating herbal remedies and potions, wildcrafting and foraging plants, and exploring the poison path, which involves the careful and mindful use of poisonous plants for transformative magic.

See Chapter 14 for more information and methods about green witchcraft.

Cosmic witchcraft

Cosmic witches align their magical practice with celestial forces, such as the moon, stars, planets, and cosmic cycles. Attuned to the rhythms of the universe and using this connection to enhance their spells, rituals, and intentions, cosmic witches view celestial bodies as energetic influences that shape life on earth and offer guidance, clarity, and power. By observing planetary and lunar movements, they time their magic to align with universal energies, maximizing its effectiveness.

Cosmic witches include four types:

- **Astrologers:** Studying celestial movements, reading birth charts, and conducting planetary magic and rituals
- **Lunar witches:** Working specifically with moon phases and lunar cycles and events, like eclipses

- **Sidereal witches:** Attuning their magic to the stars, constellations, and mythologies, and observing cosmic phenomena such as meteor showers
- **Alien witches:** Focusing on connecting with life on other planets, developing alien-inspired aesthetics, and imagining radical futures

Cosmic witchcraft often employs the stars and planets for divinatory purposes and thus overlaps with divination. These witches also engage in planetary magic, performing rituals to align with the energies of celestial bodies. Moon magic also factors prominently in cosmic magic. I detail all these concepts in Chapter 15.

Energy witchcraft

It can be argued that most witches are energy witches because they connect to energy in some way. But in this instance I refer to energy witches as those who use energy itself as their main modality, without the aid of earthly or cosmic mediums, and for purposes other than divination. Energy witches use their bodies and consciousness to focus on sensing, channeling, and manipulating unseen forces that flow within and around all living things.

Energy witches are centered on understanding and directing energy for purposes like healing, protection, transformation, and balance. They believe that energy connects all aspects of existence, and by mastering their awareness and control of it, they can enact profound changes in themselves, their environment, and others.

Energy witches can include the following:

- **Hedge riders:** "Riding the hedge" between the physical and spiritual worlds
- **Mediums:** Channeling energies and communicating with the dead
- **Necromancers and psychopomps:** Working with difficult, dark, or otherworldly energies, communicating with the dead, and ushering souls between realms of life and death (sometimes called *deathwalking*)

Energy witchcraft is diverse and includes trance states, which allow access to spiritual realms, and *astral travel*, or out-of-body experiences. Energy witches often use lucid dreams as a tool to explore subconscious energy and gain insight. Other practices include mediumship to communicate with spirits and shadow work to heal energetic wounds. Some energy witches also practice *sex magic*, using the power of sexual energy as a transformative and amplifying force. You can learn more about energy witches in Chapter 16.

IN THIS CHAPTER

» Understanding cultural appropriation

» Exploring spiritual activism

» Developing your own ethical code

Chapter 4 With Great Power Comes Great Responsibility

Witchcraft is now a multi-billion-dollar industry, for better and worse. The proliferation of occult tools is a double-edged sword. Practices and religions that were once demonized are increasingly accepted and sought after, which is usually a good thing in my book. But while the inclusive nature of modern witchcraft has been empowering and healing for millions of spiritual seekers, it has also alienated and exploited many others. This chapter covers some common pitfalls of modern practice, including cultural appropriation, environmental degradation, and conspiracy theories. I also touch on "black magic" and the ethics of hexing and cursing. The chapter ends with an introduction to spiritual activism, including ways you can develop your values around magic.

Avoiding Shady Practices

As a witch, you're never practicing in a vacuum. You're connected to everything around you, and every spell you cast has an effect. (That's the point of spells.) But nuanced discussions about the consequences of your actions rarely trend on social media, in favor of highly stylized scenes of altars, crystals, and sacred groves.

FUN FACT

Pop culture informs most modern witch initiations. I love a good witchy aesthetic as much as the next millennial. I'm convinced that the moody incantations in 1996's *The Craft* were subliminal messages activating a sub-generation of baby witches — or maybe it was just the tall black boots!

Whatever your own entry point, developing your identity as a witch will likely involve style and fashion to some extent. This can even be considered a kind of "glamour magic" that's accessible to beginners and sparks excitement for practice, which I get into in Chapter 6. I really do think witchcraft should be fun and even occasionally frivolous.

WARNING

Inevitably, trends fuel consumer demand, and witchcraft has become an industrial complex. It seems every boutique store is selling bundles of sage at the checkout counter. Over the past decade, long-secret practices have filtered into fitness studios and social media content. Influencers with hundreds of thousands of followers are offering buffets of apothecary products, readings, coaching services, and wellness retreats. Although many are experienced practitioners, some are scammers, intentionally seeking to profit off practices they have no connection to.

There's nothing inherently wrong with buying and selling spiritual resources and services, and commerce is one of the ways magical practices have been transmitted across regions and throughout time. But the extreme commodification of witchcraft has contributed to big problems for the environment, indigenous rights, and vulnerable populations, including these:

- **Spiritual tourism and environmental harm:** Overdevelopment of natural environments, overharvesting of resources, and commercialization of sacred sites have caused significant ecological damage. Popular practices like crystal mining, sacred medicine harvesting, and mass tourism to mystical locations have disrupted delicate ecosystems and depleted resources vital to local communities.
- **Cultural appropriation and indigenous erasure:** Many people are drawn by the allure of rare resources and secret practices, without pausing to consider the history, context, or people who have safeguarded these traditions for generations. Often, the commercialization of these practices strips them of their cultural roots, reducing them to trends or commodities while erasing the voices and rights of indigenous practitioners. The result is not only disrespect but also a loss of authenticity and a dilution of powerful ancestral knowledge.
- **Cult influences and marginalized communities:** The commodification of witchcraft has led to some exploitative dynamics, particularly within groups

that thrive on power imbalances. Marginalized individuals seeking community, empowerment, or healing can find themselves vulnerable to manipulative leaders or organizations. These "culty" influences often promise spiritual growth while fostering dependence among members, perpetuating cycles of oppression rather than liberation.

Traveling to magical places

I travel as much as I can, and I'd like to see many of the sacred sites, like Stonehenge and the ancient Incan citadel of Machu Picchu in Peru. *Spiritual tourism*, also known as religious or faith-based tourism, refers to traveling with the intention of experiencing spiritual growth, seeking enlightenment, participating in religious practices, or exploring culturally or spiritually significant sites. It combines travel and spirituality, often involving pilgrimages to sacred places, participation in rituals, or personal retreats aimed at learning, healing, or reflection.

Although all these are wonderful motivations, it's important to know who and what you're giving your money and time to. If you plan to travel for spiritual reasons, here are some things you can do to make sure your trip benefits you without harming others:

- Research thoroughly to learn cultural context and avoid scams.
- Respect local traditions and seek reputable sources and teachers.
- Avoid over-commercialized practices or places with vulnerable populations and resources.
- Support local communities by giving something back for use of their space and resources.
- Minimize your environmental impact as much as possible.

TIP

You don't need to spend thousands of dollars or leave the country to have a spiritual retreat. I've had great experiences with staycations near my home and on low-key hiking trips. The key is to prioritize your spiritual purpose, whether it's practicing meditation, learning from a mentor, or reconnecting with nature. Sometimes the most magical places are closer than you think.

Appreciating or appropriating?

Nothing in the world is new, so humans appropriate things all the time, often without realizing it. The word *appropriate* means "to make one's own," and plenty of things out there are fair game to appropriate, like common use images that you can feel free to remix in your event posters and social media content. Some things, however, you shouldn't take without restraint.

REMEMBER

Cultural appropriation occurs when sacred practices, symbols, or traditions are adopted without proper understanding, consent, or respect for their origins. An example is the widespread commercialization of white sage, a sacred resource to Native American and First Nations peoples. (See the sidebar on *smudging* in Chapter 14.)

Other common forms of spiritual appropriation include these:

- » Overuse of sacred resources that are historically tied to a specific region or culture, like palo santo, a traditional South American wood that's usually harvested unsustainably, shown in Figure 4-1
- » Use of derogatory or stereotypical terms or symbols, like "gypsy" imagery or "voodoo" dolls
- » Nonconsensual practice of secret or closed traditions
- » Use of deities you're not connected to as decorations

FIGURE 4-1: Palo santo incense, or "holy wood," comes from a tree native to South America.

Not all knowledge is meant to be shared or practiced universally. Closed practices often require initiation or community consent to participate. When in doubt, respect boundaries and ask questions before assuming access. Some practices have been kept secret to protect them from harm after centuries of persecution. I promise that you don't need anything that's restricted to do the best magic for yourself!

TIP

If you're curious about something outside of your culture, focus instead on *cultural exchange*, the sharing of knowledge and resources between people of different backgrounds and traditions. This fosters appreciation and consensual sharing.

Appreciation begins with education and ends with reciprocity. When incorporating cultural elements into your craft, ask yourself these questions:

- Do I understand this practice's history?
- Am I supporting the communities that steward this tradition?
- Do I have an authentic relationship to this resource or practice?
- Am I adapting it respectfully and with consent, or am I distorting its meaning?

Other examples and tips for avoiding cultural appropriation include these:

- **Using what's yours:** Use resources from your own area that aren't overharvested or sacred to one region or community, such as rosemary, lavender, or oregano. These herbs can be ethically sourced and carry healing properties.
- **Checking your language:** Words are powerful. For example, you can choose to use terms like *animal guide* or *familiar* for animals you feel connected to in your practice, rather than *spirit animal*, which is specific to some Native American and First Nations communities.
- **Reaching for universal symbols:** Use symbols that transcend cultures, like pentacles and mandalas, or make your own.
- **Identifying accurately:** Use terms like *energy worker* or *spiritual healer* to describe your practice if you engage in similar work to shamanism. Avoid claiming the title *shaman* unless you have cultural ties to a shamanic culture and have been trained accordingly.
- **Learning about your own culture:** Develop your spiritual practice with tools and symbols from your own ancestry or engage in nature-based rituals to connect with your local environment.

WARNING

Beware of fake shamans. As I introduce in Chapter 1, there has been a huge increase in demand for shamans in recent years, especially for the facilitation of ceremonies involving strong hallucinogens like ayahuasca. Ayahuasca ceremonies are increasingly commercialized by Western "shamans," often without proper training or connection to indigenous communities. Verify all credentials, and consult a medical professional before partaking in any psychoactive drugs.

TIP

Before or instead of consuming psychoactive drugs, consider other types of consciousness-altering practices. There are many kinds of pilgrimages and journeys that yield transformative effects.

Spotting "conspirituality"

One of the most troubling things I've witnessed in spiritual circles is the readiness to put all faith into a charismatic person or system that seems to have all the answers you're searching for.

FUN FACT

Conspirituality is a relatively new term for the intersection of wellness culture and conspiracy theories. Conspiritualists often leverage fear and misinformation to sell products or ideologies under the guise of "alternative truth."

One of the hallmarks of conspirituality is *toxic positivity*, the dismissal of any negative information or valid emotions like anger, grief, or pain in favor of happiness and "high vibes." This "love and light only" mindset pressures individuals to ignore their struggles and present a façade of constant positivity, stifling the deeper work required for genuine healing. This can also be referred to as *spiritual bypassing*, and it can show up as seemingly harmless platitudes like "just stay positive." But sometimes, the best work happens when you face your darkness.

WARNING

Scam alert! Always keep one eye open for cults, and beware of spiritual leaders or systems that claim you're suffering or have failed to achieve your desires because you aren't "trying hard enough" or haven't invested in their products or services. These claims often exploit vulnerability for profit, creating cycles of shame and dependency. Remember that your worth isn't tied to anyone else's formula for success.

Modern witches walk a fine line between openness to new ideas and the dangers of dogma. Cults and rigid belief systems thrive in spaces where individuals are discouraged from questioning authority or expressing doubt. They often demand blind allegiance, isolate individuals from their friends and families, and shame those who show vulnerability or dissent. See Chapter 17 for tips on how to spot red flags and avoid cult-like behavior in spiritual groups.

TIP

As a witch, it's your responsibility to question your own practices. Stay grounded by prioritizing evidence-based approaches to self-care.

Sometimes it's really hard to tell the difference between a scammer and a legitimate professional. For instance, many practitioners borrow terminology and jargon from the world of therapy even though they don't have any training in mental health themselves. Buzz terms like *boundaries* and *trauma* can be twisted to manipulate vulnerable followers. Some might even throw around diagnoses and treatments, which can be dangerous.

WARNING

Be cautious of misinformation, especially in the realm of witchcraft, where folklore, traditions, and practices are often simplified, distorted, or even fabricated for online attention. Social media platforms, in particular, can spread misleading or culturally appropriative information packaged as "easy tips" or "instant spells." Practice media literacy by critically evaluating the sources of information you encounter. Look for established authors, practitioners, or communities with a strong foundation in the tradition they discuss. Cross-reference claims, and when possible, seek out books, reputable websites, or experienced teachers to deepen your understanding. Remember that witchcraft is a complex and often deeply personal practice, and accurate, respectful information is essential for growth and integrity in your craft.

To cultivate autonomy in your practice, you can do these things:

- Question teachings or leaders that discourage critical thinking or individual interpretation.
- Build a network of practitioners who value diversity of thought and experience.
- Honor your intuition, even when it leads you to question established ideas.

TIP

Magic and therapy can often work hand in hand, blending the mystical and the practical to create holistic well-being. For example, a grounding ritual with a black tourmaline crystal can pair beautifully with deep breathing exercises to release tension and anxiety. Avoid common pitfalls of conspirituality by consulting with a variety of therapists and field experts.

SHADOWING PSYCHOLOGY

Shadow work is a buzz term that has been largely appropriated from psychology practice by modern spirituality. It's the practice of exploring and integrating the hidden, repressed, or "darker" aspects of yourself. These are often the parts of your personality or psyche that you avoid confronting — fear, anger, shame, jealousy — but that still influence your behavior, decisions, and relationships.

In witchcraft, shadow work is seen as a transformative process that aligns with magical practices, offering a way to heal, grow, and expand your self-awareness. To employ shadow work properly and safely, it's helpful to research its roots. The term originates from Carl Jung's concept of the "shadow self," referring to the unconscious aspects of the psyche.

Shadow work often involves using rituals, meditation, or journaling to shine light on these hidden parts. The goal is not to eliminate the shadow but to integrate it, learning to accept and work with your whole self. Shadow work allows witches to shed limiting beliefs, unresolved trauma, or internalized societal expectations that might block their power. By understanding and integrating the shadow self, you can channel your emotions and experiences into more profound, intentional magic.

Start simply. You can dedicate time during the waning moon to reflect on what you've avoided confronting. Use tarot or oracle cards to uncover hidden feelings or truths. Ask yourself questions like these: What makes me angry or jealous? Why? What do I fear, and how does it hold me back? What traits in others irritate me, and could they reflect parts of myself? Sit with your emotions, especially the uncomfortable ones. Visualize embracing them with compassion.

It's advisable to begin or supplement this work with a qualified mental health professional that can help you process difficult emotions.

To Hex or Not to Hex

I grew up being warned about black magic. A favorite tale in my family lore was about the evil eye. When my dad was a kid in Cuba, a stranger looked into his eyes and whispered some words, and my dad's eyes shut. The doctors couldn't do anything. My great grandmother placed him in a circle and she and other spiritualists prayed over him until his eyes opened. That's why every baby in my family gets a protective charm against the evil eye at birth. I still have mine.

The evil eye is an enduring warning featured in folk tales across the world, as mentioned in Chapter 2. It's one of countless curses that are often attributed to black magic, and it's often summoned metaphorically, as in the evil eye that watches you with envy.

REMEMBER

Witches don't agree about what black magic is. It generally refers to the use of supernatural or magical practices intended to harm, manipulate, or control others for personal gain, revenge, or malice. The term is contrasted with *white magic*, which is typically associated with benevolent or healing purposes.

WARNING

Much like the word *witchcraft*, the label of *black magic* has been leveraged against people who operate outside of accepted mainstream practices. Pagan practices and folk magic that people participate in now and perhaps consider harmless, like worshipping nature gods or making home remedies, might have been labeled black magic. And still today, people misconstrue the practices of closed religions like Vodou and Santería as black magic, as exacerbated by popular portrayals in the media. Additionally, black magic often carries racist connotations, as it disproportionately refers to the practices of people of color.

For this reason, I don't tend to use the distinction between black magic and white magic. I don't perform rituals or spells with the intent to hurt others, and I don't recommend it for beginners. Enacting harmful intentions has a way of coming back around to you.

REMEMBER

Instead of *black magic*, I use the term *baneful magic*, which I see as anything that employs dark forces or destructive intent. I don't necessarily consider these things to be bad. Sometimes you're dealing with difficult energies or need to undo a big attachment in your life or destroy something harmful in yourself, and baneful magic provides powerful tools for this.

Curses and hexes are different, and they run the gamut between good and bad intent. A *hex* is a magical act intended to cause harm, misfortune, or discomfort to a target. It can range from a minor inconvenience to a significant disruption. Although hexing is often associated with malice, many witches use it as a last resort for protection, justice, or retribution. A *curse*, on the other hand, is a more enduring form of baneful magic, designed to bring long-lasting consequences or ill fortune. Curses often require more energy and intent, making them a weighty magical choice.

I think most practitioners agree that curses are usually explicitly meant to harm and should be treated with extreme caution, but hexing is a more controversial aspect of witchcraft. For some, hexes are powerful tools for justice, protection, and energy redirection. For others, they're considered taboo or morally questionable. Understanding the different types of baneful magic and their ethical implications is essential to determine if, when, and how they fit into your practice.

The following are types of hexes and curses:

- **Justice hexes:** Directed at individuals or institutions that perpetuate harm (e.g., abusers, oppressors, corrupt systems). For example: A hex to "return harm to the sender," often using mirrors, black candles, or binding symbols.
- **Binding spells:** Intended to prevent someone from taking harmful actions, rather than directly causing them harm. For example: A spell to stop someone from spreading lies or engaging in abusive behavior.
- **Mild hexes (jinxes):** Lesser forms of baneful magic that cause temporary misfortune or inconvenience, like using a non-harmful irritant to keep someone away from you.
- **Generational or lineage curses:** Long-lasting curses intended to affect a target's descendants or entire bloodline. These are considered among the most extreme forms of magic, sometimes involving ritual sacrifices.
- **Protection hexes:** Baneful magic used defensively, often to repel harm or deter attacks. For example: A protective barrier spell that reflects negativity back to its source.

Alternatives to hexing include protection spells, cord-cutting rituals (like the one included in Chapter 12), energy reversal spells, and justice or petition spells. The ethics of hexing vary widely among witches and magical traditions. Here are some perspectives to consider:

- **The Rule of Three (Wicca):** Wiccans often follow the Rule of Three, which states that any energy sent out will return threefold. For adherents, hexing might not align with their ethical framework. Some non-Wiccan witches, however, reject this idea and believe in radical autonomy paired with personal responsibility for your actions, magical or otherwise.
- **Harm vs. justice:** Hexing for revenge may feel justified in the moment, but it's worth reflecting on whether it aligns with your deeper values. Justice hexes, aimed at addressing systemic harm or oppression, are perceived as more ethical.
- **Consent and intent:** Consider the consequences of your actions and whether the target has truly earned the energy you're sending. Reflect on your motivations. Are you acting out of anger, ego, or genuine need?
- **The burden of energy:** Hexing requires significant energy and focus. Many witches believe that baneful magic can "cling" to the caster, creating unintended side effects. This is why some prefer other forms of conflict resolution before resorting to hexing.

- **Cultural and historical context:** Hexing exists in many cultural traditions as a form of justice or protection. For example, Hoodoo practitioners might use baneful magic to resist oppression, whereas in European folklore, hexes were sometimes used to protect against curses from others. Understanding the cultural context of hexing is vital if you incorporate these practices into your craft.

Ask these questions before hexing:

- Have I tried nonmagical solutions to address the situation?
- What do I hope to achieve with this spell? Is it aligned with my values?
- Am I prepared for any potential consequences or blowback?
- Could I use a binding or protection spell as an alternative?

TIP

Whatever you choose, you should be ready to take responsibility for the consequences of your actions. When in doubt, be kind and rest on it.

For a deeper dive into the ethics and techniques of hexes, see Chapter 19. Alternatively, when you feel upset about outside forces in your life, you can turn more radically inward. Aligning with your own energy and emotions is a cornerstone of most magical practices and certainly an ethical alternative to manipulation. Your magical ethics are as unique as your craft. Embrace the gray areas, and let your practice evolve through respect and care.

Moving toward a Spiritual Activism

Witchcraft isn't just personal. It's political. Spiritual activism calls for aligning your magic with movements for justice. As Rachel Ricketts writes in *Do Better*, "Spiritual activism is the intersection of spirituality and social justice . . . it is the daily, intentional practice of dismantling oppression in all its forms."

Start by supporting grassroots efforts that resonate with your values. Whether volunteering for food banks, donating to housing cooperatives, or organizing a community event, your activism can be as magical as it is tangible.

- **Environmentalism:** Climate change demands urgent action. Crystals, for instance, carry environmental costs due to unethical mining practices. Consider alternatives like ethically sourced stones or creating your own magical tools from natural materials. Advocate for conservation efforts and animal rights as part of your practice.

- **Indigenous rights and decolonization:** Support the Land Back movement by donating to indigenous-led organizations or participating in land acknowledgments. (See Chapter 14.) Center indigenous voices, and elevate their work in your activism.
- **Anti-racism and intersectional justice:** Intersectional feminism calls for a radical inclusivity that uplifts marginalized groups. Center voices from queer, BIPOC, and disabled communities expand your understanding of justice. Gender equity and reproductive rights are intertwined with this work, especially through supporting doulas or access to reproductive healthcare.
- **Queer magic:** Queering magic is an act of resistance. Honor the unique experiences of trans, nonbinary, and queer individuals in your rituals. Celebrate identities through spells that affirm authenticity and dismantle binary structures.
- **Health and healing justice:** Mental health is an essential component of justice. Fight for accessible care, and integrate healing justice practices into your craft. These include prioritizing rest, offering mutual aid, and holding space for collective grief and joy.

If you're interested in learning more, check out Chapter 19, which is all about spiritual activism.

2

Dabbling in Witchy Mythologies

IN THIS PART . . .

Learn about the triple goddess in mythology, including the maiden, the mother, and the crone. Examine how the triple goddess has evolved to include non-Western folk figures, and start to stitch together your unique story of the witch.

Discover the power of the maiden witch, including the concepts of *extrasensory perception* (ESP), shapeshifting, and transformation. Identify your "clair" abilities and practice casting a *glamour* spell.

Immerse yourself in stories of the mother archetype, like deities connected to natural resources and powers of creation. Learn about ritual observances and conducting nurturing rituals, including land libations.

Explore the crone archetype, including stories of dark witches and spinsters. Find instructions on casting a cloak of protection and beginning to connect with ancestor crones.

IN THIS CHAPTER

» Surveying witch mythologies across the world

» Tracing how the folk image of the witch has evolved

» Identifying your own stories as a modern witch

Chapter 5 Weaving the Witch

The witch is by its nature a shapeshifter, evolving to reflect the stories of the times. Contemporary imaginings of the witch draw inspiration from folktales and mythologies across the world. Characters, deities, and spirits are constantly reinterpreted to reflect current conceptions of the witch. As such, the witch is a master of transformation, taking shapes that reflect humanity's light and dark sides alike.

This chapter introduces some of the most enduring witches in world folklore, as well as new folk icons that are being integrated into modern witchcraft. To organize the countless stories of the witch, I use the lens of the triple goddess: the maiden, the mother, and the crone. In the second half of the chapter, I prompt you to think of your own witchy inspirations and how you can start weaving your own stories. (Each chapter in Part 2 begins with stories of the witch from around the world, followed by hands-on advice to help you start your own practice.)

REMEMBER

The definition of the witch is a moving target. Historically, people who don't fit neatly into established society have been called witches. Sometimes those singled out and persecuted as witches do not even identify as such. In any case, they tend to be people who so clearly defy norms that their actions take on supernatural qualities over time.

When I use the term *witch folklore*, I'm referring to a modern mixture of magical histories and cultural stories, ranging from humans in history to gods and spirits of the collective imagination. Keep in mind that most mythologies considered part of the witchcraft canon today were not originally related to witches. The world is forever weaving the witch.

Around the World: Exploring the Divine Feminine in Folklore

As a child, I was captivated by my grandmother's bedtime tale of a witch who haunted streets at night. She first took the form of a warning for me — don't miss curfew, or she'll get you! But that only made me want to stay out late to meet the witch for myself. Over time, I threaded her story through my own, and the nighttime witch transformed with me.

In witch folklore, it's hard to know where history ends and legend begins. Biographies, mythologies, and pop culture braid together into a constantly evolving tapestry of the witch. That's part of her charm and why she continues to capture the imagination. Some of her stories break cultural barriers, told around the world with slight variations in names and details. As society passes these stories down, the witch takes on local flair.

REMEMBER

Witches can be any gender, and male witches were historically persecuted and killed along with female witches. But in contemporary representations, witches typically take on feminine forms. The witch can be said to reflect notions about female power, the patriarchy, and gender roles. When I write about the witch, I use the pronoun *she*, but I mean it as inclusive of all potential gender identities and expressions.

In adulthood, I realized that my grandmother's story of the night witch was told all over Latin America. The spirit known as *La Llorona*, or the weeping woman (see Figure 5-1), is a notorious mother who drowned her own children. She roams the earth calling for them, stealing stray kids along the way. I'm just one of millions of Latin American kids who grew up with this chilling story, and folktales of similar spirits have traveled the world for centuries. My grandmother inserted her own town's name, just as so many other grandmothers have done, so the weeping woman now seems to roam the entire world!

Stories like these capture the human imagination consistently enough to make it into the folkloric canon, providing universal reflections of the witch. They carry a cultural wisdom that allows you to tell a great deal about yourself. Witches are metaphors; they embody and challenge tropes that are woven into society, especially the ones about women's roles.

FIGURE 5-1: La Llorona forever roams, looking for her children.

The triple goddess

The witch is multifaceted and notoriously hard to pin down. In western folktales, she often shows up in three forms: the maiden, the mother, or the crone. These archetypes make up the *triple goddess* in neopagan traditions. The maiden represents the first third of your life, when you're just coming to understand yourself and your powers. The mother represents your middle age, when you nurture others and use your powers in service to the world. The crone represents your old age, when you share your wisdom to empower others to carry on your legacy. The triple goddess is significant in witchcraft, representing all phases of womanhood.

When applied to stories of the witch, each archetype embodies a duality that helps you reflect on your relationships to power, as I outline here:

- **The maiden has the power to inspire and to allure.** The witch can take on the form of a beautiful, territorial figure who beckons trespassers. She assumes a bewitching guise, sometimes tricking her targets into trusting her. She rewards her favorite humans with powers, or she shapeshifts into another creature to protect herself or go in for the kill. The maiden does not abide by outside expectations; she is full of potential energy. She is budding, always on the edge of bloom. She represents curiosity, intuition, freedom, and experimentation.
- **The mother has the power to heal or to destroy.** The witch sometimes shows up as a matriarch in folktales, whether she's a goddess who protects

tradition or a wrathful mother who has lost her children. Sometimes she illuminates your spiritual path, empowering you to find your own way, and sometimes she lashes out in grief and vengeance, threatening the things you thought were most secure.

» **The crone has the power to guide or to punish.** The crone possesses supernatural skills, usually connected to nature or the spirit world. She's a free agent who chooses how to use her powers, sometimes helping those in her community, sometimes punishing those who bring harm on her or others. In some stories, she's a wise protector or caregiver who supports her people in the absence of institutional care, while in others she's a shadow over her village, posing a warning to those who would cross her. The crone is a common representation of the witch in pop culture, often showing up as an elderly woman.

REMEMBER

The three archetypes of the witch are modern interpretations of a wide range of ancient goddess folklore, so you probably won't find an exact reference to them in original texts or nonwestern tales of the witch. Neopagan and Wiccan traditions took up the concept of the triple goddess, inspired by ancient Greek, Celtic, and Norse mythologies. It pulls together related deities or spirits who are historically considered separate beings.

The threefold witch of the west

The concept of female power manifesting in threes is a recurring theme in western mythology, and triads of goddesses represent the cyclical nature of life, death, and rebirth. These triads serve as powerful symbols within witchcraft, offering a way to appreciate the transformative power that each phase of life offers. Among the more famous triple goddesses are these:

» **Persephone/Demeter/Hecate:** Hecate is a Greek goddess associated with magic, witchcraft, and ghosts. She's depicted as a three-faced form at the crossroads between worlds, each face pointing down a different path. Although she's often considered her own goddess, she's closely linked to the myth of Persephone, the archetypal maiden, and Demeter, Persephone's mother. In her ultimate form, Hecate is the crone, and she serves as a guide into the underworld.

» **Brigid/Anu/Cailleach**: Brigid is a Celtic goddess most associated with her maiden aspect, representing the youthful, fiery force of spring, inspiration, and new beginnings. In some stories, she's connected with the mother archetype of Anu, the earth goddess who births and sustains life. As the crone, she's Cailleach, the wise old woman of winter who presides over death and rebirth, bringing the cold that cleanses the land and prepares it for the renewal of spring.

THREADS OF FATE

Sister-witches associated with weaving hold a significant place in various mythologies, symbolizing the intricate connection between fate, life, and the passage of time. The Norns of Norse mythology — Urd, Verdandi, and Skuld — are powerful weavers who spin, measure, and cut the threads of destiny. Urd represents the past, Verdandi the present, and Skuld the future, each holding immense power over the lives of gods and men alike. Their weaving isn't just a physical act but a metaphor for the complex web of fate that binds all beings.

The Greek Fates — Clotho, Lachesis, and Atropos — are another well-known trio of weavers. Clotho spins the thread of life, Lachesis measures it, and Atropos cuts it, deciding when a life ends. They represent the profound power of creation, preservation, and destruction.

» **The Morrigan:** The Morrigan is a shapeshifting deity in Irish mythology linked to fate, death, and prophecy. Her forms are collectively called the *Morrigna*, but there are conflicting understandings of how she fits the maiden, mother, and crone schema. Like Brigid, who's cited as her mother in some stories, the Morrigan is associated with the goddess Anu, sometimes spelled Anand or Anann. Her other forms include the warrior queen Macha (a fierce mother type) and the battle crow Babd, sometimes interchangeable with Nemain (both crone types associated with battle).

The classic triple goddess encapsulates the full spectrum of life's transitions, helping you connect to your powers at different phases of your life. Some trinities illustrate how the same goddess can manifest differently depending on the time of year, comprising the eternal cycle of nature. Others focus on a progression from light to dark, speaking to witches who embrace the darker aspects of the craft.

The evolving triad

Not all witches are goddesses, and not all goddesses are witches. As modern witches continue to redefine the witchcraft tradition, they often expand the concept of the triple goddess beyond its Western origins, incorporating figures from global pantheons, most of which precede the triple goddess and who may not have been considered witches, historically.

WARNING

Some of the deities I cover in this chapter were never originally part of the triple goddess structure. They have only recently begun to be considered in terms of popular witchcraft, as witches from diverse backgrounds look for parallels to the triplicate goddesses in their own cultural folklore. (See Chapter 1 about how modern witchcraft is a constant process of "reclaiming" old folk tales.)

Deities from non-Western pantheons that have begun to creep into modern witch lore include, but aren't limited to, the following:

- **Oshun/Yemaya/Oya:** In the Yoruba tradition, these female *orishas* are divine spirits who are distinct from one another. In recent years, practitioners of West African and Afro-Caribbean traditions have drawn comparisons between them and the threefold goddess. Oshun, the orisha of love, fertility, and fresh waters, aligns most with the maiden archetype and is sometimes referred to as the queen of the witches. Yemaya is a nurturing mother figure who represents oceans and healing waters, providing sustenance and protection to her children. Oya is the orisha most associated with the crone archetype, as she's a fierce deity of storms, winds, and transformation. She's also said to govern the threshold between life and death.
- **Nephthys/Isis/Hathor:** From the Egyptian pantheon, the goddess Nephthys can be considered a crone in modern interpretations, as she's associated with the night, death, and the afterlife. Her sister Isis embodies the divine mother, as she's a protector and healer linked to the earth. Hathor, who closely aligns with the maiden archetype, is a goddess of love, beauty, and joy.
- **The Tridevi:** In Hinduism, Saraswati, Lakshmi, and Parvati/Kali are often considered a unit. Saraswati is the goddess of wisdom, music, and learning, associated with youth and the pursuit of knowledge. Lakshmi is the goddess of wealth, prosperity, and fertility, representing the nurturing and sustaining aspects of life. Parvati can also be seen as the archetypal mother, but in her fierce form as Kali, she represents destruction and transformation, akin to the crone archetype.

WARNING

Be careful not to take modern interpretations of deities as gospel because the goddesses discussed have rich histories all their own and can logically fit multiple archetypes. Many of these deities are central to religious beliefs that adhere more strictly to original or secret texts, so approach them with respect for the old stories. This is especially true of those that are part of closed religious systems, like the orishas of Yoruba. Some practitioners of those systems would take issue with associating their deities with witchcraft. I include them because I've observed that modern witches are increasingly turning to regional folklore that better reflects their cultures, and it's important to stay abreast of the ways witchcraft is shifting.

TIP

I leave it to the individual to choose how and when to incorporate their spirits into their practices, and I keep to my own cultural stories, as I recommend you do as well. (See Chapter 4 on the dangers of cultural appropriation.)

The potential for modern interpretations of ancient lore is endless. Because oral traditions are increasingly recorded in writing, you can reimagine more obscure deities and add your own spin to their stories. As folk retellings breathe fresh life into the triple goddess, witches of various cultural backgrounds make new connections between their childhood witches and the maiden, mother, and crone archetypes. These retellings associate traditional deities with modern witchcraft, transforming them into feminist icons.

The Maiden: Tales of seduction and illusion

Persephone is the quintessential maiden of world mythology. Her progression from innocence to dread queen of the underworld has captured humankind's imagination for centuries. (Persephone's full story appears in Chapter 6.) In witch lore, the maiden is pure desire, reflected through beauty, raw power, or natural forces. The maiden witch is associated with springtime and the period of the month between the new and waxing moons. Brimming with creativity, she possesses a powerful magnetism, drawing energy from unseen sources to attract attention or hide from scrutiny. But the dream she represents can quickly turn to danger because her unbridled wildness can yield violence and disrupt traditional roles. Due to this threat, she's sometimes cast to the margins.

In witch folklore, the maiden beckons the weak-willed and the spiritually inclined alike, luring them in with her *glamour*, or illusions. She usually resides in wilderness areas close to towns, like forests, caves, or oceans. She lingers at borders, sometimes crossing into worlds that most dare not go. The maiden witch tests human intentions, bestowing gifts on her favorites but killing those who threaten or bore her. Her form constantly shifts, and she's sometimes represented by the forces of nature she wields.

The maiden defies the roles imposed upon her, rejecting marriage and domestic life in favor of absolute freedom — a quality seen in Artemis, the eternal huntress, and Brigid, the fiery goddess of inspiration and independence. The maiden exists in a liminal state, neither wholly belonging to the mortal world nor entirely lost to the mystical, a mirror for those who seek to chart their own course beyond societal expectations. Through her pure individuality, the maiden represents an emerging feminism that appeals to novice witches just discovering their latent powers.

TIP

Check out modern retellings of the witch in pop culture. Reimagining the witch is an increasingly popular pastime because younger generations are showing a renewed interest in mythology. New spins on old tales have exploded in literature, television, and podcasts. Through contemporary media, the stories of the witch now reflect the new ways she's enchanting others.

Bewitching waters

Water entities like mermaids and sirens feature prominently in stories of the maiden witch. They embody the dual nature of beauty and danger by seducing unsuspecting trespassers into their depths. They represent the perilous allure of youth, but their charm doesn't just rest on physical attraction.

They also awaken subconscious desires in those who encounter them. They sometimes create altered states of awareness where the usual rules no longer apply and deeper truths are revealed. Tales of sea spirits abound, including these:

- **The Lorelei:** The Lorelei is a siren-like figure from German folklore who sits atop a cliff overlooking the Rhine River. With her long golden hair and mesmerizing song, she lures sailors to their doom.
- **The Havfrue:** The Havfrue, or sea maiden, is a Danish water spirit known for her beauty and enchanting voice. She seduces fishermen and sailors, drawing them into the sea.
- **The Ningyo:** The Ningyo is a mermaid-like creature from Japanese folklore that presents as a blessing and a curse. Unlike other sirens, eating the flesh of a Ningyo can grant immortality, but it also brings misfortune to the one who has consumed it.
- **The Rusalka:** The Rusalka is a water spirit or nymph in Slavic folklore, often depicted as a beautiful woman who dwells in lakes and rivers. She is usually the spirit of a young woman who died violently or tragically. She lives on the fringes of society, haunting the waters and dragging those she lures down to their watery deaths.

TIP

Call on these magical water maidens as inspiration to dive into your emotional depths and invite new powers of perception.

Shapeshifting tricksters

In some stories, the maiden can manipulate her form, reflecting the unstable nature of desire. Usually disguised as beautiful humans by day, shapeshifters reveal their true nature by night. They represent a warning for those who wander where they shouldn't or who too easily give into their lusts.

Recent retellings focus on shapeshifters' vengeance against misogynists and the defense of those who don't fit conventional beauty standards. Legendary shapeshifters across the world include these:

- **La Patasola:** La Patasola is a witch from Colombian folklore, known for her ability to shapeshift. She's typically depicted as a beautiful maiden who lures men deep into the jungle by appearing as a lost or wounded woman. Once they're far from safety, she reveals her true form — a hideous, one-legged creature with sharp teeth — and attacks them. In modern terms, she's a type of *femme fatale*, or dangerous woman, who resists the male gaze and defends those with disabilities.

- **The Selkie:** Selkies are shapeshifting seal-folk from Scottish and Irish folklore who shed their sealskin to become human. Depicted as beautiful women trapped on land when men steal their sealskins, they represent themes of stolen autonomy and the struggle for freedom from patriarchal control. While traditional tales emphasize their longing for the sea, modern retellings frame them as symbols of reclaiming personal power and escaping forced domesticity.
- **The Huldra:** The Huldra is a forest spirit or witch from Scandinavian folklore, typically depicted as a beautiful maiden with a hidden tail, usually of a cow or fox. With the ability to appear as an ordinary human woman, her true nature is revealed by her tail or by her hollow back, which looks like the trunk of a tree. The Huldra can shapeshift to blend in with humans or to lure them into the forest, where she may lead them astray or seduce them. She represents nature that won't be colonized.

TIP

Use stories of shapeshifters to imagine how you might manipulate your image. They can also inspire you to think about the intentions behind your choices so that you can make changes purposefully.

Roaming specters

The lady in white, a recurring figure in witch folklore, embodies the duality of purity and loss. Her appearance is usually locked to a place — on deserted roads, inside manors, or near water — her ethereal attire lulling those who encounter her into a false sense of security. Although she may initially seem innocent, she disrupts the notion of safety by embodying the unknown and uncontrollable. Stories frequently portray her as a vengeful or sorrowful spirit, transformed by betrayal or loss. Here are some ways she shows up across world folktales:

- **The White Lady of Castle Houska:** Castle Houska, located in the Czech Republic, is said to be haunted by a White Lady. The legend goes that she was a noblewoman who died tragically, and her spirit now roams the castle, particularly near the chapel. Some versions of the story suggest she was a victim of unrequited love or betrayal.
- **The White Lady of Balete Drive:** The White Lady of Balete Drive is a popular urban legend in the Philippines, particularly in the capital, Manila. The story tells of a ghostly woman who haunts the road, appearing to motorists at night. According to the legend, a taxi driver raped and murdered her as a young woman in the 1950s, and now her spirit haunts the area seeking justice or revenge.
- **The White Lady of Bernardsville:** The White Lady of Bernardsville is a ghostly figure said to haunt the roads and woods of Bernardsville, New Jersey. The legend claims she was a bride who died in a car crash on her wedding night. Heartbroken and lost, her spirit roams the area in her wedding dress, searching for her lost groom.

» **The White Lady of Kinsale:** The White Lady of Kinsale is associated with Charles Fort in Kinsale, Ireland. The legend tells of a young bride whose husband was killed on their wedding night due to a tragic misunderstanding. In her grief, she threw herself off the fort's walls and died. Her spirit is said to haunt the fort, mourning her lost love.

TIP

Reflect on the lady in white when accessing memories tied to loss and grief. Consider what places you're tied to and what you're most nostalgic for. How can you turn the sad story of the lady in white into something hopeful?

UNRAVELING AND REWEAVING LA LLORONA

Studying the triple goddess helps me reframe *La Llorona* of my grandmother's bedtime tales. As I learn more of her origin story, I'm able to imagine her as a real person with relatable problems. As the legend goes, she was once called Maria, a beautiful young woman who loved to bathe in the river. A man who was passing by became entranced by her and seduced her. They had two children, and for a time she was happy in her role of lover and mother. But their passionate love soured into jealousy and betrayal as the man left her for a woman in a neighboring village. In a moment of madness, La Llorona drowned her own children, a tragic act that sealed her fate as a wandering spirit. Now, as she haunts the rivers and streets at night, La Llorona is forever trapped between the innocence of youth, her hopes as a mother, and the weight of her own monstrous deeds.

In showing her evolution from a young woman to the weeping wraith, modern stories humanize La Llorona. Some even portray her as a feminist who stands up to an abusive man. The witch of my grandmother's stories started off as a monster to fear, but as I grew, I realized that she represents everything my grandmother was scared of. Now when I imagine the young Maria who became the weeping woman, I overlay her with an old photo of my grandmother when she was 15 years old in Soledad, Colombia. In the photo, she wears a white dress, and her long dark braid rests over one shoulder.

My grandmother was an immigrant who had a hard life in her maiden years, and her marriage to my grandfather was a great hope for her. They had six children. My grandfather left her for other women, and she single-handedly moved all her children to the United States, without him. When I picture her telling me about La Llorona, I see her as the crone trying to share her wisdom. In telling her scary stories, she was protecting her grandchildren from the scary ending. She was cloaking me in her love so I might have an easier life. Today I add the threads of my memories to the ever-evolving tale of the weeping woman.

The Mother: Tales of creation and destruction

The mother archetype in witch mythologies represents the nurturing and life-giving force of nature. The mother is associated with the full moon and the cycles of birth and growth and the season of the harvest. She's the protector of the earth and all its inhabitants, representing the abundance and generosity of the natural world.

Demeter is the consummate mother of mythology. She's the goddess of the harvest and agriculture, and the maiden Persephone is her daughter. Her grief over Hades's abduction of her daughter leads to the changing seasons. (Find more on Demeter's story in Chapter 7.) This cycle of mourning and reunion reflects the mother's power to sustain life through both abundance and scarcity, teaching about the rhythms of nature and the necessity of balance in all things.

Nurturing earth deities

Witch lore draws heavily on goddess mythology across cultures, and the mother archetype arises from stories of the earth and the cycles of life, especially the cycle of fertility and birth. These include the following:

- **Gaia:** Gaia, or Mother Earth in Greek mythology, is the primordial mother of gods and humans, emerging from the void of Chaos to birth the Titans and shape the world. She represents fertility, creation, and the sustaining force of nature. Worshipped in ancient Greece through sacred groves and oracles, Gaia's influence persists today as a symbol of ecological balance and the interconnectedness of all life.
- **Pachamama:** Pachamama is the Andean earth goddess and a central figure in Incan mythology, revered as the provider of food, sustenance, and protection. She oversees agricultural abundance, ensuring the fertility of crops and the well-being of communities. Though colonization suppressed traditional reverence for her, Pachamama remains woven into modern indigenous rituals, where offerings, known as *pagos*, are still made to honor and appease her, demonstrating her resilience as a spiritual force across centuries.
- **Tlazolteotl:** Tlazolteotl is an Aztec goddess associated with fertility and purification. She embodies both the nurturing aspects of the earth and the transformative power of nature. As a midwife and pardoner, she was revered for overseeing childbirth and granting absolution for sins. Despite Spanish colonization and the suppression of indigenous traditions, Tlazolteotl's influence endured, surviving through syncretic practices that blended Aztec and Catholic beliefs, ensuring her continued presence in Mexican spiritual traditions.

- **Aphrodite/Venus:** Although the Greek Aphrodite (Roman Venus) is primarily known as the goddess of love and beauty, she's also closely connected to fertility and the earth's bounty. In some traditions, she's associated with the fertility of the land and the growth of crops, making her a symbol of the life-giving power of nature.

TIP

Call on earth goddesses with ties to your ancestry or homeland for their ability to heal, guide, and protect.

Raging matriarchs

Some stories of the mother focus on her wrath and vengeance when she or those she loves is threatened. Her stories reflect the violent power of nature, as listed here:

- **Medea:** In the Greek tragedy *Euripides*, Medea, a sorceress and the wife of Jason, exacts a terrifying revenge when he betrays her by marrying another woman. Medea's wrath is so intense that she murders her own children to punish Jason. Her actions reflect the extreme and destructive potential of maternal wrath when love turns into vengeance.
- **Pele:** Pele, the Hawaiian goddess of volcanoes, is usually depicted as a vengeful figure, particularly in stories where her children or followers are harmed. She's known for her fiery temper and her ability to cause volcanic eruptions when angered. In some stories, Pele's wrath is directed at those who disrespect the land, which she considers her child.
- **Tiamat:** A primordial goddess of the ocean in Mesopotamian mythology, Tiamat is depicted as a monstrous serpent or dragon. Initially a creator and mother of gods, Tiamat becomes a vengeful force after the younger gods kill her husband, Apsu. She gives birth to a host of monsters to wage war against them, embodying the mother archetype's fierce vengeance when her role as a creator is violated.

TIP

Petition a fierce matriarch when you feel vulnerable, when you need to remove obstacles, or when you're called to protect others.

The crone: Tales of guidance and reckoning

The crone in witchcraft is the embodiment of wisdom, transformation, and the profound mysteries of life's final stages. She's associated with the winter and the waning moon. As the elder, she's the keeper of ancient knowledge and the guide through the shadowy realms that people fear to tread. Unlike the maiden and mother, whose energies are vibrant and outward-facing, the crone's power is introspective, rooted in experience and steeped in the cycles of death and rebirth. She's the witch who has walked through life's trials, emerging not just unscathed, but stronger, wiser, and more attuned to the unseen forces that shape the world.

Hecate is the ultimate crone in mythology. (You can read more about her in Chapter 8.) She teaches that endings aren't to be feared but embraced as necessary transitions, making way for new beginnings. Her presence in witchcraft is a reminder that true power comes from within, honed through time, and is wielded with the kind of quiet confidence that only age and experience can bring. Hecate and the "hag" are being reclaimed by modern witches as a reminder that older females possess great powers and that aging can be a transformative experience.

Haunting the woods

The crone is depicted as an old, deformed witch who resides in remote and mysterious places, like the deep woods. She represents wildness that can't be tamed and the aspects of nature that restore balance, indifferent to the danger it imposes on humanity.

- **Baba Yaga:** Baba Yaga is a formidable witch from Slavic folklore, known for her fearsome appearance and dwelling in a hut that stands on chicken legs deep within the forest. (See Figure 5-2 for an example.) She embodies both the nurturing and the vengeful aspects of the crone, offering guidance or destruction depending on how she's approached, and is a powerful symbol of the unpredictable and untamed forces of nature.
- **La Befana:** La Befana is a crone from Italian folklore who lives in the countryside and is depicted as an old woman flying on a broomstick. Although she's more commonly associated with gifts to children, La Befana also has deep connections to nature and the changing of the seasons. She's a solitary, wise woman living on the outskirts of society.
- **The Wood Wives:** The Wood Wives are spirits from German folklore who inhabit the deep forests and appear as old, crone-like women. They're protectors of the forest and its creatures, rewarding those who respect the woods and punishing those who harm it. The Wood Wives reflect the crone's protective and nurturing aspects as well as the forest's ancient, mystical power.

TIP

Call on the witch of the woods to invite solitude, peace, and a closeness to nature.

FIGURE 5-2: Baba Yaga's dwelling is a hut on chicken legs.

Embodying the monstrous

Sometimes the crone takes on the form of a *cryptid* or legendary creature or is accompanied by a *familiar*, a magical companion. Although any of the three witch archetypes can manifest as shapeshifters, the crone's forms are most closely associated with animals and the more dangerous forces of nature.

REMEMBER

A *cryptid* is a creature whose existence is rumored but unproven, often woven into the fabric of local legends and whispered tales. These elusive beings challenge the human understanding of the natural world, occupying the space between myth and reality. While distinct from witches, many cryptids have become associated with witch folklore in modern times:

- **Skinwalkers:** In Navajo culture, skinwalkers are typically elders who have gained the ability to transform into animals, usually predators like wolves or bears. Known as *yee naaldlooshii*, they're revered as experienced practitioners in their communities. The transformation into a skinwalker is believed to require significant knowledge of and proficiency in witchcraft, which is typically accumulated over a long period of time.
- **Naguals:** In Mexican and Central American folklore, naguals are witches or sorcerers who can transform into animals, frequently powerful felines like jaguars. They're usually considered shamans or sorcerers with great powers.

» **Mona Bruja:** In Central America, the Mona Bruja or "Monkey Witch" is typically depicted as a shape-shifting witch who can transform into a monkey or a half-monkey, half-human creature. The Mona Bruja is known for her mischievous and sometimes malevolent behavior, such as causing trouble for those who cross her path or venturing into people's homes to steal or create chaos. Recently, new reports of her sightings have circulated around Nicaragua.

TIP

Imagine what creature or force of nature you would assume to bring balance to the world.

The witch is complicated because she is, above all, an image of humanity. Although she's connected to goddess energy, she can also be a monster. She creates and she destroys. As she reflects the best and worst aspects of humanity, she challenges notions of what the divine feminine should be. She can destroy your sense of security, but she can also show you your power. As a feminist, she evolves beyond the monster to break stereotypes, showing you how to get what you want and stand for what you believe in.

For Your Practice: Crafting an Image

When you weave and reweave the witch in your image, you're inspired to reimagine yourself in the process. You thread her stories with your own, and her shifting forms guide you through the phases of your life.

TIP

Think of your image as a cloak that you're weaving. As a new witch, you'll be honing your own image of magic as you learn and practice.

Spinning yarns

Childhood stories provide a rich trove of lore that you can pull on to develop your own unique image of the witch. Some stories stay with you for a reason. With every tale that captures your imagination, you'll find patterns that reflect your life. As you practice your magic, you'll work these patterns into your own stories. Over time, you'll create an image all your own, and the magic of your story will inspire others.

An image is more than skin deep. It might seem superficial, but your style reflects the things you care about. As you gather the stories, artifacts, skills, and tools that resonate with you, you hone your extrasensory perceptions, covered in detail in Chapter 6. Just as the witch takes various forms in the world's folklore, she also shows you how you've grown and changed. And if you're lucky, she'll remind you of the parts of yourself that have remained the same.

TIP

Search for the witch in an old story from your childhood. It can come from anywhere: a family story, a book, or a movie. Reflect on why the story has stayed with you. Imagine how you can recast the witch as a feminist icon today. Then retell the story, shifting her from a monster to a source of inspiration and wisdom that says something about your own life and experience.

Stitching together your story

Keeping a journal is one of the best ways to track your practice and growth. You can start by researching mythologies and deities you're connected to. You'll want a safe place to reflect and jot down experiences so you can return to them. I like to review these notes on a scheduled basis and journal about what I think it all means. I weave these threads into a meaningful story about my abilities as a witch and the image I'm cultivating. Often, these become the seeds for larger writings, services I offer, or curriculum I teach. My journal is the foundation for the image I'm building and the legacy I'm creating.

TIP

Start with stories and mythologies that are connected to your own home or lineage. These tend to be the most powerful, and you won't run the risk of appropriating from other cultures. That said, it's okay to learn about most deities as long as you approach your study with a respectful curiosity.

It's helpful to have a structure to your journals. I like to organize pages by different types of exercises, including but not limited to these:

- **Ritual notes:** A log of the magical exercises I engage in and notes and impressions that arise during practice. You might include ideas for the kinds of tools and processes you're exploring and developing.
- **Theory notes:** Ideas about what it all means. Sometimes you'll have big strokes of inspiration, and having your journal near will help you capture those lightning bolts.
- **Personal notes:** Every now and then I like to sit with my messy notes and wrangle them into something that makes sense. I take the threads from my practices, the threads from the moments of inspiration, the threads of my memories, and the threads of my dreams, and I weave them into a vision of what I'm creating for myself. I write these in the form of intentions for the month or the season or the year.

TIP

If you keep this practice journal faithfully, you might find that it includes many rituals and spells of your own creation. At that point, you might want to transfer those tried-and-true methods into a spell book, or *grimoire* (which I cover in detail in Chapter 9).

Weaving magic

The word *cloak* appears often in topics of the occult. Witches have historically cloaked themselves in secrecy to protect their powers. As discussed in Chapter 2, they *occult*, or hide, their practices through languages and symbols that only they can understand so that those who aren't ready or can't be trusted can't access their magic. Cloaking is also a type of ritual performed during many kinds of ceremonies, including initiations. The cloak represents achieving a level of proficiency and gaining recognition and protection within an established group.

At this point of your practice, if you've been honing your perceptive abilities and developing your personal story as a witch, you might have gathered enough energy to weave a cloak around yourself. The cloak is a metaphor I'm using to bring all these concepts together, but it's also a real thing that witches make. Witches weave different kinds of energetic cloaks to conceal and protect their powers or to project an image and attract their targets. These are sometimes referred to as *shields* or *wards*.

The act of cloaking is a kind of *glamour magic*. Glamour magic is a form of enchantment that affects your appearance and influences others' perceptions of you. It involves using energy, intention, spell work, and tools to create an "aura" or illusion around you. A *glamour* is basically an image of your own making; it's a cloak you wear that can protect your power and attract what you desire. I cover glamour magic in more detail in Chapter 6, but here are some tips to prepare for this practice:

- **Knowing your purpose:** As you learn about your special talents of perception and establish practices for developing them, a purpose for your craft will start to clarify. You're doing this work for a reason. Maybe it's to empower yourself, or maybe it's to help others. My purpose has evolved to offering beginners ways to enter witchcraft with a good base of knowledge and a sense of responsibility.
- **Setting your intentions:** The next step is to state this purpose clearly in the form of a wish. I like to write my intentions in my journal on a regular basis, usually on each new moon. (I cover intention setting with the stars in Chapter 15.) Keep intentions simple and actionable. For instance, because my purpose is to offer beginner witches resources to get started, my intention

might be this: I want to become known as a helper for new witch initiates, and I want to attract those seeking help along their magical journey of discovery.

» **Visualizing your power:** In my early days of practice, I visualized the witches and goddesses of lore that resonated with me. I was inspired by stories of shapeshifting and connection to the land. Over time, my own image started to emerge, and now I can see her clearly. She's grounded in nature and the weather, especially rain. She creates environments that people want to visit and experience. She shifts with the seasons. Her element is earth, and her colors reflect the turning of the leaves.

Your image is made of the threads of energy you pull from the web of everything — called the universe. It's uniquely yours and yet part of a larger pattern. As you grow, you'll weave your own patterns into the fabric of things, attracting other seekers. One day, as new witches pull at the universe searching for the immortal tales of the witch, they'll inevitably tug at the threads of your story and all the stories that came before.

IN THIS CHAPTER

» Drawing inspiration from stories of the maiden

» Finding potential entry points to magic

» Developing powers of perception as a novice witch

Chapter 6
Pulling Threads of Energy

Energy is the conduit of witchcraft, the invisible thread that connects the physical world to the spiritual world and that runs through all spells and rituals. Just as a spider spins her web, a witch manipulates energy, pulling it from the space between worlds to shape her desires into reality. A witch learns to feel this energy in her bones, to recognize its ebb and flow, and to channel it with purpose. Energy is never static. It always responds to attention and actions.

Mythologies of the maiden witch revolve around beings with extraordinary powers of perception. These witches access the web of energy through their unique abilities to bend their consciousness with intention. In this chapter, I explore stories of the maiden as sources of inspiration for novice witches just discovering their intuitive powers. I outline potential entry points into magical practice and offer tips to train your attention to experience the world through more than just your usual senses.

REMEMBER

Extrasensory perception (ESP) refers to the ability to sense or perceive energy beyond the normal range of the five senses. It's like tapping into a deeper, more intuitive layer of awareness where you can receive information, insights, or messages in ways that go beyond ordinary seeing, hearing, or feeling. *Energy* means different things to different people, and witchcraft encompasses many belief systems, but most witches agree that they tune into subtle, often hidden, aspects of reality in some way.

Around the World: Exploring the Maiden Archetype

When I was a kid, I knew there was something more to the world than what was generally accepted as reality. It called to me in the early mornings when the light was hazy yellow through my window. I could feel the tendrils of something reaching in, and I would follow it out my window before anyone woke up. I walked the borders of my neighborhood and climbed to the top branches of trees. I felt the tendrils in every leaf and bug, reaching up and reaching into me.

I didn't perceive a difference between science and the occult, so observing tiny things seemed like magic, and feeling the energy of the objects of my attention was something like scientific exploration. This melding of sensory input and potential realities is known as *imagination*, which is easily accessible to children who haven't learned to separate the real from the unreal. Children can often access the energetic world much easier than adults, before they're taught to ignore their natural perceptions.

REMEMBER

Anyone can train to manipulate energy, but learning to pull on energetic threads requires discipline. To work with energy is to know that there's no such thing as linear time. Energy is a pattern of relationships that encompasses past, present, and future. With practice, you can perceive these patterns and see how threads are connected. Often, this requires a process of questioning assumptions and unlearning the rules that pulled you away from your childlike vision.

To the novice witch, powers of perception are central. Mythologies of the maiden offer keys to discovery, marking the beginning of magical journeys full of innocence and naivete. From the maiden's perspective, power is the ability to perceive different worlds and access energy. She hasn't yet learned how to wield the threads of energy beyond her own desires. While the mother archetype weaves patterns of energy, and the crone archetype cloaks in the wisdom of energetic interconnectedness, the maiden accesses pure, untrained intuition. What matters in these stories are her magical abilities and the transformative nature of power.

Becoming Persephone

Persephone is the archetypal maiden whose journey connects the physical and the spiritual worlds. Her evolution from passive maiden to queen of the underworld encompasses themes of natural powers, liminal spaces, and shifting forms. Her duality is her greatest challenge and ultimately her strength because it grants her transcendent powers of perception.

Springing from the earth

Before she becomes Persephone, she's known as Kore, daughter of the earth goddess Demeter. Kore is the embodiment of spring. She roams the meadows near her home, surrounded by blooming flowers, her every step bringing new life to the earth. But beneath her youthful innocence is a deeper power, a unique sensitivity to the hidden currents of the world. Kore can feel the whispers of the earth, the subtle shifts in the air, and the unseen forces that connect all living things. This heightened perception makes her not just a bringer of life but a beacon to those who dwell in the shadows.

One day, as Kore wanders far from her mother's watchful eye, her path crosses with a rare and beautiful narcissus flower, more vibrant than any she has ever seen. She reaches down to pick it, and the earth beneath her feet trembles and splits open. Hades, the mysterious lord of the underworld, emerges. He has long been captivated by Kore's ethereal presence and her connection to the natural and spiritual worlds. He seizes the opportunity and abducts her (see Figure 6-1), pulling her down through the earth she loves, into the depths of his realm.

FIGURE 6-1: Hades's abduction of Persephone.

Scarsellino/Sotheby's/Public domain

Journeying to the underworld

In the underworld, Kore's perception becomes her greatest strength. Whereas others might be consumed by fear or despair, she begins to attune herself to the rhythms of this new world. She feels the echoes of lost souls, the flow of the river Styx, and the pulse of life that still exists even in death. As she adapts to her surroundings, Kore's innocence fades, and she begins to embrace the power and wisdom that comes with understanding life and death. With the shedding of her youth, Kore becomes Persephone. Her journey from the light of the earth to the shadows of the underworld teaches that true perception lies in embracing both realms.

Although traditional interpretations of Persephone depict her as a victim of Hades, recent retellings highlight her personal choice. In ancient Greek tales, Hades tricks her into eating pomegranate seeds, binding her to forever return to the underworld. In many modern stories, she knows the contract she enters into by eating the pomegranate, and she does so willingly. Her evolution from victim to free agent is, in itself, a journey that reflects the way feminists have reclaimed the story of Persephone for themselves.

Transforming into the dread queen

As Kore becomes Persephone, she learns to wield the darkness just as she once nurtured the light, becoming a guide for the souls that wander the shadowy realm. Her perception, once focused on the surface world, expands to include the mysteries of the underworld. She rules with compassion and strength, knowing that death isn't an end but a transition, a part of the cycle she had once overseen as Kore. When Persephone emerges from the underworld each year, she brings with her the wisdom of both worlds. Her return marks the spring equinox, and she descends back into the underworld on the fall equinox.

As she moves between worlds, Persephone reveals humankind's natural ability to navigate the seen and unseen. She's a reminder that transformation isn't just about change, but about deepening an understanding of yourself. She demonstrates that the power of the maiden isn't only in her allure but in her ability to perceive the hidden truths that others might overlook. She harnesses that wisdom as she shifts between phases of life, from the budding potential of spring to the depth of winter's introspection. To her followers, she's "Dread Persephone," a title that reflects the reverence and fear she commands in this role as both a nurturer and a sovereign of the afterlife, capable of bestowing blessings or meting out judgment.

Embodying dualities

Through the myth of Persephone, modern witches find a powerful guide for navigating their own seasons of change, understanding that the descent into the depths of their being is necessary for the blossoming of new possibilities. In recent reimaginings, Persephone has been cast as a feminist icon who takes control of her circumstances. In some stories, she's even a willing consort to Hades. In others, her passivity is reframed as a positive quality that evolves into patience and powers of observation.

Other stories of the maiden witch are marked by similar themes, including these:

» **The thread of nature:** The witch connects to the environment, perceiving natural energies that others can't. She wields both the light and the dark aspects of nature.

» **The thread of place:** The witch perceives the border between worlds and has the courage to go where others dare not traverse. She lingers on the margins and moves in liminal spaces, embodying in-between spaces.

» **The thread of transformation:** The witch represents a radical departure from tradition. Her journey connects physical and spiritual realms. She often comes up against some hardship that she transforms into power.

REMEMBER

I use the maiden archetype to organize world myths that connect to themes of duality. Some of the following myths and folk tales may not have originally been associated with the maiden, but they inspire modern witches learning to tap into their powers and embrace their light and dark sides equally.

Connecting to nature

Tales of the maiden usually involve a connection with nature, as her powers are associated with the elements and the seasons. These stories inspire modern witches who use natural forces as their entry point for magical practice. Nature represents innocence and beauty as well as indifferent brutality, a duality inherent in nature witches.

Vasilisa, the beautiful

In the Russian folk tale called "Vasilisa the Beautiful," Vasilisa is sent by her wicked stepmother into the dark forest to seek fire from Baba Yaga, a powerful and fearsome witch who lives in a hut that stands on chicken legs. Armed only with a magical doll given to her by her late mother, Vasilisa navigates the gifts and perils of the forest to satisfy Baba Yaga's daunting tasks, with the doll offering guidance and protection. Vasilisa's ancestral magic helps her overcome Baba Yaga's challenges and survive the wild of the forest. Although she begins as an untouched beauty, her true beauty reveals itself amid hardship. Her doll symbolizes the depth of her perception, bestowed to her through her ancestral line's connection to nature.

Circe, the untamed

Circe, the enchantress of Greek mythology, is one of the most iconic figures associated with witchcraft, embodying the attraction and peril of nature. She resides on the island of Aeaea, surrounded by animals and lush landscapes, which she protects and controls. Circe is a master of herbal potions and spells that transform men into animals. In modern interpretations, Circe is often seen as a symbol of female empowerment, a witch who embraces her power unapologetically, challenging the boundaries imposed by both society and the divine. She's a force of nature who can't be tamed.

TIP

Nature is a great entry point for beginner witches. Find an environment that helps you feel connected to your own natural abilities. I found my connection to witchcraft through trees. I was an anxious kid, and their presence soothed me. When I touched their trunks, I could feel the streams of energy that flowed from roots to the branches that held me.

Living in the margins

Maidens are typically portrayed as innocents who are abducted or cast out by forces they can't control. Recent stories of the maiden empower her to choose her fate. One of her powers is the ability to walk in the liminal, or in-between, spaces and to perceive the borders between worlds. Her powers of perception reside in her movement between the physical and the spiritual realms.

La Ciguapa, the elusive

La Ciguapa is a haunting figure in Dominican folklore who dwells on the fringes of society, at the borders of forests and mountains. She captivates with her enchanting beauty and the melodic, eerie sounds she makes. Yet, beneath her allure lies danger. La Ciguapa's feet are backward, her footprints leading in the opposite direction from where she's going, making her difficult to track and capture. La Ciguapa tricks her pursuers, often coaxing them deeper into the wilderness, where they become lost or meet their doom. She serves as a cautionary tale, warning against the temptations and dangers of the untamed world, especially for those in search of conquests.

La Sirène, the portal

La Sirène is a siren in Haitian mythology. Portrayed as a beautiful woman with a fish's tail who hovers at the borders of the sea and the earth, she holds a mirror that serves as a portal between the mundane world and mystical realms. La Sirène serves as a bridge between worlds, the point where the known and the unknown meet. La Sirène's dual nature, being both nurturing and potentially dangerous, reflects the unpredictable and transformative power of the sea. She's also a symbol of the subconscious state of mind and the spiritual journey. She holds the key to deep, hidden knowledge and the mysteries of the spirit world, offering guidance, wealth, and wisdom to those who honor her while reminding them of the perils of venturing too far into the unknown.

TIP

Modern witchcraft operates at the borders separating worlds. Think of the in-between spaces in your life and the places you're able to pass through that are inaccessible to others.

As I grew, I realized that I preserved my childhood ability to be in nature for long periods of time. I love to go into the wilderness, away from modern amenities. I often hike into areas that many would consider too challenging, having walked more than 200 miles on the Appalachian Trail. Although most people would consider that an athletic achievement, I experience it as a deeply spiritual one, drawing energy from the peace and patience of trees.

THE SPINNING MAIDEN

As a weaver of unparalleled skill, the Greek mortal Arachne challenged the goddess Athena, a patroness of crafts, to a weaving contest. In defiance of divine order, she created a tapestry that depicted the god's misdeeds, showcasing her mastery but also her audacity. Athena, in response, transformed Arachne into a spider (as shown in the figure), condemning her to weave for eternity. This metamorphosis links Arachne to the archetypal witch, a figure often associated with rebellion against divine or societal norms and the wielding of forbidden knowledge. Her ability to weave can be seen as a metaphor for the witch's power to craft and manipulate reality, drawing threads from unseen worlds into the tangible realm.

(continued)

(continued)

Pallas et Arachne, from "Game of Mythology" (Jeu de la Mythologie), print, etched by Stefano della Bella, designed by Jean Desmarets de Saint-Sorlin

Otto Henry Bacher/Wikimedia Commons/CC0 1.0

Arachne's association with witchcraft extends beyond her defiance and transformation; it also resides in the symbolism of the spider. In many cultures, spiders are creatures of mystery and darkness, weaving intricate webs that ensnare and control. Similarly, witches in folklore are depicted as masters of spells and charms, weaving enchantments that bind and alter the fabric of reality. The web itself, a delicate yet powerful creation, mirrors the witch's spell work — complex, hidden, and potent. Moreover, spiders are often seen as liminal beings, residing in the shadows and the in-between spaces, much like witches who operate on the fringes of society, harnessing both creative and destructive powers. Arachne, through her transformation into a spider, thus becomes a symbol of the witch's dual nature — an outcast who embodies both creativity and the dark arts.

Transforming energies

Ultimately, stories of the maiden hinge on some sort of transformation. She's often portrayed as a shapeshifter or traveler of worlds whose powers rest on manipulating perceptions. She represents the ways you can take control of your life and change your circumstances.

Tamamo-no-Mae, the shapeshifter

Beauty and danger mix in the story of Tamamo-no-Mae, a legendary figure in Asian mythology (shown in Figure 6-2). She's a gorgeous woman with the power to shapeshift into a fox spirit. These rare beings are called *kitsune*, an evolution of the Chinese *huli jing*, commonly depicted with nine tails. Tamamo-no-Mae escapes her life as a concubine in China and disguises herself to find a home in Emperor Toba's court in Japan. She gains the emperor's favor due to her charm and intelligence, which seems almost supernatural. When the emperor falls gravely sick, Tamamo-no-Mae is exposed as a kitsune and accused of draining his power. As the legend goes, she escapes through shapeshifting, but she's captured and killed. She then transforms into a vengeful spirit in the form of a stone known as the *Sessho-seki*, or the killing stone, striking down anybody who encounters it.

FIGURE 6-2: A painting of a warrior Tamamo-no-Mae as she turns into the nine-tailed fox.

Yashima Gakutei/The Metropolitan Museum of Art/Public domain

FUN FACT

Today, kitsune are popular in literature and video games, which celebrate their powers of duality and transformation. In modern history, a rock in the volcanic mountains of Nasu of the Tochigi Prefecture in Japan was identified as the official killing stone. The stone is still widely believed to contain the kitsune spirit. In 2022, it split in half, reinvigorating the legend of the fox witch. After all, the kitsune is too clever to ever be boxed in for long.

Hermaphroditus, the integrator

Hermaphroditus, in Greek mythology, was the beautiful child of Hermes and Aphrodite. Their story is one of transformation and the merging of identities. While bathing in a secluded pool, the water nymph Salmacis became infatuated with Hermaphroditus and prayed to the gods to be united with him forever. Her wish was granted, and their bodies fused into one, creating a being that was both male and female, embodying both genders. This transformation of Hermaphroditus represents the blurring of boundaries and the merging of dualities, symbolizing the fluid nature of identity. The myth also explores themes of unity, balance, and the integration of opposites within the self. Today, the story of Hermaphroditus resonates with gender fluid, nonbinary, and trans people.

TIP

As a novice witch, you're on a journey of transformation. You might not see where you're headed, but start with reflecting on what traditions or expectations you're departing from.

Today's witches are reimagining folk characters who weren't originally linked to witchcraft, like La Ciguapa in the Caribbean and Tamamo-no-Mae in Asia (see the previous sections), transforming them into powerful icons. These figures, though not traditionally seen as witches, offer powerful insights and serve as reminders of resilience. By reclaiming their narratives, modern witches not only honor their roots but also create a more inclusive and expansive vision of what witchcraft can be. See Chapter 1 about the reclaiming movements in modern witchcraft, and Chapter 2 about redefining folk monsters.

For Your Practice: Crafting a Perception

The maiden archetype illustrates how perception can be used to direct energy in powerful ways, whether for connecting to forces of nature, staying undetected, or assuming a new form. *Perception* refers to the ability to sense, interpret, and connect with energies, subtle forces, and the unseen aspects of reality. It involves tuning into both the physical and non-physical worlds through heightened awareness, intuition, and extrasensory abilities. This allows practitioners to access hidden knowledge, recognize patterns, and interact with spiritual or energetic realms.

TIP

You can hone your own perception as a novice witch. Think of the things you are naturally drawn to. What calls your attention? What you're intensely interested in can be a clue to a skill of perception that's just waiting to be trained.

Those witches who master their senses of perception can direct energy to their will. When you're ready to take your practice to the next level, see "Casting a glamour," later in this chapter, for instructions on how to wield your powers of perception to alter your appearance or the way others perceive you.

Identifying your abilities

In witchcraft, attention directs energy. When witches *attend* to things, they pull energy toward them, like tugging on the thread of a giant web. You can think of this web as everything in the universe, with all possibilities occurring at once. As a witch, you can sometimes perceive the web through one or more senses. This ability is called *intuition*, or *extrasensory perception* (ESP), and it takes many forms, or *clairs*, including these:

- **Clairvoyance (clear seeing):** *Clairvoyants* can see images, symbols, colors, or full scenes invisible with the naked eye.
- **Clairaudience (clear hearing):** *Clairaudients* can hear sounds, music, voices, or messages inaudible to the human ear.
- **Clairsentience (clear feeling):** *Clairsentients* can experience sudden changes in emotion or physical sensations in their body. They may sense energies or the presence of spirits in certain locations.
- **Claircognizance (clear knowing):** *Claircognizants* can receive sudden knowledge, insights, or thoughts that seem to come from nowhere. This can be experienced as a gut feeling.
- **Clairalience (clear smelling):** *Clairaliens* can smell odors that don't have a physical source. This can include perfume, flowers, smoke, or other odors that seem to have a message attached to them.
- **Clairgustance (clear tasting):** *Clairgustants* can taste without a physical source. Like clairaliens, the tastes sometimes come attached with symbolic messages or memories.
- **Clairtangency (clear touching or psychometry):** *Clairtangents* can obtain information about an object or its owner by touching or holding the object.

These abilities are sometimes lumped in with the word *psychic*. The objects of ESP can appear as real and clear as waking life. Many people can tap into some form of ESP, and it's not uncommon to hear stories about regular people experiencing unexpected psychic moments. Some have a strong natural inclination toward one or more forms of ESP. Novices tend to experience these perceptions spontaneously, often in early childhood or adolescence. With time and practice, you can develop these powers of perception to be called upon on demand.

TIP

Before you explore ESP, take a few minutes to meditate and clear your mind. Set a timer for ten minutes. Sit or lie in a safe, private, quiet place. Take a few deep breaths, and allow thoughts and sensations to come and go. Don't try to hold them back or hold onto them. As you observe them passing, they'll gradually get quieter, and more space will appear between them. As you become more comfortable sitting in meditation, you can increase the time you sit. The quieter your mind is when you're going into these exercises, the more effective they'll be.

Each kind of ESP requires specific practices for development. In a private, peaceful place, try the following exercises and make note of anything that you perceive in the process:

- **Scrying for clairvoyance:** *Scrying* is the process of using a reflective surface to receive visual impressions. You may use a crystal ball, a black mirror, water, or any other reflective material. Sit in front of the object with a relaxed gaze for ten minutes and note what you see.
- **Deep listening for clairaudience:** It's simple: sit and listen and take note of what you hear. You can do this in a quiet room, taking in the faintest sounds around you. Or you can listen to music and hear what's between the notes. You can also use a white noise machine, opening yourself to the sounds that may emerge among the noise.
- **Body scan for clairsentience:** Lie down. Mentally scan your body from head to toe, paying attention to arising sensations or emotions.
- **Automatic writing for claircognizance:** *Automatic writing* allows you to tap into your subconscious and receive intuitive messages through writing. Sit with a pen and paper. After a few deep breaths to relax your mind, write a specific question at the top of the page. Then allow your hand to write or draw whatever comes to mind without overthinking. These can be strings of words or symbols.
- **Memory recall for clairalience:** Recall a specific memory that has a strong associated scent. Focus on the memory and try to recall the smell. Note any emotions or impressions that arrive with the scent.
- **Food tasting for clairgustance:** Set up a variety of food or drinks that remind you of childhood. Taste each item and focus on the emotion it evokes. Note any emotions or impressions that arrive with the taste.
- **Object reading for clairtangency:** Choose an object with a history, such as an heirloom or an old photograph. Focus on the object and allow any images, emotions, or thoughts to come to mind. Record your impressions.

TIP

To avoid burnout, create a sustainable routine around your ESP practice by setting a timer. In the beginning, set the time for ten minutes. As you continue to practice, increase the time incrementally to further build your skills.

REMEMBER

Many of these ESP abilities can overlap. It will take practice to distinguish between them and to be able to call them forth on demand. Have patience with yourself as you explore the different realms of perception.

Attuning your skills

Attuning means to bring into harmony. You'll grow and change a lot in your practice, and your special abilities will shift with you. When I was a child, I was a strong clairvoyant, and I often saw spirits in my room. In my twenties, I experienced clairaudience, hearing voices that were only sometimes understandable. As I've expanded my skills into offering tarot and astrology readings, I've honed my claircognizance and clairtangency skills. It seems that the more I practice on developing one form of perception, others open themselves.

WARNING

Sometimes what's experienced as extrasensory perception can be a symptom of a physical or mental illness. It's important to keep up with your medical checks and seek out therapy if you feel that any experiences are causing you harm or distress, or if there's any indication that something dangerous is going on. If that's the case, keeping a journal will serve a double duty, helping you document your experiences to communicate them clearly with health professionals.

Building relationships with nature

The word *practice* is often used in witchcraft because that's really what it entails. Skills are practiced for the sheer joy of it. Nature offers many opportunities to practice, including these:

- **Communing with trees and plants:** Witches often see trees, plants, and other natural elements as sentient beings with their own spirits. They might form relationships with specific trees or plants by regularly visiting them, offering gifts (such as water, crystals, or flowers), and listening to their wisdom.
- **Honoring animal spirits:** Witches see some animals as powerful spiritual beings. They may connect with the spirits of animals they encounter in the wild or those that appear in dreams or meditations. This connection can involve seeking guidance or protection or learning from the animal's natural behaviors and traits.

- **Connecting to the land:** Many witches believe that the land itself is alive and has its own spirit. Working with the spirit of the land might involve making offerings, participating in rituals that honor the land, supporting indigenous peoples, or simply practicing gratitude for the earth's resources.
- **Working with spirit allies and familiars:** Witches may work with spirit *allies,* which are non-human spirits that assist in magical workings. Traditionally, *familiars* are thought to be spirits that assist witches in their magical practices. These could be animal spirits or other spiritual entities that have formed a close bond with the witch.
- **Gathering ethically:** With great care and respect, witches often gather materials for their magical work, such as herbs, stones, or wood. They may ask permission from the spirit of the object they're taking and leave an offering in return.
- **Infusing objects with spirit:** Objects can be imbued with spiritual energy. Witches craft magical tools, such as wands, amulets, or potions, with the intention of awakening or honoring the spirit within the materials used.

I've made a point of getting myself out into the forest at least a couple of times a year, knowing that it replenishes my energy. Forest bathing has become part of my spiritual practice, and over time, I've felt a transformation in myself. I've gradually divested from the expectations of having more and more things. Success isn't about having more as much as it's about needing less. I've learned this from the trees, whose messages I receive through meditation and dreams.

Casting a glamour

The maiden witches I cover earlier in this chapter are masters of perception, directing energy to their will. When you've identified your greatest perceptive powers and have honed them through consistent practice, you might be ready to direct energy. One such way to manipulate energy is by *casting a glamour*—or using your perception to create an illusion or alter your appearance. The term *glamour* has its roots in the idea of enchanting or bewitching someone with an illusion. In modern witchcraft, it's often used to make oneself more attractive or persuasive or to project a specific energy or aura. It's a good entry point into working with threads of energy. In essence, you're using your perceptive powers to alter your perceptions of yourself, and by extension, the world's perception of you.

The following sections are a general guide on how to cast a glamour spell. See Chapter 11 for a breakdown of spell work and step-by-step instructions for spellcasting.

Setting your intention

In witchcraft, *intention* is the focused purpose or desire behind any spell or ritual. It's the driving force that directs the energy you're working with toward a specific outcome. When you set an intention, you're clearly defining what you want to achieve, whether it's protection, healing, love, or any other goal. Intention is more than just a wish; it's a deliberate and concentrated mental state that channels threads of energy, thoughts, and emotions to manifest your desired result. In essence, your intention is the blueprint that guides the magic you're creating.

Before casting a glamour, clarify what you want to achieve. Are you seeking to enhance your physical appearance, project confidence, or create a specific illusion? The more specific your intention, the more focused and effective your spell will be.

TIP

Take inspiration from the images of the maiden witches you most connect with.

You may want to write an incantation or chant for your intention. An *incantation* is a sequence of words or phrases spoken or sung with focused intent to evoke a specific effect or power. Often used in rituals and spell work, these rhythmic and repetitive expressions are believed to channel energy, communicate with spirits, or activate magical forces, aligning your will with your desired outcome. See Chapter 11 for more on incantations.

TIP

Approach the spell with positivity and self-confidence. Glamour magic is about enhancing your own qualities and projecting your inner beauty or desired energy outward.

Choosing your tools

Tools are personal to witches, and you'll develop your own over time. Some beginner-friendly tools include these:

- **Mirror:** A mirror is often used in glamour spells to reflect the desired changes. It can help you focus your intention and visualize your result. (Find more information about assembling tools in Chapter 9.)
- **Candles:** Use candles to symbolize your intent. Pink or red ones are common for love and attraction, whereas white ones can be used for purity and general enhancement. (Chapter 12 offers a deeper guide to performing candle magic.)
- **Crystals:** Crystals like rose quartz (for love and beauty), clear quartz (for amplification), and amethyst (for enhancing your aura) can be incorporated into the spell. (See the appendix for a list of crystal associations.)

- **Herbs and oils:** Use herbs like lavender, rose petals, or chamomile and oils like rose or jasmine to anoint candles or yourself to enhance the glamour effect. (See the appendix for the magical properties of specific herbs and plants.)

Preparing your space

Choose a quiet, undisturbed area where you can focus. Cleanse the space with incense or by burning a smoke bundle to remove any negative energy, and then place your mirror, candles, crystals, and any other tools on your altar or workspace. (Chapter 10 has more detail about setting up altars and sacred spaces.)

Creating your glamour

Sit or stand in front of the mirror and light your candles. Then follow these steps:

1. **Gaze into your reflection and begin to visualize the desired outcome.**

   Imagine yourself looking the way you wish to appear — whether it's more attractive, confident, or projecting a specific aura.

2. **As you focus on your reflection, see the changes taking place.**

   Imagine a glowing light surrounding you, infusing your appearance with the qualities you seek. Feel the energy of the glamour filling you and radiating outward.

3. **Recite your incantation/intention, repeating it several times.**

   Allow the words to align with your visualization and intention. Feel the energy building with each repetition.

4. **Seal the spell by snuffing out your candle.**

   If using oils and herbs, anoint your pulse points (wrists, neck, and heart area) with the oil or rub the herbs gently onto your skin, focusing on your intention.

5. **Close the ritual by thanking any deities, spirits, or energies you called upon.**

   Imagine the energy of the spell settling into your being, ready to manifest in the physical world.

TIP

After spell work, it's important to release any extra energy and give attention to your body. Some common practices include putting your feet and hands on the grass or eating salty foods.

Carrying the glamour with you

After casting the spell, carry the energy of the glamour with you. Act with confidence and believe in the illusion or enhancement you've created. Glamour magic is as much about belief and attitude as it is about the spell itself. Glamours can fade over time, so you may need to reinforce them periodically, especially before important events or interactions.

TIP

You can infuse a piece of jewelry, makeup, or clothing with the glamour by holding it during the ritual and focusing your intention on it. Wear or use this item when you want to activate the glamour. See Chapter 12 for more on ritually crafted objects.

Being mindful of your ethics

Use glamour magic responsibly and ethically. Ensure your intentions are positive and don't harm others or manipulate their free will. Glamour spells should enhance your natural qualities and help you project the best version of yourself. Remember, the effectiveness of a glamour spell depends on your focus, intention, and belief in the magic you're performing. Combining this with real-world actions, such as self-care and confidence-building, will amplify the results of your glamour.

IN THIS CHAPTER

» Connecting to the mother archetype

» Committing to a spiritual practice

» Creating your own rituals

Chapter 7
Spinning Magic Rituals

The mother archetype is a bridge between the spiritual and the physical worlds. Whereas the maiden accesses the web of energy, the mother channels and sustains it. The mother witch threads together the strands of her power through years of commitment to her craft. She creates a pattern all her own, which she nurtures and protects. She ebbs and flows with the cycles of nature that are reflected in her own bodily cycles. She shares her fullness with others, and she gradually recedes to allow for those who come after her. Once she's gone from the earthly plane, her lineage continues through her energetic mark on the world.

This chapter delves into the mythologies of mother witches and the ways they create and sustain spiritual communities and traditions. These witches are the bedrock of their communities, their power rooted in their capacity to channel energy and nourish culture. In these next pages, explore how the mother archetype can help you develop your craft with patience, open you to the flow of energy, and guide you through your journey. The chapter ends with practices to begin mastering your own creative energies through rituals.

Around the World: Exploring the Mother Archetype

REMEMBER

A *ritual* is a set of actions or behaviors performed in a specific sequence, often with symbolic meaning. These actions can be part of religious ceremonies, cultural traditions, or personal routines, and they're usually carried out in a prescribed manner. Rituals can mark important events, create a sense of order or structure, foster a connection to the sacred or spiritual, or provide comfort and consistency in daily life.

To me, a ritual is anything I practice with the intention to connect more fully with the earth and with the spiritual world. An example is making a libation to the land, as I show you later in this chapter. Rituals aren't beliefs, and they're not the point of witchcraft in themselves. Instead, they're a means to practice presence, attention, and connection. Developing my own rituals has helped me harness intense energies toward creativity and healing. I've learned many of these rituals through the stories of mother witches who have mastered and shared their powers. I continue to look up to them as I enter my middle years.

The methods that mother witches use to channel energies define their craft. They're the conduit for many powers, including these:

- **Power of the Earth:** The power of the earth is central to the mother witch, grounding her in the rhythms of nature and connecting her to the primal forces of life. Through this connection, she channels the earth's restorative energies to mend what's broken and to restore balance to both body and spirit.
- **Power of Creation:** The mother witch is the bearer of fertility, and not just in the literal sense. She's a creator of new possibilities, new forms, and new realities. Whether through the birth of children, the creation of sacred spaces, or the crafting of spells, her energy is one of *manifestation* — the process of bringing the unseen into the seen, the imagined into the real.
- **Power of Lineage:** The power of lineage is perhaps the mother witch's most profound gift. She's the keeper of wisdom, the guardian of traditions, and the protector of her community. Her practice is rooted in the understanding that she's part of a greater whole, a lineage that extends back through time and forward into the future. Through ceremonies and rituals, she weaves together the threads of her ancestors' knowledge with her own, passing down wisdom to her descendants.

Becoming Demeter

In witchcraft, Demeter is revered as a mother goddess who provides sustenance and represents the cycle of life. As the archetypal mother of Greek mythology, she's the goddess of the harvest and agriculture who's responsible for the growth and fertility of the earth. Her grief over Hades's abduction of her daughter Persephone leads to the alternating patterns of growth and dormancy represented by the seasons.

Personifying the land

Demeter's essence is intertwined with the land. Just as Persephone, her daughter, embodies the seasonal bloom of spring, Demeter represents the nurturing soil that brings forth life. She's not only the goddess who ensures the growth of crops, but also the protector of the sacred bond between humans and the earth.

When Persephone is taken to the underworld, Demeter's grief is so overwhelming that she withdraws her gifts from the earth, causing the fields to wither and the world to descend into a barren winter. Demeter's sorrow is reflected in the dormancy of the earth, while her joy at Persephone's return brings about the renewal of life. For modern witches, Demeter's connection to the land teaches the importance of honoring the earth's cycles and recognizing that humans aren't separate from the land, but an integral part of its ongoing dance of life and death. Figure 7-1 depicts Persephone and Demeter, from *Proserpine: A Book of Myths* (1915).

FIGURE 7-1: Persephone and Demeter are often shown together in natural settings.

Helen Stratton/New York Public Library/Public domain

Committing to creation

Demeter signifies the harvest, which is the transition point between times of plenty and fallow periods. But even in the deepest winter is life, and dormancy is part of the process of creation. In her grief, Demeter turns inward instead of ignoring her pain, but she doesn't abandon you. She provides time for your own incubation. When winter breaks, she offers fertile soil. Seeds grow, your creations ripen, and you reap what you sow. You celebrate your harvest, and you store away the sustenance you can because another winter surely lies ahead. Demeter's story is a reminder that creation is not only about the growth and harvest. And your bounty is a sign that you have endured harder times and allowed yourself the grace of change. Even in her deepest grief, Demeter never abandons her commitment to the earth and its people. She continues to evolve in her motherhood.

Sustaining tradition

Demeter's influence extends beyond her role as a goddess of the harvest; she's also a guardian of lineage and the keeper of ancestral knowledge. In her is the embodiment of the mother archetype in its most protective form. Her connection to Persephone is not just one of maternal love, but also of spiritual lineage. Through Persephone, Demeter's wisdom and power are passed down in new forms, ensuring the continuity of life and the preservation of sacred traditions. The myth of Demeter and Persephone highlights the importance of lineage in witchcraft, the passing down of knowledge, rituals, and practices from one generation to the next. In this way, Demeter is not just Persephone's mother, but a mother of humanity.

FUN FACT

The Eleusinian Mysteries were ancient religious rites and ceremonies held in honor of the goddess Demeter and her daughter Persephone in the city of Eleusis, near Athens. These mysteries were among the most significant religious events in ancient Greece, celebrated annually for nearly two millennia, from around 1600 BCE to the 4th century CE.

Their rituals remain a secret, but it's likely that devotees reenacted the stories of Persephone and Demeter to honor the cycles of life, death, and rebirth. As a modern witch, this reverence for lineage may inspire you to honor your own land and ancestors, to seek wisdom in the traditions passed down to you, and to understand that you're part of a continuum that stretches back to the dawn of time and forward into the unknown future. Demeter's story is a reminder that the power of the mother isn't just in creation, but in the preservation and transmission of knowledge, ensuring that the cycles of life continue unbroken.

Connecting to the land

The land offers modern witches many opportunities to harness powers. Each step of land holds the history of all that came before it — the flora, fungi, fauna — and its original stewards. The land shares what it will sustain. If you're open, it trains you how to grow things with its help. The land provides resources you can use to create your own art. Through this melding of humanity and environment, traditions arise. The land helps you mark time and remember your earthly connections.

TIP

Although Demeter represents the predictable cycles of Earth, modern witches know of the many threats to the planet that are making Earth's movements increasingly unpredictable. These include the stripping of indigenous rights to the land and environmental issues like pollution and climate change. Identify a land-based issue you can devote yourself to in honor of Demeter or the mother spirit of your choice.

Gaia, birthed from chaos

Gaia is the personification of the earth and the primordial mother of all life in Greek mythology. Her name comes from the root *ge*, as in geography. Although Gaia encompasses the typical archetypal associations to the mother — fertility, creation, and protection — she emerges from chaos in her origin story. Modern witches are inspired by the more esoteric details of her myths, like Gaia's priestesses, called *pythonesses*. They inhaled underground vapors to commune with the earth goddess, and some consider them the first oracles of Delphi, before it was rededicated to Apollo.

Modern witches honor Gaia by tuning into the cycles of the seasons, the rhythms of the natural world, and the interconnectedness of all living things. Practices to Gaia might include creating altars with natural elements like stones, plants, and soil, or engaging in earth-centered rituals during the solstices and equinoxes to align with the energy of the land. Gaia has transcended local mythology and provides a template for earth worship across the world.

Pachamama, a fertile protector

Pachamama, the Andean goddess of the earth and fertility, embodies both nurturing and protective qualities. As another personification of the earth itself, Pachamama is revered for her ability to grant fertility, abundance, and prosperity to those who honor her. Modern witches who seek to connect with the earth's energies can channel Pachamama's power through rituals, offerings, and acts of reverence toward nature. By engaging with her, witches tap into the ancient wisdom of the Andes, learning to cultivate a deep respect for the earth and its resources.

WARNING

Pachamama's power is dual in nature — while she's a benevolent and nurturing force, she also demands respect and care for the earth, punishing those who exploit or harm the natural world. For modern witches, channeling Pachamama involves not only seeking her blessings but also committing to the protection and stewardship of the environment. This includes knowing when some natural resources are off-limits. The Andes is currently under great threat from spiritual tourism and climate change.

Pachamama will respond most to those who are tied by ancestry or who have committed to the protection of the land. Offerings such as food, flowers, and libations are traditionally given to her in gratitude and to ensure her favor. Witches can adapt these practices today to honor the earth's abundance everywhere.

Pele, the wrathful mother

Pele, the Hawaiian goddess of fire and volcanoes (see Figure 7-2), also embodies the dual forces of creation and destruction, making her a complex and powerful mother figure in Hawaiian mythology that continues to fascinate those familiar with her. As the creator of the Hawaiian Islands, Pele nurtures the land by bringing forth new earth through her volcanic activity, constantly reshaping the landscape and giving rise to new life. This softer side of Pele is inseparable from her fierce and wrathful nature. Her fiery temper and the untamable force of her eruptions are a reminder that creation often comes through destruction, as the old must be consumed to make way for new.

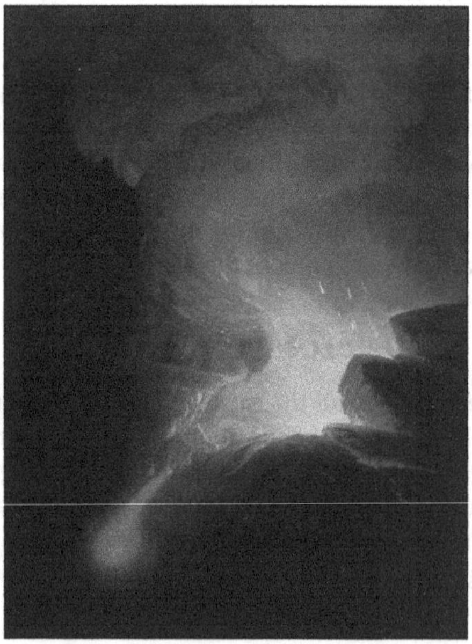

FIGURE 7-2: A painting of Pele, by David Howard Hitchcock (1929).

D. Howard Hitchcock/Wikimedia Commons/Public domain

Legends of Pele have endured, and today, it's believed that taking rocks or foliage from Hawaii will result in a curse. Every year, Hawaii Volcanoes National Park receives thousands of rocks in the mail from tourists who had taken them from prohibited places. The tourists consistently report terrible luck upon arriving home from their travels. This interpretation of Pele's wrath is especially poignant today, as native Hawaiians struggle to keep their homes, especially the residents of Lahaina, which experienced a devastating fire in 2023 that's believed to have been caused by development-related drought. Pele is a reminder of the consequences of damaging the land in this way.

Defining motherhood

The divine mother shows that motherhood isn't just one thing. Some mothers birth and raise children. Others adopt children. Some lose children and continue to be mothers. Still others mother chosen family or the community. Some mother the land, art, or science. Some women aren't mothers, and some mothers aren't women. The mother witch breaks with tradition as often as she creates new traditions.

TIP

Notice what kinds of mother figures you're attracted to. What they stand for can be a key to the kinds of traditions that are calling you. What they nurture can be a key for the things you'd like to mother in your own life.

Cerridwen, the cauldron-bearer

Cerridwen, the Welsh goddess of fertility, rebirth, and transformation, bestows her greatest secrets to her children. In some myths, she has two children: a daughter of light and a son of darkness, representing the dual forces inside of herself. In other myths, she adopts children, who then benefit from her protection. Cerridwen's stories center on transformation, as she expands the definition of what it means to be a mother. Her primary symbol is the cauldron and the potion she creates to bestow knowledge on humanity. In some stories, Cerridwen mothers through her dedication to teaching and expanding consciousness.

Modern witches evoke Cerridwen when seeking wisdom, inspiration, and fertility, as her cauldron is said to contain the divine inspiration that flows from the goddess to her followers. Through this sacred vessel, Cerridwen embodies the cyclical nature of life — birth, death, and rebirth — offering guidance and sustenance to those on their spiritual journeys. Initiates under Cerridwen receive nurturing through education and serious occult practice.

Isis, mother of the oppressed

Isis, the Egyptian goddess of motherhood, magic, and fertility, plays a significant role in modern witchcraft. She's arguably the most worshipped goddess in the history of goddesses, spanning continents from Africa to Asia to Europe. Goddesses like Persephone and Demeter and even Aphrodite are thought to be later versions of Isis. Her devotees included marginalized people and women, who were suppressed as Rome abolished paganism. Isis worshippers persisted, and it's still believed that Isis protects the most vulnerable populations. Modern witches are inspired by her because she defies institutional oppression. She's often portrayed holding a baby and is believed to have inspired modern depictions of Madonna.

Known for her profound magical abilities and protective nature, Isis is often evoked in rituals for protection. Witches who honor Isis may draw upon her maternal energy to support healing and the protection of those in need. Rituals dedicated to Isis involve evoking her presence through offerings, chants, or visualizations, calling upon her to provide protection and empowerment in personal and spiritual endeavors.

Kuan Yin, the compassionate

Kuan Yin, sometimes spelled Kwan Yin, Guanyin, Quan Âm, or Kannon, is a goddess with strong historical ties throughout Asia, namely India, China, Vietnam, and Japan. She has been traced to the bodhisattva Avalokiteśvara, a key figure in Mahayana Buddhism. Avalokiteśvara is traditionally known as the bodhisattva of compassion, someone who has attained enlightenment but chooses to remain in the cycle of birth and death (*samsara*) to help all sentient beings reach liberation from suffering. As Buddhism spread to China and Avalokiteśvara became more integrated into Chinese culture and religious practices, the figure gradually transformed into Guanyin, a female or androgynous representation.

This shift in gender was partly influenced by Chinese culture, where feminine qualities like nurturing and compassion were closely associated with the idea of mercy and care. In Chinese, the name *Guanyin* means "Observing the Cries of the World," reflecting her role in hearing and responding to the suffering. Kuan Yin holds a particularly important place in Vietnamese Buddhism, and altars to her (as Quan Âm) are common in Vietnamese homes. Across all these regions, Kuan Yin is primarily associated with mercy, compassion, and protection. She's the mother of all, often depicted holding a vase of pure water, symbolizing her ability to purify and alleviate suffering, or with a willow branch, which represents her flexibility and resilience. Her gender-bending defies common conceptions of what a mother looks like.

Nurturing matriarchal societies

Real witch practitioners embody the mother archetype more than any other archetype because mothering is woven into everyday life. People turn to mother witches for help when things go wrong because they possess supernatural healing powers. They're sometimes called medicine people or shamans. They're the *curanderas*, the *root workers*, the *sangomas*, and the *Iyanifás*. In contrast to the outcast witch, they're often seen as leaders in their local communities, as they're experts in natural remedies like herbalism.

Unlike mainstream healers, their primary source of power is the spirit world, which they channel through nature. While they employ practical healing modalities like salves and tinctures, they also evoke the spirits to clear energy and lift curses. They do possess the power to harm, but they're generally accepted as an integral part of their communities. Some become spiritual matriarchs and serve as cultural ancestors for new generations who want to learn their healing practices.

WARNING

Some indigenous cultures don't use the word *witch* to this day because it carries negative connotations from histories of persecution. Be careful when referring to some of these magical practitioners as witches. Although they inspire modern witchcraft, and although newer generations of these traditions have started to redefine the witch, the word continues to carry a stigma in some contexts. Because their practices are rooted in histories of oppression, you shouldn't appropriate their specific methods and tools.

Marie Laveau, the rootworker

One of the most famous healers in U.S. history is Marie Laveau, the legendary "Voodoo Queen" of New Orleans. Her life and practices are deeply entwined with the folklore and cultural history of Louisiana to this day. Marie Laveau was born a free woman of color in New Orleans to a Creole woman and a white planter. She was raised Catholic, and her practices mixed the saints of Roman Catholicism with African systems like Vodou and indigenous folk magic. She was widely respected for her ability to heal and protect members of her communities. She wasn't the first Voodoo practitioner in Louisiana, but her life's work greatly contributed to the preservation and evolution of Louisiana Voodoo.

Marie Laveau was known as a matriarch of Voodoo, routinely organizing rituals and ceremonies, many taking place around Lake Pontchartrain. She had a daughter called Marie Laveau II, because she was the spitting image of her mother and shared her powers. She helped extend her mother's networks and legend through her own work in rootwork and conjure (see Chapter 2 for an overview of Hoodoo). Over time, the stories of Marie Laveau became larger than life, and she was feared for her uncanny knowledge of the secrets and inner workings of society. Today, separating the historical record from legend is difficult. Her legacy lives on in the strong folk magic traditions of the southern U.S. Today, witches of color who are returning to their occult roots see Marie Laveau as a magical ancestor.

María Sabina, the curandera

Curanderas are traditional folk healers living predominantly in Mexico and South America. The most famous one is María Sabina (see Figure 7-3), a Mazatec curandera from Huautla de Jiménez in Oaxaca. She became a legend for her extraordinary healing practices with psilocybin mushrooms. María Sabina's healing sessions, or *veladas*, were mystical ceremonies full of chanting and singing to evoke the healing power of the mushrooms. Patients claimed to experience visions and spiritual journeys that led to profound healing and insight. Stories of her life often blend fact and myth, portraying her as a bridge between the material and the spiritual worlds.

FIGURE 7-3: A photo of María Sabina.

Juan Carlos Rangel/Public domain

Although María Sabina didn't call herself a witch, many perceive her work with mushrooms and her spiritual ceremonies to be magical. They involved practices often associated with witchcraft, such as the use of natural substances to achieve altered states of consciousness and communicate with the spiritual realm. She used her visions and spiritual connections to diagnose and heal illnesses, and she helped her followers access powers while in different states of consciousness. Today, psychedelics and indigenous medicine form a cornerstone of magical practice yet pose unique opportunities and challenges. (I explore these in Chapter 4.)

Mami Wata, the charmer

Mami Wata (or Waters) wasn't a historical figure like María Sabina or Marie Laveau, but rather a spirit who manifests in real flesh and blood people of the African diaspora. As her name suggests, her dominion is water, the source of life and fertility. As the embodiment of rivers, oceans, and the mysteries of the deep, she influences the natural world, bringing abundance, fertility, and prosperity to those who honor her. Her power over the waters mirrors the land's cycles of growth and renewal, and her blessings are sought by those who depend on the earth's bounty. Although she's not traditionally associated with witchcraft, her followers engage in rituals and offerings that could be perceived as magical, reflecting a deep spiritual connection to the land and its resources.

TIP

Find the spiritual matriarchs in your life. Take note of the traditions they sustain and the services they provide that might nurture your spiritual path. Trace the history of those traditions. You might be surprised to find that what they so openly practice today was once considered taboo or even illegal.

In the diaspora, Mami Wata's influence has blended with local traditions, making her a central figure in Afro-Caribbean and Afro-Brazilian religions such as Vodou, Santería, Candomblé, and Obeah. She's particularly associated with real community healers. She's both feared and revered for her knowledge of herbalism, healing, and magical practices, which can sometimes take the form of curses and vengeance. This duality is represented in common depictions of Mami Wata as a snake charmer, as shown in Figure 7-4, because she harnesses both natural and dangerous forces.

FIGURE 7-4: A depiction of Mami Wata as a snake charmer.

Unknown Source/Wikimedia Commons/Public domain

THE WEAVING MOTHER

Neith is an Egyptian primordial goddess with Libyan roots. In creation myths, she gave birth to Ra, the Sun, and wove the world with her loom. Because of this, she's sometimes considered the "Great Mother" or the "Mother of the Gods." Believed to have woven individual fates into the greater web of the world, she's ritually summoned when a decision needs to be made or when a problem needs solving. She's also associated with witchcraft because of her love of literal crafting. Some mythologists say that Athena, the Greek goddess of wisdom and justice is the Greek version of Neith. A similar myth is Spider Grandmother, a creator goddess in Native American mythologies.

WARNING

Mami Wata is also more intimately connected to real histories than most deities. During slavery, colonial laws like Jamaica's Obeah Act made her worship illegal, so Mami Wata and other African traditional spirits became *syncretized*, or blended, with Catholic saints (as covered in detail in Chapter 2). Many African traditional religions continue to be demonized today. That's why it's so important to take precautions when worshipping spirits like Mami Wata in countries that continue to persecute practitioners.

For true initiates in traditional African religions, Mami Wata is an important protector of the occult and old wisdom. In modern times, Mami Wata has experienced a cultural revival, and her devotees among modern witches are growing rapidly.

For Your Practice: Crafting a Process

The mother archetype inspires personal practice through connection with the land and a dedication to creativity. The wisdom of the mother is that everything is always in process. As a witch, you are the medium for energy, and after learning to access energy, your next task is to learn how to direct it toward your goals in sustainable ways.

Channeling the elements

The elements present beginner-friendly opportunities to connect to patterns of energy and develop sustainable rituals that feel like a natural part of your life. Here are ways you can ritually connect to each element:

- **Grounding with earth:** Earth is the element of stability, nurturing, and growth. Grounding practices involve physically connecting with the earth, whether through walking barefoot, gardening, or simply sitting on the ground, to help draw on the earth's steady and calming energy. Earth spirits include *gnomes*, who are guardians of minerals and underground treasures, and *dryads*, the tree spirits who protect forests. Additionally, the energy of ancestral spirits is often tied to the earth, symbolizing the roots of heritage and tradition. Working with earth might also involve using crystals and stones, which are imbued with the earth's energies.

- **Flowing with water:** Water embodies the qualities of emotion, intuition, and healing. Water magic taps into the ebb and flow of rivers, lakes, and oceans, aligning with the natural rhythms of the world. Conduct rituals by water bodies, collect and consecrate rainwater, or commune with water spirits like *undines*, which are elemental beings associated with streams and springs. Other water spirits include mermaids, who are guardians of the ocean's mysteries, and *naiads*, the nymphs of freshwater springs. Water's energy is fluid and adaptable, making it ideal for rituals focused on emotional healing, divination, or spiritual cleansing.
- **Inspiring with fire:** Fire is the element of transformation, passion, and energy. Fire magic is centered on harnessing the power of flames for purification, protection, and inspiration. Witches might work with the spirit of fire through candle magic, bonfires, or rituals dedicated to the sun, such as solstice celebrations. Fire spirits include salamanders, elemental beings of fire, and *phoenixes*, mythological birds that rise from their ashes, symbolizing rebirth and resilience. Fire practices often aim to ignite personal power, spark creativity, and facilitate big life changes.
- **Communicating with air:** Air represents intellect, communication, and the breath of life. Air magic involves working with the intangible and ethereal, often focusing on thoughts, ideas, and spiritual communication. Air spirits include *sylphs*, elemental beings of the wind, or fairies, who are often associated with the gentle breezes and the natural world's unseen forces. Rituals might include breathing exercises to enhance mental clarity, working with feathers as symbols of flight and freedom, or performing ceremonies during windy weather to capture the air's dynamic energy. Practices might also involve using incense or chanting to send prayers and intentions into the universe.

TIP

Use what's accessible to you. Take stock of your local environment. Patches of native plants, local watering holes, fire pits, and lookout points are great places to spark your spiritual practice. I'm a beekeeper, and I like to sit close to my bees when connecting to the elements. Their movement touches all four: I watch the bees fly from flower to flower, shining bright in the sun, or drinking water from the pond. They need all the elements to survive, and they remind me that I do, too.

Starting traditions and habits

Traditions like days of observance and ceremonies help you mark time and track the subtle ways you've grown. Some ways beginner witches can start to solidify their practices into milestones include these:

- **Adjusting to the seasons:** Most witches observe the cycles of nature, such as the changing seasons and solstices. These times are seen as opportunities to honor the spirits of nature and the land and your connection to the cycles of the world. Each season is associated with different kinds of rituals. For example, spring is a great time for clearing energy and planting seeds, and winter offers the right conditions for spirit communication. There are also specific rituals connected to each phase of the moon, which are also connected to the phases of the average ovulation/menstrual cycles (covered more in Chapter 15).
- **Observing holidays:** Although many witches celebrate established euro-pagan days of observance (see Chapter 22 for a list of days of observance in modern witchcraft), modern witches observe holidays from a wide range of religions and spiritual traditions. Many witches create their own unique calendar of holidays from personal, cultural, and national days of observance. They conduct specific ceremonies for each day.
- **Keeping a grimoire:** A *grimoire* (discussed more in Chapter 12) is an invaluable tool for witches to track their spiritual journeys and growth. By documenting rituals, spells, insights, and experiences, a grimoire allows witches to reflect on their evolving practices, recognize patterns in their progress, and build personalized records of their magical paths. Over time, it becomes a rich resource for understanding one's strengths, deepening connections with the craft, and preserving wisdom.

TIP

If you're like me, being consistent with your magical practice is sometimes hard. The demands of work and home often challenge me, and when I'm under a lot of stress, my practice is the first thing to go. I've found that having seasonal observances helps me return to my rituals and refresh them to reflect my growth and current goals.

Making a libation to the land

The foundation of all witches' practices is the land. A *libation* to the land is a ritualistic offering of liquid, usually wine, water, milk, or oil, poured onto the ground as an act of reverence or devotion to the earth or to deities associated with nature and fertility. This practice is common in many cultures and religious traditions, where the offering symbolizes a gift to the spirits of the land, ancestors, or gods. The mother archetype is a helpful symbol for the land, as mother deities and spirits typically personify nature and earthly resources. I recommend choosing a mother spirit to visualize when making libations.

The exact rituals associated with libations are specific to each tradition, but libations are open for anyone to practice. In ancient traditions, libations were often part of larger ceremonies and could be offered to ensure a good harvest, to sanctify the land, or to mark important occasions. The act of pouring the libation onto the earth signifies a direct connection between the giver and the land, reinforcing the relationship between humans and the natural world.

TIP

Research where you live to learn about the indigenous people who previously inhabited your area and the spirits and deities associated with them and the land. This research can help you decide who you're making the libation to, as well as which offerings are appropriate. See Chapter 14 for more tips about acknowledging the land.

Gathering tools

Before you make your libation, collect the following items:

- A natural liquid for the offering (such as water, wine, milk, or herbal tea) in a cup or chalice
- A small offering of food, like grains, bread, or fruit
- A candle or incense (optional)
- A quiet outdoor space where you can connect with the earth, such as a garden, a park, or another natural setting

Preparing yourself

When you have all your tools, take time to prepare yourself for the libation by doing these three simple things:

- **Ground and center yourself:** Take a few moments to breathe deeply and connect with your surroundings. Feel your energy settling and your mind becoming calm and focused.
- **Gather your materials:** Place your chalice, offering, and any other ritual tools in the chosen space. Stand or sit comfortably with your feet planted firmly on the ground.
- **Connect with the land:** Take a moment to close your eyes and sense the energy of the land around you. Feel the earth beneath you, the air around you, and any natural elements present — trees, plants, water, stones.

Performing the ritual

After you've prepared yourself, follow these steps to make your libation to the land:

1. **Call upon the land spirits.**

   Begin by addressing the indigenous people of the area and the spirits and deities associated with the land. You might say something like: *"Spirits of the land, guardians of the earth, first stewards of this place, I honor you. I give thanks for the shelter you provide, the sustenance you offer, and the life that flourishes here. I ask for your presence as I offer this libation in gratitude and respect."* Adjust to something that makes sense for your particular land and experience.

2. **Pour your libation.**

   Hold the chalice or cup in both hands, lifting it to the sky. Visualize the energy of the earth rising up to meet you as you offer your thanks. Slowly pour the liquid onto the ground, saying something like: *"To the earth, from which all life springs, I offer this libation. May it nourish and strengthen the land as the land nourishes and strengthens me. May our bond be one of respect, balance, and harmony."*

3. **Offer the food.**

   Place the food offering gently on the ground, near the libation. You might say: "I offer this food in thanks for the abundance you provide. May it return to the earth, sustaining the cycle of life and death, growth and decay. May we always remember the gifts of the land and honor them with care and gratitude." If applicable, light the candle or incense and let it burn down all the way, making sure to practice fire safety.

4. **Close the ritual.**

   Take a moment to reflect on your connection with the land. Feel the energy of the earth beneath you and offer your final words of thanks. You might place your hands on the ground, feeling the solid earth beneath your palms. Visualize any excess energy flowing from you back into the earth, grounding and centering you. Take a few more deep breaths, slowly coming back to your ordinary awareness. Leave any biodegradable, nontoxic offerings where they are, allowing the land to receive them fully.

TIP

Every year around springtime, I offer a libation in my yard, and I pair it with a donation to local indigenous or environmental organizations that act as stewards of preservation in my area. Think of an organization that you might want to support in tandem with your own libation to the land.

IN THIS CHAPTER

» Exploring the crone archetype

» Practicing protection magic

» Calling on your ancestor spirits

Chapter 8 Cloaking in Wisdom

The crone is a master of her craft. After a lifetime of practice, she has learned how to traverse worlds. She guards the threshold between them, holding the keys to the doors of perception. She's a guide through the shadows, as well as a protective light. She's wise, but she's not always nice. She tricks those who haven't mastered their energy or who don't approach her with proper intentions. She can show you how to navigate energy, or she can watch as you become entangled in energetic threads beyond your control. The crone answers only to herself, but she isn't disinterested — she plays her part in the cycle of magic, aware that everyone is connected in a web of energy.

This chapter explores the stories of crone witches and the legacies they leave behind. In some mythologies, the crone creates magical paths to follow. In others, she shines the light on darkness, ready or not. The crone transmits wisdom — sometimes gently, sometimes in ways that can break you open. In the second part of this chapter, I guide you through casting a cloak of protection and preparing to call on your ancestor crones.

Around the World: Exploring the Crone Archetype

The crone witch has spent her life mapping energetic paths between worlds. She's like a spider sitting in the middle of her web, patient for what comes her way. When you're just starting out with your witchcraft, you'll sometimes stumble across a glimmer of the spells she has cast. With a little luck and courage, you can pull on her threads to make your own spells. To master your own craft, however, you'll have to intentionally approach the crone and all that she reflects about you.

REMEMBER

A *spell* is a focused intention or ritual designed to manifest a specific outcome or change in perception of reality. Spells often involve a combination of spoken words, gestures, symbolic objects (like candles, herbs, or crystals), and personal energy to direct the practitioner's will toward a desired goal. The ritual act of performing spells is called *spellcasting*, whereas the broader practice of spellcasting is referred to as *spell work* (covered in Chapter 11).

As discussed in Chapter 6, the maiden witch enters into magic through the power of her *intention*, or the internal purpose that she wants to manifest into reality through her will. She has accessed the threads of energy coming through from other worlds, and she has awakened her intuitive powers. Chapter 7 talks about the mother witch who evolves her ritual practice toward sustaining those beyond herself. She channels energy and shares it through her earthly work. Having mastered the *mundane*, or the physical realm, the crone witch circles back to her beginnings, returning to the point of her magical entry to find that she can now cross paths into other worlds at will.

The triple goddess of maiden, mother, and crone can be considered in terms of three worlds. The concept of the *underworld*, *middle world*, and *upper world* — often referred to as the three realms or three worlds framework — appears in many cultures and spiritual traditions around the globe. These realms are typically understood as distinct planes of existence that represent different aspects of life, the cosmos, or spiritual development. As I cover in Chapter 2, many cosmologies, such as Norse and Celtic systems, are structured in the three worlds. Modern witches still use the concept of three worlds in their practices.

REMEMBER

In myths, the crone archetype is often depicted as a liminal figure who travels between these worlds. As a symbol of wisdom and transformation, she moves through realms to guide others, retrieve knowledge, and mediate between life and death.

I associate each world with one of the triple goddess archetypes, as follows:

- **The Underworld:** This is the world of Persephone, maiden goddess of Hades. Persephone's perception of the underworld awakened her intuitive powers. She became a guide for the dead, a light in the shadows. The underworld is associated with death, but it's where transformation occurs, leading the way to rebirth. The underworld is also associated to the past and *karma*, or the effects of past actions that manifest as patterns you live out again and again until you learn your lessons.
- **The Upper World:** Demeter is both the mother goddess connected to the divine power of the earth and a deity that casts a web of protection. To call on her is to feel the light of the upper world, a space of angels, ancestors, and guardians. The upper world is associated with *enlightenment*, or the release from the cycles of birth, death, and rebirth. Spirit guides can help you learn your lessons and break difficult patterns, shepherding you toward a future free of the limits of space and time.
- **The Middle World:** This is the physical world or everyday reality where humans and other living beings exist. It's the present moment. You're probably perceiving these words while in the middle world, unless there's something you're not telling me. The crone is often depicted as a wise old woman having great powers of discernment and residing in liminal spaces. Hecate is the quintessential crone; she is a guide and protector, helping others navigate life's complexities while maintaining ties to both spiritual and earthly concerns.

Becoming Hecate

Hecate is one of the most famous crones in mythology, widely considered the final phase of the archetypal journey of Persephone and Demeter. No history of witchcraft folklore is complete without her. Hecate, sometimes spelled *Hekate*, may or may not be the first witch that appears in written history depending on who you ask, but she's definitely the quintessential witch of modern times. She first appears as a Titan in Hesiod's "Theogony" in 700 BC. Distinct from other Greek goddesses, the myths surrounding Hecate associate her with witchcraft and the night.

In the *Eleusinian Mysteries*, Hecate witnesses Hades's abduction of Persephone and traverses the underworld to search for her with her iconic torches in hand. She consoles Demeter, goddess of the harvest and Persephone's mother, in her grief at the loss of her child. She carries the torch of wisdom for all those who seek her out.

REMEMBER

Hecate as a crone is a fairly modern interpretation of a complex being that takes many forms in mythology. Her origins and ancestry are contested, and she's associated with many more deities than Persephone and Demeter. Modern witchcraft has cast her as a triple goddess, sometimes also associated with Circe and Medea, but she's an independent deity in her own right. Hecate aligns with many other crones or dark goddesses across pantheons, which I explore in this chapter.

Hecate is popularly depicted as the witch at the crossroads. Each of her three faces points to a different path, and she holds various tools to symbolize each, as shown in Figure 8-1: keys often represent access at the gates of the middle world, the torch lights the path to the underworld, and daggers or serpents often appear as protective symbols of the upper world. Hecate is also associated with dogs, particularly Cerberus, the three-headed dog of Greek mythology who guards the crossroads.

FIGURE 8-1: A popular image of Hecate as a three-faced goddess.

Illustrated by Engravings on Wood/Wikimedia Commons/ Public domain

I've been drawn to Hecate and her many forms all my life. To me, she represents the ultimate mysteries of life, and I've encountered her in times of transition, when I need help seeing clearly and choosing a path. She's shown up to me in dreams, a dark figure who gives me a word of direction or points to something I'd been ignoring. She is sometimes scary looking, and I have to overcome my fear and face her. In those moments, I've felt her open my sight to the truth of what I've been forcing and what's naturally unfolding. She's helped me let go of control and realign with my powers of perception. And most of all, she's led me to connect with my ancestors.

Navigating the crossroads

Hecate's essence is bound to the crossroads, both literal and metaphorical. Often depicted with three faces, she represents the choices presented in your life — the moments where paths diverge, where you must decide which direction to take. For witches, the crossroads symbolize the space between worlds, a place where magic is potent and transformation is possible. Hecate is the guide who stands at these junctures, offering wisdom to those who seek her counsel. She embodies the unseen forces at work in the universe, and her presence is a reminder that every decision carries weight, shaping the path ahead.

Hecate's power is felt most keenly in the spaces where the veil between worlds thins — at dusk and dawn, at the new and waning moons, at the edges of life and death. For modern witches, her connection to the crossroads teaches the importance of embracing the transformative power of choice, trusting in your ability to navigate life's uncertainties, and honoring the cycles of beginning, ending, and renewal.

Hecate's role as a goddess of the crossroads extends beyond physical locations; she also stands at the crossroads of time. As a keeper of ancient wisdom, she preserves the knowledge of those who came before, acting as a bridge between past, present, and future. In her aspect as crone, she represents the culmination of experience, the wisdom that comes with age, and the lessons learned through life's challenges.

Guiding through shadows

Hecate's most sacred role is as guide for souls transitioning between worlds. Her mysteries inspire modern witches to embrace the unknown, to seek wisdom in the dark, and to honor the cycles of transformation that are life-shaping. Hecate is a goddess of the unseen and the mysterious. She walks in darkness, holding a torch to light the way for those who are willing to confront their own shadows. In witchcraft, she's revered for her ability to move through the hidden realms, granting insight into the mysteries that lie beyond the physical world. Hecate is a reminder that there's power in the shadows and that the unknown is not to be feared, but to be explored and understood.

REMEMBER

Hecate is also the goddess of *necromancy*, the practice of communicating with the dead, so she presides over mediumship and death rites.

The mythological Hecate is often depicted as a solitary figure, moving through the shadows with her torches and hounds, yet she's never truly alone. She's accompanied by the spirits of the dead, those who have crossed over and now dwell in the underworld. Hecate's connection to the dead makes her a powerful ally in ancestral work, helping witches commune with their lineage and tap into the deep well of wisdom that flows through time. For modern witches, Hecate's role as a guardian of ancestral knowledge encourages cultivating a relationship with your ancestors, learning from their experiences, and understanding that you're part of an unbroken line that stretches back through history.

Keeping the secrets of the occult

Hecate is a goddess of magic, and her influence calls upon witches to commit to their craft with dedication and discipline. She's sometimes depicted holding keys, symbolizing her role as a keeper of esoteric knowledge and the gates to other realms. Hecate's magic isn't easy or instantaneous; it requires patience, focus, and a willingness to delve deep into the mysteries. Her teachings are a reminder that true magic is a lifelong journey that involves constant learning and introspection.

Hecate is a reminder that people grow stronger with age and experience. This isn't a popular concept in Western culture, which glorifies youth. Although the crone has moved past her fertile years, she still wields powers of seduction and sexual attraction. She has learned to harness her energies and align them with her earthly body. Her beauty is unique and all for herself. She doesn't cater to the patriarchal gaze, and to those who seek to judge or control or use her, she can appear as a terrifying form.

In her role as a guide through the magical arts, Hecate is both a protector and a challenger. She offers the keys to unlock hidden truths, but she also demands that you face your fears and limitations. Magic, in her eyes, is a tool for growth, not for control. She's a reminder that to wield power, you must first understand yourself and your place within the greater web of existence. For witches, Hecate's commitment to magic teaches the importance of integrity and self-awareness in your practice. She shows that magic isn't about bending the world to your will, but about aligning yourself with the natural forces that shape the universe.

Walking the crooked path

A saying in my culture goes like this: "El diablo no es sabio por diablo, sino por viejo." It means that the devil isn't wise because he's the devil, but because he's old. In other words, wisdom comes with age and experience, not necessarily from inherent qualities like cleverness or trickery. A lifetime of experience has no shortcut, and the great gift of aging is insight if you remain committed to transformation.

REMEMBER

In the realms of modern witchcraft, the devil isn't necessarily evil. In certain pagan and occult traditions, the devil is often viewed as a symbol of personal empowerment, rebellion against oppressive systems, or the embodiment of natural forces.

I love the saying about the devil because it suggests to me that there's no such thing as pure evil. This was probably not my mother's intention in saying it to me because she very much believes in the biblical binary of good and evil. But to me, the saying humanized the devil and reinforced my belief that everyone carries light and dark inside of them. Wisdom is the power to discern between the two and to choose which forces to wield. Sometimes working with the shadows is a necessary part of your journey.

If you're dedicated to your spiritual growth, you'll inevitably come to a crossroads or two along the way. You'll have to decide which paths to take. The *crooked path* in witchcraft refers to the path less traveled in society: a nonlinear, individualized approach to magic, where practitioners follow their own intuition and experiences rather than strict dogma or tradition. The crooked path embraces shadow work, personal transformation, and the balance between light and dark, allowing witches to walk between worlds. The crone has walked the crooked path herself, and she can show you the way if you know where to find her and have the courage to face her.

Baba Yaga, the forest crone

Baba Yaga is one of the most iconic witches of all time. She isn't a crone in the modern triple goddess conception. In Slavic lore, she has only ever appeared as a crone, or old woman. *Baba* literally means "woman," and the word was used to refer to grandmothers and sometimes to witches. The etymological roots of *Yaga* are more difficult to pin down, linked to the words *serpent*, *horror*, and *wood nymph*.

Baba Yaga is said to live deep in the forest in a hut propped up by chicken legs. Shown in Figure 8-2, she looks like a common caricature of a witch, with a broom, big nose, prominent chin, and moles. But just as she can cast her home in illusion, she can shapeshift into various forms, including animals and even weather phenomena like storms. Baba Yaga attracts people with her strange challenges, appealing to their egos. She's usually a fearsome figure, but she can be ambivalent or, in rare cases, benevolent. Baba Yaga hails from the birthplace of shamanism and is sometimes considered an outcast shaman.

FIGURE 8-2: A depiction of Baba Yaga from *Vasilisa the Beautiful*, 1900.

Ivan Bilibin/Wikimedia Commons/Public domain

FUN FACT

Baba Yaga is sometimes depicted flying around in a mortar, using a pestle to propel herself. She's been known to eat wanderers who fail her tasks, but if you catch her on a good day and prove yourself worthy, she might offer a bit of treasure.

Whenever you encounter Baba Yaga, you'll measure yourself up against her challenges. She can be called on as an ancestral spirit or during rituals of initiation. But it's unlikely you'll find her on a map. Those chicken legs have a mind of their own.

Holda, the winter spinster

Holda is a Germanic goddess who, in her crone form, is associated with winter, spinning, and the underworld. In some traditions, she leads the "Wild Hunt," a procession of spirits across the night sky, an event associated with death or transformation. She's said to be both a protector of women and children and a bringer of storms and harsh weather.

Holda is the archetypal old spinster. Her very presence is a threat to some, who perceive her as a cautionary tale about women who never marry or have children. But she's also known as a protective force for women and children. She can be harsh, bringing on destructive winter storms. Like many crones, she walks the line between nurturing and death, embodying the wisdom of the crooked path.

ORIGINS OF THE "SPINSTER"

The term *spinster* originally referred to a woman whose occupation was spinning thread or yarn, a critical and respected skill in preindustrial societies. Over time, the word evolved to take on additional social and cultural connotations, particularly in relation to unmarried women.

The word *spinster* comes from the Middle English word *spinnestere*, which means "female spinner." In medieval and early modern Europe, spinning wool or flax into thread was a common and essential household task, especially for women. Thus, *spinster* was simply an occupation-based title.

By the 17th century, the term began to take on additional social meaning. Spinning was often a task performed by unmarried women because it was a domestic skill they could do in the home. Married women, on the other hand, were generally occupied with running the household, raising children, and other family responsibilities. Unmarried women, often without financial or family support, would continue spinning to earn a living.

By the 18th and 19th centuries, *spinster* took on a more negative connotation. It began to be used as a pejorative term for an older, unmarried woman, often with the implication that she had been unable to marry or was socially undesirable. The word came to be synonymous with the stereotype of the "old maid," portraying an image of loneliness or being past one's prime in terms of marriageability.

In more recent decades, the term has been re-examined and, in some cases, reclaimed by feminists and independent women as a symbol of autonomy. Historically, spinsters were often women who lived outside the traditional norms of family and marriage, and some modern thinkers have begun to view this status as a sign of independence rather than social failure. Modern witches have even started to take the term literally, turning to actual weaving and *knot magic*, a form of folk magic that uses cords, ropes, or other materials to bind, store, and release magical energy.

Making friends with darkness

The crone can be seen as a *shadow worker*, one who uncovers your hidden aspects and helps you heal and integrate them into wholeness. (I cover shadow work in Chapter 4.) As the later stage of the triple goddess, the crone is the embodiment of the darker, often uncomfortable journeys of self-discovery. The crone archetype helps witches and practitioners embrace their full selves, integrating both light and shadow to attain deeper wisdom and spiritual maturity.

Lilith, the night demon

Although Lilith isn't traditionally considered a crone in the strict sense, she embodies many qualities associated with the crone archetype — namely, the dark side of femininity. Lilith first appears in ancient Sumerian and Babylonian texts as a female demon who terrorizes women in childbirth and steals babies. She's depicted as a shapeshifter who takes on the form of a nocturnal bird or a monster-bird hybrid. Some stories mention her marriage to the archangel Samael, the king of all demons, also known as the angel of death. In modern times, she's been recast as a witch — perhaps the first witch in recorded history.

Lilith is Adam's first wife in medieval Jewish and Kabbalistic lore, expelled from Eden for failing to obey her husband. She transforms into a female demon to haunt the margins of paradise, posing a constant threat to the family unit. In more recent lore, she's seen as the snake who lures Eve to the apple. In modern times, her story inspires new waves of witches. She's reimagined as a feminist who resists gender norms and takes her own freedom into her hands. Rather than a malicious stealer of babies, she empowers those who need to leave abusive relationships and reclaim freedom of choice over their bodies. Lilith's darkness serves to challenge the patriarchy.

La Santa Muerte, the saint of death

La Santa Muerte is a powerful and complex folk saint venerated primarily in Mexico. Often depicted as a skeletal figure draped in a robe, she's associated with death but also serves as a protector and guide for those navigating life's challenges. Her name translates to "Holy Death," and devotees pray to her for protection, love, financial success, justice, and healing. Despite her ties to death, La Santa Muerte is seen as a figure of mercy and neutrality, offering aid without judgment.

Her worship blends elements of indigenous beliefs, Catholicism, and folk magic, making her a unique symbol of devotion for those on the fringes of society or in need of spiritual help. Though controversial, especially among traditional religious institutions, La Santa Muerte's following has grown significantly, with many turning to her for strength and support in difficult times. La Santa Muerte's origins are shrouded in mystery, but devotion to La Santa Muerte is a highly personal experience. La Santa Muerte reveals her mysteries to those who petition her consistently. One of the major ways devotees worship La Santa Muerte is by maintaining her shrine and conducting death rites.

REMEMBER

A *shrine* is a sacred or holy place dedicated to a specific deity, saint, ancestor, or spiritual figure. It's often a physical space where people go to pray, make offerings, or engage in acts of devotion.

Her most famous devotee is Doña Queta, the first person on record to publicly display a statue of La Santa Muerte outside her home in plain sight. This was a taboo and even dangerous act because pagan practitioners were historically persecuted. La Santa Muerte is now worshipped openly, and millions of people around the world build shrines to her on November 1, the Day of the Dead. Despite her popularity, she remains a mystery to all but her most devoted followers.

Protecting the craft

The crone is a protector, but not in the same way as the mother witch. In her wisdom, she sees the bigger spiritual picture and the ways you're connected. Instead of nurturing the body, the crone nurtures the soul through the occult. Sometimes the crone can make you face uncomfortable realities, so her workings aren't always welcome. In modern retellings of crone stories, her dark and harsh sides are likened to the forces of nature and the wheel of karma. The crone challenges you, so you practice with integrity and contribute to the strength of the collective craft.

The Cailleach, a primordial power

The Cailleach, sometimes known as Beira, queen of winter, is a figure in Celtic and Anglo-Saxon mythology. She is often depicted as a hag or witch associated with winter and storms. In some stories, the Cailleach takes vengeance on those who disrespect her or her domain. For instance, she might unleash terrible storms, prolong winter, or cause blizzards to punish those who offend her. One such tale involves her transforming people into stones for disrespecting her sacred mountains. The Cailleach takes on a new resonance today as the world faces swift changes in climate due to human impacts. Her story is a reminder of the effects of human encroaching and an encouragement to seek balance and sustainability.

Cailleach means "veiled one," or wise woman. Although she's terrifying to behold, she represents true wisdom and the primordial power of the land. She's a foil to Brigid, the goddess of spring, as she brings on the winter, forcing the world to slow. Her time is said to begin on Samhain, or October 31, and ends on Imbolc in early February, as the frost begins to thaw ahead of the Spring Equinox, when Brigid takes over. In modern times, these moments of transition are often referred to as *veils*, like the cloak of wisdom that Cailleach bestows onto those who exhibit gentleness and patience.

Oya, the transformer

Oya isn't traditionally a crone, but she reflects the crone archetype. She's an orisha of the Yoruba pantheon who oversees the winds of change, death, and rebirth. She's also a guardian of the cemetery and the gatekeeper between life and the afterlife. As a deity of storms, Oya works through destruction, sometimes violently removing obstacles from life, regardless of any attachment to them.

WARNING

To work with orishas beyond reading about them, you must be an initiate of a Yoruba religion like Santería, Lucumí, or Candomblé. The ceremony of initiation is called *Kariocha*, a "crowning" ritual that assigns a guardian orisha to initiates.

Working with crone spirits can be transformative if you manage to follow them into the liminal spaces of uncertainty and transition. If you're open to processing the difficult feelings that working with them can bring up — especially feelings of fear and grief — the crone will show you paths you never knew existed.

For Your Practice: Crafting a Legacy

The term *legacy* refers to something handed down from the past, like an inheritance, achievement, or tradition. As you deepen your practices, you will want to learn how to protect yourself, as you will open yourself up to energies that are increasingly difficult to control. After you have protection magic down, you might be ready to reach out to spirits for guidance on your path. You can start by making offerings to them, working your way up to petitioning them for protection. In this section, I guide you through connecting with your ancestor crones. You can think of these crones as reflecting the legacy you want to build in your life, and you can begin to explore your legacy by engaging with them.

REMEMBER

Spirits are non-human entities that exist in various forms, such as nature spirits, elemental forces, guardians, or ancestors. Spirits may be tied to places, elements, or specific functions, and can be benevolent, neutral, or malevolent depending on the tradition and belief system. Deities are all typically considered spirits, but not all spirits are deities.

Casting a cloak of protection

Most kinds of connections with spirits are considered advanced, so before you ever attempt contacts with spirits, you will want to learn how to protect yourself and others. This spell is designed to create a spiritual *shield* or energetic *ward* around you, commonly known as *cloaking*. This spell can be used to guard against negative energy, psychic attacks, harmful influences, or unwanted attention.

You will see throughout this book that I use the terms shield, ward, and cloak interchangeably, as do many practitioners. They're all used in protection magic. See more on protection in Chapter 10.

The best form of protection is to be responsible with your practice. Always do your own research, approach your spells with clear intention, and practice ethical magic.

You can perform this spell at any time, especially when you feel vulnerable or need extra protection. But to sustain the power of the spell work, only cast the spell properly and with patience, and wait at least a month between cloaking spells, so its potency doesn't wane. First, gather the following tools:

- A black or white candle
- A piece of fabric (optional, ideally a dark cloak, shawl, or even a scarf to symbolize the cloak you're crafting energetically)
- Salt (preferably black) or protective herbs (such as rosemary or basil)
- A small piece of obsidian, black tourmaline, or other protective stone
- Incense (like frankincense, myrrh, or dragon's blood for protection)

After you've gathered your tools, perform your ritual in this order:

1. **Prepare your space.**

   Cleanse your ritual space by burning protective herbs or lighting protective incense. Walk around your space with the incense, allowing the smoke to clear any negativity or stagnant energy.

2. **Light the candle.**

   Place your candle in front of you, and as you light it, focus on the flame. See it as a beacon of protection and purity.

3. **Create your protective circle.**

   Surround yourself with a circle of salt or scatter protective herbs around you. This forms the first layer of protection, grounding and shielding you from harm. If you have a protective stone, place it in the center or hold it in your hand to strengthen your shield.

4. **Visualize the cloak.**

   Close your eyes and take several deep breaths. Visualize a glowing cloak or veil of light slowly descending over your body. It can be any color you associate with protection — deep violet, white, silver, or even black. As this cloak settles around your shoulders and drapes over your entire body, imagine it growing stronger and more impenetrable with every breath. Picture it wrapping you in warmth, safety, and light, deflecting any negative energy or ill intent.

You may say:

"By thread and weave, I craft a shield,

To protect my mind, my heart, my field.

No harm may pass, no ill shall stay,

This cloak of power keeps danger at bay."

5. **Seal the spell and close the ritual.**

   Focus on your intention one final time and let the feeling of protection solidify within and around you. Feel the cloak becoming a strong, permanent shield that moves with you, unseen but always present. Extinguish the candle, thanking it for its light and protection.

6. **Wear the cloak.**

   If you used a physical item (like a cloak or scarf), you can wear it whenever you feel you need extra protection, or you can leave it on your altar, charged with protective energy.

Now you're ready to walk your magical path, knowing that you're part of a vast web of energy, a legacy that you'll continue with your magic and that you'll pass on in your own crone years.

Offerings at personal crossroads

When I had a handle on my practice and was ready to become more committed to my path, I called on Hecate on the night of a dark moon at a personal crossroads. That night opened a path of practice for me that continues to be full of twists and turns. It's a nontraditional path that sometimes leads me through pain and grief, but it also keeps me true to my purpose and values.

WARNING

Working with spirits at the crossroads is an advanced practice, especially when you're dealing with deities (and even more so if your deity is Hecate!). I want you to know about these practices but also to beware that opening communication to spirits can lead to intense experiences. Before performing a ritual like an offering at a crossroads, make sure you're well practiced in your protection magic and ready to receive messages that could possibly disrupt your status quo and lead to big changes in your life. I recommend waiting until you are fully initiated into your path (see Chapter 9) or involved with a coven (see Chapter 17), when you've learned the guidelines for working with spirits and practiced with support from others.

REMEMBER

Crossroads are one of the most sacred sites for spirit work, liminal spaces where many paths converge. They are associated with the crone in particular, who uses energetic axes like the crossroads to access different worlds. Crossroads are actual sites, but they're also metaphorical. Humans often reach to spirits at times of uncertainty, seeking guidance along the path, when they need to be shown new paths, or when they need to know for certain that a path isn't for them. Personal crossroads provide powerful energies for calling on spirits.

Over the course of your practice, you'll probably connect to various spirits. I recommend reaching for a friendly ancestor crone to start, like a grandparent who recently passed. The first step in your devotion to your spirit is to learn about them and make offerings to them. In Chapter 10, I cover creating sacred spaces and altars, important sites for ancestral communication.

REMEMBER

An *evocation* is the act of calling on a deity, spirit, or other supernatural entity within a defined sacred space to engage with its energy. Evocation typically involves creating an external connection with the entity for communication, aid, or collaboration with spirits.

WARNING

An evocation is distinct from *invocation*, which is a highly advanced practice where the deity's essence is summoned to dwell in the sacred space or within the practitioner. I do not recommend invoking deities until you are an experienced practitioner. Witches take years to learn to safely invoke deities, as it can be considered a form of possession and highly dangerous.

To open the connection to your ancestor spirit, you can start small, at your home altar. You can research offerings that your ancestor likes. Typically, you'll light candles for your spirit, lay out your offerings, and speak directly to them, using an evocation like: "[Name of Spirit], I call upon you. Come forth and lend me your wisdom." Before making any requests, take time to get to know each other. You may sit in meditation at your altar, visualize your ancestor spirit, and write in your journal. Close your session by snuffing out your candles and thank your ancestor spirits. Remain open to any messages that might come through the following days after evoking a spirit, including in dreams. You can also use a form of divination like tarot cards to interpret divine messages.

REMEMBER

Over time, you can work up to petitioning your spirits. A *petition* is a written or spoken request made to a deity, spirit, or the universe, asking for help, guidance, or the fulfillment of a specific desire or goal. Petitions are often part of spell work or rituals and serve as a clear and focused statement of intent. Make sure to always close your petition by thanking your spirits. Petitions are particularly powerful at night and on big lunar moments like new and full moons.

Your relationship with your ancestor crone will be stronger if you make consistent offerings and give of your time and energy without expectation. See Chapter 2 for more on working with your ancestors. If you keep at it, you can work up to conducting full ceremonies on important ritual days of observance. The energy of the crone will illuminate your path in times of uncertainty and help you cast your sights to your future with confidence while growing steadily toward your own crone years.

3

Practicing Your Craft

IN THIS PART . . .

Discover ways to connect to your ancestry and different occult traditions. Explore several kinds of witchcraft initiation. Learn about grimoires and how to keep one of your own.

Create a sacred space for your magic. Find out how to clear energy, cleanse your practice area, and cast protections. Choose your go-to ritual tools and materials to set up your home altar.

Understand the basics of spellcasting and spell work. Learn to set intentions, choose the right spells, gather magical ingredients, design incantations and symbols, and time your spells. Get acquainted with common tools and the process of consecration.

Incorporate rituals into your daily life. Explore how to craft ritual objects such as amulets, talismans, sigils, and spell jars. Learn to perform ceremonies and conduct candle magic rituals.

IN THIS CHAPTER

» Studying traditional frameworks of witchcraft

» Designing your magical initiation

» Developing a personal grimoire

Chapter 9
Initiating Your Magic

Practicing witchcraft isn't just a matter of memorizing spells and rituals. Becoming a witch involves no standardized tests or widely accepted certifications. (But if you're a school-loving nerd like me, you probably wish there were!) The witchcraft journey is a highly personal, creative, and ever-evolving process. The most adept witches cultivate curiosity and humility, and they commit to life-long learning. The path to witchcraft is varied, but the foundation of any witch's path is a dedication to education and practice.

Studying the occult requires patience and discipline, but it's also exciting to explore your personal experience through the lens of the traditions and practices you're studying. As you develop your own craft, keeping a *grimoire* is an essential part of your practice, serving as a living record of your growth, discoveries, and personal insights. This chapter explores different paradigms of traditional witchcraft and folk magic, outlines ways you can initiate your unique path, and guides you in creating your first grimoire, a powerful tool for self-reflection and mastery.

Laying the Foundation: Your Occult Studies

The occult has called to me since adolescence. Maybe it was wishful thinking — what teenager doesn't hope for special powers? — but I had the sense that life had some hidden design just under the surface of my mundane world. I spent hours in libraries and bookstores, scouring books on mythology and witchcraft. I jumped through different ages of time and across regions of the world, looking for something that would explain the order of the universe. Over time, I started to get a sense of my own beliefs and cobbled together my own practice. But no matter how much I've learned, the occult has always remained, well, occult.

FUN FACT

The word *occult* comes from the Latin adjective *occultus*, which means "hidden," "secret," or "concealed."

The etymology of *occult* calls to mind secret orders and hidden truths. It's an appropriate term to refer to the myriad magical practices that have been historically veiled from ordinary life. Some mystical traditions have kept their knowledge occulted to remain exclusive, whereas others have protected their practices to avoid persecution.

REMEMBER

The occult isn't synonymous with witchcraft. It's an umbrella term that covers a variety of systems and practices, including ceremonial magic, divination, astrology, and mystical philosophies. Although witchcraft practices often fall under the occult umbrella, not all witches consider themselves occultists.

Historically, groups that officially referred to themselves as occultists were highly exclusive and often required initiation. They typically organized around *esotericism*, the pursuit of hidden or inner knowledge.

TUGGING AT ALCHEMICAL ROOTS

Alchemy is an ancient philosophical and proto-scientific practice that seeks to transform and purify matter while exploring the mysteries of existence. It is often symbolized by the pursuit of turning base metals into gold. Its principles combine elements of chemistry, mysticism, and philosophy.

Alchemy has roots in Egypt, China, and Mesopotamia as early as 2000 BCE. In Egypt, alchemy centered on transformation, symbolized by the fertile black soil of the Nile. In China, Taoist alchemists pursued the elixir of immortality, focusing on balancing yin and yang while advancing herbal and mineral medicine.

Greek and Roman influences enriched alchemy during the Hellenistic period. Thinkers like Zosimos of Panopolis combined Egyptian spiritualism with Greek philosophy, focusing on purifying substances as metaphors for spiritual refinement. This knowledge spread through the Roman Empire, later reaching the Islamic world.

During the Islamic Golden Age (8th–13th centuries), scholars like Jabir ibn Hayyan advanced alchemical methods, introducing experimental techniques that laid the foundation for modern chemistry. When these texts were translated into Latin in the 12th century, European alchemy flourished. Medieval practitioners like Roger Bacon and Paracelsus pursued the Philosopher's Stone, believed to transform base metals into gold and grant eternal life.

The Renaissance elevated alchemy as a mystical and scientific discipline, with figures like John Dee exploring its Hermetic dimensions. By the 17th century, however, alchemy began transitioning into modern chemistry, as pioneers like Robert Boyle emphasized empirical experimentation over mysticism.

In the 19th and 20th centuries, alchemy experienced a revival through Carl Jung, who reinterpreted it as a symbolic process for personal transformation. Today it serves as both a precursor to chemistry and a metaphor for spiritual growth, reflecting humanity's enduring quest for enlightenment and perfection.

Among the historical organizations that committed themselves to secrecy in their search for esoteric truths were these:

- **Hermetic Order of the Golden Dawn:** A ceremonial magic group founded in 1888, blending Kabbalah, alchemy, and astrology to create a structured system of magical training.
- **Thelema:** A spiritual philosophy founded by Aleister Crowley, emphasizing personal will and magical practices inspired by *The Book of the Law*.
- **Freemasonry:** A fraternal organization with esoteric rituals and symbolic traditions that influenced many occult movements, including ceremonial magic.
- **Rosicrucians:** A mystical society centered on spiritual enlightenment, alchemy, and esoteric Christianity, originating in 17th-century Europe.
- **Theosophical Society:** An organization promoting Eastern and Western esoteric traditions, emphasizing reincarnation, karma, and hidden spiritual truths.

Many of these occult and esoteric organizations were male-dominated in their early formations because they were largely products of patriarchal societies where men held most positions of authority and access to education, resources, and networks. Partially because of this, some modern witches choose not to associate with the occult. Because witchcraft is practiced more openly than ever, the occult has become more niche and less representative of all witches.

I still like using the words *occult* and *esoteric* in terms of witchcraft studies because the roots of modern practices remain underground. It's up to you as a modern witch to seek the wisdom that came before, even as you're developing new systems of belief and practice. In my experience, occult studies have opened avenues of self-exploration I wouldn't have known were available to me, including ancestral work, covered in the next section.

Tracing your ancestry

When I got serious about my witchcraft practice as a young adult, I felt called to explore my ancestry, spurred by my great-grandmother's occupation as a spiritualist and medium. By the time I was born, my family had fully embraced Catholicism, and I dutifully completed all my sacraments. But as I came of age, I started to feel that I was missing something that was hidden in my family's past.

I decided to trace my ancestral traditions in Cuba, and through my research, I found that my great-grandmother most likely practiced a form of spiritism called Espiritismo de Cordón, a belief system that blends elements of Catholicism, African traditions, indigenous spirituality, and 19th-century Spiritist philosophy as developed by Allan Kardec. Espiritismo de Cordón emphasizes collective spiritual work, involving physical movement, rhythmic chanting, and direct communication with spirits.

FUN FACT

Like many spiritualities of the Caribbean, Espiritismo is *syncretic*, incorporating symbols from different religions and traditions.

In researching my great-grandmother's spiritual past, I learned so much about different religions and traditions, including African *Yoruba*, which informed parts of Cuban *Santería*. The histories of these traditions are tied to the Transatlantic slave trade and the politics of Cuba. Tracing my ancestry revealed so much about where my family came from and what generations before me experienced.

Researching your own ancestry can deepen your connection to your lineage, enhance your magical practice, and root your spirituality in personal and cultural history. Here are some practices you can try:

- **Genealogical research:** Use online genealogy tools, family records, and archives to trace your family tree. Sites like `Ancestry.com` and `FamilySearch.org` can help you map your lineage.
- **Interviews with family members:** Speak with elders in your family to learn about traditions, stories, or practices that may have been passed down through generations.

- **Cultural traditions:** Investigate the cultural or regional practices tied to your ancestry. These often include folklore, rituals, and magical customs.
- **Heirlooms:** Look to the objects, photos, and diaries that were passed down to you or your family members. These could also serve as ritual items (covered in Chapter 10).
- **Pilgrimages to homelands:** If applicable and possible, travel to your ancestral lands.

As you learn about your ancestors, you might decide to create an altar to honor them, featuring photos, heirlooms, candles, and offerings like food, drink, or incense. In Chapter 10, I guide you in creating a sacred space and a home altar.

TIP

When possible, start with ancestors you loved and had healthy relationships with. Ancestral work should be approached knowledgeably with firm boundaries, as working with a stranger who is not at peace can be harmful. You might find that some of your ancestors did things you disagree with. Some ancestral stories present opportunities to face hard truths and clarify generational lessons, but you should proceed with the utmost care.

WARNING

Sometimes ancestral work can trigger *generational trauma*, also known as *intergenerational* or *transgenerational* trauma. It refers to the psychological and emotional effects of trauma that are passed down from one generation to the next. This occurs when unresolved trauma experienced by one generation influences the behaviors, beliefs, and emotional well-being of subsequent generations, even if they didn't directly experience the original traumatic events. If you find that your ancestral journey leads to difficult emotions, I recommend talking to a therapist about how you're feeling.

In my experience digging into my roots and talking to family members, I learned that my great-grandmother gave up her practice because of her daughter's death. That made me realize that the pain of her loss was passed down to my father, and in turn, to me. I was named after my grandmother who passed, and I felt the weight of responsibility in carrying her name. I've incorporated her into my altars as part of my ancestral practice, to feel the grief that the generations before me didn't fully process because of the stress of exile and assimilation.

Not all ancestors are related by blood. If working with your natal lineage becomes difficult, you can also reach out to any of the following:

- **Cultural ancestors:** Individuals who shared your cultural heritage, traditions, or community but aren't directly related to you by blood. This includes historical figures, artists, or leaders from your culture.

- **Spiritual ancestors:** People who practiced or upheld spiritual traditions similar to yours, even if they're not part of your family tree. This includes elders in a spiritual lineage, founders of a magical tradition, or mystics whose teachings resonate with you.
- **Ancestors of the land:** Spirits of the people who lived on or cared for the land where you currently reside, including indigenous peoples or early settlers and indigenous ancestors who lived in harmony with the land.
- **Ancestors of the craft:** Individuals who shared your craft, profession, or passion, serving as inspirational predecessors.
- **Chosen ancestors:** People you admire, respect, or feel deeply connected to, whom you choose to honor as part of your spiritual lineage.
- **Mythical or fictional characters:** Legendary or symbolic figures from myths, folklore, or archetypes who resonate with you on a spiritual level.

TIP

If you feel stuck, start with yourself and the kind of legacy you want to leave to the world. You might journal about the following questions: Who do you imagine your descendants will be? What kind of ancestor would you be to them, if they were searching for you?

REMEMBER

You don't necessarily need to have an ancestral connection to a magical tradition or spiritual person to have a strong witchcraft practice. Not all spiritual traditions are ancestral, and a tradition doesn't need to have spanned generations to be valid. Insisting that a tradition be "ancient" is a common way that people *gatekeep* magic, or keep people new to the craft from identifying as witches. (You can read more about gatekeeping in Chapter 17.)

Learning about other traditions

Sometimes your ancestral search brushes up against different religions and traditions than the ones you grew up knowing, and it sparks your interest. Or sometimes your research into your ancestors hits a dead end and you decide to look into traditions that are completely new to you.

REMEMBER

A *pantheon* refers to a group or collection of deities worshipped within a specific religious, mythological, or cultural tradition. The term is often used to describe the gods and goddesses of ancient polytheistic religions or spiritual systems.

In Chapter 1, I introduce some of the ways different pantheons inform pagan practice and modern witchcraft traditions, and in Part 2, I review archetypes and deities across cultures that have become associated with modern witchcraft.

The core pantheons that inspire modern witchcraft, offering key deities and practices, include but are not limited to these:

- **Mesopotamian:** Modern witches are inspired by the ancient stories of Inanna (love and war), Ereshkigal (underworld), Marduk (creation and order), and Nergal (plague and protection).
- **Egyptian:** Key deities observed by modern witches include Isis (magic and healing), Hathor (joy and motherhood), Thoth (wisdom and writing), Anubis (protection of the dead), and Bastet (protection and home life).
- **Greek and Roman:** The Eleusinian Mysteries present the stories of Persephone, Demeter, and Hecate and focus on *chthonic* rituals dealing with the underworld and the cycle of death and rebirth.
- **Celtic:** Ancient Celtic polytheism centers around nature worship and seasonal cycles. This includes celebrations of the Wheel of the Year (such as Samhain and Beltane), sacred groves, and reverence for natural elements and deities like Brigid and the Cerridwen.
- **Norse:** Pre-Christian Norse spiritual practices include *Seidr* (a form of Norse magic) and honor deities like Odin and Freyja. Norse Heathenry employs runes for divination, rituals for protection, and ancestor veneration.

In addition to these pantheons, some regional folk religions and pagan traditions have more recently inspired witchcraft and other modern spiritual practices, including these:

- **African diasporic religions:** Mainstream exposure to Yoruba, Vodou, and Santería is increasing, although they are closed practices that require initiation (see Chapter 4 for more on closed practices). Practices include charms, spiritual baths, offerings to deities, and ancestor veneration.
- **Asian religions:** Practices from Hinduism, Buddhism, Shinto, and Taoism include meditation, chakra work, and the use of mantras.
- **Middle Eastern mysticism:** Sufi mysticism, Jewish Kabbalah, and ancient Mesopotamian practices involve the invocation of angels, study of sacred texts, and divination methods.
- **Slavic folk practices:** Pagan traditions and folk magic practices from Slavic regions employ the use of talismans, seasonal rituals, and nature-based spells. Baba Yaga is a key figure in Slavic folklore.
- **Indigenous practices:** Animistic practices of Native American, First Nations, and other indigenous peoples involve practices like smudging with sacred herbs, vision quests, and honoring the spirits of the land.

- **Hoodoo, rootwork, and conjure:** African American folk magic is rooted in African traditions, blended with European and Native American influences. It's prevalent across the Southern U.S. and varies by region (such as Appalachian folk magic). It employs candle magic, mojo bags, and spell jars, among other rituals.
- **Christian mysticism:** Practices from mystical branches of Christianity, such as Gnosticism and Rosicrucianism, involve angelic invocations, sacred geometry, and psalm magic.
- **Latin American spiritualities:** Practices from Brujería, Curanderismo, and folk Catholicism involve saints and spirits, healing rituals, and spiritual cleansing.
- **European folk magic:** Practices like hedge-witchery, cunning folk magic, and village witchcraft involve healing with herbs, protective charms, and divination techniques.

WARNING

Many folk, pagan, and indigenous practitioners don't refer to themselves as witches because the label *witch* has historically been used to stigmatize or dismiss them, and many practitioners still experience persecution.

In Chapter 1, I distinguish between paganism, neopaganism, and witchcraft. Chapter 2 includes more detail about folk practices.

WARNING

A fine line separates cultural appreciation and cultural appropriation, as discussed in detail in Chapter 4. Approach your studies with respect for other cultures, and refrain from intruding into initiation-based religions and practices where you're not invited.

Modern witchcraft is constantly evolving, and it's impossible to pin down its boundaries. Every witch will give you a different definition of their beliefs and practices. (See Chapter 1 for my own definition and treatment of modern witchcraft for the purposes of this book.) That said, some modern and neopagan traditions have solidified into specific sets of beliefs and practices, and some have even become widely recognized religions, such as these:

- **Wicca:** Wicca, a religion founded in the mid-20th century by Gerald Gardner, typically involves worship of a god and a goddess and practices of nature worship and ritual magic.
- **Traditional witchcraft:** Distinct from Wicca, traditional witchcraft encompasses a wider range of practices from different regions and cultures, including Europe, the Americas, and other parts of the world. British traditional witchcraft is one of the more robust subsets of traditional witchcraft,

including folk magic practices rooted in the cultural and historical heritage of the British Isles.

- **Druidry:** Druidry, which arose in the 18th century, is inspired by ancient Celtic practices of nature reverence, connection to the land, and honoring sacred groves.
- **Hellenistic polytheism:** Inspired by ancient Greek religion, Hellenistic polytheism involves worship of the Greek gods and participation in festivals honoring ancient traditions.
- **Kemeticism:** Kemeticism, a type of Egyptian Reconstructionism inspired by ancient Egyptian deities, focuses on maintaining cosmic balance.
- **Rodnovery:** Rodnovery is a type of Slavic neopaganism, a revival of pre-Christian Slavic practices that observe the Slavic gods and seasonal rituals.
- **Heathenry:** Inspired by ancient Norse traditions, Heathenry involves reverence for Norse gods, ancestor veneration, and practices like blót (sacrificial offerings). Ásatrú is a subset of Heathenry concentrated in Iceland.

Many witches today practice a kind of eclectic paganism that centers on personal experience and organic connection to certain traditions, whether through loose ancestral ties or special interests. As they grow in their practice, they borrow from various traditions and add their own flair. New systems and practices are constantly arising, and it's a challenge to keep track, even for the experts.

Choosing your initiation

In witchcraft, *initiation* is a transformative and symbolic act marking a person's formal entry into a magical tradition, spiritual path, or coven. It represents a commitment to the craft, a connection to magical forces, and, often, a rite of passage into a deeper level of spiritual understanding or practice.

Initiations can vary widely depending on the tradition, but they generally involve rituals designed to connect the initiate with specific energies, deities, or the collective wisdom of a group. They can range from private affairs to public demonstrations. Different kinds of initiation practices share some common rituals:

- **Purification:** Cleansing the body or spirit, such as with water, smoke, or salt.
- **Casting a circle:** Creating a sacred, protected space for the ritual.
- **Oaths and vows:** Pledging secrecy, loyalty, or dedication to the craft, coven, or deities.

- **Symbolic acts:** Blindfolding, walking through a doorway, standing in a circle, or anointing with oil.
- **Evocation of deities or spirits:** Calling on specific entities to witness or bless the initiation.
- **Gift or tool presentation:** Receiving a magical name, tools, or symbols representing the new role within the tradition.

REMEMBER

No matter the details, the purpose of initiation is transformation and commitment to the craft.

Initiating on your own

Initiation can be a solitary rite performed by an individual to dedicate themselves to witchcraft. This kind of initiation can happen as many times as needed. It's the type of initiation I've undergone because I'm not part of a formal coven.

FUN FACT

My first initiation took place in my childhood bedroom. I was 12 and feeling lost in the midst of so many hormonal changes. I don't remember exactly what I did. But I believe I must have copied something I saw on *The Craft*, perhaps calling to the directions and declaring myself a witch. I do remember writing *witch* on the inside wall of my closet.

TIP

Solo initiation rituals can include things like casting a circle, lighting candles, and reciting vows or affirmations. You may call upon deities, spirits, or elements to witness and bless your dedication. Following are four methods to claim your identity as a witch and begin your personal magical journey:

- **Lunar or nature-based rituals:** You can choose to initiate yourself during a full or new moon, symbolizing new beginnings and heightened magical energy.
- **Vision quest or pilgrimage:** A solo journey or quest to seek spiritual insight and connection can involve fasting, meditating, or spending time alone in nature. The purpose is to gain clarity about your path and receive spiritual guidance.
- **Spirit or deity petitioning:** You might choose to call upon your patron deities or spirits or even require a response before you consider yourself initiated.
- **Customized initiation:** You might design your own ritual, using items like crystals, herbs, or personal tools to set intentions and declare your commitment to the craft. Sometimes a personal crisis like a big loss or change can serve as an impetus for an initiation, though impulsive initiations aren't recommended.

Initiating by formal coven

Within a coven, initiation is a more structured affair, usually performed through a ceremony to welcome a new member. It often involves a series of steps, such as purification, oaths, and symbolic acts (for example, anointing with oils or receiving a magical name). You may undergo training or study beforehand to prepare for initiation. In this context, it's important to establish a spiritual bond with the coven, its tradition, and its deities or spirits.

Many covens employ *ceremonial magic* during initiations. Also known as *high magic* or *ritual magic*, it's a system of highly structured and formalized magical practices that often involve elaborate rituals, precise symbolism, and the invocation of spiritual or supernatural forces. It's rooted in esoteric traditions and aims to achieve spiritual enlightenment, personal transformation, or specific magical goals.

Following are examples of traditions that might employ ceremonial magic during initiations:

- **Gardnerian Wicca:** Initiation involves symbolic rituals, such as being blindfolded, bound with a cord, and ritually purified. This is meant to represent death and rebirth into the tradition, where you pledge to secrecy and devotion to the coven.
- **Alexandrian Wicca:** Similar to Gardnerian practices, this branch of Wicca may allow more adaptation and creativity or incorporate different kinds of ceremonial magic. Initiations typically follow traditional Wiccan practices, like bestowing initiates with magical names.
- **Feri Tradition:** This initiation involves deep, personal training and connection to a mentor who passes on mysteries to the initiate.

FUN FACT

The word *coven* evolved from Latin roots meaning "to come together" and passed through French and English with associations of assembly and conspiracy, eventually taking on its modern meaning as a gathering of witches. See Chapter 17 for more on covens.

Although the word has been largely used by Wicca and traditional witchcraft to represent a group of initiates into a specific system, modern witches have stretched the meaning of the word to encompass a wide range of gatherings. Sometimes the use of the term is contested among witches.

TIP

You might find in your studies that there's much controversy in the world of witchcraft because witches have widely differing opinions on many topics. Part of being a witch is being comfortable with uncertainty and dedicating yourself to constant learning and unlearning. I've found that it pays to be humble and remain open to differing perceptions. But also trust that your practice is yours to make what you will.

Initiation by ancestry or lineage

This kind of initiation connects the practitioner to a magical lineage or tradition, often passed down through mentors or elders. It may involve secret knowledge or symbols unique to the lineage, and it's often accompanied by oaths of loyalty and discretion. Different kinds of ancestral or lineage initiation might be found in the following traditions:

- **Cunning folk traditions:** A mentor or elder in a folk magic tradition might pass on specific charms, spells, and techniques as part of an informal initiation.
- **Ancestral religions:** Religions have specific services, altars, and ancestor or guardian spirit knowledge transmission that takes place during initiation.
- **Traditional witchcraft:** Lineage is passed through storytelling, personal instruction, and rituals that connect the initiate to the tradition's spiritual current.
- **Apprenticeships:** Initiations can also be more secular, as in the final ceremony following a long training under an herbalist or other traditional healer.

TIP

Whatever the tradition or path you choose, remember that you're a modern witch, walking the line between the past and the future. If you do nothing else, write down this line, filling in the blank: "I'm a modern witch with roots in _________."
In doing so, you acknowledge the foundation that you're building on through your own personal experience.

Assembling Your Tools: The Grimoire

A *grimoire* is a book of magic containing instructions on magical tools, spells, rituals, and other esoteric knowledge. It serves as both a journal and a manual. Grimoires include a range of information on topics as varied as astrology, herbology, summoning spirits, and crafting talismans.

Grimoires serve as repositories of occult knowledge. Historically, grimoires were personalized and kept secret due to the societal and legal risks associated with practicing magic. The history of the grimoire is entwined with the evolution of magical practices and spiritual beliefs across cultures. Following are some historical examples of grimoires:

- **Ancient Egypt and Mesopotamia:** Some of the earliest examples of written magical instructions were found in ancient Mesopotamia and Egypt, where texts inscribed on papyri or clay tablets included protective charms and rituals to call upon gods or spirits.
- **Greek and Roman antiquity:** During classical antiquity, magical knowledge was often recorded in philosophical texts. Hermetic works like *The Emerald Tablet* and the *Corpus Hermeticum*, attributed to Hermes Trismegistus, laid the groundwork for magical systems that would later influence European grimoires.
- **Medieval Europe:** With the rise of Christianity in Europe, many grimoires integrated Christian prayers, psalms, and the names of angels into magical practices. Books like *The Key of Solomon* (see Figure 9-1) and *The Sworn Book of Honorius* emerged as foundational texts for ceremonial magic. The medieval period also saw the translation of Arabic and Jewish texts into Latin. Works like the *Picatrix*, an Arabic text on astrological magic, heavily influenced European occultism.
- **Renaissance and early modern period:** The advent of the printing press in the 15th century allowed grimoires to become more accessible. Titles such as the *Heptameron* and *The Lesser Key of Solomon* were widely disseminated. *The Malleus Maleficarum* was also popular, though less a true occult text than a guide for identifying and persecuting witches.
- **Reformation and witch hunts:** This era spanning the 16th and 17th centuries also saw increased scrutiny of magical practices. Grimoires were often associated with witchcraft, leading to persecution during witch hunts.
- **Esoteric revival:** The 18th and 19th centuries saw a revival of interest in occultism, with figures like Eliphas Levi and the Hermetic Order of the Golden Dawn reinterpreting older grimoires. This period contributed to the blending of mystical, magical, and spiritual traditions. Grimoires began to influence literature and popular culture, cementing their place as both practical tools for practitioners and objects of fascination for the public.

Today grimoires remain central to practices such as Wicca, neopaganism, and other modern magical traditions. Often referred to as "Books of Shadows," they serve as personal or communal records of magical knowledge. Grimoires frequently appear in literature, film, and television, where they symbolize arcane knowledge and mystical power.

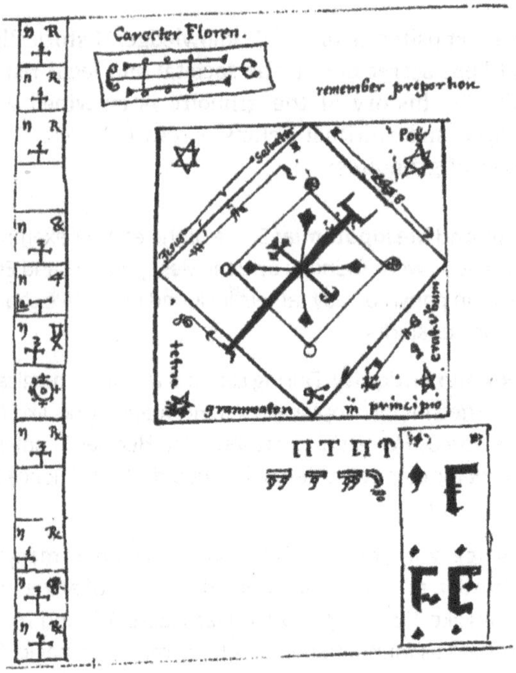

FIGURE 9-1: A page from *The Key of Solomon.*

Joseph H. Peterson/Wikimedia Commons/Public domain

FUN FACT

Although fictional, *The Necronomicon* is a "forbidden book" created by H. P. Lovecraft that has become a cultural icon in the occult community, inspiring modern magical systems and occult fiction. Lovecraft fans have even re-created the famous grimoire, as shown in Figure 9-2.

FIGURE 9-2: This grimoire prop, designed to represent H. P. Lovecraft's *The Necronomicon,* is a typical pop-culture portrayal of a book of shadows.

Shubi/Wikimedia Commons/Public domain

Modern interpretations of grimoires have expanded, incorporating elements of self-discovery, personal growth, and cultural heritage. In this way, the modern grimoire plays an important role in documenting your spiritual practice and weaving it into a cohesive narrative.

REMEMBER

Grimoires serve as a record of your spiritual journey. The modern grimoire is much like a personal diary, blending the mystical with the mundane. In my own grimoire, I mix regular journal entries about my days with my spiritual goals. A page might include a note about a personal intention along with the current astrological transit or my interpretation about the tarot card I pulled that day.

TIP

You can keep a grimoire in any form that works for you. You can write by hand in a traditional journal; type and print your pages to put in a binder; or keep an electronic grimoire. Grimoires can also be collective, updated by a group of contributors.

In addition to personal reflection, here are some things you can include in your own grimoire:

- **Philosophies and mythologies:** Notes on your occult studies and readings.
- **Methods and techniques:** Records of best practices for spellcasting and rituals.
- **Magical correspondences:** Tables of the symbolic meanings of colors, herbs, stones, or planetary influences.
- **Tools and symbols:** Lists of objects and instruments or drawings of sigils along with their uses and meanings.
- **Spells and rituals:** "Recipes" for spells and instructions for rituals and ceremonies, as well as outcomes of spells and any divinatory messages connected with them.
- **Dream diary:** Log of your dreams, along with dates and interpretations.
- **Astrological transits:** Notes on important cosmic events.
- **Divination log:** Records of your divination practices, interpretations, and outcomes.

TIP

Keep it simple. Grimoires depicted in pop culture tend to be elaborate and mystical looking, but your grimoire can be simple and unadorned.

Grimoires are wonderful visual representations of your ever-evolving magical journey. It's not just a relic of history, but a product of your enduring curiosity and imagination.

IN THIS CHAPTER

» Working with energy in your space

» Creating your home altar

» Choosing your ritual objects

Chapter 10

Setting Up Your Practice Space

Creating a sacred space is one of the most vital steps in establishing a meaningful and consistent magical practice. Your sacred space is your practice space and the foundation of your work, a place where intention and energy come together to support transformation. Choosing the location and purpose of your altar — the heart of your practice — is equally important because it will house your go-to tools and ritual objects.

Your practice space is a sanctuary for connection, growth, and magic. In this chapter, you learn how to clear the energy in your home, set protections to guard your space, and call in desired energy to support your intentions. I guide you through the different types of altars you can build and describe common ritual objects to start your spell work and rituals.

Laying the Foundation: Sacred Sites

REMEMBER

Although the mundane world is full of opportunities to connect spiritually, a distinction marks the ordinary and the sacred. The formal definition of *sacred* is anything that's considered holy or related to spiritual observance. Something becomes sacred when you imbue it with special meaning and create specific boundaries around the way you use or experience it.

Sacredness can relate to religious objects, spaces, or practices, such as a temple, scripture, or ritual, but it also extends to personal values, like the sanctity of nature. The sacred is treated with honor, care, and a sense of connection to something greater than yourself.

TIP

Sacredness is a special state, but it doesn't have to be overly complicated. You can cultivate the sacred in your life in many ways, including these:

- **The body:** Your body offers you the ability to work with energy, and it's most in tune when you treat it with care and respect. Practices like mindful movement, meditation, and self-care rituals can help you honor it as a vessel for your spirit.
- **Nature:** The natural world is one of the most accessible and profound sources of sacredness, whether it's found in the serenity of a forest, the rhythm of the ocean, or the quiet power of a mountain.
- **Community spaces:** Shared spaces, like libraries, parks, and spiritual centers, can serve as sacred sites where people gather for collective growth and connection. Chapters 17 and 18 explore how to create and honor shared spaces.
- **New experiences:** Sacredness can emerge in moments of novelty, whether you're traveling to a new place, engaging in creative endeavors, or stepping outside your comfort zone to discover fresh perspectives and possibilities.
- **Home:** Your living space can be a sacred sanctuary designed to reflect your values and intentions. By arranging it with care and infusing it with personal meaning, you can create a haven that nurtures and grounds you daily.

Each time I move to a new home, I work with its energy to create a sacred space within it. For the rest of this chapter, I focus on setting up a sacred practice space within your home, but you can use these methods for any kind of practice space.

Clearing the energy

Have you ever walked into a place that felt "heavy" or "haunted?" Just as physical spaces collect dust and clutter, homes can accumulate emotional and spiritual "residue" from stress, conflict, or external influences. Clearing energy in the home involves practices that remove stagnant or negative energies. It's a way to reset the environment, creating a more harmonious and inviting space that can support a sacred magical practice. Here are some techniques for clearing energy in a space:

- **Smoke cleansing:** Use herbs to cleanse the space. Light a dried herb bundle and let the smoke waft through each room, focusing on corners and entryways where energy tends to stagnate. Open windows so the energy has somewhere to go. Be mindful of sourcing materials ethically. (Chapter 14 covers smoke clearing rituals in more detail.)
- **Salt cleansing:** Sprinkle salt along windowsills, doorways, and corners to absorb negative energy. You can also create a saltwater solution to wipe down surfaces or floors, symbolically washing away unwanted influences.
- **Sound cleansing:** Use bells, chimes, or singing bowls to break up stagnant energy. Moving through the space with rhythmic sounds or chanting can shift vibrations and bring harmony.
- **Decluttering:** Physical clutter often carries emotional or energetic weight. Decluttering and organizing your space can free up stagnant energy and promote flow.
- **Plants:** Introduce air-purifying and energy-cleansing plants like aloe vera, peace lilies, and snake plants to naturally refresh the atmosphere.
- **Essential oils or sprays:** Create a cleansing spray with water, an essential oil like lavender, eucalyptus, or lemon, and a pinch of salt. Spritz the mixture throughout the home to refresh and uplift the energy. (See Chapter 14 for how to make and use "Florida water.")

PERFORMING "LIMPIAS"

I grew up referring to the act of clearing energy as a *limpia*. Limpia means "clean" in Spanish. In a spiritual context, limpias are traditional cleansing rituals performed by cultures throughout Latin America, particularly Curanderismo. (See Chapter 2 for more on Latin American folk magic.) Limpias are used to clear negative energy, restore balance, and promote overall well-being.

Typically performed by curanderos or healers, limpias may involve the use of herbs, eggs, smoke, or sacred tools. Each element carries symbolic meaning: herbs like rue and copal are believed to absorb negativity, whereas an egg is thought to draw out dense or harmful energy when passed over the body (referred to as *pasar el huevo*). The ritual may include prayers, chants, or blessings to evoke spiritual protection and healing.

Limpias aren't just about physical purification. They address the mind and spirit, removing emotional blockages, alleviating stress, and resolving spiritual dilemmas. Modern interpretations have made limpias increasingly accessible, blending ancient techniques with contemporary spiritual practices.

Putting down protections

After clearing your space of unwanted energies, you'll want to employ protections so that negative energies or spirits can't re-enter. You can create energetic boundaries in several ways, including these:

- **Symbolic barriers:** Use protective symbols such as pentagrams, crosses, and sigils. You can draw these symbols over doorways and windows with a finger, chalk, or water infused with herbs like rosemary and basil. (See Chapter 11 for commonly used symbols and sigils.)
- **Defensive crystals:** Place crystals like black tourmaline, obsidian, or selenite around the perimeter of your space. These stones act as energetic guardians, absorbing or deflecting negativity.
- **Protective herbs:** Scatter herbs like sage, bay leaves, or lavender around the room or hang bundles near entryways. You can also brew protective herbal sprays to mist over surfaces.
- **Energetic shields:** Visualize an energetic barrier enveloping your space. Imagine a glowing, impenetrable light encircling the area, protecting it from harm. You can pair this practice with spoken affirmations, such as, "Only positive energy may enter here." (I offer protective spells in Chapters 8 and 21.)
- **Wards or charms:** Place objects imbued with protective intent, like a witch's bottle, evil eye talisman, or a charm you've consecrated, in strategic areas to safeguard your space. (See Chapter 11 for instructions on consecrating tools.)

Setting intentions

Once you've done the clearing and put protections in place, you're ready to start designing your space for your purposes. Here are some ways you can set your intentions for your sacred space:

- **Define your purpose:** Reflect on why you're creating the space — whether it's for meditation, magical workings, relaxation, or creative inspiration. Write this intention down or say it aloud to reinforce your focus.
- **Infuse your space with energy:** Hold a visualization or meditation session to channel your intentions into the space. Picture the energy of peace, creativity, or spiritual connection filling every corner.
- **Use correspondences:** Enhance your intentions with symbolic elements that align with your purpose. For example, if your space is for meditation, you might use calming blue and green tones in your decor and burn soothing scents like sandalwood or lavender.

- Speak **affirmations or blessings:** Words of affirmation or blessings over your space can solidify its purpose. For instance, you might say, "May this space be a sanctuary of peace and inspiration."
- Feature **sacred objects:** Place meaningful objects, like a favorite crystal, statue, or photograph, in the space to anchor your intention. These objects can act as a focal point, constantly radiating your chosen energy.

TIP

The most effective way to focus on intention for a spiritual practice space is to build an altar, which serves as a kind of "hearth," or focal point, for your magical work.

Assembling Your Tools: The Home Altar

In witchcraft, an *altar* is a sacred, designated space used for rituals, spell work, meditation, and connecting with spiritual energies. It serves as the center of your workings, acting as a bridge between the physical and spiritual worlds. An altar can be as simple or elaborate as you want, reflecting your personal intentions, beliefs, and the type of work you want to perform.

REMEMBER

Altars have long histories across the world, but in contemporary witchcraft and neopagan traditions, altars blend ancient practices with modern interpretations and are always evolving to fit individual needs.

Choosing an altar space

First, choose a location for your altar. Your altar serves as the focal point for rituals, meditations, and offerings, so its placement should reflect intention, accessibility, and alignment with your energy.

TIP

Work with what you've got. Not everyone has a picture-perfect home or a huge space to work with. Maybe you share space with a family member, partner, or roommate. For most of my time practicing, I had my altar on my night table in a corner of my bedroom.

Although you don't need anything fancy, you should follow a few parameters:

- **Privacy and quiet:** Choose a spot where you can practice without frequent interruptions. A private corner of a room, a shelf in a bedroom, or a dedicated nook in a quiet area can provide the solitude necessary for focus and reflection.

- **Energetic alignment and direction:** Consider the energy of the space. Spaces near windows can invite natural light and fresh energy, whereas enclosed areas may feel grounding and introspective. Some witches face altars in specific directions, commonly to the north or east. Trust your intuition to guide you to a location that feels energetically right.
- **Accessibility:** Your altar should be easy to access for regular use, encouraging consistent engagement. Avoid spaces that are difficult to reach or that require significant rearranging to use. At the same time, you might want to avoid high-traffic areas.
- **Sacred proximity:** You may prefer placing your altar near an entrance to guard the home, whereas someone else may situate it in an area associated with certain activities, like a kitchen for hearth magic or a garden for nature-based rituals.
- **Size and surface area:** You'll want a usable surface. Choose one that accommodates your needs, whether it's a small windowsill for a minimalist setup or a larger table for an elaborate altar. Make sure the surface is stable and can safely hold your tools and decorations.
- **Cleanliness and order:** Your altar space should be physically clean and free from unrelated items. A clutter-free environment helps maintain focus and ensures the area remains sacred.
- **Safety:** If your practice involves candles, incense, or other flammable items, select a fire-safe location away from curtains, papers, or anything else that could ignite.

By choosing an altar location that resonates with your intentions and aligns with the energy of your home, you can effortlessly create a sacred environment that supports and enhances your spiritual journey.

Homing in on a purpose

Home altars are deeply personal and can be tailored to reflect your spiritual needs and cultural background. Although the possibilities for your altar are endless, here are some common types of home altars and their unique purposes:

- **Devotional spirit altars:** Devotional altars are similar to shrines, dedicated to honoring a specific deity, spirit, ancestor, or spiritual tradition. These altars often feature statues, images, or symbols representing the entity being venerated, along with offerings such as candles, flowers, food, or incense. For example, a devotional altar for a goddess like Hecate might include keys, moon symbols, and black candles.

- **Ancestor altars:** A type of devotional altar, the ancestor altar honors the spirits of loved ones who have passed away, serving as a space for remembrance and connection. These altars often include photographs, heirlooms, or objects associated with the ancestors, alongside offerings like food, drink, or flowers. This type of altar is a common feature in cultures worldwide, such as the Día de los Muertos altars in Mexico.
- **Seasonal or sabbat altars:** These altars change with the seasons or mark specific celebrations, such as solstices, equinoxes, or sabbats in pagan traditions. Decorations might include seasonal flowers, fruits, or objects that symbolize the time of year. For instance, a Yule altar could feature evergreen branches, red candles, and symbols of rebirth like sun wheels.
- **Working altars:** Working altars are used for active magical practices, such as spell work, rituals, and meditation. These altars often include tools like wands, athames (ceremonial daggers), and chalices, as well as ingredients like herbs, oils, and candles. A working altar is typically designed for flexibility and functionality, allowing you to set up or rearrange items as needed for different workings.
- **Nature altars:** Nature altars celebrate the elements and the natural world, often incorporating objects like stones, feathers, shells, and dried herbs. They may also include representations of the elements of earth, air, fire, and water, such as bowls of water, candles, or soil. These altars are ideal if you feel a connection to nature and want to honor its cycles and energies.
- **Healing or self-care altars:** These altars are focused on personal well-being and can be used for meditation, relaxation, or emotional healing. They may include calming items like crystals (for example, rose quartz or amethyst), scented candles, essential oils, or affirmations. Healing altars are often placed in quiet, comfortable spaces to encourage introspection and self-care.
- **Creative altars:** Creative altars reflect your individuality and artistic expression. These altars can include unique or nontraditional items like artwork, handmade crafts, or objects with personal meaning. They may focus on a theme, such as creativity, inspiration, or empowerment, and evolve as your interests and goals change.

Sourcing your ritual objects

Altars typically include meaningful items like candles, crystals, herbs, and representations of deities, ancestors, or nature. Tools such as wands, athames (ceremonial knives), and chalices are often placed on the altar, along with objects related to the elements of earth, air, fire, and water. Seasonal decorations or offerings, like flowers or food, may also be added to honor cycles of nature or specific spirits.

Although there are no strict rules, the altar's arrangement is often intentional, with each item chosen and placed to enhance focus and channel energy. Choosing the right ritual objects for your altar is an essential part of crafting a space that resonates with your intentions and supports your spiritual or magical practices.

REMEMBER

Ritual objects aren't just tools; they're symbols of your energy and the elements you want to bring into your work.

Start by reflecting on the purpose of your altar. Is it for devotion, spell work, meditation, or seasonal celebration? Your intention will guide your choice of objects. For instance, a devotional altar may feature a statue or image of a deity, but a working altar might include tools for spellcasting, like candles or a mortar and pestle.

TIP

Many practitioners include items that symbolize the elements of earth, air, fire, and water to create a balanced energy on their altar.

Following are some elemental associations for your altar:

- **Earth:** Stones, crystals, or a small bowl of soil represent grounding and stability.
- **Air:** Feathers, incense, bells, or books symbolize intellect and communication.
- **Fire:** Candles, incense, or a small cauldron embody transformation and passion.
- **Water:** A bowl of water or a chalice represents intuition and emotion.

Depending on your practice, certain tools might become staples on your altar. Some of the most common categories of tools for an altar include these items:

- **Ingredients for spells:** Spells may call for specific kinds of candles, herbs, or stones.
- **Divination tools:** Items such as tarot cards, pendulums, runes, and crystal balls provide guidance and insight, linking the altar to spiritual communication.
- **Sacred vessels:** Often, spells and rituals call for liquids like water or alcohol, food offerings, or soil, and it's nice to have special containers for them, such as chalices or bowls. Vessels like cauldrons and mortar and pestles are more than decorative; they're used for burning or mixing ingredients.
- **Ritual tools:** Objects like athames, wands, bells, scissors, brooms, and mirrors are used to direct energy, evoke spirits, and mark ritual boundaries.

- **Personal or ancestral touches:** Include items that hold personal significance, such as photographs, heirlooms, or trinkets that inspire you. These objects infuse your altar with your unique energy and make it a space that feels deeply personal.
- **Seasonal or rotating objects:** Your altar can change with the seasons or specific rituals. Incorporating seasonal decorations, like flowers in spring or pumpkins in autumn, keeps your altar alive and connected to natural cycles.
- **Offerings and symbols:** If your altar is devotional, consider offerings such as food, drink, or symbolic items that honor the deity or spirit you're working with, like statues. You might also use markings and sigils.

The ritual objects on your altar should resonate with you and serve as both practical tools and symbols of your spiritual journey. There's no right or wrong way to choose your items. What matters most is that they reflect your intentions, inspire you, and help you create a sacred space where you feel empowered and connected. Chapter 11 provides more details about these tools, along with their ritual uses and accompanying spells.

TIP

If you want a more discreet setup, a curio cabinet can double as an altar. These cabinets allow you to store and display your tools, symbols, and treasures while keeping them organized and out of sight when they're not in use. Glass-fronted cabinets can showcase items while protecting them, blending seamlessly into your home decor. Figure 10-1 shows an example of a curio cabinet with simple shelves.

Often called metaphysical shops (or *botanicas*, in Latin American and Afro-Caribbean cultures), spiritual supply stores are treasure troves for finding the perfect ritual objects and tools. From candles and incense to crystals, herbs, and oils, the offerings are curated to support various rituals and traditions. Add shopping at your local spiritual supply store to your weekly errand list. Wandering through a spiritual supply store allows practitioners to explore intuitively, selecting tools that resonate personally or align with their intentions. Many of these stores also offer specialized items alongside cultural artifacts tied to specific spiritual paths.

The experience of visiting a shop that you connect with often feels sacred because the energy of the space invites curiosity and connection. Whether you're seeking an object to cleanse your energy, enhance a spell, or simply deepen your connection to the divine, a spiritual supply store offers a tangible gateway into your practice.

FIGURE 10-1: A typical curio cabinet for storing ritual objects.

Working with your altar

Creating and maintaining your altar is an ongoing practice that enhances your connection to your spiritual path. Thoughtful setup and consistent engagement transform your altar into a powerful tool for focus, intention, and growth. Here are some best practices for setting up your altar and establishing a routine:

- **Start with clean energy:** Begin by thoroughly cleaning the physical space where your altar will sit. Use an energy-clearing method, like smoke or sound cleansing, to ensure the area is free of lingering negativity. (See tips on energy clearing earlier in this chapter.)
- **Arrange with intention:** Thoughtfully place items on your altar to reflect its purpose. For example, center a deity statue or candle for devotion or arrange your tools in a way that's functional for spell work. Symmetry or intuitive placement can create a harmonious and aesthetically pleasing arrangement.
- **Leave room for growth:** Design your altar to be flexible so that you can add or change items as your practice evolves. Seasonal decorations or temporary tools can keep your space dynamic and inspiring.

- **Keep it clean and sacred:** Regularly clean your altar, both physically and energetically, to keep its energy vibrant. At least once a week, dust surfaces, replace spent candles or wilted flowers, refresh offerings, and cleanse tools as needed.

Once you've set up your altar, establish a sustainable routine. Follow these tips for getting started with your altar:

- **Start small and consistent:** Begin by engaging with your altar regularly, even if only for a few minutes each day. Light a candle, say a prayer, or meditate in front of your altar to build a habit of connection.
- **Create a daily or weekly ritual:** Dedicate time to work with your altar consistently. This might involve journaling, practicing divination, or refreshing the items on your altar. For example, a Sunday ritual might include cleansing your altar, setting intentions for the week, or drawing a tarot spread.
- **Use your altar for reflection:** Spend time in front of your altar to reflect on your goals, practice gratitude, or seek guidance. This can be as formal as a ritual or as simple as sitting quietly with your thoughts.
- **Adapt to your needs:** Let your routine evolve to fit your lifestyle and spiritual goals. Some days might call for extensive rituals, whereas others might only require a brief moment of mindfulness.
- **Mark special occasions:** Use your altar to celebrate milestones, seasonal shifts, or spiritual festivals. Decorate and dedicate your altar to align with the energies of the occasion, such as adding flowers for a spring equinox or pumpkins for Samhain.
- **Honor your intentions:** Approach your altar with respect and purpose. Before engaging, take a moment to center yourself and clarify your intentions, ensuring your time with your altar is meaningful and focused.

TIP

The altar is there to help you. Try to keep your altar offerings fresh and your space clean because your magic will be stronger if you devote yourself to your space in a consistent way. But don't get down on yourself if you drop your practice or neglect your altar. It happens to everyone. Ask yourself what you need to adjust — whether it's location, purpose, tools, or frequency of practice — and pick back up where you left off.

IN THIS CHAPTER

» **Understanding the basic parts of a spell**

» **Creating intentions, incantations, and symbols for spell work**

» **Cleansing, charging, and consecrating tools**

Chapter 11 Casting Spells

If there's one thing witches are known for, it's their spells. In pop culture portrayals of the witch, spells are uttered in ancient languages, read from big dusty grimoires. Movie witches raise their wands and speak their spells dramatically, leading to immediate results. Although that sounds like loads of fun, real spells are more subtle. Spell work involves, first and foremost, being honest about what you want. When you strip spells of fancy ingredients, esoteric tools, and archaic symbols, you're left with your intention, the foundation of most spells.

In this chapter, you learn about the components of spell work, including developing intentions, writing incantations, creating symbols, and timing your spells for optimal energetic conditions. I also cover some of the major categories of beginner spells. The second half of this chapter guides you through consecrating your go-to tools and ritual objects so you're equipped to start your practice with confidence.

Laying the Foundation: Spell Work Basics

First, I cover some important terms. A *spell* is a focused act of intention and energy that seeks to bring about a desired outcome. It involves the use of tools, words, gestures, and symbolism to align with natural or supernatural energies.

FUN FACT

The term *spell* derives from Old English *spel*, meaning "speech," "story," or "narration." By the Middle Ages, the term began to take on its magical connotations, associated with the use of special words, incantations, or charms to enact change.

REMEMBER

Spellcasting is the act of performing a spell. Like following a recipe, spellcasting employs a specific sequence of actions. *Spell work* is a broader term that encompasses not just the act of spellcasting but also the preparation, planning, and ongoing practices related to spells. This includes crafting intentions, gathering tools and ingredients, and maintaining the energy of a spell over time (all of which I cover in this chapter).

While the terms *spell*, *spellcasting*, *spell work*, and *ritual* are often used interchangeably, I make some distinctions between them. I see spells as specific workings that focus on narrow intentions or outcomes. In contrast, rituals are a series of prescribed actions, sometimes performed routinely or repetitively. Although spellcasting and spell work can be considered rituals, rituals don't necessarily have to involve spells, or they can encompass multiple spells.

To make that less confusing, here's a simple example involving candle magic. (I cover candle magic rituals in more detail in the next chapter.) In this case, the magical practice involves lighting a green candle symbolizing abundance to attract financial prosperity, which can be considered in these different ways:

- **Spell:** In this scenario, *spell* can refer to the concept itself — that is, a financial prosperity spell. Or it can be the intention of the spell, like "I sustainably attract wealth into my life." It can also be the incantation of the spell, like "Money flows to me freely and abundantly."
- **Spellcasting:** *Spellcasting* is the active execution of the spell — the moment when the magical intention is enacted. This might involve physically lighting the green candle, reciting the incantation, and visualizing your desired outcome as the flame burns. In other words, this is the action phase of the spell, which can also be considered a simple ritual.
- **Spell work:** *Spell work* is a broader term that encompasses all aspects of preparing for and performing the spell. It includes gathering your tools (a green candle, oils, herbs), carving symbols into the candle, anointing it with oil, choosing the right timing (for example, during a waxing moon), and casting the spell itself. Spell work reflects the entire process, from intention setting to follow-up actions. It can involve multiple spells and castings and can be considered a more involved ritual.
- **Ritual:** Spell work and rituals are closely related and can be considered synonymous in many cases. In candle magic, a complex ritual might involve multiple forms of spell work, like preparing a sacred space, calling

the four elements or deities associated with prosperity, lighting multiple candles, and performing a ceremony that includes the wealth-attracting spell. The ritual might also involve routine symbolic acts that extend beyond the limited scope of spells, such as meditating on gratitude or offering thanks to the universe.

TIP

Don't worry too much about semantics. You can come to your own decisions about the words you use to describe magical *workings* (an all-inclusive term for all sorts of spells and rituals). Hopefully, this helps you parse through the varied terms you're likely to encounter as you begin to perform spells. Now that those terms are out of the way, check out the basic components of spell work:

- **Intention:** This is the most important aspect of any spell because it defines what the practitioner is aiming to achieve. Clear, focused intention ensures that you choose a spell that aligns with the desired outcome.
- **Tools and ingredients:** Each spell requires specific items used to amplify or direct energy, like herbs, crystals, candles, oils, or symbols. These are chosen based on their correspondences to the spell's goal. Tools are consecrated before use and reconsecrated following prolonged use. (I cover consecration in the second half of this chapter.)
- **Words, gestures, and symbols:** This entails a combination of incantations, chants, movements, and sigils that form the core action involved in spellcasting. Words may act as carriers of intention, whereas symbols can focus energy.
- **Energy:** Ultimately, spells seek to harness energy toward an intention. Energy is accessed through specific conditions, including timing and the practitioner's will. This can include aligning with natural cycles, carrying out certain movements or gestures, and ensuring the energy raised during the spell is consistently directed and maintained.

Declaring your intentions

You'll hear the word *intention* a lot in the witchcraft world, and I use it throughout this book. An intention is a clear, concise statement of purpose that defines what your spell aims to achieve, transforming abstract desires into a concrete goal. Declaring intentions for spells is a foundational step in spellcasting because it aligns your energy with a desired outcome.

This declaration acts as a guiding thread, ensuring that all elements of the spell — tools, words, symbols, and energy — are attuned to the same purpose. When crafting an intention, phrase it positively and specifically, avoiding vague or negative language that could misdirect the energy.

FUN FACT

Writing down or speaking an intention engages cognitive and neurological pathways to enhance focus and effectiveness. Neuroscience research, particularly from the work of James Doty, MD, demonstrates that the act of writing down intentions activates the prefrontal cortex, the area of the brain responsible for decision-making and goal-setting. This process reinforces neural pathways, making the goal more tangible and achievable.

Simply put, by committing intentions to paper or speaking them aloud with conviction, you increase your ability to achieve your goals.

WARNING

Be certain that your desires and emotions really align with your intention. Sometimes you might wish for things you don't actually want because of outside pressure or expectation. When desires don't align with intentions, spells might be ineffective, or you might get something you're not ready for. The adage applies — "be careful what you wish for!"

A well-crafted magical intention is the foundation of effective spell work, and you can think of its structure as a formula for focusing energy and manifesting results. A good intention is clear, specific, and positive.

TIP

First, think of what you desire, and visualize already embodying, possessing, or experiencing your desire. It might help to simply state your desire with the phrase "I wish," "I want," or — more on the nose — "I intend." This helps center what you truly want and prevents you from overthinking your intention.

I'll use one of my recent intentions as an example. A couple years ago, I wanted a dog. I kept saying, simply, "I want a dog." I fully imagined a dog in my home. I visualized walking my dog, snuggling with my dog on the couch, and taking my dog to coffee shops. My desire was strong, and the image behind it was clear.

REMEMBER

Sometimes the desire or visualization underpinning an intention is so strong that it doesn't require any further action in terms of spell work. Simply being honest and stating your intention confidently, clearly, and consistently can serve as a spell in itself.

If I'm being honest, my intention to have a dog was like this. I wanted the dog, and one kind of fell into my lap. After a few weeks of visualizing my perfect dog, my brother called and asked me to adopt one of his dogs before he was deployed on a military assignment. Everything I visualized about her has come true!

For the sake of this example, pretend that I cast a formal spell to attract the dog into my life. I would have started by strengthening my intention into a more specific statement that followed these guidelines:

- **Start with "I":** Intentions should always center you and your desires, not anybody else's. If you catch yourself starting an intention with another subject, ask yourself if you're trying to influence someone or something that's actually out of your control. Spells that seek to manipulate others are advanced and highly controversial.
- **Use positive construction:** By positive, I don't necessarily mean feel-good. A positive statement, in the sense of language structure, is constructed in an affirmative manner, without the use of negating words like *can't, don't*, or *won't*. Most especially, avoid double negatives like, "I will *not fail* to attract a dog." That's just confusing.
- **Be precise:** Clarify your intention as much as possible by including specific details. Here's where visualization helps. If I had pressed myself to be more specific, "I want a dog" may have evolved into "I want a sweet, friendly, fun dog that will keep me company and show me how to enjoy my life more." Although that's specific, it's still open-ended, not overly constraining. I decided to focus on the values that were most important to me rather than a specific breed.
- **Focus on the present:** Use the present tense. There's nothing wrong with keeping to "I want" or "I wish" statements, but sometimes it might feel right to phrase your intention as if you already have the thing you want. For example, "I have a sweet, friendly, fun dog . . ."
- **Use dynamic words:** Sometimes it's appropriate to use a strong action phrase, like "I create," "I attract," or "I manifest." Reach to phrases that feel true to you and the change you want to see in your life.
- **Include a timeframe:** Timing is everything, but it's often neglected. Make sure you include *when* you want your intention to take place or occur. Your greatest wish might not be so great if it comes too soon or too late.

Given more time to develop my dog intention, I might have settled on something like, "I have a sweet, friendly, fun dog. She is my loving companion, filling my life with comfort and enjoyment." (Yes, your intention can be more than one sentence, provided it generally follows the guidelines.)

TIP

Although words are important, your desire is the core of your intention. Try your best to craft clear and specific statements, but it's the thought that counts. Don't worry that you'll accidentally go wrong; worry and fear are energies you certainly don't want to introduce into your formula.

Pick a spell, any (well, not just any) spell

Choosing a spell once you've settled on your intention involves aligning the method and components of the spell with the energy and purpose of your goal. Here are some key steps to guide you in selecting the right spell:

- **Define the core energy:** Reflect on the type of energy your intention requires. Do you need to attract something (e.g., love, success) or release something (e.g., negativity, obstacles)? This will help you narrow down spells that are designed to match that energy, such as attraction spells for drawing in abundance or banishing spells for letting go of unwanted influences. Use a trusted reference book or research spells online.
- **Consider correspondences:** Certain ingredients and symbols are associated with specific intentions and energies. The appendix of this book includes correspondences for herbs, crystals, and planetary energies, but there are countless correspondences. Look for spells that utilize tools, ingredients, or colors that align with your intention. For example, a love spell might involve pink or red candles, rose petals, and Venusian energy, whereas a protection spell might include black candles, salt, or iron.
- **Match complexity to your comfort level:** Choose a spell that suits your experience level and available resources. If you're a beginner, you might prefer straightforward candle spells or affirmations, whereas if you're advanced, you might work with elaborate rituals involving sigils or planetary alignments.
- **Timing and context:** Select a spell that aligns with natural or astrological timing, such as moon phases or days of the week. For example, a waxing moon supports spells for growth, whereas a waning moon aids in banishing. (See more on lunar timing in Chapter 15.) If timing doesn't align immediately, you can adapt or wait for the optimal energetic window.
- **Adapt or personalize:** If you find a spell that resonates but doesn't perfectly fit your intention, don't hesitate to modify it. Incorporate elements that feel authentic to you, ensuring the spell aligns with your personal energy and magical style.
- **Check for ethical alignment:** Ensure the spell aligns with your ethical principles and feels right to you intuitively. Consider the potential consequences and whether the spell respects the free will and boundaries of others.

You can choose from countless spells, but most spells fall under one of the following categories:

- **Attraction spells:** These spells focus on drawing something into your life, such as love, wealth, friendship, or opportunities. Examples include love spells to attract a romantic partner, abundance spells to invite financial prosperity, and friendship spells to build connections with like-minded people. Attraction spells focus on *manifestation*, or making a desire materialize into reality, which I cover more in the next chapter.
- **Release spells:** These spells deal with letting go of unwanted energies, emotions, relationships, habits, or obstacles. These can include "cord-cutting" (see Chapter 16) and banishing spells.
- **Binding spells:** These spells seek to restrict or neutralize harmful forces, actions, or behaviors. They include spells like preventing bad habits, binding harmful actions from having negative effects, and stopping gossip. They can include justice spells and even ethical revenge spells, curses, or hexes (carefully approached by advanced practitioners) to redirect harm.
- **Protection spells:** These spells create a barrier against harm, negativity, and unwanted influences. They're sometimes called shielding spells, and include casting protective circles and using protective charms or talismans.
- **Transformation spells:** These spells facilitate personal growth, change, or evolution. They can include spells for confidence and self-esteem, breaking old patterns, and cultivating new habits. Some transformation spells can focus on shadow work and confronting traumas to clarify hidden powers.
- **Knowledge or guidance spells:** These spells seek to enhance memory, learning, or intuition, including spells to absorb knowledge or connect with the wisdom of spirit guides. They can facilitate dreamwork or other forms of consciousness.
- **Healing or cleansing spells:** These spells promote physical, emotional, or spiritual healing, including energy-clearing spells and spells to heal emotional wounds. They can boost energy and help with grounding.

REMEMBER

In Chapter 21, I offer ten spells you can start practicing, each with ingredient lists and step-by-step instructions, including incantations and timing recommendations.

Gathering your ingredients and tools

The previous chapter went over common groups of tools and ingredients you can use to equip your altar, including herbs, crystals, and divination mediums. In the second half of this chapter, I take a closer look at some of the commonly used tools in spell work, and I guide you through consecrating your tools so they're ready to be used at a moment's notice.

TIP

Casting spells is kind of like cooking. If you set up your kitchen and stock it with staple groceries, you'll be able to whip up many meals without having to go to the store or start at square one each time you want to cook. When you've spent time assembling your altar and gathering your go-to tools and ingredients, casting spells will feel less daunting.

When I'm preparing for a spell, I like to look at what I already have laying around my house. I'm a big proponent of not spending money when you don't have to. Some of my go-to ingredients come from my backyard, for instance, like my garden dirt or the *Bidens alba* that grows rampantly around my property.

Similarly, the strongest tools are sometimes found right under your nose, like your favorite scissors or an heirloom that's closely intertwined with your ancestral energy. In Table 15-1, in the "Assembling Your Tools: Materia Magica" section, I include alternatives that are commonly found around most houses.

Even when you're organized and well stocked, you'll often have to source additional materials to fulfill the requirements of your spell. See Chapter 10 on metaphysical shops that carry most of the tools and ingredients you would need. But you can get many ingredients at more routine places like grocery or craft stores.

TIP

Study your spell carefully, and make sure you know the ingredients and tools that the spell is calling for. If you don't, look them up in a trusted reference book or online. Figure out what you have, what you need to acquire, and how you'll go about gathering everything you need, just as you would if you were preparing a grocery list.

Designing your incantations

Once you've set your intention, picked your spell, and gathered your tools and ingredients, you're ready to prepare the action steps of your spell work. *Incantations* are verbal expressions of intent that amplify and direct energy. Whether phrased as prayers, chants, affirmations, or poetic verses, incantations lend the force of words to spells.

Incantations are sometimes confused with intentions. Although they're informed by intent, incantations can be more abstract or varied in structure. Intentions define the goal of a spell, whereas the incantation activates and channels the energy during spellcasting. Intentions are a guiding principle and don't have to be vocalized, whereas incantations, by their definition, are spoken symbols that trigger the effects of a spell.

TIP

If intentions are the "why" of your spell, then incantations are the "how."

Incantations can take a variety of forms, including these:

- **Affirmations:** These focus on building confidence and personal growth more than a specific outcome. For example, "I'm strong and capable of doing difficult things," or "I'm enough, and I'll rest when I need to."
- **Petitions and prayers:** These are requests for assistance from spiritual entities, deities, ancestors, or the universe. They evoke external aid for guidance, protection, or achieving goals. For example, "Goddess, grant me clarity and wisdom as I make this decision." (In this case, you can petition on behalf of someone else, though I would still caution you to get consent from the subject and use "I" statements, as in "I ask that you aid my friend in her healing journey.") You might even reach to prayers from your childhood that have great resonance to you.
- **Chants or songs:** Chants and songs are rhythmic or melodic repetitions of phrases, words, or sounds that focus energy and intention. These forms often use repetition to build a meditative or trance-like state, allowing the practitioner to align with their desired goal. *Mantras* are commonly used; they're single words or short phrases repeated continuously to focus energy or create a specific vibration.
- **Divination induction:** Sometimes you might write an incantation in tandem with a form of divination, such as cartomancy and pendulum work. (See Chapter 13.) A divination-focused incantation might read something like, "I open to the messages coming through to me," or "I hear the words of my ancestors."
- **Poetry:** Poetry offers a creative and symbolic way to express intentions. Using metaphor, rhyme, and rhythm, poems can elevate incantations into a form of art that channels deeply personal or archetypal energy. You can write your own poetry or recite poems that speak to you and your intention.

The simplest incantations are often short phrases or combinations of words that encapsulate the spell's purpose or seal the spell with closing words. A few phrases have been part of the witchcraft lexicon in pop culture for ages, including these:

- **"As above, so below":** This is a well-known magical axiom that reflects the interconnectedness of all realms, evoking harmony between the spiritual and physical worlds. The phrase originates from the Hermetic text *The Emerald Tablet*, attributed to Hermes Trismegistus. It encapsulates the principle of correspondence: that the microcosm reflects the macrocosm, and vice versa.
- **"Abracadabra":** Far from just a stage magician's phrase, this word has ancient origins. Derived from Aramaic, it means "I create as I speak," underscoring the power of spoken words to shape reality. Historically, it was used as a charm

for protection or healing, with the word written in a triangular pattern to diminish negative energies as it was repeated.

- **"So mote it be":** This is a phrase commonly used to seal or conclude a spell, similar to saying "Amen" in a prayer. It was popularized in Wiccan and modern witchcraft traditions, though it has historical ties to Freemasonry. It emphasizes your will that the spell's intention manifests.
- **"By the power of three":** This phrase evokes the symbolic power of the number three, which is associated with balance, unity, and the divine. The "rule of three" holds significance in many traditions, including Wicca, representing the triple aspects of deity (e.g., maiden, mother, crone) and the idea that actions return threefold.
- **"Harm none, and do what ye will":** This is a guiding ethical principle in modern witchcraft, particularly Wicca, that serves as both a spell incantation and a reminder to act with responsibility. It's a modern adaptation of the Wiccan Rede, a foundational text in contemporary witchcraft practices.

FUN FACT

In modern witchcraft, witches often repurpose affirmations or sacred declarations from their ancestral religions as kinds of incantations. The Abrahamic *Amen* can be a powerful seal, as is *Ase* (Ashé) used in African diasporic religions. I suggest only using these if you have a strong personal or cultural connection to them. Following are other tips for crafting your own incantations:

- Keep them concise and rhythmic for easier repetition. Repetition helps anchor the intent and build momentum.
- Use present-tense language to affirm that your intention is already coming into being.
- Select words that resonate with your personal energy or the specific goal of the spell.

Regardless of form, the effectiveness of an incantation lies in the energy and intent behind it. When speaking or chanting, focus on the words' meaning and visualize the desired outcome. Your voice — whether whispered, spoken, or sung — becomes a vessel that carries your intention into the universe.

Using symbols

Symbols are powerful tools in spellcasting, serving as visual representations of intention and energy. By using marks that resonate with your practice, you can enhance the potency of your magic, personalize your tools, and create lasting connections to your work. Whether carved into objects, drawn on paper, or imagined during meditation, symbols can help you better channel energies.

Symbols are universal or personal marks that hold significant meaning in a magical context. These can include:

- **Runes:** Ancient alphabets, like the *Elder Futhark*, that hold symbolic and energetic meanings. Each rune can be used for a specific intention, such as protection, abundance, or transformation.
- **Universal symbols:** Common motifs like the pentacle, crescent moon, or triquetra, which are imbued with layers of cultural and spiritual significance.
- **Personalized symbols:** Marks or images you create to represent unique aspects of your craft, deities, or personal goals. *Sigils* are symbols created with the intention of manifesting a specific desire or outcome, which I cover in more detail in the next chapter.

WARNING

Runic alphabets have been appropriated by white supremacists, due to the fact that Nazi Germany used some of the symbols in their propaganda. Before you learn about or use runes, evaluate their context to make sure they're not being co-opted by racist values or for nefarious purposes.

You can enhance the power of your tools by marking them with symbols. For example:

- **Carving or drawing:** Inscribe symbols onto candles, wands, or stones with a knife or pen.
- **Anointing:** Draw the symbol using an oil, herbal infusion, or chalk.
- **Visualizing:** Visualize the symbol glowing on the tool, even if it's not physically present.

Over time, you can develop your own sets of symbols unique to your practice. These *sigils*, or crafted symbols, can represent specific intentions, deities, or elements. As you work with your sigils, they become connected to your energy and more effective in your magic. Some become so iconic that you might feel like they're part of your very being — and you might even permanently tattoo them on your body, as I have!

Here are some tips to get started with symbols:

- **Experiment and record:** Begin by designing symbols for common themes in your practice, such as protection, healing, or manifestation. Keep a record in your grimoire.
- **Evolve with practice:** Let your symbols evolve as your craft deepens, adapting their meanings and designs to reflect your growth.

- **Combine traditions:** If you work within a specific tradition (e.g., Wicca, chaos magic, or Norse), combine traditional symbols with personal ones to create a hybrid language.

Timing for specific energies

Timing is pivotal to spell work. The right spell at the wrong time can turn out to be a dud or even lead to an undesirable outcome. By understanding the energetic qualities of different times and cycles, you can optimize the power of your spells.

The moon is a wonderful timekeeper, and each phase is associated with specific intentions, as discussed in more detail in Chapter 15:

- **New Moon:** A time for reflection, clearing, new beginnings, setting intentions, and planting seeds for future growth.
- **Waxing Moon:** Ideal for spells that encourage growth, attraction, and expansion.
- **Full Moon:** Amplifies power, making it suitable for manifestation, enhancing, and illumination rituals.
- **Waning Moon:** Best for banishing, releasing, and letting go of old energies.

TIP

These days, plenty of magic-oriented almanacs include guidance on best times for specific spells and rituals, including factors like lunar phases, astrological transits, planetary hours, and seasonal correspondences.

You can also time your spells by the day of the week. Each day is traditionally linked to planetary energies:

- **Monday (Moon):** Introspection, emotions, and psychic abilities.
- **Tuesday (Mars):** Action, courage, and conflict resolution.
- **Wednesday (Mercury):** Communication, intellect, and travel.
- **Thursday (Jupiter):** Abundance, growth, and luck.
- **Friday (Venus):** Love, beauty, and harmony.
- **Saturday (Saturn):** Discipline, protection, and banishment.
- **Sunday (Sun):** Success, health, and vitality.

Or if you're looking for more substantial seasonal spells, the Wheel of the Year can help you connect your intentions to the changing seasons:

- **Spring:** A time for renewal, growth, attraction, and fertility spells.
- **Summer:** Focused on abundance, energy, and fulfillment.
- **Autumn:** A season for harvesting results, gratitude, and introspection.
- **Winter:** Associated with rest, reflection, and preparation for new beginnings.

See the appendix for more information on the Wheel of the Year.

Casting your spells

Once you've prepared for spell work (setting your intention, choosing your spell, gathering your materials, designing your incantations and symbols, and deciding on timing), you're ready to perform your spell.

REMEMBER

Before casting your spell, you'll want to cleanse your space (see Chapter 10) and perform a grounding exercise (see Chapter 21), preparing your mind and energy for spell work. You might choose to cast a circle (see next chapter) or protective ward (see Chapter 21) to guard yourself and set energetic boundaries.

The steps of spellcasting are as follows:

1. **Hold your intention in your mind.**
2. **Combine tools, actions, and words to direct energy toward your intention.**
3. **Close the spell by thanking the elements, spirits, or deities you called on.**

After you've cast your spell, ground yourself once more. If applicable, dissolve your circle by walking the circle in reverse. Using your dominant hand or your ritual tool (like an athame or wand), walk the circle counterclockwise (referred to by some witches as *widdershins*) to symbolically undo the boundary of the circle.

Dispose of your spell materials in an environmentally friendly way that preserves the integrity of the spell, such as the following:

- **Burying:** Best for spells related to growth, grounding, or protection.
- **Burning:** Best for releasing, banishing, or transformative spells.
- **Releasing into water:** Best for cleansing, emotional healing, or letting-go spells.

» **Trash disposal:** Best for banishing or spells where the goal is to remove something from your life.

» **Offering to nature or composting:** Best for gratitude, abundance, or nature-based spells.

» **Re-using and recycling:** Best for spells where tools like jars, crystals, or candles are not completely consumed in the process.

TIP

Once your spell is cast, release control and trust that it's doing its work. Document your work by recording your spell in your *grimoire*, or magic journal. Record any outcomes and notes that would prove useful in future spell work.

Assembling Your Tools: Materia Magica

Materia magica refers to the physical items, ingredients, or tools used in magical practices, rituals, or spell work. The term originates from Latin, where *materia* means "substance" or "material."

Table 11-1 outlines some classic witch tools you're likely to need in your spells, along with their traditional purposes, and household alternatives that you might use — because it's always best to use what you already have.

TABLE 11-1 The Witch's Toolkit

Tool	Tool Name	Traditional Purpose	Modern Alternatives
	Cauldron	A vessel of transformation, used for brewing potions, burning herbs, or mixing spell ingredients.	A cooking pot, slow cooker, or heat-safe bowl.
	Broom	For sweeping away negative energy, cleansing sacred spaces, and symbolizing movement between worlds.	A regular household broom or even a hand brush.
	Athame	A ritual blade used to direct energy, cast circles, or symbolically "cut" spiritual ties.	A kitchen knife, letter opener, or favorite scissors.
	Wand	Used to channel and direct energy in spells and rituals.	A wooden spoon, pencil, or decorative stick from nature.
	Mirror	For scrying, reflecting energy, or as a portal for divination and spiritual work.	A compact makeup mirror or any reflective surface like a phone screen.

Tool	Tool Name	Traditional Purpose	Modern Alternatives
	Bell	To cleanse spaces with sound, mark the beginning and end of rituals, or call upon spirits or deities.	A wind chime, sound bowl, kitchen timer, or even a ringtone on your phone.
	Chalice	Represents the element of water; used in rituals for offerings, blessings, or as a drinking vessel.	A wine glass, mug, vase, jar, or any vessel that can hold liquid.
	Mortar & pestle	For grinding herbs, spices, or other ingredients in spell work.	A food processor, rolling pin, or even the back of a spoon and a bowl.
	Key	Symbolizes access to hidden knowledge, unlocking opportunities, or connecting with other realms.	A literal house key, skeleton key, or decorative key necklace.
	Crystal ball (tarot cards; pendulum)	Used for scrying, divination, and focusing intuitive energies.	A glass paperweight, a reflective ornament, or a clear glass of water. Other divination tools: tarot cards, pendulum.
	Hat	Traditionally a symbol of power and connection to otherworldly forces; sometimes worn during rituals to protect the crown chakra.	A wide-brimmed hat, hoodie, or scarf to symbolize focus and intention.

There's a reason these tools endure in pop culture and common practice. Although they're practical, they're also powerfully symbolic, and in my own practice, I've found that they keep growing stronger and, in turn, strengthen my confidence. In the next chapter, I cover other ritual objects that require ritual creation, like talismans, amulets, charms, satchels, spell jars, and intention candles.

Still, objects are just objects until you've consecrated them. *Consecrating* is the act of dedicating an object to a specific purpose, infusing it with your energy and intention. Once you've gathered your tools, you can transform them into materia magica by consecrating them.

REMEMBER

Consecration is a spell in itself. One of the foundational spells in witchcraft, it ensures the integrity of the tools you use to cast. Consecration transforms mundane objects into powerful tools, reinforcing the connection between you and your tool, ensuring it resonates with your personal practice and the energies you seek to channel.

Although each object has a standard use, it's important to create meaning and associations for each, depending on your work. Hold the tool in your hands and focus on its intended purpose. Visualize its role in your practice — whether it will direct energy, protect your space, or act as a vessel for offerings.

TIP

Speak aloud or silently affirm its purpose, such as:

> "I consecrate this tool to guide and channel energy in alignment with my will and its highest purpose."

You can substitute "highest purpose" with the tool's specific use.

Cleansing your tools

Begin by purifying your tool to remove any residual energies it may have accumulated. This process is similar to the kinds of things you would do to clear energy in your home, which I cover in Chapter 10. All of the following are cleansing techniques:

- **Smoke cleansing:** Pass the tool through the smoke of incense or a cleansing herb like rosemary.
- **Water cleansing:** If the material allows, rinse the tool in natural water, such as spring or ocean water. For water-sensitive items, sprinkle a few drops instead.
- **Salt cleansing:** Bury the tool in a bowl of salt overnight to draw out unwanted energies.
- **Sound cleansing:** Use bells, singing bowls, or chants to clear the energy.

Charging the connection

Over time, your tool may need to be reconsecrated, especially after intense usage or if it feels "off." Regular cleansing and charging will keep it attuned to your energy. Store your tools in a sacred place, treating them with respect and intention to maintain their power.

TIP

Reconsecration can be paired with regular rituals to help you build your long-term relationship with your tools. You can incorporate consecration and charging into larger cleansing and protection rituals.

Many witches choose to charge their tools under the light of the moon or the sun, laying them outside with a clear view of the sky so they can absorb celestial energy. You can also bless your tools with the elements like so:

- **Earth:** For infusing your tool with grounding and stability, you can bury it in fertile soil.
- **Air:** For clarity and communication, you can find a high lookout point and hold your tools up to the wind as you recite your incantation.
- **Fire:** For passion and transformation, you can cleanse your tools with smoke.
- **Water:** For intuition and emotional depth, you can recharge your tool with water from your favorite river or pond.

TIP

If you're short on time, you can simply sit in meditation and visualize channeling your own energy into the tool.

IN THIS CHAPTER

» Incorporating regular rituals into your routine

» Crafting ritual objects, ingredients, and symbols

» Casting circles, "calling the quarters," and working with candle magic

Chapter 12 Ritualizing Your Life

Rituals set the rhythm of your practice and inform the ways you maneuver through the magical and the mundane each day. While you bend spells to your will, you *abide* by rituals. To abide means to bear, endure, or accept something you can't control, like the rules of magic or the constraints of time and energy. To abide also means to dwell, as in, to be at home. So, as I see it, to perform a ritual is to be fully present with what is rather than trying to change something forcefully. By respecting the timing and opportunities of your own crooked path, you open yourself to growth and transformation.

In this chapter, I offer tips to incorporate rituals into your days, create sustainable magical routines, craft your own ritual objects, and perform ceremonies. The second half of the chapter is dedicated to candle magic, including color correspondences and preparing candles for ritual work. I guide you through a candle ritual you can perform each season to evoke new creative energies.

Laying the Foundation: A Magical Routine

REMEMBER

A *ritual* is a set of intentional actions performed in a specific sequence. Rituals can be mundane, focusing on the ordinary parts of life, or they can be magical, following prescribed instructions.

Studies in psychology have shown that performing ritualized actions, like lighting a candle, saying specific words, or following a set sequence of steps, can create a sense of control and calm, especially in uncertain or stressful situations. This is why rituals are so universal across cultures and history — they tap into your brain's natural desire for structure and meaning, making you feel grounded and focused. Rituals can help build routine or even become routines in themselves. The repetition and consistency help you integrate magic into your everyday life. Rituals create safe containers for you to explore your practice. They help you maintain energetic balance and sustainably grow as a witch.

REMEMBER

Although a ritual doesn't have to include spells, many magical rituals involve spell work. In Chapter 11, I cover the basics of spellcasting. Here, I explore ways to incorporate spells with rituals. Some rituals use simple spells, such as clearing spells while sweeping. Others involve a series of spells and strict ritual observance to intention and timing.

Enchanting the mundane

The witch life seems glamorous on the outside, but really, I've felt most "like a witch" during (seemingly) mundane periods of life. Looking back at these times, I realize that I was at the best points of my practice when I had a consistent routine. Examples are the six-week period I woke up early to meditate and the summer I ate on a schedule and went to sleep at the same time every night. Whenever I was enjoying a good work/life balance and taking care of myself, I had more energy to devote to my magical practice.

TIP

Everyday rituals aren't rigid. They flow with you, as you flow with them. Not all rituals will be daily ones. Some will be weekly, others monthly, and the most involved ones can be reserved for seasonal practice.

Start building your rituals with slow and steady routines. I started with a daily practice of sitting at my altar, grounding my energy, and pulling one card from my tarot deck. Slowly, I added on things like lighting candles and making petitions. As I continued in my practice, I realized there were things I felt called to do weekly, like cleansing and gratitude rituals. On a biweekly or monthly basis, I performed more involved release and attraction rituals timed with the moon phases.

I offer some examples of simple rituals you can begin to incorporate. To start, choose one to do daily, one to do weekly, one for monthly practice, and one for special occasions. I keep more complex rituals like petitioning spirits and calling for transformation for occasional practice, like during the transition between seasons. These are some of my go-to rituals to sustain my energy for my practice, paired with a few tools I discuss in Chapter 11:

- **Cleansing with my broom:** To clear away stagnant or negative energy from my home or space, I open the nearest door to the outside; starting in the center of the room I make my way toward the door. I sweep lightly, hovering the bristles just above the floor, moving in a clockwise direction, imagining clearing away all negativity or unwanted energy.
- **Attracting by planting a garden:** Each season I turn my garden and plant new seeds that correspond with energies I want to call into my life. Each time I water the plants, I think about my intentions, knowing that I'm slowly growing toward them, as my plants grow toward the sun.
- **Banishing by cutting cords:** Sometimes I feel like I'm having a hard time letting go of something, like a bad habit or relationship dynamic. In these moments, I visualize a "cord" connecting me to the thing I want to release. I use a ribbon or piece of rope to represent the connection, and I cut it with my ritual scissors or athame (small dagger). See the instructions for a full cord-cutting ritual in Chapter 16.
- **Protecting through visualization:** When I sit in front of the mirror, I create an energetic shield around me by visualizing a glowing sphere of light enveloping me, keeping all harmful energies away.
- **Transforming with a pot or cauldron:** I simmer herbs and oils to create a wonderful aroma in my kitchen. Transforming ingredients into something else is gratifying and reminds me that change is possible. See Chapter 14 for a sachet simmer pot recipe.
- **Evoking with my wand:** Sometimes I'm feeling under-resourced and want to call upon specific energies, deities, or elements to aid in my magical work. At my altar, I hold up my wand, raise my voice, and speak my incantations to the spirits I'm petitioning. It sometimes feels silly, but overcoming my insecurity, taking up a lot of space, and making a lot of noise is energizing and makes me feel confident.
- **Healing with nature:** Every now and then I need to reconnect with the earth. I go on long walks in nature. I've occasionally spent a couple of weeks at a time hiking and backpacking. I find it takes a few days among trees to ease the chatter in my mind.

REMEMBER

You might notice that the themes of these rituals match closely with the ones I outline for common spells. (You can pair these rituals with the corresponding spells I outline in Chapter 21.) Although the general intentions are similar, spells are focused on a narrow outcome, and rituals usually serve a larger purpose. They might not seem as flashy as some spells, but they create space for spiritual growth. That said, some rituals do call for complex spell work, and some involve multiple forms of spellcasting.

TIP

Trust the process of your everyday rituals and magical routine. Start small, and gradually customize as you feel comfortable. Have fun, and document your rituals and experiences in your grimoire.

Crafting magical objects and symbols

As I've gotten more seasoned in my practice, I've started to make some of my own tools and ritual objects, like brooms and wands. Magical tools and ingredients become powerful allies when they're ritually constructed, meaning they're intentionally crafted, blessed, or charged to hold and direct specific magical energy. The act of creating these items transforms them from mundane objects into vessels of spiritual and energetic power. The construction process itself is a sacred ritual, as you can imbue your essence into your objects. Think of the rings of *Lord of the Rings*, or the horcruxes in *Harry Potter* — except they don't have to be negative or possess people.

In Chapter 11, I cover consecrating tools, which is a simple spell you can use to dedicate your tools toward their purpose. You can craft many of the tools from scratch to increase their magic. You can also create other kinds of ritual objects by combining tools, symbols, and ingredients, including:

- **Amulets:** Primarily protective tools, *amulets* are designed to shield the wearer from harm, negativity, or spiritual attacks. Often made from metals, stones, or carved symbols, they're ritually blessed, anointed with protective oils, or infused with protective herbs. Example: A piece of obsidian wrapped in wire and worn as a necklace to ward off psychic harm.
- **Charms:** *Charms* are small, portable objects that can serve multiple purposes, from bringing luck to providing emotional strength. Often crafted with small items like beads, feathers, or carved wood, charms are personalized and infused with intent during their creation. They might be blessed with breath, smoke, or specific incantations. Example: A small pouch filled with a rabbit's foot and a four-leaf clover to carry good fortune. They're often carried on the person, kept in a special place, or integrated into spell work.
- **Sachets:** *Sachets* (sometimes spelled *satchels*) are portable pouches filled with magical items to attract, protect, or manifest energies. A small cloth bag is filled with ingredients aligned to the purpose, such as herbs, stones, and charms. The sachet is tied shut and ritually blessed or "fed" with oils or incense to maintain its energy. Example: A green sachet filled with basil, coins, and a citrine crystal for prosperity.
- **Intention candles:** Candles crafted for intention focus energy during spell work, often representing intention through color, scent, or engraving. You can create and pour candles during important cosmic events for extra power.

Candles are inscribed with symbols, anointed with oils, or rolled in herbs and *charged*, or imbued with energy, before being lit in rituals. I cover candle magic in the later section "Preparing and dressing candles."

- **Potions:** Potions are liquid preparations intended to be consumed, applied, or used in rituals for magical purposes, such as healing, love, or spiritual cleansing. Potions are crafted by brewing herbs, roots, and other magical ingredients together, often while chanting or focusing on the desired outcome. They're sometimes charged under specific moon phases or planetary alignments for added potency. Example: A healing potion brewed with chamomile, lavender, and honey to restore calm and balance.
- **Oils, salves, and tinctures:** Magical oils, salves, and tinctures are crafted to anoint objects, candles, or the body, serving to amplify intentions, evoke specific energies, or create sacred spaces. You can use them for protection, attraction, healing, or other magical purposes.

WARNING

Find a maker or teacher to learn from, and follow instructions closely when ritually crafting objects. Unlike mundane rituals, making your own magical objects can involve higher standards or more restrictions. For instance, you need to ensure tinctures are safe for ingestion. Or if you're making an intention candle to capture the energy of a current planetary transit, you'll have a specific window to do so.

Ritually crafted objects and ingredients are aligned with your goals, so you can personalize them through rituals or specific designs to resonate with your desired intention. You might even become known for your tools and ingredients over time. One of the most wonderful things about practicing for a while is getting to share your specific brand of magic in your witchy community.

BUNDLING THE MAGIC

Witches bundles or *sachets* are collections of magical items — such as herbs, flowers, feathers, or other natural objects — wrapped or tied together with twine. They're often hung in sacred spaces or burned as offerings and are commonly used to purify spaces, ward against negative energy, or attract prosperity. Cultures have different names for bundling, and exact practices are highly influenced by local resources and regional influences. For example, *mojo bags*, also known as *gris-gris*, are small pouches filled with items chosen for their symbolic or energetic properties. They originate from Hoodoo, a syncretic magical tradition that blends African, Native American, and European influences (which I cover in more depth in Chapter 2). They're carried on the body or placed in a meaningful location, in contrast to the average witches bundle, which is typically displayed or burned.

Transforming energy with talismans

Talismans are typically created to attract specific energies or outcomes, such as success, love, or courage. Made by adding ingredients and intentions to a base object, they can be engraved or inscribed with symbols or sacred words, charged through visualization, or aligned with astrological timings. Basically, it's all about creating something unique that represents what you're trying to call in. Before you begin, hold a strong intention in your mind about what you're looking to attract, repel, or transform.

I recently started creating "shadow boxes" to transform hard things I'm dealing with into empowerment. Here are the steps I take to make my shadow box talismans:

1. **Choose the base object:** Select an item that resonates with your intention and can serve as the foundation for your talisman. Talismans can start from anything, but because I'm making shadow boxes, I choose a small object that can hold other things, like a box or a locket.
2. **Gather corresponding materials:** Choose colors, symbols, crystals, herbs, personal items, or anything else that you feel resonates with your intention. Cleanse the box and other ingredients and materials.
3. **Assemble the box:** I like to line the back of the shadow box with a fabric or paper that complements my intention. Arrange your items carefully. I use a small amount of glue to affix my items.
4. **Empower the box:** When you're satisfied with your arrangement, you can empower the box by visualizing your intention flowing into it, or you can charge it with moonlight or sunlight. You can also burn incense or a candle to charge it with fire. Because I make my boxes for transformation, I visualize the unwanted parts of myself or my circumstances clarifying into the more lovely things I've represented in the box.
5. **Place the box:** Keep your box somewhere safe, or in a place that matches its intention (such as your night table, if it's a box for dreams).
6. **Consecrate the box:** Just like any other ritual object, you'll have to maintain the energy through occasional reconsecration and cleansing.

Making your own sigils

Sigils are custom-made symbols designed to represent a specific intention or desire. They're widely used in modern magic, particularly in chaos magic, due to their flexibility and adaptability. A sigil functions as a condensed, symbolic "seal" of the practitioner's will, charged with energy and released into the universe to manifest the desired outcome.

FUN FACT

In *chaos magic*, sigils are particularly important because they rely on your belief and creativity rather than predefined symbols or traditions. Chaos magic emphasizes flexibility, allowing you to adapt the sigil-making process to suit your personal style and energy.

To create a sigil, like the one I've created here, you can follow these basic steps that I learned from an expert sigil master:

1. **Start with your written intention:** For example: "I create beautiful, irresistible cupcakes, and by the end of the year, I will win an international baking competition."
2. **Strike out parts of the intention:** For instance, you can remove all vowels and any consonants that repeat anywhere in the phrase, leaving only unique consonants. Taking the cupcake statement mentioned in step 1, that would leave only the letters Y and G. (You can make your own rules for how to narrow down letters.)
3. **Arrange the remaining letters:** Your goal is to create a unique symbol. Overlap, rotate, and combine the letters until they no longer resemble the original words. Focus on aesthetics and how the design resonates with your intention.
4. **Charge the sigil:** Much like charging tools, you can infuse the sigil with energy through meditation, visualization, or rituals. Some practitioners gaze at the sigil while visualizing their intention or incorporate it into a spell using candles, herbs, or other tools.
5. **Release the intention:** Burn, bury, or destroy the sigil to release its energy into the universe. You can choose to keep it as a focal point for ongoing work, but I've been taught that forgetting about it is best because then it becomes occult magic, doing its work under the surface. Above all else, sigil magic is about releasing control and being ready for what might unexpectedly come (so you can delight in the surprise when you're informed that you've made the World Cupcake finals).

Manifesting with spell jars

I've always been a bit of a magpie, collecting little treasures that represent things I love. When I feel ready to make something beautiful, I arrange them in a jar, thinking about each object or ingredient as I drop it in, holding in my mind what the objects mean to me and the energies they will call into my life. I seal them with the wax from a burning candle and place them somewhere I can see them.

REMEMBER

Spell jars are containers that hold a mix of symbolic and magical ingredients sealed to manifest a specific intention. Practitioners layer ingredients such as herbs, crystals, written petitions, and liquids in a jar. Each layer is added with intention, and the jar is sealed with wax to "lock" the energy inside.

Manifesting is a bit of a buzz word thrown around in spiritual circles. It simply means to bring something into reality — to, say, make a wish come true. I find that the easiest manifestation rituals are ones that use physical objects to represent what I'm trying to make reality. Much like the shadow box ritual (in the earlier section "Transforming energy with talismans"), the contents of spell jars connect with your wishes. Here are the steps I've taken to make a common kind of spell jar called a *honey jar* to manifest love:

1. **Gather your materials:** You'll need a small jar with a lid, preferably glass; honey or another natural sweetener like syrup; a piece of paper and a pen; personal items like a photo, strands of hair, or another token representing love; love-drawing herbs such as rose petals and lavender; and a pink or red taper candle.
2. **Write your intention:** Write your name and the kind of love you want to attract. Remember that it's best not to manipulate others' energies, so try to stick to ideals of love rather than trying to "get" one person at all costs. (Those things have a way of backfiring.) Fold the paper three times toward you, symbolizing drawing love into your life.
3. **Add the ingredients:** Place the folded paper into the jar. Add the love-drawing herbs, visualizing the qualities you want in your love relationships as you do. While adding rose petals, imagine love blossoming in your life. If you have personal items, add them on top.
4. **Pour the honey:** Slowly pour honey into the jar, covering the paper and ingredients. As you pour, focus on the sweetness of love coming into your life or the relationship. Say an incantation aloud, like, "As this honey is sweet, so too is the love I attract into my life."
5. **Seal and charge the jar:** Close the jar tightly and hold it in your hands. Focus on your intention, imagining it as already fulfilled. Visualize the love, harmony, and joy flowing into your life. Light the pink or red candle and place it on top of the jar. Allow the wax to drip and seal the lid. (I light the bottom of the candle so the melting wax sticks to the surface of my jar top or cork.) For safety, sit with your candle until it burns out.
6. **Maintain the spell:** Place the honey jar on your altar, near your bed, or somewhere meaningful. Light another pink or red candle on top of the jar (or next to it) periodically to recharge the spell, especially on Fridays, because it's associated with Venus, the planet of love.

Performing ceremonies

Some rituals mark special occasions, such as those performed on *sabbats* (see Chapter 22) or *handfasting* during weddings, involving binding a couple's hands together as a symbol of their union. Ceremonial rituals often employ multiple kinds of spells, such as clearing and protection spells, before and after the performance of the main ritual.

Ritual ceremonies in witchcraft could include seasonal or lunar celebrations, initiation rites, or other rites of passage. Two common spells that are used during larger rituals are *circle casting* and *calling the quarters.*

Casting a circle

Casting a circle is a time-honored traditional spell and ritual among witches. First focus on the purpose of the circle, such as protection, concentration, or sacred connection. Hold your wand, athame, or hand up and walk clockwise around the perimeter of your space, visualizing a glowing circle of light forming around you. Say something like: "I cast this circle, a boundary of light, to protect and hold this sacred rite." (I do love a good rhyme!) Once the circle is complete, feel its protective energy surrounding you.

Calling the quarters

Calling the quarters is a ritual practice in modern witchcraft and pagan traditions, particularly Wicca, used to call on the energies of the four cardinal directions — East, South, West, and North — and their associated elements (Air, Fire, Water, and Earth). This practice creates sacred space, balances energies, and aligns you with the natural world. The steps involve facing in each of the directions in turn, as depicted in Figure 12-1. Although the specifics depend on your practice, feel free to use this template and adjust as you gain confidence:

1. **Face East (Air):** Light a yellow candle while speaking an incantation like this one: "Spirits of the East, guardians of Air, I call upon you to bring clarity, inspiration, and breath to this circle. Be with me now."
2. **Face South (Fire):** Light a red candle while speaking an incantation like this: "Spirits of the South, guardians of Fire, I call upon you to bring passion, energy, and transformation to this circle. Be with me now."
3. **Face West (Water):** Light a blue candle while speaking an incantation like this: "Spirits of the West, guardians of Water, I call upon you to bring intuition, healing, and emotional flow to this circle. Be with me now."
4. **Face North (Earth):** Light a green candle while speaking an incantation like this: "Spirits of the North, guardians of Earth, I call upon you to bring stability, strength, and grounding to this circle. Be with me now."

FIGURE 12-1: Diagrams of the four directions and their associations.

Assembling Your Tools: Candle Magic

FUN FACT

I grew up with candle magic rituals. *Novenas*, or nine-day devotionals, are a common tradition among Catholics. The term comes from the Latin word *novem*, meaning "nine." Novenas are often used to seek intercession from saints for a specific intention, such as healing, guidance, protection, or a particular blessing. Everyone does novenas a little differently, but I remember lighting one candle per day and praying over it, for a total of nine candles over nine prayers. It's only since beginning my journey in witchcraft that I learned to view this as petitionary candle magic.

REMEMBER

Candle magic is one of the most accessible and versatile forms of magical practice, spanning vastly different religions and traditions. With a candle's flame acting as a symbol of transformation, intention, and focus, this practice allows you to channel your desires into the physical and spiritual realms.

FUN FACT

Candles were used in ancient Egypt, Greece, and Rome during ceremonies and offerings. Their flames symbolized light, guidance, and divine presence, and the flames were often used in divination practices. In Christianity, Judaism, and other faiths, candles are lit to honor deities, ancestors, or saints, symbolizing prayers carried upward through the smoke. Candle magic became a staple in European folk magic and later Wiccan traditions, valued for its simplicity and symbolic power.

Candle magic's appeal lies in its universality — fire is a primal element, and its transformative energy is recognized across cultures.

Knowing your colors

The color of a candle is believed to enhance specific intentions by aligning with its corresponding energy; see Table 12-1.

TABLE 12-1 Candle Color Meanings

Color	Meaning
White	Purity, protection, clarity, peace, and new beginnings
Black	Banishing negativity, protection, and shadow work
Red	Passion, love, courage, and vitality
Pink	Friendship, self-love, romantic love, and harmony
Green	Abundance, prosperity, fertility, and growth
Blue	Healing, wisdom, communication, and calm
Yellow	Creativity, confidence, success, and intellectual clarity
Purple	Psychic abilities, intuition, spiritual connection, and ambition
Orange	Joy, energy, attraction, and opportunity
Brown	Stability, grounding, and matters of the home

Choosing your form

Different types of candles can be used in candle magic, depending on the spell or ritual, as shown in Table 12-2.

TABLE 12-2 Candle Type Uses

Candle Type	Description	Use
Taper candles	Long and slender	Single-use spells because they burn quickly
Pillar candles	Larger and longer-lasting	Ongoing intentions or repeated rituals
Tea lights	Small and convenient	Quick spells or as part of larger setups
Chime candles (birthday candles)	Small, colorful candles that burn in 1-2 hours	Specific spell work
Jar or votive candles	Encased in glass	Protection or devotional work
Figure candles	Molded into shapes like humans, animals, or symbols	Personal spells or sympathetic magic

Preparing and dressing candles

Before using a candle in magic, prepare it to hold your intention by cleansing it to remove any residual energies. You can do this by passing it through incense smoke, sprinkling it with salt, or wiping it with moon water, as I describe in Chapter 10.

Dressing a candle involves *anointing* it, or rubbing it with oils or in herbs to amplify its energy:

- **Taper candles:** Use oils that correspond to your intention (for example, lavender for peace, cinnamon for attraction).
- **Pillar candles:** Apply the oil from the base to the wick if drawing energy toward you, and from the wick to the base if sending energy away.
- **Tea lights:** Roll the oiled candle in herbs or powders for added potency.

TIP

Hold the candle in your hands and focus on your intention. Visualize the energy of your desire flowing into the candle. Speak your intention aloud or silently as you infuse it with your will.

Waxing poetic

As I've worked with candles, I've circled back around to my cultural prayers, but with renewed focus as a confident practitioner. Petitioning and prayer are common practices in candle magic, connecting your intentions to higher spiritual forces. I find this to be a highly creative and even poetic process because I write my intentions as part of a sort of performance for my ancestors, spirits, or the gods.

Refer to Chapter 11 on how to create an intention. In this case, the intention serves as a *petition*, a request to the spirits.

TIP

Place the petition under or near the candle, or burn it in the flame to release your intention into the universe. As you do, address deities, ancestors, or spiritual entities, asking for guidance or support. Combine your prayer with visualization, imagining your desired outcome as you speak.

Bringing it together in ceremony

If you're comfortable with your tools and the basics of spellcasting and ritual work, you can try putting all these concepts together with a candle ceremony. This ritual incorporates the sequence of cleansing your space, casting a circle, calling the quarters, and evoking energies. It's a foundational ritual that you can adapt to fit a variety of purposes, from setting up for spell work to creating sacred space for meditation or even initiation. You'll need the following materials:

» A cleansing tool.

Choose herbs, incense, or salt water.

» A wand or athame.

This tool is for circle casting.

» Candles representing the four elements/directions.

Choose colors and forms that represent the spiritual entities you'd like to evoke.

» A bell, rattle, or chime.

This one is optional.

» Personal items for the altar.

This one is also optional — crystals or symbols.

Prepare by cleansing the space and grounding, if you haven't already. (See Chapters 10 and 21 for cleansing and grounding spells.) Next, cast your circle and call the quarters (see instructions for each of these spells under the section "Performing ceremonies" earlier in this chapter).

Now it's time for the main act. Stand in the center of the circle, close your eyes, and take a few deep breaths to center yourself. If applicable, you can ring your bell to start your petition or present your offerings in the center of the circle.

If petitioning a deity or spiritual energy, speak their name aloud. Example: "I call upon the Goddess of the Moon. Guide me with your wisdom and light." If evoking abstract energies, such as love, courage, or protection, you can say something like, "I call in the energy of courage. Fill this space and my being with strength and resilience."

Picture the energy or entity entering the circle. Imagine it filling the space with its presence, radiating power, or enveloping you in its light. Now is the time to ask your question or make your petition, if you have one.

WARNING

Only call on spirits that you're confident you're ready to work with, and avoid *invoking*, or summoning a presence, unless you're trained. *Invocation* is considered an advanced practice that should be preceded by foundational work like consistent petitions and offerings. If you don't feel ready, stick to a loving ancestor or a general energy you want to evoke (see Chapter 8 for the difference between evoking and invoking).

When you are done, to seal your ritual, say: "I thank you for your presence and guidance. May your energy align with my purpose." Stand in each direction and thank the elements, saying something like, "Spirits of the East, thank you for your clarity and presence. Depart in peace." (Repeat for South, West, and North.)

Walk counterclockwise (or *widdershins*, an old Scottish term meaning "against the way") around the circle, visualizing the protective light dissolving.

Say an incantation like, "I release this circle, its purpose complete. The energy returns to the Earth, in perfect peace."

Touch the ground or place your hands on your heart. Take deep breaths to center your energy. Spend a moment journaling or meditating on the experience if desired. Documenting your rituals will help you adjust as you make yourself at home, so you can find your own words and movements.

TIP

Your power as a witch isn't measured in the number of spells that come true for you. It's in how well you integrate magic into your everyday life.

4 Exploring Paths of the Modern Witch

IN THIS PART . . .

Learn about different forms of divination. Practice tapping into your intuition. Explore divination methods including cartomancy, pendulum dowsing, and scrying.

Discover green witchery, including wildcrafting, foraging, gardening, and kitchen magic. Find instructions for making herbal sachets and Florida water for cleansing.

Get acquainted with the basics of cosmic magic, including the correspondences of lunar cycles. Dive into the parts of the astrological birth chart and learn about planetary energies.

Tap into healing energy modalities used across the world. Learn about mediumship and different states of consciousness, including dreams and spirit communication. Practice visualizing your chakras and find instructions for a ritual to release energetic ties.

IN THIS CHAPTER

- » **Discovering ancient and modern forms of divination**
- » **Tapping into your intuitive powers as a diviner**
- » **Learning methods and tools to start or expand your divination practices**

Chapter 13 The Divination Witch

When you hear the word *divination*, you probably think of fortune tellers and psychics. Although that's not completely off the mark, divination is primarily a practice of interpretation that leads to revelatory insights about life experiences. Sometimes that includes making predictions or reading minds, but the pillars of any divination practice are actually *intuition* (the connection to unconscious or subconscious processes) and the *divine* (the connection to a higher consciousness). Witches who specialize in divination have varying definitions of the divine, which is open to any faith. What most divination witches have in common is that they use the *mundane* — aspects of the ordinary, conscious world — to access their personal intuition and divinity.

This chapter covers common divination practices, explores techniques to expand your intuitive abilities, and outlines a few of the most beginner-friendly methods and tools for divination. From tarot cards to pendulums, crystal balls to runes, I demystify divination and help you choose the tools that are right for your own practices.

Tapping into Your Power: Psychic Magic

Anyone can be a diviner. It's sometimes predictive, but in modern divination, the focus of fortune-telling is more on interpreting current energies than determining sequences of events in fatalistic ways. In other words, divination is always about your perceptions and the ways you act as a unique interpreter between the mystical and the mundane. No matter your level of knowledge and practice with your specific tools, your divinatory power comes from your openness and awareness.

REMEMBER

In divination, a *reading* is the process of interpreting information using a divinatory tool or method. The purpose of a reading is to provide guidance, answers, or a deeper understanding of a question, situation, or general life path. During a reading, the diviner uses a specific technique to access hidden knowledge, like drawing tarot cards or reading palm lines on a hand. Reading is also a verb, as in "they're reading the cards."

Common assumptions can perpetuate the idea that divination is narrowly about predicting the future. As a professional tarot reader, I've been asked to "look the part," and I just interpret that as meaning I can fully show up as my authentic self. Readers and diviners have no specific look, and you don't have to assume a uniform. Sometimes I show up to an event in jeans, and sometimes I wear all black. Every time, I tune into my present self.

WARNING

Whether you call them *fortune tellers* or *psychic readers* or something else, diviners are often stereotyped in popular culture. A go-to "look" often appears in media portrayals (as though all diviners wear the same costume): flowing skirts, head scarves, and heavy jewelry. These stereotypes often appropriate Romani culture, sometimes calling to mind the word *gypsy*, which is a derogatory term now widely considered a slur.

CULTIVATING PRESENCE IN READINGS

Being completely present during a reading is important. As a diviner, I try to be fully grounded and focused on the reading rather than anything that's going on in my personal life. Presence helps when I encounter clients who might have the stereotypical view of a reader in mind, whether consciously or unconsciously. Maybe they're scared or skeptical, or maybe they're silent, waiting for me to "prove" my psychic powers. Being sensitive to body language and perceived expectations helps me adjust my communication to encourage my clients to open up, achieve their own presence, and connect to the readings.

I believe in free will, so even if I'm addressing the past or the future, my reading is always a *present* interpretation of the past or the future. The reading picks up on current energies, so a reading tomorrow will yield a completely different interpretation than one today. When I read for myself, I open a channel to my sources of power. When I read for someone else, I consider it a collaboration between me and them, and between us both and the divine messages coming through.

Divination is about possibilities more than fate. If you can let go of your predisposed notions — whether reading for yourself or others — you'll open yourself to the surprises that will undoubtedly arise.

As a divination witch, you must develop your intuition and learn to trust the messages you receive and your interpretations of those messages. This ability to discern symbols and see patterns requires both study and practice. Anybody can hone these skills. Over time, you'll blend your learned techniques with your own gifts, tapping into your special powers of divination.

Getting to the roots of divination

Divination is one of the oldest spiritual practices on earth, with roots stretching back thousands of years across nearly every culture. The earliest divinatory practices were usually concerned with the will of the gods. In ancient Greece, for example, kings and commoners alike consulted the Oracle of Delphi to know whether they had divine favor for their actions or decisions.

Early divination methods varied greatly across the ancient world. Here are a few examples, keeping in mind that many of the methods I list were found in multiple regions across the world:

- **Dreams in Egypt:** Dreams were believed to be messages from the gods, and priests and oracles conducted *oneiromancy*, interpreting the dreams as divine signs.
- **Entrails in Mesopotamia:** Diviners called *haruspex* inspected the livers of sacrificed animals to divine the will of the gods, a process referred to as *haruspicy*. *Extispicy*, in contrast, is the process of examining and interpreting any entrails of sacrificed animals.
- **Auguries in Greece:** *Augurs*, or seers, observed the flight patterns of birds to predict future events.
- **Omens in Rome:** *Omenologists* interpreted natural phenomena like lightning strikes, unusual animal behavior, and celestial events as signs from the gods.
- **Energy flows in China:** Also known as *Yi Jing*, the *I Ching* is a system of divination using a set of 64 hexagrams, each representing energetic qualities. China is also the birthplace of *Feng Shui*, the ancient art of divining energy flows in living spaces.
- **Earth divination in the Arabian Peninsula and North Africa:** Originating in the Islamic world and spreading to medieval Europe, geomancy involved interpreting patterns created by casting handfuls of soil or drawing dots on the ground.

- **Staves in Celtic and Druid tribes:** Diviners used sticks or wooden pieces inscribed with the ancient alphabet known as *Ogham* to connect with natural forces.
- **Bone throwing in Africa:** *Hakata* is the casting of bones, shells, or other natural objects and the interpretation of how they fall to determine messages from ancestors or spirits.
- **Trance in shamanic tribes:** *Vision quests* are a form of divination practiced by many shamanic peoples, including Siberian, Native American, and Norse tribes. They are personal spiritual journeys induced by fasting, isolation, mind-altering substances, or rhythmic drumming that provoke altered states of consciousness.
- **Turtle shells in Japan:** *Kame-Boku* is a form of divination similar to the Chinese oracle bones. Turtle shells were used in ancient Japan to divine messages from the gods by interpreting cracks formed after heating.
- **Runes in Norse/Viking tribes:** *Runes*, an ancient alphabet used by the Norse, were cast or drawn to provide insight into personal questions.
- **Calendar divination in Mesoamerica:** The Mayans and Aztecs used their complex calendar systems, known as *Tonalpohualli*, to interpret cosmic energies on specific days to predict events.
- **Fire scrying in Persia:** In *scrying*, a reflective surface like water, a mirror, or oil is used to perceive visions or gain insight. Because fire was a central element in Zoroastrianism, Persian diviners interpreted the movements and forms of fire to receive guidance from the spirits.

Throughout history, diviners have often operated like consultants, becoming part of the fabric of royal families and governments. Divining was not only mystical but also an earthly source of power.

WARNING

Although divination is a core practice in modern witchcraft, the first recorded diviners were rarely considered *witches*, a term that largely held negative connotations in ancient times.

As discussed in Chapter 1, divination practices were periodically condemned by religious authorities. But the persecution continues even today because divination is considered heretical by the Catholic Church and other religions. Much divination has persisted in secret, blending folk magic and cultural rituals into practices that survived even the most intense periods of persecution. These clandestine traditions passed through generations, evolving into the various forms of divination seen today.

Which "mancy" do you fancy?

In recent years, divination has shed some of its stigma and been embraced as a tool for self-exploration and spiritual insight. Symbolic systems like tarot cards, runes, and astrology have regained mainstream interest, no longer widely viewed as mere superstition, on the one end, or heresy, on the other.

FUN FACT

These methods and the messages that arise from using them are commonly referred to as *oracles*. In terms of divination, the suffix *-mancy* comes from the ancient Greek word *manteia*, meaning divination or prophecy. The suffix is attached to the root of the word that indicates the type of oracle used for divination. For example:

- **Cartomancy:** Divination using cards (for example, tarot or playing cards)
- **Astromancy:** Divination by interpreting the stars, planets, and other celestial bodies, closely tied to the practice of astrology
- **Tasseomancy:** Divination by reading tea leaves
- **Chiromancy:** Divination by reading the lines and features of human hands
- **Necromancy:** Divination by communicating with the dead or spirits
- **Oneiromancy:** Divination through the interpretation of dreams
- **Cleromancy:** Divination by casting lots, such as stones, bones, or dice
- **Osteomancy:** Divination by throwing bones, specifically
- **Bibliomancy:** Divination by randomly flipping to words in a book
- **Carromancy:** Divination by reading wax droplet formations, which is often conducted in tandem with fire scrying
- **Graphomancy:** Divination based on handwriting, including any form of writing believed to have a supernatural or mystical origin, such as automatic writing

You can choose from countless *-mancys* out there. Anything in the world can be an oracle! Divination isn't so much about the mundane object that you use but how it helps you connect to your intuition. Some people have go-to oracles, whereas others spontaneously use what's available in the moment. If you don't know where to start, working with the elements can help you explore possibilities.

Methods of divination are tied to each element:

- **Geomancy:** Divination through casting earthly objects such as stones, sand, or dirt, and interpreting their patterns

- **Hydromancy:** Divination through water, ink, or oil, such as observing ripples, currents, or reflections (including water dowsing, using tools to locate water sources)
- **Pyromancy:** Divination through fire, flames, or smoke, usually via close observation or scrying
- **Aeromancy:** Divination through atmospheric conditions, such as wind patterns and cloud formations

TIP

Try as many methods of divination as you can, and keep a journal to log your experiences and interpretations. Don't despair if you don't immediately have great results. Focus more on what tools feel right or what methods make you excited. Take special note of ones you feel have potential given more practice.

Expanding your consciousness

The pillars of any divination practice, no matter the methods or tools you choose to employ, are intuition and divinity. Intuition is the ability to understand, know, or sense something without the need for conscious reasoning or analysis. It's often described as a "gut feeling" or inner sense that guides decisions and judgments without relying on logical or deliberate thought processes. For the divination witch, this inner knowing becomes the key to interpreting messages from the universe, the spirits, or the deeper layers of the subconscious or even the unconscious.

The second pillar of divination is divinity itself. The divine is highly personal. Divine sources may include gods, angelic beings, ancestors, spirits, or the universe. Atheist or agnostic witches may also use divination, and some diviners even consult the theoretical sciences, like quantum physics, to explain the ways they tap into the unknown. No matter your beliefs, divination is about using your intuitive powers to connect to your personal divinity, the higher power that you aspire to know. Through divination, this power rushes through you and provides understanding and guidance. This is sometimes referred to as the *superconscious*, a consciousness that transcends human experience.

REMEMBER

When you say someone is *psychic*, you're usually talking about someone who can tap into their intuitive abilities to connect to the divine. They become a *medium*, or channel, between planes of consciousness. I explore mediumship further in Chapter 16.

In my experience, diviners evolve from raw intuition to channeling the divine through their dedication to their craft. Over their practice, they learn to trust themselves, expand their consciousness, and harmonize mind, body, and spirit.

Intuition is connected to the body. Your perceptions are honed through your human experiences, including what you keep in your subconscious and unconscious mind. Your craft occupies your conscious, waking mind, as you become an expert in your methods and master the theory and language of divination. And your connection to the divine aligns you with spirit and your higher consciousness.

Intuition as a practice of the body

Each psychic reader possesses their own special powers of perception. In Chapter 6, I dive into the concept of *clair* abilities, forms of extrasensory perception (ESP) that allow you to receive information beyond the normal senses, such as seeing, hearing, feeling, or knowing things that aren't physically present or observable. Two examples of these forms of ESP are clairaudience (clear hearing) and clairsentience (clear feeling).

Everyone has intuitive abilities. Developing intuition is a gradual process, requiring years of practice, patience, and self-trust. Some witches may find they're more naturally inclined toward one of these abilities, whereas others may develop several over time.

TIP

Meditation is one of the most powerful tools for sharpening this inner sight, as it helps quiet the mind and connect with the subtle energies that you embody. Consult Chapter 6 for more detailed exercises to develop your own "clair" abilities. Honing your perception through regular exercises is like going to the gym; it's a muscle you work out. As your perception expands, your divination practices improve over time.

Method as a practice of the mind

A good reading combines intuition and learned techniques. Readers constantly develop their technical skills, learning the symbolism of their methods of choice until they become second nature. For beginners, learning a method is a good entry point to conducting readings because it involves using universal symbols they can study.

TIP

Study the commonly understood meanings of the symbols you're working with. In my own practice, until I learned to trust my intuition, I focused on learning the language of the tarot. Each day, I drew a card and read about its symbolism, either by referencing the guidebook that came with the deck or by searching universal meanings online.

Over time, your intuition will whisper to you to add your own meanings to the common meanings of symbols. Sometimes, based on context and other information, you'll depart completely from widely accepted interpretations, as you access a higher understanding.

REMEMBER

You assign meaning to symbols through a process of *interpretation*. Interpretation involves analyzing information, symbols, or events and offering an explanation or perspective based on your unique understanding and knowledge.

Methods of divination primarily aid your interpretation. They don't represent objective truth. For example, the Fool card in the traditional Rider-Waite-Smith deck typically represents new beginnings, adventure, and the willingness to take risks. The character on the card is depicted as about to step off a cliff. Depending on context, this could be interpreted in a positive light, as someone who completely trusts the journey and exudes positivity. On the other hand, the Fool could be interpreted as a naïve person who's about to throw away opportunities in their perpetual need to escape. Other, nontraditional interpretations of the Fool are possible. (Maybe instead of stepping off a cliff, they're about to fly.) Your intellect and your intuition will meld to help you arrive at your unique interpretation.

TIP

Never stop learning. Even after two decades of working with the tarot, I'm still learning the method. The beautiful thing about using a system of symbolism is that you can continue to study different interpretations of the same symbols you've been working with forever, and it refreshes your practice. It also helps to lean on your method studies on days you don't feel particularly intuitive.

Altered consciousness as a practice of the spirit

It's okay if your divination practice focuses on opening your intuition and learning your craft, without incorporating the divine or reaching higher levels of consciousness — especially as you're starting out. For many people, coming to a deeper understanding of human experience through divinatory methods is satisfying enough and can be a healing and transformative process. That said, ultimately, the highest expression of divination opens a channel to the mysteries of your existence. Through divination, you have the potential to connect to the spiritual world, whatever that means to you.

Some readers have an innate connection to the divine, but for most, channeling higher powers requires lots of practice. Although I had spontaneous experiences with the spiritual world in my childhood, I could never control them, and they came at random. Through steady practice with divination in adulthood, I've slowly opened the channel to the divine, and now I more regularly make connection to ancestors and spirit guardians.

In Chapter 16 about the Energy Witch, I cover mediumship in more detail because divination and energy work have a lot of overlap.

TIP

To promote connection to the spirit world, create a sacred space for your readings. If your intention is to connect with a divine being or spirit guide, you can make offerings to them on your altar and address them directly. (See Chapter 10 on how to set up sacred space for spirit communication.)

For Your Grimoire: Divination Methods

Although there are countless methods of divination, a few have become go-to's for beginners. Among these are cartomancy, pendulum dowsing, and scrying. (Astrology is another popular system that can be used for divination, but it extends to other practices besides divination, so I cover it in more detail in Chapter 14.) If you're looking for where to start, consider the following beginner-friendly tools that are open to all.

Cartomancy

Cartomancy, or divination using cards, arose following the introduction of playing cards in 14th century Europe, after Egyptian and Arab traders shared their *Mamluk* decks of four suits and court cards. Whether the decks developed from trade with Asia is contested, but early playing cards were possibly adapted from Chinese games played with strips of bamboo. Europeans called these early decks *Saracen* or *Moorish* decks due to their Arabic origins, and Italians later referred to them as *carte da trionfi*, or trump cards.

FUN FACT

By the late 15th century, the cards evolved into the Italian *tarocchi* and started being used for occult purposes. Their use in divination took off in the 1700s, when Antoine Court de Gébelin published a volume about their divinatory origins. Whether his claims were true or not, by the late 18th century, Jean-Baptiste Alliette had coined the term *cartonomancy*, which he later shortened to cartomancy.

By the 19th century, cartomancy had become widespread across Europe, with different forms emerging. The Tarot de Marseille became a foundational tool for divination in France, while in England, simple playing cards were adapted into a system for fortune-telling. The 19th-century occult revival further propelled cartomancy, with Arthur Edward Waite and Pamela Colman Smith creating the now iconic Rider-Waite-Smith tarot deck in 1909, which remains one of the most popular decks.

TIP

In recent years, scholars have started to refer to the deck as the Waite-Smith Tarot — cutting out Rider, the publisher — recognizing the importance of Smith's contribution because she wasn't honored or paid for her achievements in her life.

Kinds of cards

Thousands of interpretations of traditional cartomancy decks exist today as artists spin traditional imagery or create their own unique oracle decks. The five most popular kinds of decks today are these:

- **Tarot cards:** Usually a deck of 78 cards based on the Waite-Smith deck, which focuses on the hero's journey. (You can find a breakdown of the parts of the Waite-Smith deck in the appendix.)
- **Lenormand:** A 36-card system offering more straightforward, practical readings compared to tarot.
- **Playing cards:** A standard deck of 52 playing cards repurposed for fortune-telling and predictive readings.
- **Lotería cards:** A set of colorful, symbolic images traditionally used in a Mexican game of chance, but they're also employed in modern folk magic and divination practices to gain insights and interpret messages.
- **Oracle cards:** Divination cards with varied, nonstandardized decks that may include images, phrases, or themes for intuitive guidance.

TIP

I recommend starting with the Waite-Smith deck or a deck based closely on it because it's the most used deck in the world. Most decks come with a guidebook, offering the creators' interpretations of the symbols. Some also include sample spreads. Until you develop your intuitive skills, you can read the descriptions for each card. Seeing different interpretations of cards across decks can help you understand the nuances of the cards. Ask yourself how the description connects to the question you asked or the card position you pulled it for if you're using a spread. If you pulled multiple cards, try telling a story about how the cards connect, moving from one card theme to the next.

Starter spreads

One of the most common tarot card spreads you're likely to encounter is the Celtic Cross. This classic 10-card spread offers a comprehensive reading that covers various aspects of a situation, such as the present, past influences, challenges, potential outcomes, and advice. The Celtic Cross is widely used due to its depth and ability to provide detailed insights into complex questions or situations, but it can be overwhelming for beginners. While I was learning, these starter spreads helped me focus on the symbolism of the cards rather than memorizing sophisticated card positions:

- **One-card pull:** Pull a single card to answer a specific question or provide daily guidance. This is a great way to develop a personal connection with your deck and focus on interpreting the meaning of each card. You can also try a Yes/No spread for quick, direct answers. Shuffle and draw one card. Assign meanings in advance where upright indicates "yes" and reversed (or certain negative cards) indicates "no."

- **Three-card spread:** This versatile spread is commonly used for past-present-future readings or to explore the situation, challenge, and outcome of a particular issue. Other three-card ideas include body, mind, spirit readings, or you can pull a card for each month in a season.
- **Four-card spread:** You can use this spread to pull a card for the energy of each season: spring, summer, fall, and winter, forecasting your year ahead. Or you can use a manifestation spread: the first card is what you want; the second card is what you require to get what you want; the third card is the obstacle that stands between you and what you want or indicates something you need to let go; and the fourth card is what's coming if you overcome these obstacles.

TIP

Always shuffle your deck well. Knowing when to stop shuffling and which card to choose is part of the intuitive process. I shuffle until I feel a little tingle in my neck. That's super specific, so you'll probably experience something completely different. Some people feel a warmth in their hand, whereas others perceive a shine to their card. Still others just unceremoniously cut the deck in half and pick the top card. Sometimes the card just pops right out of the deck! Don't overthink it, and over time you might become sensitive to your own "tingle."

As an example of how to interpret a spread, I pulled the three cards shown in Figure 13-1 for myself as I wrote this. Look at the cards in terms of the past, present, and future. I pulled Justice in the past position (*reversed*, or upside down), Lovers in the present position, and Wheel of Fortune in the future position.

FIGURE 13-1: An example of a three-card spread using the major arcana cards of the Waite-Smith deck.

Pamela Colman Smith/Arthur Edward Waite/Public domain

REMEMBER

Reversed tarot cards can indicate blockages or delays in the energy of the upright card, suggesting that the qualities or lessons of the card are present but not fully realized. They can also signify the opposite or shadow aspect of the card's meaning, such as strength becoming weakness or abundance turning into scarcity. Some readers view reversals as a call for introspection or internal work, pointing to hidden aspects, personal growth, or the need for a deeper understanding of the situation. I like to see reversed cards as potentials that could be realized through awareness or action.

Justice represents fairness, truth, balance, and the law. I pulled it reversed, which could mean the opposite: unfairness, dishonesty, imbalance, and chaos. Or it could mean that I internalized these themes, or there was unrealized potential, blocking the more positive meanings of Justice. In the past position, I interpret this to mean that I experienced an injustice that might have held me back, but it was largely a perception, not a material reality.

The Lovers card represents love (obviously!), harmony, alignment with values, and choices. In the present position, I interpret this to mean that I should see the beautiful things right in front of me, and I have wonderful opportunities that I can choose to pursue that will bring me a great sense of connection.

The Wheel of Fortune represents the cycles of life, the connection between all things, and destiny. In the future position, I interpret this to mean that I'm part of something larger that I can't always understand or control, but everything always comes back around, so good things will come to me in time, and I should take challenges in stride.

REMEMBER

It's in your power to create a helpful story from your spread, no matter how difficult the cards appear.

When I look at these three cards together, a story appears. I went through a difficult period that left me feeling that I was treated unfairly, but if I can just let that go, I might be able to be more present with all the love and support that surrounds me right now. And if I can remain present with what's good in my life, I might be able to roll with the punches and notice the blessings when they come my way. (I realize I'm being a little vague, but I'm not about to air out all my dirty laundry!)

Pendulum dowsing

Pendulum dowsing is a form of divination that involves using a pendulum — typically a small, weighted object suspended from a chain or string — to gain insight, answer questions, or locate objects or energies. The word *dowsing* comes from the 17th-century English term, likely derived from a Germanic or French root meaning "to strike" or "probe," referring to the movement of the dowsing tool in response to hidden energies or forces. Traditionally, dowsing was performed with a rod or stick (often a Y-shaped branch) to locate underground water or other substances, a technique that dates to ancient Egypt and China and was widely used in Europe during the Middle Ages. Over time, this practice evolved to include pendulums.

At metaphysical shops, you're likely to find crystal pendulums that are shaped like diamonds. Many of them come with their own reading mats with guides for use, as depicted in Figure 13-2. Today, pendulum dowsing remains popular in metaphysical and spiritual circles, expanding beyond resource-finding into divination and personal insight.

FIGURE 13-2: A pendulum hovering over a reading mat.

The pendulum is held still, and when a question is asked, it begins to move in certain patterns, such as swinging in a straight line or circular motion, to indicate "yes," "no," or other answers. Often used to tap into the subconscious mind or connect with spiritual energies, pendulum dowsing relies on interpreting the pendulum's movements as responses to specific inquiries. It can be used for a variety of purposes, including decision-making, energy healing, and finding lost items, making it a versatile and accessible tool for both beginners and experienced practitioners in metaphysical practices.

Here are some tips to get started with pendulum dowsing:

- **Choosing a pendulum:** You can use any object with a bit of weight on a chain or string, but many prefer to use crystals or metal pendulums. Pick one that resonates with you or feels comfortable in your hand.
- **Establishing yes/no signals:** Before asking questions, establish how the pendulum will indicate yes, no, and maybe answers. Hold the pendulum still and ask it to show you these responses — typically, movements will be circular or back-and-forth swings, but each person's pendulum may behave differently.
- **Clearing your mind:** Clear your mind and be neutral when asking questions. Emotional bias or a desired outcome can influence the pendulum's movements. Staying calm and open is essential.
- **Starting simple:** Begin with simple yes/no questions, like "Is my name [*your name*]?" or "Is today Monday?" This will help you build confidence in the pendulum's responses.

TIP

If you're combining pendulum dowsing with tarot cards, the pendulum can act as a complementary tool to refine or enhance the reading. For example, you can spread your tarot cards out on a table and hover your pendulum over them and choose the card that the pendulum swings toward. Additionally, you can use the pendulum after pulling a card to verify or further explore the interpretation by asking yes/no questions related to the card's meaning, helping the reader gain more specific insight or direction.

Scrying

Scrying is a form of divination that involves gazing into a reflective or translucent surface — such as a crystal ball, mirror, water, or even smoke — to receive visions or insights about the past, present, or future. The history of scrying spans many cultures and time periods. Ancient civilizations, such as the Egyptians, Greeks, and Celts, employed various forms of scrying, often using water or polished stone to commune with the divine or seek guidance from spirits.

Perhaps the most famous historical example is Nostradamus, the 16th-century French seer, who reportedly used a bowl of water to "see" his famous predictions. During the Middle Ages and the Renaissance, scrying was associated with occult practices and magic, and objects like crystal balls became emblematic of fortune tellers, as shown in Figure 13-3.

FIGURE 13-3: A painting called "The Crystal Ball" by John William Waterhouse, 1902.

John William Waterhouse/Wikimedia Commons/Public domain

Often described as a type of "second sight," the practitioner enters a meditative or trance-like state while focusing on the surface, allowing their subconscious mind or spiritual entities to reveal symbolic images, impressions, or messages. Scrying is a deeply intuitive practice, with the reader interpreting the often abstract or metaphorical visions based on personal insight or established symbolic meanings. It's a great method to build your intuition.

Follow these steps to get started with scrying:

1. **Choose a scrying tool.**

   Select a reflective or translucent surface that resonates with you, such as a crystal ball, a black mirror, a bowl of water, or even a candle flame. Some people also use smoke or clouds for scrying.

2. **Create a calm environment.**

   Find a quiet, comfortable space where you won't be disturbed. Dim the lights or use candlelight to enhance the reflective properties of your scrying tool. You may also want to play soft music or burn incense to set a meditative atmosphere.

3. **Center yourself.**

   Take a few deep breaths, clear your mind, and relax your body. Some beginners find it helpful to meditate for a few minutes to enter a calm, receptive state.

4. **Focus on your tool.**

   Gaze gently at your scrying tool without straining your eyes. Let your focus soften and try to enter a relaxed, almost trance-like state. Avoid forcing yourself to "see" something. Just allow images, shapes, or impressions to arise naturally.

5. **Set an intention or ask a question.**

   You can scry with a general openness to receiving whatever comes, or you can ask a specific question. Keep this intention in mind as you gaze into the surface.

6. **Observe and interpret.**

   As you relax into the process, you may begin to see images, colors, patterns, or symbols. These may be clear or abstract. Don't rush to analyze them; instead, make a mental note of what you see or feel. Trust your intuition when interpreting the images or impressions you receive.

7. **Closing the session.**

   After about 10–15 minutes, gently pull your eyes away from your tool, perhaps closing your eyes. Thank any energies or spirits you may have connected with, and ground yourself by taking a few deep breaths or touching the earth. You may want to journal your experiences for later reflections.

DIVINATION METHODS FOR THE VISUALLY IMPAIRED

Divination is for everyone, including the visually impaired. Most tools that are traditionally visual can be adapted to focus on tactile, auditory, or intuitive methods. *Auditory scrying* uses sounds like wind chimes, water, or bells to interpret patterns or energies based on the sounds rather than visual cues. Rune stones typically have engraved symbols you can identify by touch. Braille playing cards can be used for divination; after all, tarot actually started with decks of playing cards. Hexagonal dice with raised symbols are also a great alternative. For a more intuitive experience, *psychometry* involves feeling and interpreting the energy or vibrations of objects through touch alone.

TIP

Whatever your methods of choice, you'll want to energetically cleanse your tools regularly to improve the accuracy of readings, especially if you begin to read for multiple people. You can do this with smoke, moonlight, crystals, or salt, among other things. Chapter 11 covers techniques for cleansing and consecrating tools.

WARNING

Don't be afraid of negative readings. Sometimes you'll come across symbols with difficult themes. Remember that there are no fated outcomes, only present conditions. Use these as opportunities to accept what you feel, and ask yourself how you can use the symbolism as motivation to extend more care to yourself or others, make a healthy change, or communicate your needs.

IN THIS CHAPTER

- **Understanding the roots of green witchery**
- **Uncovering your nature-based skills**
- **Gathering tools for your practical magic rituals**

Chapter 14
The Green Witch

When I was a kid just discovering witchcraft, I was enamored by mythology and the dramatic glamor of fictional witches. As I've gotten older, my interests have simmered down to an appreciation for *practical magic*, the ordinary rituals that I incorporate into my routine to inspire my days. These rituals are at the core of *green witchcraft*, based in the magic of the earth, the flora and fauna, and the seasons. Green witches draw their power from the land they call home, using herbs, flowers, roots, and other natural resources in their spells and healing practices.

Green witches believe in the interconnectedness of all life, with a deep respect for the environment and a desire to live sustainably. They often align their magic with lunar phases, seasonal changes, and the natural rhythms of the world around them. They're resourceful and dedicate themselves to their communities and the needs of the material world. Green witches are often healers. This chapter touches on the history of green witchcraft and outlines the ways you can connect to practical magic in your daily life.

Tapping into Your Power: Nature Magic

Green witchcraft is based on a strong connection to the land and natural resources. As I cover in Chapter 2, the places known as home were once stewarded by indigenous peoples who lived in reverence and harmony with the land and its wildlife. Currently, indigenous lands make up 20% of the world's territory, while containing 80% of what remains of Earth's biodiversity. This is due to indigenous knowledge and the deep roots of sustainability they continue to pass down culturally. To authentically practice green witchcraft, it's important to acknowledge society's roles in the colonization that displaced indigenous peoples and dedicate time and energy to sustainable practices that repair Earth.

Green witchcraft has roots in folk magic across the world, particularly in the work of medicine people who provided nature-based healing services to their communities. There are the *shamans* in Siberia and the Native Americas, the *curanderos* and *curanderas* of Latin America, the *sangomas* of Africa, and the *rootworkers* of the US South, among many others who served as caregivers in the absence of institutional support. Folk magic practitioners didn't necessarily consider themselves witches, and many were persecuted for their healing work during the witch trials and the slave trades, as I cover in Chapters 1 and 2.

The Celts, Druids, and other pagan societies of pre-Christian Europe paved the way for the reclamation movements of modern witchcraft (also discussed in more detail in Chapter 1). Healers of these cultures were the keepers of plant knowledge, using herbs to treat illness and to perform rituals for things like protection and fertility. Many of these practices form the backbone of what's now recognized as green witchcraft.

CUNNING FOLK

Cunning folk played a crucial role in the history of green witchcraft and the preservation of traditional, nature-based practices throughout Europe, particularly during the Middle Ages and early modern period. These individuals were often local healers, herbalists, and practitioners of folk magic who served their communities by offering remedies for physical ailments, protection against malevolent forces, and assistance with everyday problems through charms, spells, and divination.

Cunning folk were deeply connected to the natural world, using plants, herbs, and the cycles of the moon and seasons in their magical and healing practices — elements that are central to modern green witchcraft. They were regarded as wise and knowledgeable, often serving as intermediaries between the human world and spiritual or natural forces.

During the rise of Christianity, many of these nature-based practices were suppressed. Despite persecution, wisdom survived, and rituals were passed down through generations in rural communities, hidden in folk traditions, herbal remedies, and even midwifery. The modern revival of green witchcraft emerged in the 20th century, alongside the broader resurgence of neo-paganism and the environmental movement.

Although green witchcraft has a long history, it remains a highly personal and regional practice that's always evolving. Each green witch tends to develop their own unique connection with nature, learning from the land, plants, and animals to craft an earth-centered spiritual path. Green witches are also intimately connected with natural cycles of life and death, and modern witches are increasingly taking on traditional folk occupations such as midwives and death doulas.

Acknowledging the land

Green witchcraft starts with the land. Practicing land acknowledgment involves recognizing and honoring the indigenous peoples who have historically lived on the land where you currently practice, while cultivating respect and responsibility toward the land itself. Here are some ways to integrate land acknowledgment into your practice:

- **Research the land's history:** Learn about the indigenous tribes and communities who originally inhabited your area. Understand their cultural, spiritual, and historical connection to the land, and acknowledge the impact of colonization.
- **Verbal acknowledgment:** At the beginning of your rituals, spells, or outdoor activities, offer a verbal acknowledgment of the indigenous peoples who once stewarded the land. Express gratitude and respect for their connection to nature, and recognize your role as a current caretaker of that space.
- **Incorporate indigenous teachings respectfully:** If possible, study indigenous perspectives on land stewardship, but do so with respect, ensuring you're not appropriating sacred practices thoughtlessly. Instead, focus on principles such as sustainability, reciprocity, and living harmoniously with the earth.
- **Support indigenous communities:** If you own land or are thinking of owning land, ask yourself if you're contributing to the displacement of native peoples or marginalized communities. Contribute to local indigenous causes or organizations that work to preserve their heritage, lands, and rights. Many cities now have reparations programs you can contribute to as a self-imposed tax for owning land or operating a business. You could also participate in local events or education to promote understanding and reconciliation.

- **Give offerings to the land:** As a regular ritual, you can offer gifts to the land, such as flowers, herbs, or biodegradable objects, to show gratitude and foster a deeper connection with the earth. (In Chapter 6, I outline the steps to make a ritual libation to the land.)
- **Join a movement:** The world needs a lot of healing as climate change ravages the environment. That means increasingly contending with storms that cause landslides, droughts that deplete water sources, pollution from fossil fuels, and soil degradation from factory farming, among so many other ecological issues. By dedicating yourself to an environmental cause, practicing sustainability, and making some sacrifices, you can help preserve biodiversity for generations to come.

When the land is properly acknowledged and cared for, it provides for its citizens. Green witches often forage for special ingredients, grow their own herbs, or work with plant and nature spirits to gain wisdom and insight. In all these endeavors, green witches are eco-conscious, incorporating sustainable practices as a core tenet of their work. When approached with patience, consistency, and respect, green witchcraft empowers people to fully enjoy earthly existence.

Making mundane magic

Mundane magic is another way of saying practical magic. The mundane is the ordinary, material world. It's not flashy. It's not primarily concerned with channeling deities or understanding the great mysteries of life. Instead, mundane magic is grounded in everyday things. It's your cup of tea in the morning, your mindful walk, or your favorite recipe that's been handed down to you from generations of ancestors. At the core of mundane magic is gratitude for the small things in life and an attention to care for yourself and others.

Green witchcraft is based in the mundane because its medium is the earthly elements and the seasons. *Elemental witches* are a subset of green witches who primarily work with air, fire, water, and earth. Elements are a great way to get started with your practical magic. A common practice in modern witchcraft is to *call the quarters*, a ritual used to evoke the elements and their energies (see instructions in Chapter 12). Each quarter represents one of the cardinal points and is associated with a specific element, energy, and spiritual significance. The common names for the four corners and their corresponding elements follow:

- **North:** Associated with the earth element, the north represents stability, grounding, and the material world. Earth rituals to evoke the energy of the north might include tending to a garden or working with the soil.

» **East:** Associated with the air element, the east represents intellect, communication, new beginnings, and inspiration. Air offerings to evoke the energy of the east might include breathwork or chanting.

» **South:** Associated with the fire element, the south represents transformation, passion, willpower, and energy. Fire offerings to evoke the energy of the south might include candle magic or burning herbs.

» **West:** Associated with the water element, the west represents emotions, intuition, healing, and the subconscious. Water rituals to evoke the energy of the west might include brewing tea, making soups, or taking a ritual bath. You can also make moon water by placing a jar full of water outside under a specific lunar phase that aligns with your intentions (see Chapter 15 for lunar magic correspondences). Moon water can be used for cleansing, drinking, bathing, or as a ritual ingredient.

TIP

If you were as obsessed with the 90s cult classic *The Craft* as I was, you might remember that each of the protagonists aligned with one of the directions. (In my middle school crew, I was the witch of the east direction, like Fairuza Balk's character.) Elements provide a great organizing structure for small covens, explored more in Chapter 17.

Another way to practice mundane magic is to spruce up your home for each season. In the spring, you might bring in fresh flowers. In the summer, you could make cooling tonics. In the fall, you might decorate with cinnamon brooms and gourds. And in the winter, you could put up twinkling lights. These little things mark time and refresh the energies of your space. You might also rethink your home altar seasonally, switching out the kinds of offerings you make (see Chapter 10). You can consult the Wheel of the Year for witchy days of observance (see Chapter 22) or follow the cycles of the moon (see Chapter 15).

Whatever you choose, remember that practical magic is all about creating practices of care for yourself and others. Remember, self-care isn't selfish, and the more you care for yourself with mundane magic, the more you can care for those around you.

Wildcrafting and foraging

Wildcrafting and foraging are essential practices in green witchcraft, involving the respectful and sustainable gathering of wild plants, herbs, and natural materials from the environment for magical and medicinal use. Green witches rely on their knowledge of plants to identify useful species for healing, spell work, or ritual. This should be done with great care, respecting the natural ecosystems, and ensuring that plants are harvested in ways that don't harm the local environment or deplete resources.

Wildcrafting is more than just collecting herbs. It's an act of communion with nature, where the witch builds relationships with the plants, honors their spirit, and expresses gratitude for the gifts the earth provides. Through foraging, green witches may seek out edible plants, berries, mushrooms, and roots that can be used in both culinary and magical practices. Foraging can also align with the cycles of the seasons. Many green witches harvest plants and herbs at specific times to capture their peak magical energy.

WARNING

This process requires knowledge of local flora and a keen understanding of which plants are safe to consume or use in spells, as many plants and fungi are poisonous.

TIP

Learn about the native plants in your local environment and their magical correspondences. To get started with common herbs and plants, consult the list of species used in introductory plant magic in the appendix.

Here are the different kinds of things you could forage:

- Herbs
- Wildflowers
- Edible plants
- Mushrooms
- Roots
- Berries and seeds
- Feathers
- Bones

WARNING

Do your research about your area, and avoid foraging for endangered, protected, or overharvested plants. One of the most harvested plants in the spiritual market is white sage (*Salvia apiana*), a sacred plant that indigenous tribes use, particularly in the southwestern United States, for ceremonies, cleansing, and healing rituals. It's now vulnerable due to overharvesting driven by commercial demand, particularly by non-indigenous people, which threatens both the plant's survival and the cultural traditions of Native communities.

The mining and harvesting of crystals can also be problematic because much of it leads to land degradation and water quality issues. It disturbs local biodiversity and sometimes employs child labor.

TIP

Check the sustainability of the tools and products you use. If something hurts the environment, it's not going to translate to the best magic for you. These tips can help keep your foraging sustainable:

- **Research where to forage:** Stay away from private property, indigenous reservations, and dangerous areas. Learn the local regulations for foraging on public lands.
- **Know your plants:** Educate yourself about the plants in the area. Learn what's edible and when to harvest each one. Consult field guides, and never ingest something you're not sure is safe. Many poisonous plants look like safe plants, so always triple-check!
- **Don't take more than you need:** To avoid overharvesting, only take what you need, and find out ahead of time how to harvest appropriately. Some plants should be harvested with specific techniques to promote maximum growth and preserve the safety of its surrounding ecosystem.
- **Make an offering:** Leave a natural, biodegradable offering when you forage, such as native plant seeds, as an act of gratitude and a good-faith exchange with nature.
- **Leave no trace:** Tread lightly and leave no waste. Don't disturb wildlife.

FUN FACT

I was motivated to start foraging when I realized that the smoke bundles for cleansing energies available at the metaphysical shops were mostly made with white sage. In Florida, local plants that work well for smoke clearing include rosemary, pine needles, and lemongrass.

TIP

Ask yourself what materials you might be able to make yourself to cut back on shipping costs and environmental impacts. After you collect your herbs, hang them to dry in a dark, dry place. Once dried, you can cut and wind them tightly in a thin hemp string to create a smoke bundle. You can also create your own incense by grinding your herbs with a mortar and pestle.

WARNING

"SMUDGING" IN NATIVE AMERICAN CULTURES

Smoke clearing through the burning of herbs is practiced in many ways under many names by cultures across the world and is open to anyone. *Smudging* typically refers to a specific spiritual practice that involves burning plants like white sage in Native American ceremonies for purification, healing, and connecting with the spirit world.

(continued)

(continued)

The use of the term is controversial; some say the word should only be used by Native American and First Nations practitioners, or that using the term outside of its cultural context without understanding its significance is considered cultural appropriation. Others argue that the term is of English origin, and since each indigenous group has their own name for smoke clearing, "smudging" is fair game. Sometimes we get caught up in semantics and lose sight of what's important: respect for other cultures and endangered species.

To play it safe and respect the sacredness of the practice of indigenous smoke rituals, I personally use terms like *smoke cleansing* or *smoke clearing* when referring to my own rituals, and I avoid using white sage and other overharvested resources. I also avoid terms like *powwow*, *tribe*, *clan*, and so forth, that are specific to indigenous cultures. I encourage you to do your own research and make an informed decision about the words and resources you use.

Reimagining your kitchen

The kitchen is usually considered the hearth of a home. I came from a household of adults who never cooked, so I was never taught the basics of cooking or passed down family recipes. There were no cooking rituals like you see in holiday movies, with multigenerational families gathered in the kitchen. I've always been nostalgic for that kind of thing, so I've started to build my own kitchen rituals in my adulthood. I hope to one day have recipes to pass on.

Kitchen witchery is a form of witchcraft that focuses on the magic of the home and hearth, where everyday cooking, cleaning, and domestic tasks become opportunities for ritual and spell work. Kitchen witches typically have experience in herbalism, using herbs, spices, and other ingredients with intention. They transform meals and brews into magical workings for protection, healing, prosperity, or love. They see the kitchen as a sacred space where mundane and magical activities blend.

You can start your practice of kitchen witchery by setting up your home pantry or *apothecary*. This is usually a cabinet, shelf, or closet containing ingredients for culinary or magical purposes. These could include:

- **Dried herbs:** You can buy these already dried and storied in jars, or you can hang them to dry yourself, which makes for a quintessentially witchy kitchen scene. You can also mix herbs to create herbal tea blends.

- **Essential oils:** Essential oils are concentrated plant extracts to be used in aromatherapy and topical ointments. (Use caution, though, because you should dilute most oils before application.)
- **Tinctures and infusions:** These are concentrated herbal extracts made by soaking plants in alcohol, glycerin, or vinegar (tinctures) or water (infusions) to draw out their medicinal and therapeutic properties.
- **Salves:** Made from herbs, oils, and beeswax, these are used to soothe, heal, or protect the skin, often incorporating medicinal or magical properties.
- **Spell jars and potion bottles:** Every good witch has a healthy collection of mason jars and unique containers — you can never have enough, in my opinion!

TIP

Make sure to set up your apothecary in a cool, dry, and dark space to preserve your ingredients, or use dark containers to keep light from breaking down the potency of what you're storing.

For ideas of other non-plant stores you can keep, see the part in Chapter 10 about *curio cabinets* or witches cabinets, depositories of meaningful curiosities like fossils, talismans, and crystals. Another practice of kitchen witchery is to keep a *grimoire*, or book of spells, for magical recipes. (See Chapter 9 for how to start your own grimoire). Think of each recipe as a spell you're casting, and apply all the usual rules of spell work, including clearing the energy of the space and setting an intention. (See Chapter 11 on spell work.) This makes all the difference between ritual and plain old cooking. You might organize your recipes by the season, including things like:

- **Love-infused tea for the spring:** Choose herbs associated with love, like rose and jasmine, and think about the things you love as you brew your tea.
- **Cooling elixirs for the summer:** Blend hydrating fruits, and garnish with fresh herbs from the garden, a few drops of a tincture or infusion, and a sweetener like honey. You can also make *sun tea* by placing herbs, flowers, or other ingredients in water and allowing them to steep in direct sunlight.
- **Abundance stews for the fall:** Make a stew in a big cauldron in the fall or winter with veggies harvested in your garden. The stew should be enough to share with friends or to eat from over a whole week. This is an expression of gratitude and generosity.
- **Protection soup for the winter:** Bring together grounding ingredients like root veggies for a nourishing soup that fights illness.

TIP

Once you're stocked with ingredients, you can add some easy, go-to rituals to your grimoire. Try organizing them by daily, weekly, monthly, and seasonal rituals. Here are a few beginner-friendly kitchen rituals:

- **Morning beverage as a daily practice:** Wake up early, and before you get on your screen or talk to anybody, make yourself a cup of coffee, tea, or juice as mindfully as possible, adding ingredients from your apothecary as you see fit. You might sit near a bright window in a favorite chair, or out in the garden, if you have access to outside space.
- **Stocking up as a weekly practice:** At the beginning or the end of each week, take stock of your pantry and apothecary (see Figure 14-1) and think of the meals you'll need for the week. Make a little time to shop and replenish your stock. This can include things for the rest of your house, too, like toiletries or hygiene products. Make it a joyful practice by treating yourself to a new or exciting product or ingredient each week, maybe making a stop at your local metaphysical shop.
- **Deep cleansing as a monthly practice:** Each month, do a deep clean of the kitchen and other high-traffic spaces of your house, maybe even blending your own floor washes and herbal sprays. Clear the energy with sustainable smoke bundles. I like to have a beautiful broom dedicated to intentional cleaning, and I listen to instrumental music.
- **Protection as a seasonal practice:** At the beginning of each season, you can refresh your charms and warding spells. A common technique is to create salt boundaries at thresholds. (See Chapter 10 on creating sacred space and the warding spell in Chapter 21.)

FIGURE 14-1: A home apothecary stocked with herbs.

TIP

Every house has a spirit, sometimes referred to as a *hearth spirit*. You can call on your house spirit for protection and inspiration during any or all of your rituals. You can say something like, "Spirit of my hearth, protect this space," or "House spirit, help me bless this food." You can also make offerings of food, drink, or flowers to your house spirit on your altar.

Cultivating a witches garden

During the Middle Ages, when witchcraft was feared and witches persecuted, the gardens of accused "witches" were often seen as places of mystery and danger. Witches were associated with poisonous herbs such as belladonna, mandrake, and henbane, further fueling the association of herbal healers with malevolent magic. Despite the risks, herbalists and healers continued to secretly tend their gardens, preserving the knowledge of plant magic through generations. These gardens represent the light and dark of green witchcraft; just as they're spaces of protection and healing, they also cultivate the raw materials for cursing, hexes, or shadow work (see Chapter 4). Today, witches around the world grow both healing herbs and baneful plants, honoring the duality of nature in their magical work.

TIP

Think of gardens as sacred spaces, outdoor altars of sorts (or indoor altars near windows or under a grow light, if you're an apartment dweller). You might also build a collective garden that's accessible to all your neighbors, or a "secret" garden in a public space that people can stumble upon, like along a trail, in a grove, or in a clearing.

The garden is like a living spell, nurturing and protecting the area around your home. It honors the spirits of nature and can feature a combination of native plants, vegetables, herbs, flowers, and trees.

TIP

If you have limited space, try *companion planting*, or planting mutually beneficial crops close together. For example, the *Three Sisters* garden is a Native American technique that involves growing corn, beans, and squash together. The corn provides a natural trellis for the beans to climb, the beans enrich the soil with nitrogen, and the squash's broad leaves shade the ground, helping retain moisture and suppress weeds. You can also try planting dill and basil with tomatoes as a natural pest repellant that attracts beneficial insects.

Here are some brief tips for starting your own garden:

- **Know your purpose:** Ask yourself what the focus of your garden is. Do you want to primarily eat from it, grow medicinal herbs, or focus on growing the most beautiful plants? Do you have a spiritual theme, like plants associated with certain spirits or gods?

- **Choosing strategically:** Do some research about the plants you want to use and their magical properties. Choose plants that are native to your environment to support native flora and fauna. How much space and sun do you need? Do you want a private or a public space? A raised bed or in-ground? Should you protect the garden against animals or the elements?
- **Planting the garden:** Mix your own soil and plant your seeds or seedlings with intention, perhaps speaking a spell as you do so.
- **Inviting spirits and whimsical energies:** Here's the fun part. How are you making this a magical space? I like incorporating elements of *faery* and *druid* gardens, adding statues, flowers, shiny objects, water features, or bird feeders. You can make tiny altars and ask the faeries to watch over the garden.
- **Caring on a schedule:** Dedicate yourself to small daily tasks and larger weekly or biweekly tasks to keep your garden healthy, such as weeding, pest control, fertilization, and harvesting. You can create your own plant care products and fertilizers to add to the intentionality of your garden.

TIP

Start simple. Plant what grows easily for you at first and add from there. The best garden is one that's alive!

WARNING

Baneful plants or herbs contain toxic or poisonous properties and can be harmful or even deadly if ingested improperly or mishandled. These plants have historically been used in witchcraft for protection, banishing, shadow work, and spirit communication.

Plants like belladonna (deadly nightshade), datura, brugmansia, hemlock, wolfsbane, mandrake (see Figure 14-2), henbane, and foxglove are considered baneful due to their toxic properties, but their potent energies make them valuable in magical practices when wielded by experienced practitioners. Although they're dangerous in their lethal or toxic doses, these plants can be medicinal in trace doses, and they can be energetically used to repel negative forces, break curses, or create protective barriers. Some advanced witches use baneful plants in rituals of transformation, embracing their symbolic connection to death, rebirth, and the darker aspects of magic.

WARNING

Although it is important to be aware of poison plants, working with them is not a beginner practice. If you do choose to work with these plants, use them in non-toxic concentrations and handle them with an abundance of caution, especially around children and pets. Working with these plants requires great respect because their physical toxicity can be dangerous, even deadly, if not handled properly. Ask yourself if your practice might hurt anyone; I don't condone working with curses or hexes as a beginner because they're highly likely to get out of control, with negative energy rebounding back to you. (See Chapter 4 to learn more about the ethics around hexing.)

FIGURE 14-2: An illustration of a mandrake, which is thought to resemble a human body.

TIP

If you are interested in baneful plants, seek wisdom from an experienced witch or herbalist. Some witches make their own products that are safe for use, offering powerful tools for shadow work and healing. These herbs are often combined into tinctures or salves for specific uses, like altering consciousness or inducing dreams. One salve traditionally associated with witches is the *flying ointment*, which is thought to facilitate *astral travel* or spirit communication (refer to Chapter 16).

Connecting to animal spirits

The witches garden extends to care for all the living things that cross your garden path. In green witchery, you might also care for animals around your garden, like stray cats or songbirds or crows. Perhaps you keep animals as pets on the premises, or you have farm animals like chickens or goats. I'm a beekeeper, and working with insects is part of my rituals.

FUN FACT

Find your familiar. A *familiar* is an animal or spiritual entity that protects you and your space and helps you with your magic. Mine is my cat Nala, who helped me clear energy and connect to my dreams. She passed away recently, but I still feel her with me and call on her when I need clarity. Familiars are more than just pets; they help you connect spiritually.

WARNING

Avoid using the phrase *spirit animal*, as it holds deep significance for Native American and First Nations peoples and should be respected.

Here are some ways to incorporate animals into your practice:

- **Supporting native wildlife:** Create a sanctuary for local fauna by planting native species and avoiding harmful pesticides. For example, I help the possums in my area, often misunderstood because of their appearance. These harmless creatures are essential for maintaining ecological balance.
- **Advocating for animal rights:** Get involved by volunteering, attending city meetings, or supporting initiatives like wildlife crossings and habitat preservation. You might also consider reducing or eliminating meat from your diet.
- **Rescuing animals and supporting rehabilitation centers:** Adopting animals from shelters reflects the sustainable ethics of green witchcraft. Avoid supporting unethical practices, such as puppy mills. Think beyond animals as pets and consider donating to organizations that help wild animals; they deserve good lives regardless of how you personally benefit from their existence.

For Your Grimoire: Home and Hearth Rituals

A common mistake many beginner witches make is going out and spending a lot of money on tools and products. I'm here to tell you that you don't need all that stuff! When I first started in earnest with green witchery, I was a broke grad student. So I planted seeds and slowly worked my way up to keeping lots of plants. I used what I had laying around.

Be resourceful. Use the old tenets of sustainability you learned in kindergarten: reduce, reuse, and recycle. See what you have to work with already. Is there an old tool shed with materials you can repurpose? Can you share resources with your neighbors?

That said, investing in the right tools for your green witchery will lend your rituals an element of excitement and whimsy. Here are a few of my go-to tools for my kitchen and garden (for information about how to consecrate tools, see Chapter 11):

- **Gathering baskets and foraging pouches:** These are useful for holding the herbs and plants you find; they are easy to find in thrift stores, and they look great hanging in your kitchen or shed. Look out for things you can use to carry your finds when you're out on your foraging adventures.

- **Sharp shears and ceremonial scissors:** I have a cute pair of engraved silver scissors that I wear on a chain around my neck. I use them to harvest or during rituals when I need to cut something.

- **Jars and containers:** I collect old containers from used kitchen products, like jam jars and juice bottles. They make great storage for curio cabinets and apothecaries. (I describe the witches cabinet in the earlier section "Reimagining your kitchen;" it has ideas of what to stock your cabinet with.)

- **Kitchen broom:** Every witch needs a good broom. Traditionally, witch brooms, called *besoms*, were made with sticks and branches laying around the property. Today, there are many beautiful brooms made by creative artisans. I make my own simple brooms with broomcorn, and I make small versions to clear my altar, adding herbs and dried flowers to them to beautifully honor each season. Figure 14-3 shows an image of a besom.

- **Cauldron:** The cauldron is the witch's signature symbol. I love cast-iron cauldrons that are functional as well as aesthetically pleasing. You can use your cauldron for cooking, for mixing herbs, or for burning incense.

- **Mortar & pestle:** I have an heirloom mortar and pestle from my childhood home that I still use to grind garlic and other herbs. It's a must-have when preparing blends or cooking with spices.

FIGURE 14-3: A decorative besom made of sticks and dried flowers.

There are countless recipes out there for green witchery and kitchen magic. Find them online by searching green witch recipes and spells or checking out books on plant and herbal magic. The next section highlights a few of my personal favorite recipes and spells for practical magic around the home and garden.

Herbal sachets for self-care

An herbal sachet is a small pouch filled with specific herbs, flowers, and sometimes crystals, used to promote certain energies or intentions. For a dream sachet, herbs like lavender, mugwort, and chamomile are commonly placed under a pillow or near the bed to enhance restful sleep, vivid dreams, or lucid dreaming. A bath sachet is used similarly in the bath, where the herbs are submerged in the water to infuse it with their healing or magical properties. A *kitchen sachet* is to be filled with edible herbs and spices and used for cooking soups and stews, sometimes called a *simmer pot*. Sachets may be filled with rose petals for love, rosemary for cleansing, or eucalyptus for healing. All types of sachets offer a gentle, natural way to incorporate herbal magic into self-care rituals. (Consult the appendix for typical herbs and their magical correspondences.)

Gather the following or mix in your own ingredients for a unique recipe, depending on the magical properties you'd like to work with:

- **Small fabric pouch:** Muslin or cotton works well.
- **1 tablespoon each of dried herbs:** Lavender, rosemary, and chamomile are popular choices.
- **Small crystal:** Optional, for added energy. (See the appendix for a list of common crystals and their magical properties.)

Follow these steps:

1. **Combine the herbs.**

   In a small bowl, mix the lavender, rosemary, and chamomile (or whatever herbs you've chosen).

2. **Fill the pouch.**

   Place the mixed herbs into the fabric pouch. You can also add the crystal, if applicable.

3. **Tie the pouch closed.**

   Secure the pouch by tying it closed with a string or ribbon.

4. **Use your sachet.**

   Place the sachet under your pillow for restful sleep, in your bath for a calming soak, or on your person for protective energy. Some people also make special spice sachets for cooking. (In that case, make sure to place the spices in a nontoxic, nonflammable wrapping like cheesecloth.)

Florida water for cleansing

Florida water, which I introduce in Chapter 2 and 10, is a citrus-based spiritual "cologne" traditionally used in cleansing, protection, and purification rituals in various magical practices, particularly within Hoodoo, Voodoo, Santería, and Latin American folk magic. Its base notes typically include citrus, lavender, clove, and floral oils.

FUN FACT

I grew up using Florida water because it's what my grandma used to wash her floors. She called it a *limpia*. In Latin American culture, *limpias* are rituals that clear energy, and Florida water is used for some of them. It cleanses spaces, objects, and people of negative energy. You can add it to a spiritual bath, or you can apply it as an offering to spirits and deities. Though commonly available in stores, many practitioners make their own Florida water to imbue it with personalized intentions and energy. Here's a recipe to make your own.

Gather the following, and feel free to substitute ingredients to make this your own:

- **1 cup vodka:** Used as the base for extraction
- **10–15 drops each of various essential oils:** Bergamot, lavender, lemon or orange, clove, and cinnamon
- **1 tablespoon each of dried herbs:** Rose petals and lavender flowers
- **Zest of a lemon or orange peel:** Optional, for freshness
- **Distilled water:** To dilute the mixture if desired

Follow these steps:

1. **Combine the ingredients.**

   Pour the vodka into a clean glass jar or bottle. Then add all the essential oils, dried herbs, and citrus zest to the vodka.

2. **Infuse.**

   Seal the jar and shake it gently. Allow the mixture to infuse in a cool, dark place for about 2–4 weeks, shaking it gently every few days to mix the oils and herbs.

3. **Strain.**

   After the infusion period, strain out any solids (herbs and citrus peels) using a fine mesh strainer or cheesecloth.

4. **Dilute (optional).**

   If you'd like to soften the scent or make a larger batch, add a small amount of distilled water to the strained liquid. Keep in mind that this step is optional.

5. **Bottle and store.**

   Transfer the strained liquid to a dark glass bottle (to protect the essential oils from light) and label it with the date. Store in a cool, dark place, and it will last for several months.

6. **Use the solution to clear energy.**

   You can pour the Florida water into a spray bottle and mist around the area you'd like to clear. You can add a few drops to your bathwater, or you can use the liquid to anoint candles (as described in Chapter 12), consecrate your tools (see Chapter 11), or dab on your wrists for protection.

WARNING

Essential oils can be toxic in high concentrations. Always dilute them, and research pet-friendly oils (some are deadly to animals). Keep out of reach of children.

IN THIS CHAPTER

» Tracing the link between astrology and witchcraft

» Discovering planetary magic

» Finding the tools for your cosmic magic practices

Chapter 15 The Cosmic Witch

Cosmic witches are called to the mysteries of the universe. They look to the stars for guidance, working with planetary energies, moon phases, and astrological alignments to shape their magic. Many engage in star-gazing and astronomical studies, keeping abreast of the constant discoveries in the field of astrophysics. Some cosmic witches perform rituals to the planets, others create intentions and spells based on their birth charts, and still others use the stars for divination. Most modern witches work with astrology on some level, but this chapter focuses on witches who specialize in lunar and planetary energies. I delve into the history and foundations of cosmic magic, offering insight into how you can work with celestial forces and incorporate the stars into your daily rituals.

Tapping into Your Power: Planetary Magic

Astrology was one of my entry points into witchcraft. When I was a child, I spent hours at the library reading Greek and Roman mythologies, fascinated by the stories associated with the stars. Venus wasn't just a neighboring planet, but a goddess associated with love and beauty. Saturn was more than just the best planet to draw because of all its rings; it was a Titan that represented time and the toil of the earth. These stories helped me learn about the movements of the solar system while they inspired my creative side.

Tracing astrological histories

Astrological rituals and cosmic magic have roots in ancient civilizations that believed the movements of the stars and planets directly influenced earthly events.

REMEMBER

Astrology is the study of the movements and positions of celestial bodies — such as the sun, moon, planets, and stars — and their influence on human affairs. It's based on the belief that a meaningful connection exists between the cosmos and life on Earth and that the alignment and interactions of these celestial bodies at specific moments can affect an individual's personality, behavior, and destiny, as well as broader world events.

Several civilizations observed and tracked the stars to support their agrarian cycles and make social and political decisions, and these practices evolved into more sophisticated astrological systems that form the foundation for modern astrology. These ancient influences include:

- **The Babylonians:** The Babylonians are credited as some of the earliest astronomers and astrologers, meticulously tracking celestial bodies and correlating their positions with natural events, omens, and divine will. They believed the heavens reflect godly powers, and their rituals often sought to align with planetary movements to predict outcomes.
- **The Egyptians:** The ancient Egyptians further refined Babylonian knowledge, integrating cosmic beliefs into their religious practices, particularly through their worship of celestial deities like Ra, the sun god, and Thoth, associated with the moon. Astrological magic was central to their ritualistic life, where priests and magicians observed the skies to determine auspicious times for everything from religious ceremonies to the construction of monumental structures like the pyramids, designed to mirror the constellations.
- **The Vedas:** Ancient Indian texts such as the *Vedas*, particularly the *Vedanga Jyotisha*, is one of the earliest known treatises on astronomy and astrology. Vedic astrology's use of *sidereal* measurements aligns it with the observable positions of celestial bodies, reflecting a direct connection between the cosmos and earthly events (see the "Many Astrologies" sidebar for more about sidereal astrology).
- **The Greco-Romans:** In the Greco-Roman era, which lasted from the 8th century BC to the 5th century AD, astrology became even more formalized, with figures like Ptolemy developing comprehensive systems that linked celestial alignments with human affairs. This period saw the rise of planetary magic, where practitioners began invoking the spirits or deities associated with the seven classical planets (Sun, Moon, Mercury, Venus, Mars, Jupiter, and Saturn) to influence fate.

» **Medieval and Renaissance Europe:** The occult scholars such as Agrippa and Paracelsus worked with astrological charts and celestial correspondences to craft rituals, talismans, and alchemical processes. These traditions, passed down through centuries, evolved into modern forms of planetary magic.

REMEMBER

Cosmic magic refers to a branch of magical practice that draws upon the energies and influences of celestial bodies and cosmic forces. This form of magic taps into the power of the stars, planets, moons, and other cosmic phenomena to channel energy, enhance spells, and align with the broader rhythms of the universe. Practitioners of cosmic magic work with astrological alignments, lunar phases, planetary movements, and other celestial events to guide their rituals, spells, and meditations. Cosmic magic is centered around the belief that the universe is interconnected, with the heavens influencing life on Earth.

MANY ASTROLOGIES

Modern astrologers use two major systems of astrology: *tropical astrology* and *sidereal astrology*. Tropical astrology, commonly recognized as *Western astrology*, does not account for *axial precession*, or the Earth's "wobble." Similar to the wobble of a spinning top, Earth's axis traces a circular path over time, causing the direction of the axis to shift slowly. One complete precession cycle takes approximately 26,000 years. During this time, the positions of the celestial poles and equinoxes shift relative to the fixed stars.

Over centuries, this results in the alignment of the zodiac signs used in tropical astrology drifting from their original positions relative to the constellations. For example, the Sun currently rises in Pisces during the spring equinox, though tropical astrology places it in Aries. This means that although I'm a Gemini sun in tropical astrology, I'm actually a Taurus according to sidereal astrology!

Sidereal astrology, also known as *Vedic astrology* or *Jyotish*, is the primary system practiced in Hinduism and much of the "Eastern" world. Sidereal astrology acknowledges the Earth's skewed axis, which leads to ever-changing distances between the Earth and the constellations, a phenomenon known as the *precession of the equinoxes*. This distinction underscores key differences between the two astrological systems, reflecting varying cultural and astronomical approaches to interpreting celestial movements.

There was a time when the two systems were aligned, but they began to diverge around 285 AD. This year also marked the Roman Empire's split into two factions and the beginning of its decline. Over the centuries, due to factors such as conquest, colonization, and a cultural aversion to mathematical complexities, tropical astrology rose to dominance in the Western world. Meanwhile, sidereal astrology remained the guiding framework for Vedic traditions, which continue to be widely practiced.

Perhaps the most sophisticated practitioners of astrology and cosmic magic in ancient times were found in Mesoamerican civilizations, particularly the Maya, whose advanced understanding of the cosmos was central to their religious practices and daily life.

FUN FACT

The Maya were highly skilled astronomers, and they developed complex calendars, most notably the *tzolk'in* (a 260-day ritual calendar) and the *Haab'* (a 365-day solar calendar). Mayan priests performed astrological rituals to align with these celestial patterns, seeking to ensure the favor of the gods and predict future events. The Maya also constructed architectural wonders, like the pyramids of Chichen Itza, which aligned with celestial events such as the equinoxes and solstices.

Observing the lunar cycles

The moon is at the center of many modern witchcraft practices, and working with lunar magic is certainly not limited to cosmic witches. But as I progressed in my astrological studies and the moon became the focal point of my rituals, I started to think of myself primarily as a cosmic witch.

The moon is a great starting point for cosmic witchcraft because it's easily visible in the sky. The lunar cycle is one of the most fundamental and widely used natural rhythms in astrology and magic. The moon's phases, which span approximately 29.5 days, offer powerful opportunities for aligning your magical work with nature's ebb and flow. By observing and working with the moon's phases, practitioners can synchronize their intentions with the waxing and waning of lunar energy, using its natural power to enhance spells, rituals, and personal growth. Each phase carries its own significance, offering a distinct energy that can be harnessed for different types of magical work. Figure 15-1 is a diagram showing the phases of the Earth's moon and their magical correspondences.

New moon

The new moon, sometimes called the dark moon, marks the beginning of the lunar cycle, when the moon isn't visible in the night sky. This phase is associated with finding new beginnings, setting intentions, and planting seeds for the future. During the new moon, the energy is introspective, making it a perfect time to go inward, reflect on what you want to manifest, and prepare to set intentions for the upcoming lunar cycle. Rituals during this time often focus on goal-setting, fresh starts, or new projects. It's a powerful time for writing down wishes, creating vision boards, or performing spells that invoke beginnings and potential.

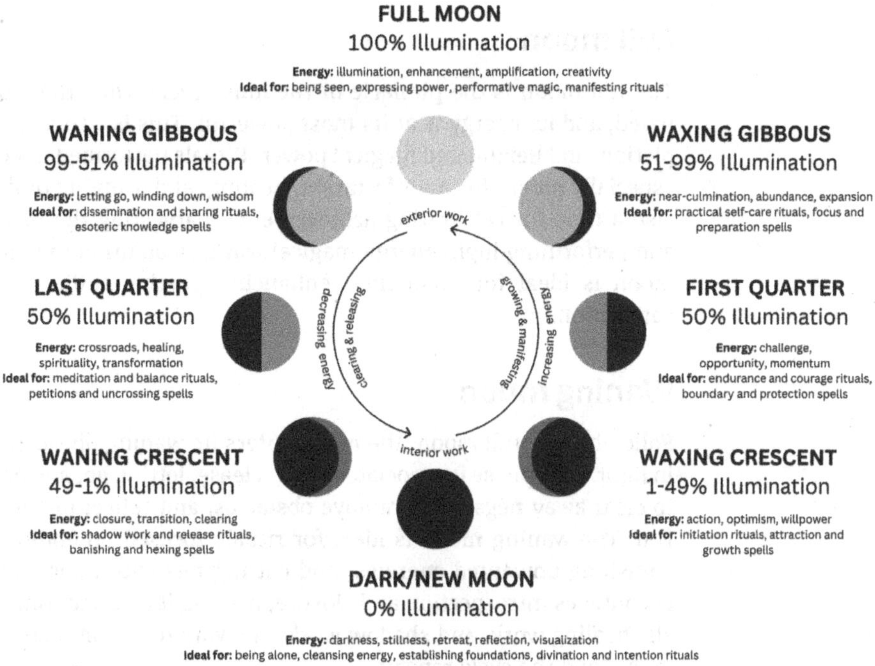

FIGURE 15-1. The lunar phases.

TIP

Some witches distinguish between the dark moon and the new moon. The dark moon can refer to when the moon is completely invisible in the sky. It occurs just before the new moon and typically lasts 1–3 days. This phase marks the end of the moon's waning phase, when no sunlight is reflected on the side of the moon visible from Earth. The dark moon is associated with rest, introspection, banishing, and letting go. It's often seen as a time to reflect and release negativity before starting a new cycle.

In technical terms, the new moon occurs when the moon is between Earth and the sun (conjunction), so the illuminated side faces away from Earth.

Waxing moon

As the moon becomes visible and grows in light during the waxing phase, the energy becomes increasingly active and expansive. This period, from the new moon to the full moon, is ideal for building momentum, taking action, and nurturing the intentions set during the new moon. The waxing moon is a time for spells that involve growth, manifestation, attraction, and drawing in positive energy. Practitioners often focus on work related to career advancement, love, health, or financial prosperity during this phase.

Full moon

The full moon is the pinnacle of the lunar cycle when the moon is fully illuminated, and its energy is at its most powerful. This is a time of culmination, completion, and heightened magical power. Rituals performed under the full moon are especially potent for manifestation, healing, and bringing projects to fruition. It's also a time for celebrating achievements, harvesting the results of past efforts, and performing high-energy magical work. In addition to manifestation, the full moon is ideal for divination, enhancing psychic abilities, and deep spiritual connection.

Waning moon

Following the full moon, the moon enters its waning phase, gradually decreasing in light. This phase is associated with release, letting go, and banishing. It's a time to clear away negativity, remove obstacles, and reflect on what no longer serves you. The waning moon is ideal for rituals focused on endings, breaking habits, banishing unwanted energies, and cutting ties with toxic situations. This phase encourages introspection and closure, making it a perfect time for cleansing rituals, healing work, and shadow work. The waning moon phase ends with the dark moon, and the cycle repeats.

Eclipses

A solar eclipse occurs when the new moon passes between Earth and the sun, temporarily blocking the sun's light. Symbolically, it marks sudden revelations and radical breakthroughs in awareness. A lunar eclipse occurs when Earth comes between the sun and the moon, casting a shadow on the moon. It aligns with a full moon, intensifying emotions and encouraging release. Both solar and lunar eclipses are viewed as cosmic reset buttons, offering a chance to release old energies and welcome new possibilities.

WARNING

Some witches believe that eclipses present chaotic and unpredictable energies, so rituals aren't recommended unless you're an experienced practitioner. Even so, eclipses may bring sudden changes that are beyond your control, so magic performed during this time is thought to have long-lasting and sometimes unintended consequences. In some Native American cultures, eclipses are even seen as malevolent events that shouldn't be observed directly.

TIP

Instead of casting complex spells, some practitioners prefer meditation, journaling, or divination to harness the eclipse's energy.

Studying the stars

My own passion for cosmic magic is fueled by astrological study. I'm constantly fascinated by the dance of the stars and the new discoveries of quantum physics. Astrology is the language of the universe's mysteries.

In popular astrology, the position of planets within the twelve signs of the zodiac is traditionally charted to create *horoscopes*, which are used to forecast and interpret potential outcomes in various areas of life, including relationships, career, health, and personal growth.

But astrology is so much more than that. Although astrology isn't a science, it has been practiced for thousands of years across many cultures, with the most widely known system today being Western astrology. Other systems include Vedic astrology from India and Chinese astrology, which follows a lunar calendar. Astrologers use tools like *natal charts* (also known as birth charts), which plot the positions of the celestial bodies at the time of a person's birth, to provide insight into personality traits, challenges, and opportunities.

Starting with the astrology chart

A birth chart, also known as a *natal chart*, is one of the most significant tools in astrology because it provides a detailed map of the sky at the exact moment and location of an individual's birth. It charts the positions of the sun, moon, planets, and other celestial points within the twelve zodiac signs and twelve astrological houses, offering insight into a person's personality, strengths, challenges, and life path.

Each planet represents a different aspect of the self, such as emotions (the moon), communication (Mercury), or love (Venus). Their placement in specific zodiac signs and houses influences how these energies manifest in an individual's life. Astrologers interpret the relationships, or aspects, between these celestial bodies to gain further insight into recurring themes, growth opportunities, and potential life events.

TIP

Although astrology is often used to create horoscopes and facilitate divination, I like to use astrology to communicate with the many different parts of myself. I've used it to clarify my perspective on problems and to heal my relationship with myself and others. In modern witchcraft, astrology is just as often applied as a healing practice as it is used to predict events.

In essence, a birth chart (see Figure 15-2) is a unique cosmic blueprint that reflects an individual's potential and guides self-understanding and personal development throughout life:

- **Planets:** Each planet in astrology represents different aspects of a person's personality, behavior, and experiences. Their placement in the chart reveals how these energies manifest in the individual's life.
- **Signs:** The twelve zodiac signs represent different qualities and archetypes. When a planet is placed in a particular sign, it colors the way that planet's energy is expressed.
- **Houses:** The birth chart is divided into twelve houses, each representing different areas of life, such as relationships, career, home, and personal growth. The planets in a person's chart fall into these houses, showing which aspects of life are most influenced by the planet's energy.
- **Aspects:** The aspects refer to the angular relationships between two or more planets in a birth chart or transit. These angles are measured in degrees along the 360-degree circle of the zodiac. Aspects describe how planets interact with each other energetically, influencing personality traits, events, or dynamics in a person's life.

TIP

I like to think of the birth chart as a theatrical production in the sky that helps me make sense of my life. The planets are the actors, the signs are the characters they play, and the houses are the stages or scenes where they act out their dramas. The aspects between planets contribute to the plot, as they represent dynamics between characters. See the appendix for a chart of the planets, signs, houses, and their associated meanings.

Tracking transits

In astrology, *transits* refer to the ongoing movements of the planets in real time as they travel through the zodiac. As the planets move, they form aspects to the planets, houses, and points in a person's natal chart. These transiting planets trigger specific energies and events based on the nature of the planets involved and the areas of life they influence.

Transits are important for understanding timing in astrology because they indicate periods of growth, challenges, or opportunities. For example, when a transiting planet like Saturn forms a significant aspect to a natal planet, such as a square or conjunction, it often signals a time of responsibility, discipline, or lessons related to the energy of the natal planet it interacts with.

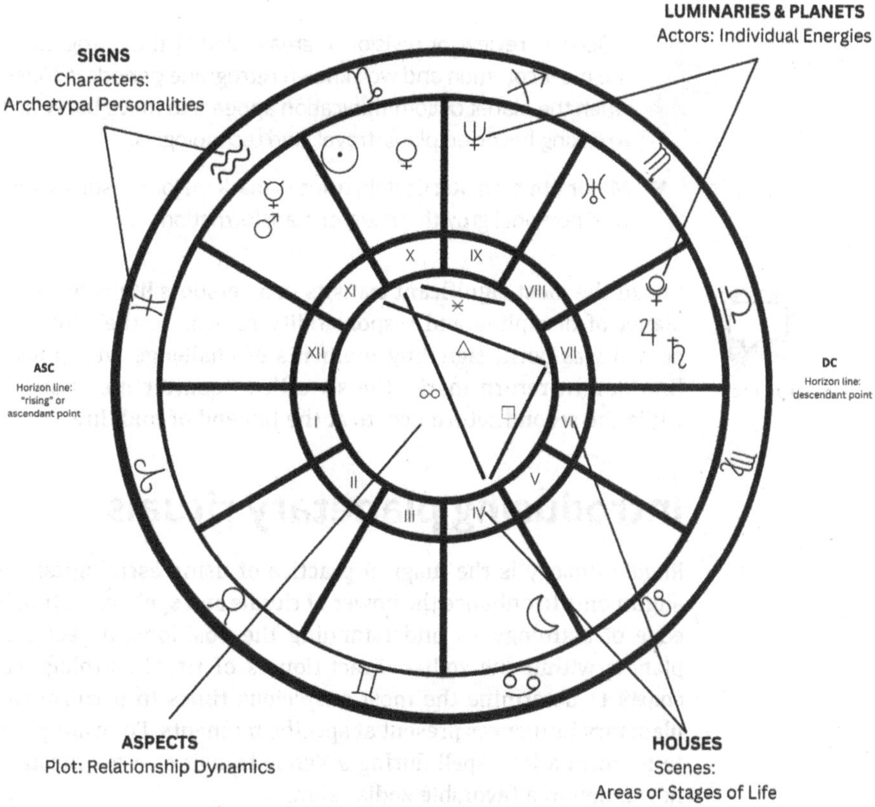

FIGURE 15-2: An example of a birth chart.

Astrologers use transits to forecast trends and events in a person's life, giving insight into periods of personal development, career changes, relationship shifts, or emotional growth. Understanding transits can help individuals prepare for both challenging and beneficial periods, aligning their actions with the cosmic energy at play. Important types of transits include these:

- **Ingresses:** An *ingress* occurs when a transiting planet enters a new zodiac sign or house in your natal chart. These transitions can mark changes in the flavor of the planet's energy and what areas of life it affects.
- **Returns:** A *planetary return* occurs when a transiting planet returns to the same degree and sign it occupied in your birth chart. These events mark significant turning points or periods of personal growth and reflection. Examples, among many others, include your solar return, also known as your birthday, and your Jupiter return, a time of expansion, growth, and opportunity that occurs approximately every 12 years.
- **Retrogrades:** *Retrogrades* happen when a planet appears to move backward in the sky from our perspective on Earth. These periods often signify a time of

reflection, review, or revision in areas ruled by the retrograding planet. One of the most common and well-known retrograde periods is *Mercury retrograde*, when the planet of communication appears to move backward, notorious for wreaking havoc on plans, travel, and technologies.

- **Major life transits:** Certain transits mark major life stages, often associated with personal growth, crises, or transformation.

FUN FACT

One of the most significant transits in a person's life is the *Saturn return* when the planet of discipline and responsibility returns to the same place it was when a person was born, signaling moments of challenge and growth assessment. The first Saturn return marks the so-called "quarter life crisis" of one's twenties, while the second return occurs at the tail end of mid-life.

Introducing planetary rituals

Ritual astrology is the magical practice of using astrological timing and celestial alignments to enhance the power of rituals and spell work. It involves deep knowledge of astrology — understanding the positions, aspects, and movements of planets within the zodiac. Practitioners of ritual astrology consult astrological charts to determine the most auspicious times to perform rituals based on the planetary influences present at specific moments. For example, they might choose to perform a love spell during a Venus transit or a manifestation ritual during a new moon in a favorable zodiac sign.

The focus of ritual astrology is on timing and aligning magical intent with the natural flow of planetary and astrological energies. Following are some uses of ritual astrology:

- Choosing *elections*, which are dates for rituals based on planetary aspects
- Consulting natal charts or transits to personalize magical workings
- Timing spells or rituals to specific astrological events, like retrogrades, eclipses, or moon phases

REMEMBER

Planetary magic is a subset of ritual astrology specifically focused on the intrinsic powers of individual planets and their corresponding energies.

Rather than primarily concentrating on astrological timing, planetary magic works directly with the symbolism and attributes of each planet to influence specific areas of life. Each planet is associated with certain themes. In planetary magic, practitioners invoke these forces through rituals, talismans, correspondences (such as herbs, colors, or metals associated with the planets), and other magical tools. The goal is to channel the planet's essence into a spell, regardless of its current astrological position.

WARNING

Don't confuse planetary energies with the deities that share their names. For example, Mars is the planet of passion and also the Roman god of war. Though they share similar properties, working with planets is a very different process than *invoking*, or summoning, deities (see Chapter 8 for more information on invoking).

Key aspects of planetary magic include these:

- Calling on planetary energies for specific purposes, such as petitioning Mercury for communication or intellect
- Creating planetary talismans or charms imbued with the power of a particular planet
- Aligning spells and rituals with planetary correspondences, such as certain colors, metals, days of the week, and deities tied to the planet's energy

See the later section "Petitioning the planets," for planetary associations used in ritual magic.

For Your Grimoire: The Natal Chart

The most important tool for the cosmic witch is an astrological chart calculator and generator. You can choose from many free ones online. You can input your birth details — date, time, and location of birth — to automatically pull your natal chart, which includes the planets' positions at the time of your birth.

TIP

You'll want to know your time of birth because it will affect which houses of astrology the planets align with. This will also set your *rising sign*, which I cover in the next section.

If you don't know your time of birth, try asking family members who might know or get a copy of your birth certificate from your local health department. If you can't find your birth time, take your best guess or choose noon as your default time. Some people who don't know their time of birth choose to set their rising sign the same as their sun sign. Certain astrologers specialize in *birth time rectification*, the process of divining the birth time based on a recounting of significant life events.

When generating a chart, you'll be asked to choose a house system. *House systems* map the houses in the chart based on a 360-degree wheel. Each chart is divided into twelve houses, and the exact number of degrees that each house spans depends on the house system, or chart mapping technology, that you choose. Planets might fall in different houses depending on which house system you choose. The two most common house systems are *Placidus*, popular in modern Western astrology, and *Whole Sign*, commonly used by traditional astrologers.

Many astrological websites also have charts of current transits, astrological calendars, and ephemeris tables. Once you're comfortable with your studies, I recommend getting acquainted with an *ephemeris* (plural: ephemerides), a great tool for tracking planetary movements. It's a table or data set that lists the precise positions of celestial bodies over a period. You can purchase ephemerides in a bookstore or download them online.

Interpreting your birth chart

As a beginner cosmic witch, you'll want to become acquainted with these three parts of your birth chart:

- **Rising sign:** The *rising sign*, also known as the *ascendant*, represents the zodiac sign that was rising on the eastern horizon at the exact moment and location of your birth. It marks the beginning of the first house in your natal chart and plays a significant role in shaping your personality, appearance, and how others perceive you. The rising sign governs how you present yourself to the world — the "mask" you wear in social situations. It influences how people see you initially, including your demeanor, style, and outward behavior. Astrologers believe the rising sign can even affect your physical traits and body language. The rising sign determines the placement of the houses in your chart, shaping how the planets influence specific areas of your life.
- **Sun sign:** The *sun sign*, or *star sign*, reflects your ego, identity, and conscious self. It symbolizes your life force, your core personality, and the traits you strive to develop throughout life. It's based on the position of the sun at the time of your birth, which corresponds to one of the 12 zodiac signs. The sun sign points to your vital energy and how you express yourself outwardly. It often governs life goals and the essence of who you are, which becomes more pronounced as you grow older.
- **Moon sign:** The *moon sign* reflects your emotions, inner world, instincts, and subconscious. It governs your emotional reactions to situations and your needs for comfort and security. The moon sign is based on the position of the moon at your birth. Because the moon moves quickly through the zodiac,

changing signs every two to three days, you need to know your exact birth time and place to determine it accurately. The moon sign shows your emotional needs and how you process feelings. It also reflects your comfort zone and your connection with close relationships.

FUN FACT

In popular culture, these three positions are referred to as your "Big 3." It's not uncommon to see people post their Big 3 to their social media —or even dating — profiles!

I like to think of the sun, moon, and rising signs as aligning with the three levels of the mind in popular psychology:

- **The conscious mind (sun sign):** The *conscious mind* refers to your present awareness — the thoughts, decisions, and perceptions that you actively focus on. It processes logic, reasoning, and willpower. When you're making decisions, planning, or solving problems, you're using your conscious mind. The sun sign is associated with the conscious mind.
- **The subconscious mind (moon sign):** The *subconscious mind* stores memories, habits, emotions, and beliefs that are below the surface of your awareness. Although you're not actively conscious of it, it influences behavior and thought patterns. It governs automatic responses and habitual behaviors. It also holds past experiences and repressed emotions that shape your actions and perceptions. The moon sign is associated with the subconscious mind.
- **The superconscious mind (rising sign):** The *superconscious mind*, which is often associated with intuition, spiritual insight, creativity, and a connection to universal consciousness, refers to a higher level of awareness that transcends the ego. In spiritual traditions, the superconscious is where you tap into universal truths, enlightenment, or deep inspiration. Some consider it the seat of higher self-awareness or a connection with divine energies. The rising sign is associated with the superconscious mind.

Research the meanings of your sun, moon, and rising signs and consider them in relation to the different states of mind. (You can start with the associations in the appendix.) In my own practices, this has given me the opportunity to see myself as multiple characters, each taking center stage depending on the scene or scenario. This puts a little distance between me and my perspectives or actions, so I can work through problems and communicate compassionately with myself, as I would talk to a friend.

TIP

When reading your horoscope, look at your rising sign instead of your sun sign because it more accurately reflects the house placements and what areas of your life will be affected by certain transits.

Aligning with the elements and qualities

Each sign of astrology is associated with one of the four elements. Working with the elements is an accessible way to begin a ritual astrology practice because it aligns with other beginner forms of witchcraft. Each element connects to different experiences, as outlined here:

- **Earth:** The Earth signs are Taurus, Virgo, and Capricorn. In astrology, the Earth element is associated with practicality, stability, structure, and material concerns. It governs aspects of life that are grounded in the physical world, including health, finances, career, and responsibilities. Earth signs tend to focus on building, maintaining, and organizing, valuing hard work, security, and tangible results. Rituals could use tangible objects, especially earth-related ones like metals, crystals, or even dirt.
- **Water:** The water signs of Cancer, Scorpio, and Pisces are associated with emotions, intuition, and deep connections. These signs govern the realm of feelings, imagination, and inner experience, emphasizing the importance of emotional depth, empathy, and sensitivity. Rituals could employ liquid, such as pouring libations or making a potion.
- **Fire:** The fire signs — Aries, Leo, and Sagittarius — are associated with energy, passion, action, and creativity. Fire signs embody enthusiasm and boldness, often acting as initiators and leaders. They're known for their dynamic, adventurous spirit and desire to take risks. Fire rituals could include dancing around a bonfire or lighting candles.
- **Air:** The air signs — Gemini, Libra, and Aquarius — are associated with intellect, communication, and social connections. Air signs govern thought processes, relationships, and the exchange of ideas, placing a strong emphasis on mental clarity, learning, and interpersonal dynamics. Air rituals could employ chanting mantras or reading prayers.

Each sign of astrology is also associated with a quality, or mode of action, including these:

- **Cardinal:** The cardinal signs — Aries, Cancer, Libra, and Capricorn — represent initiation, leadership, and action. Each of these signs begins a new season, embodying the energy of starting fresh and taking initiative. Those born under this sign are known for being dynamic, proactive, and often goal-oriented. Cardinal rituals focus on intentions and initiation.
- **Mutable:** The mutable signs — Gemini, Virgo, Sagittarius, and Pisces — represent adaptability, flexibility, and transition. These signs occur at the end of each season, embodying the energy of change and preparation for the next phase. Associated with adjustment, learning, and versatility, they often bring

closure or evolution to whatever phase they influence. Mutable rituals focus on movement, change, and releasing control.

» **Fixed:** The fixed signs — Taurus, Leo, Scorpio, and Aquarius — are known for their stability, determination, and persistence. These signs occur in the middle of their respective seasons, symbolizing a steady and consistent energy that focuses on building, maintaining, and preserving. Fixed rituals focus on endurance and manifestation.

TIP

Keep a journal as you research your birth chart and your placements' associations with cosmic rituals. As you examine planets in particular signs, note the corresponding element and qualities, and think of rituals that might align with those energies. For example, to work with placements in mutable and water signs, you might want to employ running water, such as a shower or a waterfall. A fixed fire combination might involve keeping a candle lit for a long period of time.

Petitioning the planets

Planets are sometimes referred to as *rulers* because they preside over certain houses and signs. (See the Appendix to see their rulerships, referred to as *domiciles*).

To *petition* planets means to intentionally engage with their energies to seek assistance, guidance, or blessings in areas governed by those planets. The concept stems from the idea that each planet embodies certain qualities, and by consciously working with these energies, one can manifest desired outcomes or gain clarity on specific matters. Table 15-1 shows these planetary qualities.

TABLE 15-1 Planetary Qualities

Planet	Qualities	Petition For	Ritual Day
Sun	Vitality, success, self-expression, leadership	Confidence, recognition, personal growth, enhanced creativity	Sunday
Moon	Emotions, intuition, cycles, and nurturing	Emotional healing, intuition, fertility, and deeper connections with family	Monday
Mars	Courage, action, ambition, and conflict	Motivation, strength to overcome obstacles	Tuesday
Mercury	Communication, intellect, travel, and commerce	Clear thinking, effective communication, business deals, and safe travel	Wednesday
Jupiter	Luck, expansion, abundance, and wisdom	Financial prosperity, good fortune, success in studies, and personal growth	Thursday

(continued)

TABLE 15-1 *(continued)*

Planet	Qualities	Petition For	Ritual Day
Venus	Love, beauty, harmony, and pleasure	Romance, friendships, creativity, and enhancing beauty or charm	Friday
Saturn	Discipline, structure, karma, and boundaries	Patience, perseverance, overcoming challenges	Saturday
Uranus	Revolution, innovation, breakthrough	Creativity, liberation, and navigating change	Sometimes associated with Wednesday*
Neptune	Mysticism, imagination, and dreams	Heightened intuition, psychic abilities, dreamwork, and art	Sometimes associated with Friday*
Pluto	Death, rebirth, and hidden power	Personal transformation and shadow work	Sometimes associated with Tuesday*

**Uranus, Neptune, and Pluto don't have traditional associations because they were discovered after these decisions were made in traditional astrology.*

Follow these steps to petition the planets:

1. **Select your planet of petition.**

   Choose a planet based on its themes and what you intend to invoke into your life. You might also choose a planet for its association with the day of the week of your ritual.

2. **Choose an auspicious time.**

   It's best to work during favorable aspects or transits involving the planet. Consider using a planetary hour calculator (easily found online) to choose an hour associated with your planet.

3. **Create a ritual space.**

   Use ritual items and offerings associated with the planet. Intention candles are popular options.

4. **Write the petition.**

   Draft a clear and respectful message or request to the planet, acknowledging its energy and qualities. Express gratitude in advance for the desired outcome.

5. **Meditate or pray.**

   Sit quietly and visualize the energy of the planet. You might use mantras, affirmations, or planetary symbols to connect deeper with the energy you're invoking.

Make your practice your own. Cosmic magic is about attuning yourself to the rhythms of the cosmos and feeling more connected to your place on Earth and among the mystery that is the universe.

IN THIS CHAPTER

- » **Learning about the energy centers of the body**
- » **Delving into different energy healing modalities**
- » **Getting to know the tools for clearing, protecting, and amplifying energy**

Chapter 16 The Energy Witch

No matter what path you choose as a modern witch, you'll likely be working with energy in some way. Energy work in witchcraft focuses on the unseen currents that pulse within and around you. Energy isn't bound by tools or ingredients; instead, it relies on the ability to sense, direct, and transform energy with intention and focus. Whether you're divining with tarot, concocting herbal potions, or reading star charts, you're likely also working with energy if you're reaching beyond the superficial aspects of your craft. All the witches I cover in previous chapters can be considered energy witches, but in this chapter, I focus on witches who specialize in energy healing, including *mediums*, who channel energy directly through their bodies, minds, and spirits in addition to or instead of using specific tools. I introduce the concept of energy in Chapter 5, as you access unseen sources of power. This chapter covers the energy centers of the body, different types of healing modalities, and the beginner tools to access the hidden power in your witchy practices.

Tapping into Your Power: Subtle Magic

In witchcraft, *energy* refers to the unseen, dynamic force that flows through all living beings and spaces. Energy is the life force behind every spell, ritual, and intention, a thread that binds the physical and metaphysical. This energy, considered the foundation of magic, is the medium through which witches transform thought into action and intent into reality. Unlike physical objects or visible matter, energy in witchcraft is sensed, directed, and shaped through mental focus and visualization. Energy is often directed by tools like crystals, herbs, and symbols, and *mediums* primarily move energy by employing their bodies directly. By using their personal energies, these witches can influence the surrounding world, connecting with the natural and spiritual realms to create change.

REMEMBER

The concept of working with energy is ancient and spans many cultures, each with its own understanding and terminology for this vital force. Early traditions from ancient Egypt, India, China, and the indigenous cultures of the Americas recognized a form of energy that animates life.

This is referred to as *prana* in Hinduism and yoga, *qi* or *chi* in Chinese philosophy, and *ka* in ancient Egyptian beliefs. *Meridians* are channels that run through the subtle body, used in systems like acupuncture and traditional Chinese medicine. They can be thought of as energy pathways that allow life force energy to flow throughout the body.

The modern Western understanding of energy work evolved through exposure to these ancient traditions, with practices like Reiki from Japan, chakra work from India, and the Western New Age movement embracing energy healing and meditation in the 20th century. In witchcraft, this concept of energy work has been adapted into practices such as aura cleansing, grounding, and visualization, allowing practitioners to work with energy on both personal and collective levels. By working with energy, witches today continue a long tradition of using the unseen forces of life to heal, protect, and manifest intentions, building bridges between cultures and expanding the potential of their craft.

Working with the subtle body

The *subtle body* is considered the nonphysical, energetic counterpart to the physical body, consisting of energy layers, centers, and channels that connect humankind to spiritual and emotional realms. Unlike the physical body, which is visible and tangible, the subtle body is sensed through intuition, emotion, and spiritual practices. The subtle body is a foundational concept in witchcraft because it serves as the primary conduit for sensing, channeling, and directing energy.

When I was a kid, I sensed my subtle body intuitively. I felt different emotions in different parts of my body and even saw colors when I felt certain emotions deeply enough. I didn't know that this wasn't a common experience until later in life. By then, science had conditioned me to think that the body was separate from the mind, and the colorful emotions faded. It wasn't until I started practicing yoga in my twenties that the colors returned, and I learned about the hidden energy centers of the body.

Vibing with your aura

The *aura* is an energetic field, sometimes referred to as a vibration, or *vibe*, that surrounds the physical body and expresses itself through a color. It's considered part of the subtle body and serves as a protective shield that reflects a person's emotional and spiritual state. Each color is associated with a different kind of energetic expression, and aura colors can shift depending on what energies are prominent at any given moment. Practitioners may work with the aura to cleanse negative energy, enhance psychic protection, or strengthen their personal boundaries.

FUN FACT

Although science has yet to prove the existence of auras, quantum physicists are constantly theorizing about subtle energy. For example, some studies have found that the human body emits energy that falls within the visible color spectrum when measured with certain instruments. Some new theories link these phenomena with the possibility of auras.

Unlocking the chakras

The subtle body is often visualized as being composed of centers of power, each corresponding to different aspects of one's energy and consciousness. These are commonly referred to as *chakras*, energy centers aligned along the spine, each representing different physical, emotional, and spiritual states, from grounding in the root chakra to higher intuition in the crown chakra, as outlined in Figure 16-1. *Chakra* is a Sanskrit word that literally translates to *wheel* or *cycle*. Each chakra is visualized as a turning orb of light.

FUN FACT

Although there are seven major chakras according to the most popularly practiced system, some say the body contains hundreds or even thousands of energy centers.

For energy witches, the subtle body is central to practices like grounding, cleansing, protection, and healing. Through meditation, visualization, and focused intention, you can manipulate the flow of energy within your subtle body to clear blockages, balance emotions, and enhance your natural intuition. By learning to sense and work with the subtle body, you gain a deeper awareness of how your energy interacts with the world around you, empowering you to harness that energy for healing, protection, and manifestation.

Healing modalities around the world

Various healing modalities use energy work to balance, restore, and enhance well-being on physical, emotional, and spiritual levels. Each approach has its unique philosophy and techniques for interacting with the body's energy systems.

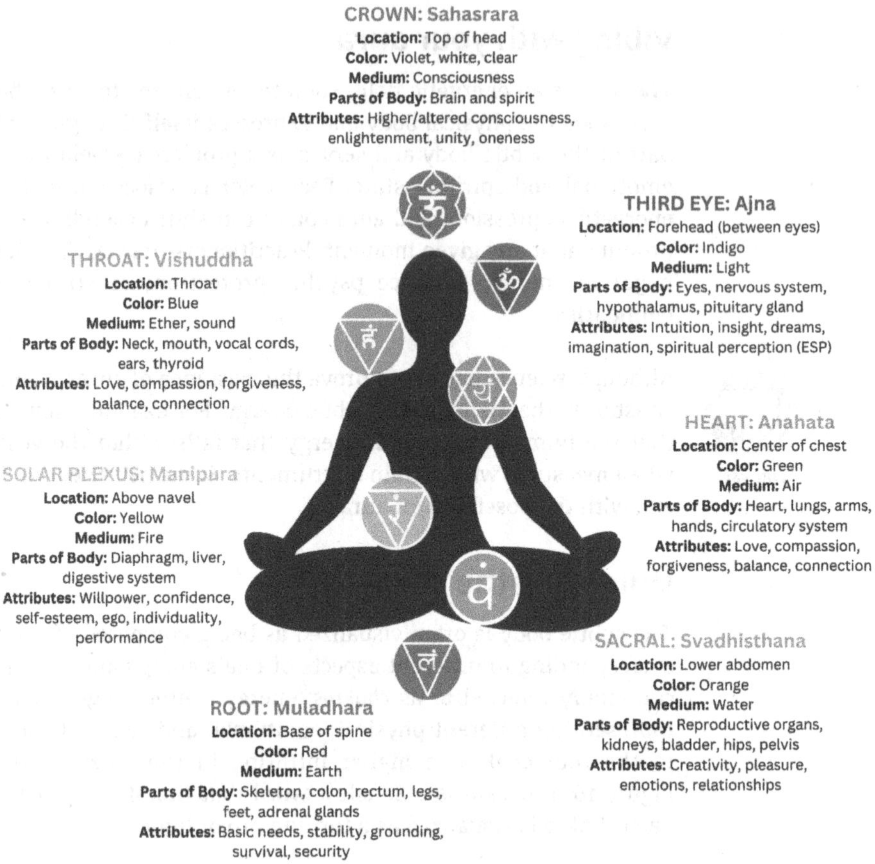

CROWN: Sahasrara
Location: Top of head
Color: Violet, white, clear
Medium: Consciousness
Parts of Body: Brain and spirit
Attributes: Higher/altered consciousness, enlightenment, unity, oneness
THIRD EYE: Ajna
Location: Forehead (between eyes)
Color: Indigo
Medium: Light
Parts of Body: Eyes, nervous system, hypothalamus, pituitary gland
Attributes: Intuition, insight, dreams, imagination, spiritual perception (ESP)
THROAT: Vishuddha
Location: Throat
Color: Blue
Medium: Ether, sound
Parts of Body: Neck, mouth, vocal cords, ears, thyroid
Attributes: Love, compassion, forgiveness, balance, connection
HEART: Anahata
Location: Center of chest
Color: Green
Medium: Air
Parts of Body: Heart, lungs, arms, hands, circulatory system
Attributes: Love, compassion, forgiveness, balance, connection
SOLAR PLEXUS: Manipura
Location: Above navel
Color: Yellow
Medium: Fire
Parts of Body: Diaphragm, liver, digestive system
Attributes: Willpower, confidence, self-esteem, ego, individuality, performance
SACRAL: Svadhisthana
Location: Lower abdomen
Color: Orange
Medium: Water
Parts of Body: Reproductive organs, kidneys, bladder, hips, pelvis
Attributes: Creativity, pleasure, emotions, relationships
ROOT: Muladhara
Location: Base of spine
Color: Red
Medium: Earth
Parts of Body: Skeleton, colon, rectum, legs, feet, adrenal glands
Attributes: Basic needs, stability, grounding, survival, security

FIGURE 16-1 The seven main chakras of the body.

LAYERING BODIES

Chakras control the flow of energy and are often thought to make up the different color layers of the aura, referred to as *bodies*:

- **The etheric body:** The etheric body is the first layer of the auric field, closest to the physical body, extending about 1–2 inches beyond the skin. This layer is often described as a bluish or grayish light, containing an energetic blueprint of the physical form. The etheric body is associated with the root chakra.
- **The emotional body:** The emotional body extends a few inches beyond the etheric layer and is associated with feelings and emotions. This layer often appears in fluctuating colors that correspond to the individual's emotional state. The emotional body is associated with the sacral chakra.

- **The mental body:** The mental body surrounds the emotional body and is linked to thoughts, beliefs, and cognitive processes. It often appears as bright yellow light and is closely related to the mind and intellect. The mental body is associated with the solar plexus chakra.
- **The astral body:** The astral body extends out from the mental body and is associated with love, relationships, and connection to others. It often appears as a soft pink or rosy light and is sometimes called the *bridge* layer because it links the lower and higher energy bodies. The astral body is associated with the heart chakra.
- **The etheric template body:** The etheric template body is an energetic "blueprint" for the physical body. It extends farther than the previous layers, typically reaching 1.5 feet from the physical body, and is associated with the throat chakra.
- **The celestial body:** The celestial body is associated with spiritual and emotional ecstasy, reaching 2–3 feet beyond the physical body. It's often described as a shimmering, radiant layer filled with light, linked to feelings of unconditional love and spiritual insight. It's associated with the third eye chakra.
- **The causal body:** The causal body, also known as the *soul* layer, is the outermost layer of the aura, extending up to three feet or more from the physical body. It appears as a golden or white light and is linked to the higher self or soul. The causal body is associated with the crown chakra.

Balancing through Traditional Chinese Medicine

Traditional Chinese Medicine (TCM) is an ancient system of healing based on balancing the body's life force, or *qi*, through various techniques that restore harmony between the body, mind, and spirit. TCM sees health as a balanced flow of energy along pathways called *meridians*, as described earlier in the chapter. These include:

- » **Acupuncture:** Involves inserting fine needles into meridian points to stimulate energy flow, release blockages, and enhance health.
- » **Herbal medicine:** Uses specific herbs to balance internal energies, tailored to the individual's unique constitution and energetic needs.
- » **Qigong:** A practice combining movement, breathwork, and meditation to cultivate and balance life force energy, promoting mental clarity and physical vitality.

Harmonizing with Ayurveda

Ayurveda is a holistic healing system from India that seeks to balance the body's energies, or *doshas*, to promote harmony and wellness. It emphasizes diet, lifestyle, and herbal therapies as ways to restore energy balance. Ayurvedic practices include:

- **Dosha balancing:** Involves using diet, herbs, and lifestyle practices to harmonize your doshas, enhancing well-being.
- **Abhyanga:** Uses warm, herbal-infused oils in massage to restore balance, detoxify the body, and calm the mind.
- **Shirodhara:** A therapy in which warm oil is poured over the forehead to calm the nervous system and promote mental clarity.
- **Yoga:** Integrates physical postures, breath control, and meditation to align the body, mind, and spirit, promoting overall health and equilibrium.

Grounding with yoga and meditation

Yoga and meditation are ancient practices that work with the body's energy centers, or *chakras*, and life force energy, or *prana*. These practices integrate physical movement, breath, and mental focus to align and balance energy within the body:

- **Pranayama:** Breath exercises regulate prana, enhancing mental clarity and physical energy.
- **Visualization:** Visualization and guided imagery are mental techniques for directing energy. By imagining specific energy flows or healing light, practitioners can influence their emotional state, relieve tension, and promote mental clarity.
- **Chakra meditation:** The focus is on visualizing and balancing the chakras, promoting emotional and spiritual well-being.
- **Kundalini yoga:** This combines breath, movement, and chanting to awaken energy at the base of the spine and guide it through the chakras.

Clearing blocks with Reiki and biofield therapies

Reiki is a Japanese healing art that involves channeling universal life force energy through your hands to promote healing. It's based on the idea that energy can flow through the body, mind, and spirit to clear blockages and balance the recipient's energy field. Practitioners place their hands on or near the body to channel energy, helping to clear blockages and promote relaxation and healing. You can also send healing energy long-distance so that you can help individuals who aren't physically present. Modern biofield therapies are similar to Reiki, involving working with the body's electromagnetic field to restore balance and vitality. These therapies include the following:

- **Polarity therapy:** Combines touch and gentle movements to balance energy flows, aligning the physical and energy bodies.
- **Magnetic therapy:** Uses magnets placed on specific points to influence the body's electromagnetic energy. This therapy is believed to improve circulation and alleviate pain.

Elevating energy with sound healing

Sound healing uses vibrational frequencies to balance the body's energy. Different sounds and vibrations resonate with specific energy centers, clearing blockages and promoting a state of harmony and relaxation. Modes of sound healing can include the following:

- **Tibetan singing bowls:** Produce sound vibrations that align chakras and clear stagnant energy.
- **Tuning forks:** Used to direct specific frequencies at acupuncture points or chakras, restoring energetic balance.
- **Crystal singing bowls and gongs:** Vibrate at frequencies that resonate with the body's natural rhythms, aiding in emotional release and relaxation.

Relaxing with massage and bodywork

Massage and bodywork stimulate energy flow by applying pressure to specific points and energy pathways, releasing tension, improving circulation, and promoting relaxation. Different bodywork techniques can enhance both physical and energetic health.

- **Shiatsu:** A Japanese massage, it uses finger pressure on meridians to enhance energy flow.
- **Thai massage:** This combines stretching and compression along energy lines to release tension and improve flexibility.
- **Reflexology:** Pressure is applied to reflex points on the feet, hands, or ears, which correspond to different areas of the body, supporting holistic health.
- **Therapeutic touch:** Practitioners assess and smooth the energy field, working above the body to relieve stress and encourage healing.

Entering different states of consciousness

Energy witchcraft expands beyond the physical realm, delving into the mystical and intangible realms of dreams, astral travel, journeying, and mediumship/necromancy. Each of these practices relies on subtle energy to bridge the worlds of consciousness, spirit, and the unknown. By tapping into your own energy and the energy of other realms, you can explore different states of reality, connect with spirits, or receive guidance from higher sources. This section talks about how energy witchcraft plays a role in each of these mystical areas.

Dreaming insights

You can perceive dreams as portals to the subconscious and the spiritual realms, offering messages from within and from the spiritual world. Practitioners often work with dreams to uncover hidden insights, confront fears, and receive guidance. Energy witches may use dream incubation techniques, setting specific intentions before sleep to receive messages or gain clarity on a question.

During sleep, the subtle body, particularly the astral body, is thought to be more active, allowing for deeper energetic exploration and experiences beyond the physical world. Tools like crystals (such as amethyst or labradorite), herbs (such as mugwort or lavender), and protective sigils can enhance dreams, increase recall, and protect energy while dreaming. Energy witches may also cleanse their energy before sleep, using visualization or grounding techniques to ensure their dreams are clear and unburdened by daily stressors.

FUN FACT

Lucid dreaming is the experience of becoming aware that you're dreaming while still in the dream, often allowing you to control and interact with the dream environment consciously. Practicing reality checks — like looking at your hands or reading text twice — can increase your chances of becoming aware in a dream, letting you take control and explore your dream worlds on your terms.

Projecting through astral travel

When I was a kid, I was an avid lucid dreamer. I would train myself to discern that I was dreaming, and then I could control my dreams. I could fly, explore worlds, and every now and then, I could astral travel. *Astral travel* (or *astral projection*) is the practice of consciously leaving the physical body to explore the astral plane, an energetic dimension where boundaries between worlds are more fluid. Figure 16-2 shows the astral body.

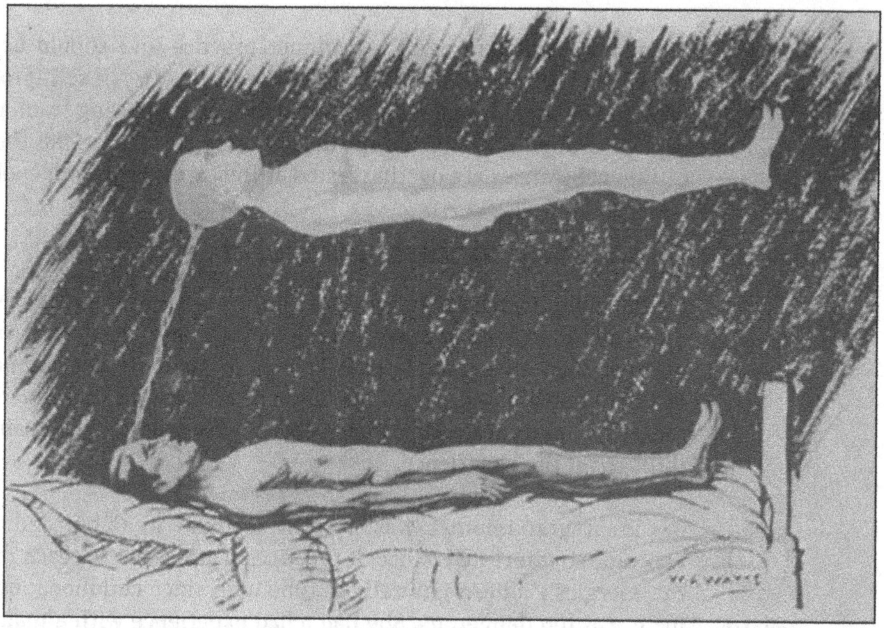

FIGURE 16-2: The astral body traveling away from the physical body during astral projection.

Hereward Carrington, Sylvan Muldoon./The Projection of the Astral Body. Rider, 1929./Wikimedia Commons/public domain

TIP

Astral travel requires a strong command of your energy because it involves expanding beyond typical boundaries while remaining connected to the self. Techniques like grounding, shielding, and centering are essential for safe astral travel. You may visualize a protective barrier around their astral body, often in the form of light, to guard against unwanted energies while you're "out of body." You can place stones like black tourmaline or obsidian near your body during astral work to provide protection and grounding. Clear quartz or moonstone can enhance the experience.

Journeying to other worlds

Shamanic journeying involves entering a trance-like state to travel within the spirit world for healing, guidance, or spiritual insight. This journey is guided by intention and the use of the subtle body, allowing you to communicate with spirit guides, animal spirits, or ancestral energies. The journey often begins with grounding, centering, and opening the energy field to prepare for travel between worlds.

Sound tools like drums or rattles are frequently used to maintain rhythm and deepen your trance, allowing you to keep your energetic focus as you move through the spirit realm. You may also call upon protective guides before beginning a journey to ensure safe passage. You might even employ psychoactive substances to achieve the trance state required for journeying.

WARNING

Shamanic journeying isn't a beginner practice and should be supervised by a trained and reputable shamanic practitioner. Be wary of self-proclaimed shamans with no ties to the indigenous cultures they're borrowing from. Psychedelics have become a popular draw for spiritual tourism to places like the Amazon, where certain substances are overharvested at the expense of indigenous communities.

Connecting to the spirit world

Mediumship involves connecting with the spirits of the deceased, either to communicate or to seek wisdom from ancestors and spirit entities. Mediums draw on their own energy and spirit energy to facilitate communication across the veil between life and death. Mediums often prepare their energy by grounding, centering, and protecting themselves, ensuring they remain safe and clear throughout the experience.

FUN FACT

My great-grandmother was a spirit medium in Cuba, and she's the reason I became so interested in occult practices. I asked her to teach me how to channel the energies I'd been naturally in tune with since childhood, but she always told me it was too dangerous. She had a bad experience with a malevolent spirit that made her quit her practice and hang up her hat long before I was born. Still, I wish I would have pressed her more while she was alive. I remain interested in mediumship as a craft.

WARNING

Necromancy, or working with the dead in a more intentional, ritualistic way, is not usually considered a beginner practice. It requires a high level of respect and skill in energy manipulation. You must approach this work with caution and a strong sense of purpose because connecting with spirits can expose you to lingering or intense energies. Protective charms, sigils, and crystals (such as onyx or smoky quartz) are often used to anchor that energy and prevent unwanted attachments.

As a beginner, you can use offerings, like candles, incense, or ancestral foods to honor and connect with spirits in a respectful manner, building a bridge of energy for clearer communication. The most popular tradition for honoring ancestor spirits is the Day of the Dead, a Mexican observance that has become popular all across the Americas.

FUN FACT

Some mediums connect with familiars. Traditionally, a *familiar* is thought to be a spirit or animal that assists a witch by offering protection, guidance, and an energetic link to the natural world or spirit realms.

These companions can amplify energy and direct intention and serve as protectors or intermediaries in ritual work. As energetic amplifiers, familiars can strengthen your own energy as a witch. When working with a familiar, you might experience heightened focus and more robust energy flow as the familiar's energy blends with your own, creating a synergistic effect. This combined energy can make spells, rituals, and energy work more potent as the familiar's presence intensifies your intentions.

For Your Grimoire: Energy Work

Much like divination, the tools that aid in energy work are widely varied and highly personal to the practitioner. The right tools can cleanse, protect, amplify, and direct energy. They can also aid in all sorts of healing modalities and entering different states of consciousness. The first step for you as a beginner witch is to learn how to clear energy and protect yourself, which I introduce in Chapter 10. Some of the most common tools of the energy witch include these:

- **Crystals:** Crystals are natural energy amplifiers, each with unique vibrational properties that influence physical, emotional, and spiritual energy. Used to clear, protect, and strengthen energy fields, crystals serve as powerful allies in grounding, healing, and manifesting intentions. See the appendix for a list of common crystals and their healing associations.
- **Sigils and sacred symbols:** *Sigils* are symbols charged with personal intention, crafted to represent and manifest specific desires, from protection to healing to empowerment. By creating and activating a sigil, energy workers infuse it with intention, making it a focal point for directing energy. These symbols can be inscribed on objects, drawn on paper, or visualized to channel focused energy and influence the surrounding environment. I cover sigils in more depth in Chapter 12.
- **Herbs:** Herbs carry their own natural energy and are used for cleansing, protection, and grounding in energy work. The herbs have distinct energetic qualities, making them versatile tools in rituals, spells, and healing practices. Whether burned, carried in sachets, or brewed into teas, herbs offer powerful support for maintaining balanced energy and aligning with nature's rhythms. See the appendix for a list of herbs and their healing properties.
- **Flower essences:** Similarly, flower essences capture the subtle energy of plants, addressing emotional and mental imbalances on an energetic level. These gentle remedies, made by infusing flowers in water, clear emotional blocks, promote resilience, and restore harmony. Often taken as drops or added to baths, flower essences are ideal for emotional healing, inner peace, and spiritual growth.
- **Salves and oils:** Salves and oils are infused with herbs and essential oils to provide physical and energetic healing. Applied directly to the body or used in rituals, they create a layer of protection, soothe emotions, or balance energy

centers. From protection oils to chakra-balancing salves, these blends connect with the skin and aura to anchor intentions and enhance energy flow.

- **Amulets and talismans:** Amulets and talismans are charged objects worn or carried for protection, luck, or specific purposes. Each is selected or crafted with intention, absorbing and radiating energy that aligns with the wearer's goals. They act as personal shields, attracting positive energy or enhancing attributes like courage and clarity, empowering the user on both physical and energetic levels.
- **Sound tools:** Sound tools such as singing bowls, bells, and drums create vibrational frequencies that cleanse, balance, and raise energy. Each instrument's unique tone resonates with specific energy centers, aiding in clearing stagnant energy and restoring harmony. Sound tools are particularly effective for aura cleansing, grounding, and aligning the energy field with higher frequencies.
- **Candles:** Candles symbolize transformation and focus in energy work, with their flame representing the dynamic force of change. Each candle color corresponds to a different type of energy, from protection to love to intuition. When lit, candles amplify intentions and serve as powerful beacons, helping practitioners direct energy toward their goals through meditation, ritual, or spell work. You can read more on candle magic in Chapter 12.

Visualizing your chakras

One of the best ways to get started with your energy practice is to visualize your chakras. This helped me train myself to control my energy instead of just being surprised by colors when I felt strong emotions. Here's a short meditation to help you visualize and connect with your chakras. This practice is grounding and can be used to balance, clear, and energize each chakra. Revisit the main chakras shown in Figure 16-1 (in the earlier section "Unlocking the chakras") and then follow these steps:

1. **Settle in.**

   Find a comfortable seated position, either on the floor or in a chair. Close your eyes, take a few deep breaths, and allow your body to relax.

2. **Ground yourself.**

   Visualize roots growing from the base of your spine or your feet, reaching deep into the earth. Feel the solid connection, grounding you firmly.

3. **Move through the chakras, starting with the root chakra.**

   Bring your attention to the base of your spine. Imagine a glowing red sphere of light there, warm and steady. Breathe into it, visualizing it growing stronger with each breath, filling you with a sense of security and stability.

4. **Move up to the sacral chakra.**

   Shift your focus to your lower abdomen, just below the navel. Visualize a bright orange light there, radiating warmth and creativity. Let it expand with each inhale, filling you with joy and inspiration.

5. **Move up to the solar plexus chakra.**

   Direct your attention to your upper abdomen, around the stomach area. See a golden-yellow sphere of light there, representing your personal power and confidence. Breathe into it, feeling it grow brighter, filling you with self-assurance and strength.

6. **Move up to the heart chakra.**

   Move to the center of your chest. Imagine a soft, green light there, glowing with love and compassion. With each breath, let this light expand, filling your heart with kindness, forgiveness, and connection.

7. **Move up to the throat chakra.**

   Bring your awareness to your throat. Visualize a calming blue light there, resonating with truth and clarity. As you breathe, feel this light expanding, empowering you to express yourself freely and honestly.

8. **Move up to the third eye chakra.**

   Focus on the space between your eyebrows. Imagine a deep indigo or violet light there, representing insight and intuition. Breathe into this light, allowing it to sharpen your inner vision and connect you with your inner wisdom.

9. **Move up to the crown chakra.**

   Finally, move to the top of your head. Visualize a radiant violet or white light there, expanding upward, connecting you to the universe and divine wisdom. Breathe deeply, feeling this connection grow, filling you with peace and clarity.

10. **Find full body awareness.**

    Envision all your chakras glowing brightly, aligned and balanced, with energy flowing smoothly between them. Take a few deep breaths, feeling calm, centered, and energized.

11. **Close the meditation.**

    Slowly bring your awareness back to your body. Wiggle your fingers and toes, take a grounding breath, and open your eyes.

TIP

Search online for free guided meditations to help with your visualization exercise until you become more comfortable with the chakras and their positions in the body.

Cord-cutting ritual

Chapter 12 covers beginner practices for setting intentions and manifestation, using tools like candles, sigils, and amulets. Sometimes instead of calling in energy, you'd like to cleanse the space or protect your energy (as I cover in Chapter 10). In rare cases, a regular clearing won't undo certain energetic ties to people, places, or things.

WARNING

While cord-cutting rituals are simple, they should not be undertaken lightly. Only use this when other forms of cleansing and protection magic have not worked, and you really need to end a connection with something or someone for good. Cord-cuttings are considered banishing rituals, performed with the intention of a permanent ending.

Gather the following items, but feel free to substitute for like ingredients to make this your own:

- **A black or white candle:** Black for protection and banishing; white for purifying and new beginnings
- **A piece of string or cord:** Symbolizing the energetic tie you want to sever
- **Scissors or a small knife:** To cut the cord
- **A fireproof bowl or plate:** For candle safety and ashes
- **Incense or smoke bundle:** For cleansing the space
- **Salt, black tourmaline, or essential oils:** Optional, for additional protection and clearing

TIP

Before proceeding with the ritual, you might want to take a cleansing bath. See Chapter 14 for instructions on how to make an herbal bath sachet and consult the appendix for herbs used for cleansing.

Follow these steps:

1. **Set up and cleanse your space.**

   Find a quiet, private space where you won't be disturbed. Cleanse the area by burning the incense or smoke bundle, allowing the smoke to purify the air. If you have salt or protective crystals, place them around your space for added grounding and protection.

2. **Light the candle.**

   Place the candle on a fireproof surface and light it, setting the intention to release any unwanted attachments. If you like, you can anoint the candle with essential oil to enhance the energy of the ritual.

3. **Hold the cord and set your intention.**

   Take the piece of string or cord in your hands. Visualize it as a representation of the energy or connection you want to release. Think about the person, habit, or situation you're cutting ties with, and set a clear intention to let go, releasing anything that no longer serves your highest good.

4. **Visualize the energetic cord.**

   Close your eyes and visualize the energetic cord that connects you to this person or situation. Imagine it as a strand of light or energy linking you to them, and focus on the feeling of this connection. Recognize any weight or emotional ties associated with it.

5. **Cut the cord.**

   When you feel ready, use the scissors or knife to physically cut the cord. As you do, visualize the energetic cord being severed completely, releasing all attachments. Say something like, "I release this connection with love and gratitude. I reclaim my energy and my power."

6. **Burn the cord (optional).**

   If you feel comfortable doing so, place the cut cord into the flame of the candle, letting it burn as a final act of release. Be sure to place it in the fireproof bowl or plate and allow it to turn to ash. As it burns, visualize any lingering energy dissolving into smoke, leaving you free and clear.

7. **Close the ritual.**

   Take a few deep breaths to center yourself. Thank any spiritual guides, ancestors, or energies that supported you during the ritual. When you feel ready, extinguish the candle, symbolizing the end of the ritual. Safely dispose of any ashes or remnants, preferably outside, as a final act of release.

8. **Ground and cleanse.**

   After the ritual, wash your hands or touch the ground to discharge any residual energy. You may also use a salt bath or even just eat a little salt to further ground yourself.

5

Expanding Beyond Personal Practice

IN THIS PART . . .

Learn about the history of covens and how to choose among the different types of covens practicing today. Find tips on how to connect with like-minded witches, as well as red flags to watch out for.

Explore strategies for creating sacred space and organizing your own communities, including guidelines for facilitating ritual circles and protecting yourself and others.

Connect your personal practice to issues you care about. Explore topics in spiritual activism and learn how to choose a cause to devote your magic to.

Imagine new forms of magical practice and creativity. Explore ways to devote yourself to becoming an ancestor witch.

IN THIS CHAPTER

- » Learning about the history of covens
- » Exploring the workings of modern covens
- » Choosing your own coven

Chapter 17
Joining a Coven

It's simple: a *coven* is a group of witches. Covens are central to the evolution of witchcraft, offering communal and structured ways to explore and practice magic. Witches gather in covens to share knowledge and perform rituals. The history of covens is highly contested, but the concept of the modern coven originated in European witchcraft lore and spread through the rise of Wicca and European traditional witchcraft. In the past couple of decades, covens have taken on a certain glamor, with Hollywood portrayals of close-knit groups who practice in style — like the witches in *The Craft*, who captured my imagination as a novice witch.

Whether you're new to the path or simply curious about what a coven is, this chapter will take you through the basics, from the history of covens to tips for finding and joining a coven to ethical considerations. By the end of this chapter, you'll have a better understanding of covens and how they can fit into your own spiritual journey.

Hedge Witches vs. Coven Witches

For most of my practice, I've been a solitary witch. The term *hedge witch* refers to a type of witch who practices a deeply personal, often solitary form of magic, rooted in nature and spirit work. The word *hedge* itself comes from the idea of a boundary — in this case, the boundary between the physical world and the spiritual or unseen realms. In contrast, coven witches grow in their power through group practice. In recent years, I've started to share my practice with groups, and though I've always been an independent witch, I've evolved greatly by joining energies with other witches. As I grow, I can see myself breaking out of my hedge witchery and committing to a coven over time.

Practicing alone

Today, hedge witchcraft continues to thrive as an alternative, personal, and nature-focused form of witchcraft. Joining a coven when you're a beginner has several benefits, but it's also a good idea to develop the basics of your own practice so that you can evaluate why you'd like to join a coven and prepare yourself for the kinds of energy exchanges you'd encounter with a group.

FUN FACT

Historically, hedge witches were rural, self-taught practitioners who worked outside of formalized religious or magical systems. They were often herbalists, healers, and wise folk, known in their communities for their knowledge of plants, natural remedies, and spiritual guidance. These individuals weren't typically part of structured covens or priesthoods, but rather practiced a folk-based form of magic passed down through generations or learned through personal experience.

The term *hedge witch* is a more modern label, but the practices it refers to are ancient. In medieval and early modern Europe, village healers or *cunning folk* might be considered hedge witches by today's standards. These individuals often lived on the edges of their communities, both physically (on the outskirts of villages) and socially, as they worked with both the material and the spiritual aspects of healing and magic.

Practicing as a collective

During the infamous witch trials in Europe and North America between the 15th and 18th centuries, it was often alleged that witches gathered in groups to worship the devil, perform dark rituals, and conspire against society. Figure 17-1 shows witches gathering with demons, as popularly imagined at the height of the European witch panic. These accusations fueled widespread fear, although the historical evidence for organized covens during this period is minimal, and much of what was reported was likely fabricated under duress or the result of religious persecution.

FUN FACT

The first recorded reference to a coven is usually attributed to Isobel Gowdie, a Scottish woman who confessed to being part of a group of witches during her trial in 1662. Gowdie's confession is one of the most detailed accounts of witchcraft from the period. She claimed that her coven consisted of thirteen members, which might have contributed to the idea that covens traditionally have this number of participants.

FIGURE 17-1: An artist's rendering of witches gathering with demons.

"Scots Witches Prepare" by J.M. Wright, illustrated for "Tam o' Shanter" by Robert Burns, 1790

Isobel Gowdie's testimony is significant because it provides one of the earliest known descriptions of a group of witches who met regularly to practice magic and attend gatherings with the devil. It's important to note, however, that her confessions were likely influenced by the torture and coercion common in witch trials of the time. Nevertheless, her case remains one of the first and most detailed recorded mentions of a coven in historical records.

REMEMBER

The modern concept of a coven was heavily influenced by the emergence of Wicca in the mid-20th century. In the 1920s, anthropologist Margaret Murray promoted her "witch-cult theory," using the word *coven* to describe pagan groups of thirteen witches who worshipped a horned god around Europe — a god that was turned into the devil by Christianity. This inspired Gerald Gardner, a key figure in the development of Wicca, who described covens as small, structured groups of witches, often led by a high priestess or high priest. Academics have largely discredited the witch-cult theory; nonetheless, Wicca's swift rise gave covens a more formalized and positive place in the world of modern witchcraft.

As witchcraft evolved into the late 20th and 21st centuries, covens became widely accepted as a legitimate way for witches and pagans to practice their craft together. No longer seen as something dark or dangerous, covens today are communities of like-minded individuals who gather to share spiritual knowledge, celebrate the cycles of nature, and practice magic.

Types of covens

Modern covens can be found all over the world, and they're not limited to Wicca or traditional witchcraft. They can also be affiliated with other spiritual paths, including Druidry, Heathenry, ceremonial magic, eclectic paganism, and many more. Some covens are more structured and hierarchical, whereas others operate in a democratic or egalitarian manner, with all members having equal say.

Modern covens can focus on a wide range of practices, from honoring the cycles of the moon and celebrating the *sabbats* (seasonal festivals outlined in Chapter 22) to working magic for healing, protection, and personal development. Some covens emphasize teaching and mentorship, whereas others focus more on mutual spiritual support and shared ritual practice.

Following are some of the most common kinds of covens found in modern witchcraft:

- **Wiccan covens:** These covens follow the teachings of Wicca, often based on the traditions that Gerald Gardner and other early Wiccan leaders established. Wiccan covens typically honor the goddess and the god, follow the Wheel of the Year (seasonal sabbats), and perform rituals aligned with the lunar cycle. They tend to have a formal structure, with ranks such as high priestess, high priest, and initiates.
- **Eclectic covens:** Eclectic covens draw from a wide range of spiritual and magical traditions, incorporating elements from different paths to create their own unique blend of practices. These covens may honor various deities from different pantheons, practice diverse forms of magic, and adapt rituals based on the members' preferences.
- **Ceremonial magic covens:** Covens that focus on ceremonial magic often work within structured magical systems, such as the Hermetic Order of the Golden Dawn and Thelema. These groups are typically more formal in their ritual work, often emphasizing the use of sacred geometry, alchemy, and the invocation of specific deities or spirits. Ceremonial magic covens may require extensive study and discipline.

- **Druidic groves:** Although technically not always referred to as covens, Druidic groves are groups of people who practice Druidry, focusing on nature worship, the veneration of ancestors, and reverence for Earth. Their rituals often take place outdoors, and they emphasize harmony with the environment and cycles of nature.
- **Heathen kindreds:** In Heathenry (or Asatru), groups of practitioners may gather in what are known as *kindreds* rather than covens. These groups are devoted to honoring the Norse gods, ancestors, and spirits of the land. Rituals, called *blóts*, involve offerings and celebrations in honor of deities such as Odin, Thor, Freyja, and others.
- **Family or hereditary covens:** Some covens are made up of family members who share a hereditary or family-based magical tradition. These covens often pass down teachings and rituals from one generation to the next. Family covens can be deeply private and are usually small in number.
- **Teaching covens:** These covens emphasize education and mentorship. They may take on new students and train them in the tradition or system that the coven practices. Teaching covens can be an excellent place for beginners to learn foundational skills in magic and witchcraft.

TIP

Many covens today have online components or operate completely online, allowing members to connect virtually or hold digital rituals. This has allowed for a broader and more accessible understanding of witchcraft and has made it easier for solitary practitioners to find communities that resonate with their beliefs.

Motivations for joining a coven

Joining a coven can offer many benefits for beginner witches. Here are some common reasons why people choose to join covens:

- **Community:** Being part of a coven provides a sense of community, where you can share experiences, knowledge, and spiritual practices with like-minded individuals. This can be especially important for those who feel isolated in their spiritual journey or lack a local pagan or magical community.
- **Guidance and support:** Many covens offer mentorship, with more experienced members guiding newcomers through the basics of witchcraft and ritual. Learning from others in a structured environment can be incredibly valuable for beginners who want to build a strong foundation in their practice.
- **Rituals and celebrations:** Covens provide an opportunity to regularly celebrate lunar and seasonal observances, which can deepen your connection to the rhythms of nature and the divine.

- **Spiritual growth:** Working within a coven can challenge you to grow both spiritually and magically. Covens often encourage members to explore their personal power, face their fears, and develop their intuition through ritual and magical work.

TIP

Although you can join a coven at any time along your magical journey, you might be ready to consider a group when you've reached a plateau with your personal practice. If your routine is starting to feel stale, learning from others and joining in group ritual could take your practice to the next level.

Finding Your Witches

Joining a coven is a personal decision. You can take the following steps when considering joining a coven to better your chances of finding one that aligns with your values, beliefs, and spiritual goals:

- **Conduct research:** Start by researching different kinds of covens, their practices, and their traditions. Look into what kind of structure you feel most comfortable with — whether it's a formal tradition like Wicca, a more eclectic group, or a specialized magical practice.
- **Attend open rituals or events:** Many covens host open rituals, workshops, or public events where you can meet members and learn more about their practices. This is a great way to get a feel for the group's energy and decide if it resonates with you.
- **Ask questions:** When you find a coven you're interested in, don't hesitate to ask questions about their beliefs, practices, and expectations. Understanding the group's structure and how they operate will help you determine if it's the right fit for you.
- **Know the commitment:** Some covens may have a trial period or a dedication process before you become a full member. This allows both you and the coven to see if the relationship is a good match. Be prepared for commitment; joining a coven often involves a process of initiation and regular participation in rituals and meetings.
- **Evaluate ethics:** It's important to join a coven that aligns with your ethical beliefs. Some covens may have rules about working with certain types of magic or engaging in specific behaviors. Make sure you're comfortable with the group's moral and ethical standards.

TIP

Before you search for covens, take a moment to list your personal values and non-negotiable ethical beliefs. This will help you use discernment to find the right match instead of being swept up in the latest interaction.

Seeking green flags

Once you're involved in a gathering of witches, pay attention to group dynamics and how you feel during and after meetings. Your intuition will guide you, but what follows are a few signs that you've found a good group:

- **Consent:** The group operates on consent. All members agree to participate in rituals, spell work, or activities. No one should ever be forced or pressured into participating in something that makes them uncomfortable. Consent is a core value in any healthy coven dynamic.
- **Respect for diversity:** Because covens are small, it's perfectly fine to limit membership to certain demographic parameters. For example, it's not uncommon to see all-women's covens. Inclusivity will vary depending on the context, but the coven should welcome people of diverse backgrounds, orientations, and identities. A respectful coven honors diversity and fosters an environment of acceptance and support.
- **Use of magic:** The ethical principles and rules for the use of magic are clearly communicated. The coven's approach to magic should align with your personal ethics, especially regarding matters like hexing, cursing, and free will.
- **Privacy and confidentiality:** The coven protects member privacy. Covens often work with sensitive spiritual and personal matters, so maintaining confidentiality is crucial. Members should respect each other's privacy and avoid sharing personal information or magical workings outside the coven.
- **Power dynamics:** The coven practices mutual respect, valuing each member equally. Some covens have hierarchical structures, but these should be approached with care. Leadership roles, such as high priestess and high priest, come with responsibilities, not unchecked authority.

TIP

Some covens have open meetings and ritual circles you might attend to get a feel for the group culture before asking to join more officially.

Avoiding red flags

Although most considerations for joining covens are a matter of comfort and preference, watch for these signs that a coven is problematic or even dangerous:

- **Pressure to join:** Beware of covens that rush you to join, demand instant commitment, or discourage personal choices. A healthy coven should allow you time to explore and respect your autonomy.
- **Lack of transparency:** Excessive secrecy about leadership, practices, or intentions is a warning sign. You should be able to get clear, honest information about the group's goals and structure.
- **Abuse of power:** Be cautious of leaders who manipulate members emotionally, financially, or sexually. Any form of coercion, control, or exploitation, especially involving money or personal vulnerabilities, is a major red flag — and might even be illegal.
- **Disrespect for boundaries:** Covens that dismiss personal boundaries, push members into uncomfortable situations, or discourage individual consent are unhealthy. Respect for boundaries should be a core value. While joining a coven is a time commitment, covens shouldn't make excessive demands on members' time.
- **Cult-like behavior:** If the coven discourages interaction with others outside the group, promotes rigid or dogmatic beliefs, or creates an "us versus them" mentality, this could signal cult-like behavior.

TIP

No is a full sentence. If you ever feel uncomfortable with an invitation or a proposition, it's okay to decline without explanation.

Growing within a Spiritual Group

Although I'm not part of a formal coven, I've grown by leaps and bounds when I've practiced with friends and participated in occult learning communities. Growth looks different for everyone. Being a witch has no prescribed curriculum, but you can find a growing number of resources to guide you, including this book! My practice has been enriched by group interaction, as I've trained to perform more ceremonially, learned about different cultural rituals, and found support from a community who cares about the same things.

TIP

You don't have to join an elaborate organization. It's generally accepted that three is the minimum number of participants required to make a coven. So if you find a couple of like-minded friends willing to practice and learn together, you have a coven!

Performing ceremonies

Covens perform a range of rituals, depending on their tradition, focus, and spiritual goals. Following are some of the most common types of rituals you might encounter in a coven setting:

- **Esbats:** Esbats are rituals held on the full moon (and sometimes the new moon), where witches gather to honor lunar energy, perform spell work, and reflect on personal or collective goals. Moon magic is a central practice in many covens because the moon's phases are believed to influence emotions, intuition, and magical power.
- **Sabbats:** Covens typically celebrate the eight sabbats of the Wheel of the Year: Samhain, Yule, Imbolc, Ostara, Beltane, Litha, Lughnasadh, and Mabon (listed in detail in Chapter 22). These festivals honor the changing seasons and the cycles of birth, death, and rebirth, often with rituals that include feasting, storytelling, and honoring deities associated with that time of year. Some covens might share other religious or cultural days of observance not traditionally associated with witchcraft.
- **Initiations:** Many covens have initiation rituals that formally welcome new members into the group. These rituals often involve symbolic acts of transformation, commitment, and purification. Initiates may be given a magical name or title as part of this process.
- **Healing rituals:** Healing rituals can be performed for individuals within the coven or for the community at large. These rituals may involve energy work, herbal magic, or evocation of deities for health and well-being.
- **Protection rituals:** Covens often perform protection rituals to safeguard their members, homes, or communities. These rituals may involve casting circles, evoking protective spirits, or using talismans and sigils to ward off negativity.
- **Spell work:** Covens may work together on shared spell work, pooling their energy for a common goal. This could include spells for abundance, love, justice, or personal empowerment. The coven might keep a collective grimoire, or book of shadows.

In Figure 17-2, a small group gathers to perform a ritual.

FIGURE 17-2: A coven forms a ritual circle.

Continuing education

Even experts can't know everything there is to know about magic and the occult. One of the best reasons to join a coven is to expose yourself to different traditions and points of view. Although most witches are self-taught, personal blind spots and limitations are a given. Joining a coven, especially one focused on teaching and personal development, can help you grow in any or all of the following areas:

- **Magical theory and practice:** Covens can fill in the gaps about foundational knowledge, the principles of rituals and spellcasting, and the "why" behind the work.
- **History and tradition:** You can learn about the roots of witchcraft and paganism, explore different traditions, and open pathways to researching your own magical lineage.
- **Coven etiquette:** Just like any other facet of society, covens have spoken and unspoken rules about how to engage with group dynamics, including roles, hierarchy, and shared responsibilities.

Supporting community

Modern covens often organize around shared ideals and humanitarian interests. *Spiritual activism* (explored in detail in Chapter 19) is a growing concept in relation to group witchcraft. It involves using collective energy toward things like social justice, environmental protection, and community healing. Spiritual activism blends magical and spiritual practices with activism to bring about positive change in the world. Covens engaged in spiritual activism might:

- Perform rituals for social justice, focusing on equality, human rights, and the protection of marginalized communities.
- Raise energy for environmental causes, such as protecting endangered species, fighting climate change, and healing damaged ecosystems.
- Offer community support, including organizing charity events, providing healing circles, or engaging in mutual aid efforts.

Gatekeeping Magic

Gatekeeping in witchcraft, particularly within coven settings, is a complex and often polarizing topic. *Gatekeeping* refers to the practice of restricting access to certain knowledge, practices, or spiritual experiences. Although the term can carry negative connotations — implying exclusion or elitism — some boundaries are necessary within certain spiritual practices. When approached mindfully, gatekeeping can help practitioners maintain respect for sacred traditions, protect their spiritual power, and foster environments that are safe and authentic.

Although some traditions do require specific initiations or training for safety or spiritual reasons, toxic gatekeeping occurs when individuals or groups attempt to control who's allowed to practice magic or identify as a witch based on arbitrary, exclusionary standards relating to control of power. In this context, gatekeeping can stifle exploration, creativity, and personal spiritual growth within the broader community.

Knowing what's open (and closed) to you

As witchcraft has grown in popularity, especially through social media and online communities, it's become easier for individuals to access and adopt practices from various cultures without fully understanding their origins or significance. Curiosity and exploration are natural parts of any spiritual journey, but there's a line between respectful cultural appreciation and harmful appropriation.

As covered in Chapter 4, *cultural appropriation* occurs when elements of one culture — often a marginalized or oppressed one — are taken and used by members of a dominant culture in ways that strip them of their original meaning, often without consent or understanding. In the context of witchcraft, this can happen when sacred rituals, symbols, or deities are co-opted by individuals who have no connection to the culture from which they originated, often commodifying or misrepresenting them.

In covens, gatekeeping around cultural practices is sometimes necessary to ensure that members engage with spiritual traditions in a respectful and authentic manner. Covens around closed practices might exclude those who don't have cultural connections to their traditions or require members to undergo initiation before participating in secret rituals.

WARNING

Although gatekeeping can protect sacred traditions, it can also be taken too far. It's tricky to be the judge of who's allowed to practice certain forms of magic. If a gatekeeper won't consider the nuances of respectful engagement and cultural appreciation, people might be excluded from connection to different traditions — or even their own cultural practices — in respectful ways.

Some tell-tale signs of toxic gatekeeping follow:

- **Elitism and superiority:** People or groups claiming that only their tradition, lineage, or path is the right or true way to practice witchcraft, often dismissing or invalidating other forms of practice. This creates a hierarchy where only certain practitioners are considered legitimate.
- **Exclusion based on experience:** Dismissing or belittling newcomers, implying that one must have years of experience, certain initiations, or extensive knowledge to be considered a real witch. This discourages beginners from learning or experimenting with their practice.
- **Rigid rules and restrictions:** Insisting that there are strict, inflexible rules everyone must follow, such as certain tools, rituals, or deities required for witchcraft to be valid. This often ignores the diversity of spiritual practices and stifles personal growth and exploration.
- **Policing identity:** Telling people they can't call themselves a witch, practitioner, or part of a tradition unless they meet specific — often arbitrary — criteria. An example is claiming that one must be part of a specific coven or cultural group to be a true witch.

Protecting your power

You can transform gatekeeping into a healthy practice by focusing on your own development rather than policing others. *Power* is the ability to influence and shape the energy around you, whether through spell work, ritual, or personal will. This power is deeply personal and can be cultivated over time through spiritual discipline, connection with nature, and alignment with divine forces. Your power belongs to you.

WARNING

Your power can become vulnerable to external influences, such as energy-draining people, toxic environments, or spiritual manipulation. You can set boundaries that protect your energy (see the protection ritual in Chapter 8), ensuring that your magical practice is rooted in strength, clarity, and autonomy. This is especially important within covens, where group dynamics can sometimes complicate individual empowerment. Following are a few tips for protecting your power:

- **Establish clear boundaries:** Both in a coven and in your personal practice, it's crucial to have clear boundaries around your energy. This might involve saying no to participating in certain rituals that don't feel aligned with your intentions or setting limits on how much energy you give to others, even within a coven setting. Boundaries are a way of protecting your personal power so that it remains focused and effective.
- **Know when to shield:** Many witches practice energy shielding, a technique used to protect oneself from unwanted energies or psychic attacks. In a coven, this might involve creating a personal energetic barrier during group rituals or using protective talismans and symbols to guard your energy. This ensures that your personal power isn't diluted or hijacked during group workings.
- **Discernment in group energy work:** Group rituals can be powerful, but they also require careful discernment. When working with others in a magical setting, trust that everyone involved is aligned with the group's intentions. If you feel uncomfortable or sense that someone is misusing energy, voice your concerns or even remove yourself from the situation if necessary.
- **Mindful leadership:** In covens with a designated leader, such as a high priestess or high priest, it's their responsibility to protect the energy of the group while ensuring that no one individual is dominating or siphoning off others' power. This is why leadership in a coven must be ethical, mindful, and transparent. Good leaders guide the coven in a way that empowers every member, rather than consolidating power for themselves.

Although the concept of the coven originated with European paganism and proliferated through Wicca, the modern coven is evolving to empower a more diverse generation of witches, each bringing their own traditions and skills to the proverbial circle. As the coven evolves outside of Wicca, new kinds of leaders emerge, in contrast to the traditional coven priesthood of early covens. Chapter 18 covers ways to create your own groups and hold space for your evolving practices.

IN THIS CHAPTER

» Organizing your own spiritual communities

» Facilitating group circles

» Sustaining your energy and protecting your members

Chapter 18
Holding Space

If you spend a significant amount of time in spiritual circles, you might hear the term *holding space*. The modern use of the term became prevalent in the mid-to-late 20th century, with the rise of humanistic psychology and the development of therapeutic models emphasizing empathy and active listening. Psychotherapists and counselors often "hold space" for their clients, meaning they offer a nonjudgmental, supportive presence to help individuals explore their thoughts and emotions safely.

Witchcraft and other forms of modern paganism have borrowed from therapeutic models of group therapy, but to witches, holding space also has a sacred connotation. It's the intentional act of creating an environment for spiritual healing and transformation. The integrity of a spiritual space rests on the group facilitator's ability to engage in mindfulness, energy management, and safety. This chapter covers how to organize your own spiritual community, facilitate ritual practice, and ethically and sustainably offer your magical services.

Creating Sacred Space

In witchcraft, one of the primary functions of holding space is to create a sacred environment where magical work, rituals, or spells can take place. The word *sacred* sounds fancy, but sacred spaces are simply respectful and intentional settings for spiritual practices, as I outline in Chapter 10. Attending to sacred space creates a feeling of safety and connection among participants and ensures that members are in alignment.

REMEMBER

In Chapter 17, I introduce covens and offer tips for joining a coven. Forming and leading a coven involves a lot of experience and continual training and should be pursued with the support and consent of your community. Some traditions require specific time commitments, education, trials, or votes before allowing candidates to assume leadership roles within covens.

In modern witchcraft, there are many ways to create sacred space outside of formal covens. I've personally never led a formal coven, but I've cofacilitated a free monthly women's moon circle at my local yoga studio. For four years, that circle met each month on the full moon without fail. In that time, I learned a great deal about myself and the way to transform for the better by connecting with others consistently. My intention in starting the circle was to create a space that I thought was missing in my community, but I quickly learned that I needed the circle just as much as anyone else.

Over the course of four years, I unexpectedly faced many of my fears and developed tremendously as a speaker and teacher. When I started, I was so nervous I could barely speak without turning red — even with a group of just a few friends. The intensity of my reaction surprised me. Because I'd never put myself out there in that way, I had no idea that I would be so uncomfortable.

REMEMBER

It's okay to be uncomfortable in group settings. When you have a gift to share and you show up as your full, vulnerable self, most people tend to relate and are even more likely to open up themselves.

When I was starting out, I dreaded leading the circle to the point of paralysis. I couldn't do anything on meeting days except wait until the late afternoon, going over my words in my head. I felt relieved when I could finally start preparing the group space and let out all my pent-up energy. The next day, I was always so spent. To make things worse, I couldn't stop revisiting what I'd said, thinking of ways I could have phrased something better or wondering if someone's blank stare meant they hated the whole thing and would never come back. I realized that I had to work on my fear of public speaking and my intense anxiety about being disliked, which were rooted in old insecurities I hadn't yet faced.

Assessing your motivations

Anyone has the potential to organize a gathering or coven and bring special gifts to the table. Leadership can take many forms. Some are comfortable delivering sermons, for example, whereas others (like me) prefer to ask questions and get people talking. Orchestrating a spiritual gathering has no defined recipe, but you should ask yourself a few questions before deciding to take on the weighty task of holding sacred space:

- **What are my motivations?** Why do you want to start your own group? Maybe you're around like-minded individuals who want to join a formal coven, and you organically decide to take the lead. Other common motivations include offering something that doesn't already exist, sharing a vision for community, and developing skills. Be honest. If your motivation is only to gain a following or to make money, you might find that the energy it takes to sustain a consistent group is worth more than any amount of fame or fortune.
- **What are my qualifications?** You don't need a degree to start your own group, but it's helpful to have some kind of qualifications to guide you and help you promote your offerings. Did you go through a course of study, or do you have a certification that applies to your group's focus? Have you been working with clients for some time? Does your identity help you access certain groups or information? You can look to leaders you admire for development guidance, but there's no right or wrong way to share your talents as long as you approach self-development and self-promotion authentically and ethically. (See Chapter 17 for more information about ethics within covens.)
- **What kind of leader am I?** Evaluate your skills as a leader. How comfortable are you at organizing others? Are you more of a teacher or more of a facilitator? Do you like to impart wisdom? What's your preferred method of communication? Knowing your strengths will help you decide what kinds of groups and events to organize.
- **What are my time and energy commitments?** Starting your own circle is a big commitment, and consistency is important to establish community and build momentum. Ask yourself how much time you can realistically dedicate to organizing a regular gathering. You'll need to set aside time to plan and promote your events. Think about the other commitments you need to balance. Can you sustain the demand this new endeavor would impose on your life? Are you willing to sacrifice time usually spent on other things or nights with friends?
- **What do I have to offer and learn?** Group work is about give and take. Identify what you would most like to share. Maybe it's an insight or a skill you've been developing. At the same time, ask yourself what you would get out of dedicating yourself to holding space for others. It's okay to benefit from leading a group. For example, growing as a teacher and gaining experience that might lead to other opportunities is a nice side effect of having your own circle.
- **How does this fit into my spiritual path?** How do your motivations and skills contribute to spiritual growth for yourself and others? This could include promoting healing, engaging in activism, or simply learning how to be more present with others.

FUN FACT

I started leading full moon women's circles while I was working on my PhD. I needed a space away from my research, where I could see the principles I was studying in action. I was writing about the ways younger generations were turning to witchcraft, especially children of immigrants who felt a rift from Christianity and wanted to explore their ancestral traditions. In group circle, I saw this story repeated in so many different forms, through such varied cultural stories and individual experiences.

The experience taught me so much more than I could find in book and journal articles alone. Although I offered my take on the philosophical concepts I was learning, I also learned through community practice and stories. It was a mutually beneficial commitment between me, my cofacilitator, and our circle that enriched all participants (or the regulars who kept coming, anyway). Not only did I grow in practical terms — from leading groups of 4 to groups of 40 — I developed spiritually as well.

Starting your own circle

Once you've decided that you're going to start holding space, you'll need to do a bit of planning before you can take your show on the road. I find it's good to home in on a theme or scheme of organization to help you design your group and space. I recommend starting a journal dedicated to planning your circle. (I use the term *circle* to refer to any kind of group or space you're designing, including covens, healing gatherings, classes, retreats, and other meetings.) Before you involve others, you might start brainstorming with the following exercises:

- **Clarify your vision:** Set a timer for five minutes and freewrite all the words that come to mind when you think of your ideal circle.
- **Imagine a gathering:** Choose one of the words and write a one-paragraph scene that puts that word into action. For example, if one of your words is *conversation*, imagine an ideal group discussion. Describe the scene: What's the setting? What's the topic of discussion? How does the conversation move along? How many people are talking? How many are listening? How long does each person get to speak? Who are the participants? Repeat this activity for a few more words from your previous exercise, writing a scene for each word. Then reread your scenes. They represent snapshots of your ideal group and space.
- **Refine a focus:** Evaluate the scenes you've written. Do any stand out as surprising or original? For example, if your most riveting scene involves participants working on a group spell, maybe the focus of your circle can be building a collective book of spells. Now you've moved from a word to something that could turn into a strong theme.

Following are common themes to organize spiritual circles around:

- **Lunar/seasonal cycles:** Many circles get together on specific phases of the moon — usually the new and full moons, but I'd love to see a good waxing gibbous meeting! Seasonal meetings are also popular on solstices and equinoxes.
- **God/dess worship:** You could have a devotion-oriented circle that practices rituals and makes offerings to a deity or rotating deities. Similarly, you could have an ancestral worship group, with members either connected to the same ancestry or land or sharing their individual ancestral rituals with each other.
- **Divination:** A circle could focus on different forms of divination (tarot, astrology, tea leaf reading, and more), with meetings or classes revolving around learning and putting concepts into practice.
- **Nature-based rituals:** Some circles gather in natural settings like forests or beaches. The focus is on connecting to the land and developing *green witchcraft* (covered in Chapter 14).
- **Healing mind, body, and spirit:** Many spiritual gatherings highlight a particular kind of healing, which can manifest as longer retreats so participants have time to develop habits and experience transformation.
- **Spiritual activism:** Other circles might be motivated by a humanitarian aim, like organizing public ritual as protest. Find more on spiritual activism in Chapter 19.

REMEMBER

Circles can also focus on specific religious or traditional practices, such as Wiccan observances or indigenous rituals. These are usually carried out in covens and other closed groups that might require initiation, as I cover in Chapter 17.

Having an organizational scheme based on a strong theme can help you promote your events and attract your ideal audience. It can guide you through all parts of the planning process and support you as you hold space for others. Ultimately, the way you organize your circle should prioritize spiritual connection, but it's also a highly practical way to approach your work.

TIP

Take this from personal experience: Sometimes a concept blows your mind, and you're really excited about it, but if it's overly complicated or too specific, others might not understand it. If your concept is on the philosophical side, make sure it's also practical and easy to communicate in simple terms. You can keep your philosophy in mind while meeting people where they are. This comes easier with practice!

Finding a container

Groups can't form without spaces. This seems obvious, but when you choose a place as an afterthought instead of a core component of your plan, you run the risk of disruptions that can mess with the vibe you're trying to cultivate. Being intentional about the gathering spaces helps build community.

TIP

You want the setting to fit your focus and your practical needs. For instance, if you plan on doing body work, a yoga studio that provides mats and bolsters is a far better choice than a concrete court or a cavernous atrium. I like to think of the spaces chosen as containers for energies. Containers come in all forms. You might want a small, cozy one with low light for a group focused on processing emotional energies. An airy and bright container lends itself to a book-learning environment.

Consider these things when choosing a space:

- **Online or in-person:** In-person spaces are great for building a local following, whereas online spaces can capture a wider audience and offer asynchronous interaction through media like chat channels.
- **Permanent or temporary:** Having a consistent space can foster familiarity and grow local community, whereas temporary spaces like markets and pop-ups can spread the word and are usually cost-effective. Some spaces are seasonal due to weather, and some lend themselves to retreat spaces for one-time travel.
- **Private or public:** For obvious reasons, private spaces are usually preferred for creating sacred spaces. Participants tend to feel more secure and are more likely to open up in emotional ways. On the other hand, sometimes public spaces are sought for certain practices or performances — like nature rituals on public lands, chants at mass protests, and shrines to memorialize the departed.
- **Intimate or open attendance:** A space can restrict the number of people you can invite. A small space might be fine if you can't energetically support more than a certain number of people. If you can manage as many people as possible, or if you're holding something like a conference, you might consider a larger event space or an online platform that can support large traffic.
- **Free or fee-based:** Free events help you reach new people and foster an inclusive environment, but charging a fee can help you build a sustainable program that incentivizes commitment and helps you include more valuable offerings. Either way, consider whether you would like to require RSVPs to anticipate attendance.

Choosing a space can be an opportunity to think of how you might join with community partners. Many businesses like retail shops and fitness studios have rentable spaces, or you might be able to strike up a mutually beneficial agreement to share the space. Collaborative spaces are becoming more common as artists come together to combat rising rents and share amenities and materials. Leveraging multiple followings can help you get the word out. Other considerations include atmosphere, safety, and accessibility.

RISE OF THE TECHNOPAGANS

Technopagans are practitioners of modern paganism, witchcraft, or related spiritual paths who gather primarily in online spaces or who use digital tools in their spiritual practices. Technopagans blend ancient traditions with modern innovations, recognizing the potential of technology to connect, create, and empower their magical work. For these witches, the digital realm serves as a sacred space where they can gather, learn, and share their craft, even when physical proximity isn't possible.

I first heard the term technopagan in *Buffy the Vampire Slayer*. Miss Calendar, the computer teacher at Sunnydale High, was an undercover witch who saved spells on floppy disks and threw around terms that were completely alien in the late 90s, like *cyber-coven*. I later found out that technopaganism is an actual thing, at least in theory. The concept explored how some people were blending modern technology with ancient, Earth-based spiritual practices like paganism and witchcraft.

In practice, technopaganism is constantly evolving. Whether they use the term or not, technopagans come together in virtual spaces such as forums, social media groups, and specialized platforms dedicated to witchcraft and paganism. These online gatherings allow for a wide exchange of knowledge, from sharing spells, rituals, and spiritual experiences to discussing how to use digital in magical practice.

Platforms like Discord, TikTok, Patreon, Reddit, and Instagram, along with blogs, podcasts, and YouTube channels, serve as modern-day covens where technopagans can meet, discuss, and celebrate their paths. For many, these digital connections provide the same sense of community and spiritual enrichment as traditional in-person covens or gatherings.

(continued)

(continued)

What sets technopagans apart is their integration of technology into their magical workings, which I explore further in Chapter 20. This might include using apps for moon phases or creating digital altars. Some technopagans view the internet itself as a kind of "virtual ether," a space that mimics the spiritual or energetic realms of magic. In this way, they see technology not as separate from nature or spirituality but as an extension of the magical and energetic networks that already exist in the world. Whether they're coding sigils into websites, using online randomizers for divination, or conducting virtual rituals via video calls, technopagans embrace the digital age as an opportunity for new forms of spiritual connection and expression.

Getting the word out

Good things take time to develop, but too often I see group leaders take the "if I build it, they will come" approach to their new endeavors. So many things are competing for our attention that it's crucial you have a promotion plan and devote as much time to communications as you do to planning the contents of your events. I know the business side of holding space doesn't come naturally to all who are spiritually inclined, and that's okay! Learning occurs by trying things and seeing what works. Here are a few ways to make sure you're reaching the people who would most connect with what you're offering:

- **Social media:** Consider creating a unique handle for your event or establishing an event page or channel where members know to look for your latest offerings. You can also leverage other organizations' social media by posting to their pages, where allowed, and tagging cosponsors or other potential partners. The more organizers who are involved, the greater your potential audience.
- **Email newsletter:** Collect members' contact information through a secure application, so they can opt into receiving regular newsletters about event info. Make sure you have their consent to contact them, and avoid spamming them, so you can foster trust and achieve a good open rate for your messages.
- **Free calendars:** Many communities have free calendars through their official city websites or news publications. Post your events everywhere you can, including at physical locations around town, like on community bulletin boards at coffee shops.
- **Content creation:** Spend a manageable amount of time offering resources via your social media accounts and websites to attract followers. This could be a valuable bit of research that calls attention but leaves people wanting more. Make sure to tag your content accordingly for search engine optimization,

so when people search within the category of your offerings, you're more likely to come up in search results.

- **Follow-ups:** I can't stress enough the importance of following up with individuals shortly after an event. Following up helps establish authentic relationships and opens avenues for feedback.

Practice patience and positivity. It took years for my following to grow and before I was filling my events to capacity. It's good to have benchmarks for the number of participants, but only you can decide what's worth your time. Having a few people who are invested and excited is better than a room full of disinterested people.

TIP

I evaluate attendance seasonally, analyzing performance against my goals, and making adjustments. It helps me keep a realistic pulse on my impact and decide if it's time to either let something go or double down my efforts.

Consecrating the space

To *consecrate* means to dedicate something for a sacred purpose. No matter the setting or audience, holding space involves creating a cohesive, focused, and energetically safe environment for all participants. As the circle leader, you'll be responsible for maintaining the energetic boundaries of the ritual space and ensuring that the group remains aligned with the circle's intent. This often includes managing the flow of energy within the group, keeping distractions or negative energies at bay, and ensuring that each participant feels welcome and included.

This can be overwhelming the first few times you hold space, especially if you're sensitive to others' energies. A few techniques can help you manage a group's collective energy within a space (covered in more detail in Chapter 10), including these:

- **Cleansing the space:** Before the gathering, you can clear the space by burning herbs and incense with open windows. This neutralizes any energy that's been hanging around from previous spiritual workings.
- **Casting a circle:** This is one of the most common ways of containing energies in witchcraft. The circle creates a boundary between the mundane world and the sacred, marking a space where magical energy can flow freely while being protected from unwanted outside influences. (See Chapters 3 and 12 for more instructions on casting circles.)
- **Calling the quarters:** Practitioners may call upon and represent the elements (earth, air, fire, water) to "hold space" at the four cardinal directions, ensuring the space is balanced and energetically aligned. (See Chapter 12 for ritual instructions for calling the quarters.)

- **Evocation of deities/spirits:** Practitioners may evoke specific deities, ancestors, or spirit guides to oversee the space and lend their energy to the ritual, providing additional spiritual protection and guidance.

REMEMBER

Although I've been using the word *circle* to represent all kinds of gatherings, the circle is the traditional formation of choice for a reason. It's one of the most foundational and ancient symbols in witchcraft and many other spiritual traditions. In ritual magic, the circle serves as a sacred boundary, a container for energy, and a symbol of unity and protection. Gathering in a circle can unite the energies of the participants; in a circle, energy is shared and flowing, taking the pressure off the leader to manage many individual energies at once. In Chapter 16, I dive more deeply into what I mean by energy and how witches work with others' energies.

Taking Responsibility

When you're holding space, you're providing a nonjudgmental, supportive container for participants to engage in deep, sometimes emotional, inner work. In transformative rituals — such as rites of passage, initiation ceremonies, or spells aimed at personal growth — holding space can involve bearing witness to someone's transformation while energetically supporting them in the process. You *hold space* by maintaining focus and presence, ensuring the ritual unfolds smoothly and that the individual feels empowered to fully step into the intentions or changes they're seeking. The act of witnessing can be sacred in itself, imbuing rituals with care and intention.

Grounding your energy

Holding space for others can be draining under the best circumstances, so prepare your energy before interacting with your circle. For solitary practitioners, holding space might be an internal practice — ensuring that they're fully present and grounded before engaging in meditation, divination, or trance work. This involves preparing the mind and environment, clearing distractions, and setting an intention to stay centered throughout the spiritual work. The same goes with holding space for others. The preparation starts with you. Holding space for yourself requires self-compassion. If you can extend compassion to yourself, you can be more present for others. You can use the following tips to ground your energy:

- **Connect with your breath:** Begin by taking slow, deep breaths. Inhale deeply through your nose, hold for a few moments, and exhale slowly through your mouth. Focus on the feeling of the air filling your lungs, and release tension with each exhale. With each breath, allow yourself to feel more present in the moment. As you breathe in, visualize pulling energy down from your head into your body, and as you exhale, release any tension, stress, or scattered thoughts.

- **Visualize grounding roots:** Imagine roots growing from the soles of your feet (or from your tailbone if you're sitting). These roots extend down through the floor, past the surface of the earth, deep into the soil, and finally connect to the earth's core. Visualize the roots getting thicker and more solid, anchoring you securely. As your roots connect to the earth, visualize yourself drawing up stabilizing energy. Picture this energy as a warm, calming light or a soothing color that rises from the earth into your body. Allow this grounding energy to fill you, providing a sense of calm, strength, and stability.
- **Release excess energy:** As you connect with Earth's energy, you may become aware of any tension, anxiety, or scattered energy within you. With each exhale, visualize sending this excess energy back down through your roots, where it can be neutralized and absorbed by the earth. Focus on reaching a balance where your energy feels steady and calm, neither too high (overactive or anxious) nor too low (lethargic or drained). Visualize your body as a clear vessel, filled only with the grounding, stable energy you need.

Communicating clearly and compassionately

Clear communication is the key to maintaining the flow of energy and the continuity of the group. You can use the following strategies to communicate effectively with your circle, especially for discussion-oriented groups:

- **Set clear intentions and ground rules:** In your announcements and promotions and at the start of the circle, clearly communicate the purpose of the gathering. Whether it's a discussion, a ritual, or a healing circle, setting an intention ensures everyone is in agreement and aligned with the energy of the gathering. Gently lay out simple guidelines to ensure respectful communication and participation.
- **Open with a centering practice:** Just as you grounded your energy before engaging with others, you may lead your group through a short exercise to settle into the space. This can look like breathing as a group, moving together, or sharing a moment of silence.
- **Create a speaking structure:** In circles where you want to ensure everyone has a chance to speak without interruption, you can use a talking stick or another sacred object. The person holding the object is the one speaking. It helps keep the flow of conversation smooth and focused.

- **Encourage active listening:** As a facilitator, show that you're fully present when someone else is speaking by making eye contact, nodding, and refraining from interrupting. Encourage others to do the same. After someone shares, you may briefly summarize their key points to demonstrate understanding and encourage the group to engage with what's been said.
- **Guide the energy with open-ended questions:** Keep the conversation flowing by asking open-ended questions that invite deeper reflection or exploration. These questions should encourage sharing without forcing anyone to participate.
- **Keep the focus on the intention:** If the discussion starts to veer off-topic or get too tangential, gently bring it back to the original intention or purpose of the gathering.

TIP

If one person dominates the conversation, don't be afraid to politely interject. You can do this by affirming something the person said and gently guiding the discussion back to the group with an open-ended question, ensuring others have a chance to speak.

Because sharing can bring out sensitive topics, remain aware of emotional responses. In my years facilitating circles, I witnessed every emotion under the sun. Every situation is different, and over time I became more comfortable being present with others' emotions and responding intuitively. Until you develop your own intuition for group facilitation, err on the side of deep listening.

Allow pauses and silences, even if they feel awkward. It's easy to rush past difficult emotions. For example, if a participant gets choked up while talking about something, you might have the impulse to say "Oh, it's okay," and change the focus. In my experience, it's best to give them time to find the words. Sometimes if you can manage to wait past the point of comfort, you can help someone make a breakthrough.

WARNING

Some expressions of emotion can be disruptive to the group as a whole, such as excessively angry rants or *trauma dumping*, the act of oversharing personal, often distressing, emotional experiences without considering consent to receiving such information. Although it might be cathartic for one person to share in this way, it could trigger others who aren't ready to face their own emotions. Remember that unless you're a licensed therapist, you're probably not fully equipped to handle a group's unbridled expression of traumatic experiences. I find it helpful to have some mental health resources on hand to share with the group.

Holding space strikes a delicate balance between fostering openness and enforcing rules of engagement. Through your rules and talents of facilitation, you can harness the group's energy toward a collective intention so that everyone feels connected and safe.

Protecting your community

For many witches, the ultimate expression of spiritual freedom and empowerment comes from holding space for others. This act of leadership and community-building requires a deep understanding of personal and collective boundaries, as well as the responsibility that comes with holding space for others' spiritual journeys. Serious facilitators will make energy management a lifelong practice.

As you begin to hold space for others, you'll want to make sure you do the following:

- **Foster inclusivity:** Holding space means making sure that all voices are heard, especially those from marginalized or underrepresented communities. This might involve ensuring that rituals are nondiscriminatory and accessible to all members equally.
- **Enforce rules for emotional safety:** Group work can involve intense emotional experiences, especially in rituals that deal with transformation, shadow work, or healing. As a space-holder, you should create an environment where members feel emotionally safe. This might involve setting clear guidelines around confidentiality, consent, and mutual respect so that members can share openly without fear of their vulnerabilities being exploited.
- **Support individual growth:** Although group work is often focused on collective goals, it's equally important to encourage each member's personal spiritual journey. Holding space means supporting others in their personal growth, whether that involves learning new magical techniques, exploring their shadow side (see Chapter 4 for information about shadow work), or deepening their connection with deities. A good leader or space-holder knows when to step back and allow members to follow their own path.
- **Encourage accountability:** Leaders (and everyone) must be accountable for their actions within the group. This means being willing to admit mistakes and being open to feedback. Transparency helps maintain the trust and integrity of the group.
- **Practice self-care:** Holding space for others can be exhausting, so it's important for leaders and members alike to practice self-care. Self-care practices include having healthy boundaries, taking time to yourself, eating well, and getting enough sleep.

» **Foster shared leadership:** Even if you're the primary leader of your circle, it's important to create a sense of shared leadership. Encourage other members to lead rituals, share their knowledge, and take on responsibilities within the group. This creates a more balanced and inclusive environment. Consider having a co-organizer to pick up the slack when you can't show up fully.

Holding space in witchcraft also entails offering energetic protection during spiritual work. For example, when someone is going through a significant emotional release or connecting with spirit guides or ancestors, a practitioner might hold space by ensuring the area is protected from outside influences or unwanted entities. This might involve protective symbols, calling upon guardian spirits, or other forms of *spiritual shielding* or *cloaking* (covered in Chapter 8) to safeguard the spiritual environment.

TIP

Consider asking participants to sign a liability waiver that includes what they can expect and any potential risk involved with participation.

Opening to feedback

Taking feedback from your group is essential for the continuous development of your offerings. When you create a space where participants feel comfortable providing input, you gain valuable insights into how your methods are resonating with the group and what changes you must make.

Criticism is difficult to process, especially when you're starting a new thing. When working with groups consistently, it's inevitable that you'll encounter someone who's unhappy with something you've said or done — or something you didn't say or didn't do. This is part of the territory of taking risks and doing new things. You'll have to use discernment about what feedback is worth taking seriously, but if you're into holding space for the long haul, you'll need to listen to your people and commit to constant self-development.

FUN FACT

This was hard for me at first. When you create something so close to your heart, criticism about your creation can feel personal. During my first year leading circle, I was so scared of feedback that I never asked for it. But that didn't stop my overthinking, and ultimately, I proved to be my own worst enemy. As I gained confidence, I became more open to hearing others' thoughts about how I could improve.

TIP

I like to build feedback into the agenda. When facilitating discussion, I ask participants to share what they love the most about the offering and what they would like to see more. It's a gentle way for them to tell me what they think, and it's a gentle way for me to receive feedback.

Feedback allows you to assess which elements of the circle are effective, such as the structure, the energy flow, or the types of activities offered, and which may need adjustment. Incorporating feedback also helps you, as the facilitator, grow and refine your skills. It can highlight areas where you may need to improve, such as communication and time management. It can open your eyes to continuing education you can engage in, like sensitivity trainings or health certifications. Over time, this process of receiving and acting on feedback will strengthen both your facilitation style and the overall quality of your circle's offerings.

Going into business

Making money holding space is a touchy subject. Many spiritual people tend to recoil at the mention of money or feel shame if they're making any profit off their offerings. Others might be on the other end of the spectrum, losing sight of why they started holding space once their ventures become profitable. I advocate for a temperate approach that balances everyone's needs.

There's nothing wrong with making a living as a space-holder or spiritual leader. The fact that people are willing to pay you indicates that you have something valuable to offer. Once I addressed the roots of my insecurity and realized that there was a big demand for my services, I started charging for some of my events, and I've gradually increased my rates over the years. What started as volunteer work evolved into part-time work. Now my client sessions and group classes make up a big part of my income, and I can fully devote myself to my spiritual offerings. Being paid has allowed me to reinvest in myself so that I can sustain the energy required to hold space consistently. It's also allowed me to open a semi-permanent space of my own within a larger collaborative.

That said, money creates new challenges, and I periodically reassess my motivations and whether certain pursuits are spiritually aligned. I've decided that I'm only comfortable teaching and offering services around my actual interests because those come from the heart. I'm not comfortable doing something just because I know it will be popular and sell out. If I'm bored, that's a good indication it's not the right choice for me. To keep things accessible, I create free or discounted options for people who might otherwise be priced out of my offerings.

WARNING

As social media influencers and life coaches have risen in popularity, *spiritual grifting*, or the exploitation of vulnerable populations for financial gain, is a growing threat. Although many spiritual workers have good intentions, some have taken advantage of trends to target individuals who are desperate for spiritual fulfillment.

The spiritual world isn't immune to multilevel marketing (MLM) schemes. In MLMs, spiritual or wellness products are often marketed as life-changing, pushing individuals to buy in and recruit others under the guise of personal growth, all while enriching those at the top of the pyramid. Similarly, cult-like organizations may manipulate followers through promises of enlightenment or community, using coercive control to extract money or labor while masking their true intentions.

Even organizers of expensive retreats, although not always exploitative, can prey on people seeking healing or spiritual transformation, charging exorbitant fees for basic services or teachings that are often commodified versions of indigenous or ancient practices. In all these cases, the grift lies in prioritizing profit over genuine spiritual growth, taking advantage of those who are in search of meaning, healing, or connection. To avoid hurting anyone — even unintentionally — make sure to center your spiritual ethics as you hold sacred space for others.

IN THIS CHAPTER

» Connecting personal practice with social justice issues

» Getting acquainted with the core principles of spiritual activism

» Choosing a cause and organizing in a collective

Chapter 19 Aligning with Spiritual Activism

Spiritual activism is the practice of engaging with social justice efforts through a personal spiritual lens. The concept emerged in late 20th and early 21st-century scholarship within feminist fields of study. Unlike activism rooted in organized religion or traditional dogma, spiritual activism is centered on the self as the foundation for change. As a spiritual activist, you aim to create a more just world by cultivating self-care and healing. You believe that changing the world begins by changing yourself, and empowering yourself nurtures the energy necessary to empower others.

For many practitioners, witchcraft isn't only a spiritual practice but also a form of resistance that honors marginalized identities and challenges systems of oppression. This perspective, sometimes referred to as *witch-activism*, holds that by cultivating inner power — through ritual, meditation, energy work, and community building — you can better support causes like environmental justice, gender equality, disability access, and LGBTQ+ rights. This chapter discusses the core principles and tools of spiritual activism and the kinds of self-care and social justice magic you can dedicate yourself to.

Organizing around Magic

As discussed in Chapter 1, witchcraft is inherently political because it has historically been rooted in resistance to patriarchy and colonization. Although you can practice without being politically minded, many modern witches are also spiritual activists. Unlike traditional activism, which often focuses on external goals and measurable outcomes, spiritual activism combines these goals with the inner values of compassion, peace, and unity. Through this lens, activism becomes a form of "sacred work" that not only seeks to change society but also transforms you, aligning the fight for justice with a journey of personal growth and ethics.

FUN FACT

Chicana intellectual Gloria Anzaldúa is credited for coining the term *spiritual activism*. She emphasized that by confronting and healing internalized oppression and expanding spiritual capacities, activists can develop the resilience and clarity they need to confront societal injustices and build inclusive, egalitarian communities.

REMEMBER

Spiritual activism is aligned with *intersectional feminism*, which is radically inclusive and serves oppressed and marginalized people. Intersectional feminism acknowledges the overlapping and interdependent systems of oppression — such as race, class, gender, sexuality, and ability — that shape individuals' unique experiences and access to power.

Many spiritual leaders have dedicated themselves to activism and could be retroactively considered spiritual activists, although they may not have identified exactly as such in their lives. For instance, Mahatma Gandhi used the term *satyagraha*, or *soul force*, which fueled India's independence movement through nonviolent resistance rooted in Hinduism, Jainism, and his personal spiritual values of truth and love. This philosophy partially inspired Martin Luther King, Jr., who grounded his teachings of love, equality, and resistance in his Christian faith.

Thich Nhat Hanh, a Vietnamese Zen Buddhist monk, introduced the concept of *engaged Buddhism* during the Vietnam War. His teachings combined mindfulness with social responsibility, urging people to recognize the suffering of others as their own and act with compassion and unity. His concept of *interbeing* highlights the interconnectedness of all beings, a foundational principle for many spiritual activists today.

Contemporary organizers who can be considered spiritual activists, based on the ways they integrate their spiritual ethics into personal practice, include these:

- **Malala Yousafzai:** Yousafzai is a Pakistani activist who advocates for girls' education. Her work is rooted in her Islamic faith and her belief in the transformative power of knowledge. She draws strength from her cultural and spiritual resilience as she resists systemic oppression of women and girls.

- **Vandana Shiva:** Shiva is an Indian scholar whose environmental activism is guided by the principles of interconnectedness and reverence for Earth. She advocates for sustainable agriculture and indigenous rights as sacred responsibilities to protect the planet.
- **Wangari Maathai:** Maathai is a Kenyan activist whose Green Belt Movement combined environmental conservation with community empowerment, grounded in her belief that caring for the earth and uplifting marginalized communities are spiritual acts of justice.
- **Adrienne Maree Brown:** Brown is a scholar of spiritual activism whose work interweaves principles of pleasure, healing, and community resilience, emphasizing that social change is most powerful when founded in joy, interconnectedness, and personal transformation. In her influential writings, she encourages activists to honor their inner lives, prioritize sustainable and regenerative practices, and view collective liberation as an act of radical love.

WARNING

Some critics of spiritual activism dismiss it as *slacktivism*, a term used to describe minimal or superficial support for a cause, often involving low-effort online actions such as liking, sharing, or commenting on social media posts, signing online petitions, or changing profile pictures to show solidarity. *Virtue signaling* is the act of publicly expressing opinions or sentiments intended to demonstrate your moral correctness or alignment with socially accepted values. Although this approach isn't necessarily ineffective, you should pair it with commitment to action and change.

One of the core tenets of true spiritual activism is dedication to the difficult work of personal awareness and evolution. As a spiritual activist, you commit yourself to a consistent practice of transformation. The most effective spiritual activists contribute their skills or share their experiences with larger groups and causes. Spiritual activists believe that there's no separation between self-development and collective change because the tools of spiritual activism foster inner resilience, a crucial factor for long-term commitment to a cause.

TIP

In this context, being "spiritual" isn't necessarily about having a specific belief system or being initiated into a tradition. It's more about knowing that you're part of a whole and learning how to take care of yourself so you can contribute to the collective.

Traditional activism can sometimes be marked by burnout, frustration, or even bitterness, especially when progress feels slow. Lacking a spiritual foundation as an activist may make it challenging to sustain your energies, leading to emotional fatigue and disillusionment. In contrast, spiritual activism is fortified by inner practices — like meditation, mindfulness, and self-reflection — that enable you to maintain your well-being, recognize your limits, and constantly find renewed purpose.

Aligning with core principles

Spiritual activism frames activism as *sacred work*, where each act of justice reflects higher values such as empathy, interconnectedness, and nonviolence. This approach to activism challenges you to move beyond merely reacting to injustice and to see your work as a conscious, purposeful expression of your beliefs. By grounding activism in spiritual practice, you become more intentional and compassionate in your actions. Here are a few core principles of spiritual activism:

» **Presence and mindfulness** allow you to engage in your work with full awareness and intention, cultivating the ability to observe rather than react impulsively. By grounding yourself in the present moment, you can better manage the emotional and mental toll of challenging work. Mindfulness practices help you bring a sense of calm and clarity to your actions, enabling you to respond thoughtfully to conflict and embody the peace you want to promote.

» **Compassion and empathy** become a guiding force, where you view others — even those who oppose you — as part of a shared human experience. This perspective allows for meaningful dialogue, reduces polarization, and fosters connections that transcend ideological divides.

» **Interconnectedness** encourages you to see the world as a web of relationships. When you fight for justice, you understand that your actions aren't isolated but influence a collective ecosystem of social, cultural, and environmental networks. This belief inspires a more holistic approach to change.

» **Nonviolence** is more than a tactic; it becomes a way of embodying peace as both a means and an end. Rooted in spiritual practice, nonviolence becomes an expression of inner peace, cultivated through mindfulness and compassion, and applied outwardly in ways that respect all beings.

» **Resistance** in spiritual activism is more than opposition; it's a sacred commitment to confront oppressive structures through resilience, courage, and love. This form of resistance is rooted in the understanding that opposing injustice isn't merely an obligation but a moral act that affirms the inherent dignity and worth of all.

Spiritual activism involves four core tools:

- **Inner reflection and therapy:** Techniques such as journaling or introspective dialogue that help you confront personal biases and internalized oppression, fostering self-awareness and integrity in your advocacy.
- **Community rituals:** Ceremonies and gatherings that build solidarity, honor shared intentions, and provide space for collective healing.
- **Storytelling and creative expression:** Art, music, and narratives that communicate values, inspire empathy, and bring attention to social issues in transformative ways.
- **Intentional rest and self-care:** Practices that prioritize physical, mental, and spiritual well-being to prevent energy drain and burnout, ensuring you have the energy and clarity to sustain long-term efforts.

Reflecting on the self

Self-reflection and personal transformation are central to the journey of spiritual activism. This process begins with an honest assessment of your own beliefs, biases, and assumptions, recognizing that effective activism requires you to address any inner barriers that might contradict the principles you aim to promote.

Through self-reflection, you can confront your own prejudices and dismantle conditioned judgments that could hinder your empathy or skew your understanding of social issues. By doing so, you can approach activism with self-awareness, knowing that you, too, are always learning and growing alongside the causes you support.

TIP

It's okay to adjust your viewpoints as you learn new information. Practice *humility*, the quality of having a modest view of your own importance, embracing openness to learning and growth. This sometimes involves *unlearning*, the conscious process of questioning, deconstructing, and letting go of ingrained beliefs, biases, and assumptions that uphold oppressive systems and social norms.

Personal transformation through self-awareness is a powerful form of preparation for the challenges of activism. It helps you develop resilience and compassion, both for yourself and for those around you. As you become more aware of your triggers, biases, and motivations, you might learn to respond with intention rather than reaction. This self-knowledge acts as an anchor during difficult moments in activism, when understanding and mutual respect are most needed.

Following are techniques for self-reflection:

- **Journaling:** Regular journaling is a powerful way to track thoughts, emotions, and biases, providing a safe space for self-exploration and honest reflection. Daily prompts or freewriting exercises can help you uncover your intentions, confront inner conflicts, and monitor your personal growth as an activist.
- **Meditation:** Practicing mindfulness meditation encourages you to observe your thoughts without judgment, fostering self-awareness and emotional regulation. Techniques like loving-kindness meditation enhance empathy through compassion rather than confrontation.
- **Affirmations and intentions:** Setting daily affirmations or intentions can help you maintain focus on personal growth and ethical alignment as an activist. By articulating values and aspirations each day, you reinforce the principles guiding your activism.

Healing through self-care

Healing and self-care are vital elements in sustaining a long-term commitment to activism, especially as you face the relentless challenges and emotional demands of social justice work. Spiritual activism recognizes that the struggle for justice must include caring for yourself as an act of resistance against systems that often dehumanize or disregard individual needs.

Activists are frequently exposed to difficult realities, stress, and even trauma, which can lead to burnout, compassion fatigue, and physical health issues. Addressing these effects requires not just momentary relief but ongoing practices that nourish your body, mind, and spirit, allowing you to continue your work from a place of strength and balance.

TIP

Integrating spiritual practices into self-care routines is an effective way to cultivate resilience, foster emotional renewal, and maintain your dedication to the cause. Practices like yoga, meditation, and ritual can help you center yourself and process your emotions.

Spiritual self-care encourages you to see self-compassion as inseparable from compassion for others, allowing you to offer support and empathy without depleting your own reserves. Through these practices, you learn to prioritize your own needs without guilt, realizing that sustained personal well-being is foundational to sustained collective action.

Spiritual self-care techniques include these:

- **Yoga:** Yoga combines physical movement, breathwork, and meditation, offering both physical and mental relief. You can use yoga to release tension, increase flexibility, and practice mindfulness, supporting both body and mind. Simple, restorative poses are especially useful for relaxation and grounding.
- **Ritual:** Rituals can mark personal milestones, set intentions, or help you release emotions. Examples include lighting candles, creating an altar, or engaging in ceremonial practices to honor personal progress or acknowledge difficult events. Rituals offer symbolic acts that deepen your spiritual commitment and sense of purpose.
- **Therapy:** Therapy provides a safe space to process stress, prevent burnout, and build emotional resilience, enabling you to sustain your work while prioritizing your mental well-being.
- **Shadow work:** Shadow work is a method of exploring aspects of yourself that are often suppressed or ignored. By acknowledging these "shadow" traits (such as anger or prejudice), you can integrate them healthily and prevent them from influencing your actions subconsciously (explored more in Chapter 4).
- **Nature connection:** Spending time in nature, whether through hiking, gardening, or simply sitting outdoors, has restorative effects. Connecting with the natural world reduces stress, provides perspective, and reminds you of the interconnectedness you strive to protect as an activist.

Expressing with sacred art and communal ritual

Creative expression plays a powerful role in spiritual activism, offering you unique tools for conveying spiritual ideals and catalyzing change. Art, music, and storytelling allow you to communicate complex emotions, ideas, and values in ways that transcend traditional discourse, resonating deeply with audiences across cultural and linguistic barriers.

REMEMBER

Sacred art is creative expression that embodies spiritual themes, rituals, or symbols, aiming to connect viewers with the divine, the transcendent, or deeper aspects of the human spirit. Through creative expression, spiritual activists can capture the soul of a movement, inspire empathy, and evoke the transformative vision of a just world.

Sacred art is especially effective for addressing issues that are often difficult to confront directly, such as systemic injustice, environmental degradation, and social inequality. Art provides a space for healing, reflection, and even confrontation, allowing you to engage with challenging topics in a transformative way.

For example, music can become a rallying cry that unites and empowers, whereas storytelling has the capacity to share diverse, often marginalized, perspectives that bring greater understanding and connection to the cause. Through these mediums, sacred art becomes not only an expression of personal belief but a powerful tool for public engagement, education, and advocacy.

Case studies of sacred art include:

- **Ai Weiwei:** The Chinese contemporary artist and activist uses sculpture, photography, and installations to speak out against government oppression and human rights abuses. Weiwei's work, influenced by his personal experiences and spiritual beliefs, often combines political critique with themes of compassion and resilience, embodying the role of art as a force for justice and awareness.
- **Ntozake Shange:** Shange used poetry, dance, and theater to explore Black womanhood, spirituality, and resilience. Her work highlights the spiritual dimensions of personal and collective healing, using art to empower, validate, and liberate voices within marginalized communities.
- **Edgar Fabián Frías:** Frías is a nonbinary, queer, indigenous (Wixarika) interdisciplinary artist whose art and installations imagine radical futures of collective care.

Examples of sacred art include:

- **Storytelling and spoken word:** Activists can share their personal journeys, cultural stories, or historical narratives to raise awareness and inspire empathy. Storytelling circles or performances encourage listeners to connect on an emotional level, building solidarity and understanding.
- **Collaborative art projects:** Murals, sculptures, memorials, and community art installations created with collective input emphasize unity and inclusivity, allowing communities to visually represent shared values and goals. These projects are not only visually impactful but foster a strong sense of community. Figure 19-1 shows a collective altar for George Floyd at the site of his death on Chicago Avenue in Minneapolis, Minnesota.
- **Music and chanting:** Music, whether traditional songs, original compositions, or protest chants, serves as a rallying tool, bringing people together in moments of empowerment, reflection, and collective action. Music can also convey complex spiritual and ethical messages, creating a deeper connection to the cause.

FIGURE 19-1: The George Floyd memorial and collective altar, a powerful site of spiritual activism.

Resisting in nonviolent ways

Resistance and political engagement form the core of spiritual activism, emphasizing action and resilience in the face of injustice. Spiritual activism views resistance not just as opposition to oppressive forces but as a positive, life-affirming commitment to justice, compassion, and equality. Activists draw from their spiritual beliefs to engage politically, advocating for policies and changes that align with values of interconnectedness, equity, and the dignity of all people.

TIP

One of the simplest ways you can resist oppression is to rest and find small joys in your daily life.

Joy and rest are acts of defiance against systems that thrive on exhaustion and division. Spiritual activists are increasingly embracing nontraditional forms of resistance, including these:

- **Joy as resistance:** Embrace joy as a form of defiance by creating and celebrating moments of happiness, gratitude, and connection within activist communities. Activities like dancing, storytelling, and sharing meals foster unity and provide strength, reminding activists of the beauty and dignity of the causes they uphold.

- **Radical rest:** Prioritize rest and self-care as essential acts of resistance against systems that devalue well-being. This can involve creating time for restorative practices, scheduling intentional breaks, and encouraging others to value and protect their own need for rest. Radical rest is born out of Audre Lorde's quote, "Caring for myself is not self-indulgence, it is self-preservation, and that is an act of political warfare." Today, Tricia Hersey, founder of The Nap Ministry, is at the helm of the "rest as resistance" movement.
- **Civil disobedience:** Engage in nonviolent protest as a means of drawing attention to injustice and catalyzing change. Acts of civil disobedience, such as sit-ins, marches, and strikes, disrupt societal norms and demand recognition of systemic issues, compelling others to acknowledge and address them.
- **Community solidarity networks:** Build networks that foster collective action and mutual aid. Community organizations, coalitions, and informal groups strengthen resistance efforts, offering practical support, shared resources, and a unified voice to stand against injustice.

W.I.T.C.H.

W.I.T.C.H., short for Women's International Conspiracy from Hell, was a radical feminist collective that emerged in the late 1960s, blending political activism with witchcraft-inspired imagery and performance art to provoke and protest patriarchy, capitalism, and social injustice. Formed in 1968 as part of the broader women's liberation and anti-war movements in the United States, W.I.T.C.H. used the figure of the witch — a historical symbol of female power, often demonized by society — as a symbol of resistance and empowerment.

By reclaiming the term *witch*, members of W.I.T.C.H. sought to challenge systems that threatened female autonomy. Their protests were theatrical and subversive; members dressed in black, wore pointed hats, and "hexed" institutions that they believed perpetuated sexism, inequality, and corporate greed. Their presence not only created a sense of fear and mystery around their activities but also drew attention to the ways in which society demonized women who challenged the status quo.

As a loosely organized network, W.I.T.C.H. chapters sprang up in cities across the U.S., each adapting the group's mission to address local issues, from economic inequality to environmental concerns. Their actions ranged from hexing Wall Street to staging "zaps," or protests, at beauty pageants and bridal fairs, aiming to dismantle societal expectations placed on women and expose the links between consumerism and female oppression.

Although the original W.I.T.C.H. disbanded in the early 1970s, its legacy has endured, inspiring later feminist groups and activists who see witchcraft as both a spiritual practice and a tool for resistance. In recent years, a resurgence of interest in W.I.T.C.H.-inspired activism has emerged, with contemporary feminists using the witch as a powerful icon for challenging patriarchy, advocating for reproductive rights, and fostering community among marginalized groups. W.I.T.C.H. remains a potent reminder of how symbols of the past can be reclaimed and reinvented as powerful tools for social change. You can read more about reclaiming movements in Chapter 1.

Attending to collective action

In Chapters 17 and 18, I discuss joining a coven and holding space for group practice, both of which provide foundational instructions on how to work with other witches and lead groups. When working toward collective action, it's important to practice cultural sensitivity and use tools for navigating potential conflicts between individual spiritual beliefs and the activist community's objectives. Spiritual activist groups center around inclusivity, resilience, and rootedness.

Practicing radical inclusivity

Practicing *radical inclusivity* within spiritual activism means creating spaces and movements that embrace people of all backgrounds, identities, and beliefs, fostering a sense of belonging that respects individual differences as essential to collective strength. This approach challenges you to go beyond mere tolerance, cultivating a deep commitment to understanding and uplifting the unique experiences and contributions of marginalized and underrepresented communities.

In spiritual activism, radical inclusivity involves actively listening to diverse perspectives, recognizing how intersecting forms of oppression affect individuals differently, and addressing unconscious biases within activist spaces. Radical inclusivity is itself an act of resistance to oppressive systems that exclude and marginalize groups of people.

Empowering the disempowered

REMEMBER

Rituals and ceremonies in activist spaces provide powerful opportunities for grounding, solidarity, and collective healing. Community resilience is built from consistent engagement and support.

These practices allow you to connect with your activist purpose on a deeper, often spiritual level, transforming the physical space of protest or gathering into a sanctuary of shared values and intentions. Rituals in activist spaces might range from simple symbolic acts, like lighting candles for remembrance or solidarity, to larger, culturally rooted ceremonies that honor the land, acknowledge ancestors, or seek guidance from spiritual sources. These rituals help you pause, reflect, and renew your commitment, building a sense of unity that transcends individual motivations and connects you to a shared vision of justice, healing, and transformation.

In addition to fostering resilience, rituals in activist spaces create a safe, sacred environment where you can process emotions, release grief, and celebrate victories, no matter how small. Ceremonies can serve as an outlet for expressing anger, loss, hope, or gratitude, allowing you to process and honor the emotional realities of your work.

Engaging community and local leaders

To ensure cultural respect and inclusivity, these rituals should be led by community elders or spiritual leaders who understand the nuances and histories of these practices.

Engaging community leaders — particularly spiritual leaders, elders, and influential local figures — can significantly enhance the reach and impact of activist initiatives. Spiritual leaders can be priests or other members of the clergy, but they don't have to be part of traditional institutions. They can be the therapists and healers in your life, or the teachers and coaches who help you navigate your body in this world. They can be your local librarian or a volunteer at the art collective.

TIP

The best way to find spiritual-minded community leaders is to be actively involved in spaces of collective activism and healing. Visit your local meditation centers, parks, art galleries, and practice studios.

These community leaders often hold positions of respect and trust. They bring cultural wisdom and ethical guidance that can anchor activism in the local context, helping to ensure that efforts are not only impactful but culturally respectful and sensitive. In practice, this engagement might look like inviting these figures to speak at events, collaborate on community programs, or provide mentorship and support to younger activists.

TIP

Building interfaith and multicultural alliances is another powerful way to strengthen activism by embracing the diverse values and beliefs that unite communities in a shared vision of justice and compassion. Practical steps to creating these alliances include hosting regular interfaith dialogues, organizing multicultural events that celebrate shared values, and establishing networks for ongoing support and communication.

Effective alliances require sensitivity to different beliefs and practices, as well as a commitment to inclusivity, ensuring all voices are respected and represented. By creating these partnerships, you can harness the unique strengths and insights of each community, forging a coalition that transcends individual differences and unites you toward a common purpose.

Paths of the Witch Activist

Witch activists draw on their spiritual powers to fuel social change, reclaiming symbols of resistance to challenge injustices. You might take many paths of spiritual activism as a witch. All spiritual activism is *embodied activism*, a form of activism that emphasizes the integration of physical, emotional, and *somatic* (body-based) awareness into social justice work. The human body carries personal and collective experiences, such as trauma, privilege, or oppression. Embodied activism encourages you to stay connected to your own body and emotions, which can prevent burnout, foster resilience, and allow for a more compassionate, empathetic engagement with others. In this section, I lay out a few common paths of spiritual activism for you to explore.

Eco-spirituality

Eco-spirituality is a path that emphasizes the sacredness of nature and its interconnected relationship with Earth. Witch activists on this path engage in environmental justice, believing that protecting the planet is a spiritual responsibility and a necessary step toward a more just and sustainable world. Eco-spiritual witches use rituals, land blessings, and nature-based practices to advocate for conservation and animal rights, fight climate change, and support sustainable living. This path honors Earth as a living being, viewing environmental activism not only as an ecological effort but as a profound spiritual mission that calls for the healing of both the planet and humankind.

You can include several types of eco-spiritual practices:

- **Nature rituals:** Conduct rituals that honor and protect animals and natural elements — such as forests, rivers, and oceans — using offerings or blessings to foster a deeper connection to Earth.
- **Land blessings:** Perform land blessings and cleansing ceremonies to promote harmony between people and the land, especially in areas affected by environmental harm. (See Chapter 7 for a libation to the land ritual.)

- **Seasonal celebrations:** Observe the wheel of the year, marking solstices, equinoxes, and harvest festivals that align with nature's cycles, reinforcing commitment to sustainable practices. (See Chapter 22 for 10 days of observance.)
- **Ecological altars:** Create an altar with natural elements like stones, leaves, or flowers as a daily reminder of your ecological commitment.
- **Community gardens:** Establish or support community gardens that provide fresh, organic produce, particularly in food deserts, promoting self-sufficiency and local food access. Gardens are great sites to trade information, save seeds, and swap plants.
- **Herbalism and plant medicine:** Learn and practice herbal medicine to promote health and well-being within the community, focusing on locally grown herbs and plants. Use food preparation as a ritual to celebrate local, sustainable ingredients, incorporating intentions of nourishment and community care. (For more, see Chapter 14 about green witchery.)
- **Conservation advocacy:** Use social platforms, letter-writing campaigns, or local council involvement to advocate for conservation policies, climate action, and sustainability.

Gender equity and reproductive rights

Many witch activists support gender equality, reproductive rights, and bodily autonomy, viewing these as fundamental to personal sovereignty and empowerment. This can involve advocating for access to reproductive healthcare, addressing gender-based violence, and challenging gender norms. Specific practices you can incorporate into your magic rituals include these:

- **Empowerment rituals:** Conduct rituals that protect bodily autonomy and empower individuals, using symbols of strength and self-sovereignty.
- **Sacred circle gatherings:** Create safe spaces for women, trans, and non-binary individuals to discuss and support reproductive rights and bodily autonomy.
- **Advocacy for reproductive healthcare:** Write to representatives, support reproductive rights organizations, and raise awareness on social media.
- **Intentional hexes:** Use spell work, sigils, and collective rituals to symbolically weaken patriarchal structures, channeling intention to disrupt oppressive systems and empower those affected by sexism and inequality. This practice often includes binding spells or protection rituals aimed at supporting gender equality and dismantling misogyny.

WARNING

Hexes are advanced forms of magic that should be approached with extreme care. When we direct magic toward outside figures, our energy can become bound with our objects of attention. Make sure you know the basics of spellcasting, including grounding, boundary, and protection spells (see 10 foundational spells in Chapter 21). Always research the kind of magic you're using and seek teachers and community for support with advanced magic. See Chapter 4 for more on the ethics of hexing.

Indigenous rights and decolonization

The path of indigenous rights within witch activism involves supporting and honoring the sovereignty, traditions, and sacred practices of indigenous peoples. This path addresses issues of cultural appropriation by encouraging non-indigenous practitioners to respect the boundaries of indigenous spiritual practices and to avoid using them out of context. Witch activists engaged in *decolonization* work strive to return stolen land, respect indigenous wisdom, and promote indigenous-led solutions to environmental and social challenges. (See more in Chapter 2.)

This path emphasizes allyship, respectful engagement, and the commitment to amplify indigenous voices, focusing on reparative justice and respect for indigenous knowledge as a cornerstone of spiritual activism. The following actions support decolonization activism:

- **Allyship with indigenous movements:** Support indigenous-led movements, such as the Land Back campaign (see Chapter 4), through donations, amplifying their messages, and participating in allyship education.
- **Decolonizing practices:** Practice decolonization within witchcraft by questioning the origins of spiritual practices and honoring the rightful cultural context of your work.
- **Land acknowledgments:** Begin rituals, gatherings, or personal practices with an acknowledgment of the indigenous peoples of the land. Include ways that people can contribute to allyship and indigenous movements with their time and money.
- **Indigenous art and knowledge:** Purchase art and spiritual resources directly from indigenous creators, and prioritize indigenous wisdom in eco-spiritual and activist practices.
- **Local partnerships:** Collaborate with local indigenous groups to support land reclamation and conservation efforts, aligning witchcraft activism with indigenous-led initiatives.

Anti-racism and intersectional justice

Many witchcraft activists focus on dismantling racism and advocating for intersectional justice that addresses the overlapping systems of oppression based on race, gender, class, and ability. This involves challenging systemic racism and promoting inclusivity within spiritual and activist communities, including the following practices:

- » **Self-reflection and unlearning biases:** Engage in shadow work or journaling to examine and dismantle internalized biases, using witchcraft as a tool for personal transformation.
- » **Altar work for justice:** Create an altar dedicated to anti-racism and inclusivity, with symbols, candles, or photos that represent the commitment to intersectional justice.
- » **Community education and dialogue:** Host or participate in workshops that address intersectionality and anti-racism within spiritual and witch communities.
- » **Spells for protection and empowerment:** Perform spells and protections for activists, marginalized communities, and justice movements.
- » **Financial and organizational support:** Donate to anti-racism organizations and amplify their work in community circles, social media, and ritual spaces.

Queer magic and LGBTQ+ rights

Queer magic within witch activism celebrates and empowers LGBTQ+ identities, reclaiming the historical connections between queerness and mystical practices. For queer witch activists, magic becomes a tool for self-acceptance, healing, and resistance against discrimination. This path explores the intersections of gender, sexuality, and spirituality, celebrating the fluid and transformative nature of both identity and magical practice. Through rituals that honor queer ancestors, gender-expansive deities, and non-binary energies, queer magic affirms the power of living authentically and fights for LGBTQ+ rights. Embracing queerness as a sacred expression of diversity creates spaces where all identities are celebrated and where spirituality fuels the movement for equality and liberation.

- » **Rituals honoring queer ancestors:** Create rituals to honor queer ancestors and historical figures who paved the way for LGBTQ+ rights, evoking their courage and resilience.
- » **Gender-expansive deities and archetypes:** Work with deities and archetypes that embrace gender fluidity, non-binary identities, and the diversity of human experience.

- **Queer circles and coven spaces:** Form or join inclusive spiritual communities or covens where LGBTQ+ individuals feel supported and celebrated. (See Chapter 17 on covens and Chapter 18 on holding space.)
- **Rituals of self-affirmation:** Use affirmations, mirror work, and self-blessing rituals to celebrate identity, fostering self-acceptance and empowerment.
- **Advocacy for LGBTQ+ rights:** Participate in or organize awareness campaigns, fundraisers, or events that support LGBTQ+ rights and promote inclusivity.

Wellness and healing justice

Witchcraft activism frequently emphasizes mental health, disability accessibility, and community healing, particularly for marginalized communities. This can include advocating for access to health resources, trauma-informed practices, and alternative healing modalities that address emotional and spiritual well-being. Try these practices to promote health and healing justice:

- **Healing circles and safe spaces:** Organize or participate in circles dedicated to emotional support and collective healing, with a focus on trauma-informed practices. (See Chapter 18 on holding space.)
- **Champion accessibility:** Ensure your community spaces and offerings provide access to people with disabilities and neurodivergent people.
- **Mindfulness and grounding practices:** Use a grounding technique, such as breathwork, meditation, or protective visualization to manage stress and emotional fatigue.
- **Rituals for releasing trauma:** Develop personalized rituals that focus on releasing stored trauma and inviting resilience, such as symbolic cleansings or cord-cutting ceremonies. (See Chapter 12.)
- **Advocacy for accessible mental health care:** Support policies and organizations that promote mental health resources, especially for marginalized communities.

TIP

Remember that spiritual activism is as much about inner transformation as it is about external impact. Sustain your journey by cultivating compassion, self-reflection, and resilience, knowing that each small, intentional action — whether a ritual, a protest, or a moment of mindful presence — contributes to a larger wave of change. Trust in the power of your own growth to inspire and uplift the collective movement for justice and healing.

IN THIS CHAPTER

» Working with challenging energies

» Imagining new forms of practice

» Becoming a magical ancestor

Chapter 20
Creating the Future

How can you adapt to today's challenges as a witch while staying true to the heart of your craft? In a world shaped by increasing climate crises, unprecedented technological leaps, and stark social inequities, witches are called to imagine new possibilities. How can you practice magic that honors the earth in an age of environmental instability? How can you build inclusive, vibrant communities in this era of artificial intelligence? And how do you create space for both innovation and tradition?

This chapter invites you to envision the future of witchcraft — one that honors its history while embracing its potential to grow, adapt, and inspire. In these next several pages, I outline contemporary challenges to magical practices and the opportunities they present for modern witchcraft.

Preparing for (More) Modern Challenges

Eventually, the current swell of pop culture interest in witchcraft will wane, and authentic, dedicated practitioners will be faced with the task of what comes next. In Chapter 13, I explain my philosophy on divination and introduce the idea that the future isn't separate from the present moment. Divining the future means seeing patterns that already exist and predicting how they will play out. In this way, predictions are forms of creative documentation — part truth, part imagination.

To state an obvious point, the present is a continuation of the past. The past undoubtedly shapes your current practices. Being a witch often means connecting to your ancestors and the traditions that came before. But as much as the past can inspire you, you're also creating something new in the present through your own unique practices.

REMEMBER

Witchcraft is a creative act. Creativity happens in the here and now, as you act on your intentions.

Modern witchcraft is rooted in the happenings of the world. If you mean to practice witchcraft faithfully, you can't ignore society's problems. It's tempting to practice magic as an escape or to momentarily feel powerful. But as I discuss in Chapter 19, a practice that empowers you while neglecting the world amounts to a form of *spiritual bypassing*, or using magic to avoid facing hard truths.

TIP

As a modern witch, you can use your creative powers to make better sense of the past and establish a long-lasting legacy of empowerment for your spiritual descendants.

Increasingly, climate change threatens the natural world you hold in reverence, systemic injustices call for social action and awareness, and technology reshapes how you connect and share your craft. These aren't problems to bypass with spells of comfort or rituals of escape. Instead, they're calls to deepen your practice and to ground your magic in real, impactful work.

Raising energy through social unrest

Witches have never existed too far from politics. As I cover in Chapter 1, during the Early Modern period in Europe and North America, political and religious upheaval fueled widespread witch hunts. Witchcraft accusations reflected fear, misogyny, and political control. In times of war, plague, or famine, witches became scapegoats for societal instability. Authorities used witch hunts to maintain control and suppress dissent, particularly targeting women, healers, and marginalized individuals.

FUN FACT

In the 1960s, witchcraft became a powerful symbol of feminist resistance and counterculture during a time of political upheaval. Emerging during the rise of second-wave feminism, W.I.T.C.H. was a radical feminist group that protested patriarchy, capitalism, and systemic oppression.

Members dressed as witches, using theatricality and symbolism to challenge societal norms. W.I.T.C.H. hexed Wall Street in 1968, criticizing the capitalist system. Their protests used satire and witchcraft-inspired imagery to empower women and draw attention to issues like gender inequality and economic exploitation. (For more, see Chapter 19.)

WARNING

The witch's political identity is complicated. In many colonized regions, witchcraft was used as a weapon against indigenous spiritual practices. Colonizers often labeled native magical practices as *witchcraft* to demonize and suppress cultural identities. To this day, some magical practitioners of indigenous traditions reject the label *witch*.

For instance, during the revolution that overthrew French colonial rule, enslaved Africans in Haiti combined African spiritual practices with Catholicism, creating *Vodou*. Rituals including spells and sacrifices were used to inspire rebellion and evoke protection and strength. Practices perceived as witchcraft by colonial powers eventually became symbols of resistance. (More on this in Chapter 2.)

REMEMBER

Today witchcraft is increasingly seen as a political statement that includes indigenous spiritualities.

Modern witches use their historical demonization to raise power and challenge systems of oppression, reclaiming the label as a symbol of power, autonomy, and defiance. Witchcraft empowers individuals to resist societal injustices while creating meaningful personal and collective movements of change. This is relevant more than ever today, as *toxic masculinity* glorifies violence, dominance, or control over others as markers of success. Witches of all genders can champion radical feminism and support all human rights.

Rebalancing energy between disasters

Witches are in tune with the earth, but in today's age it's common to associate the word *Amazon* with online shopping, not the rainforest where so many resources are extracted. As global environmental crises such as climate change, habitat destruction, and pollution intensify, witches are uniquely positioned to advocate for and model sustainable practices.

REMEMBER

In earth-based traditions like witchcraft, paganism, and indigenous beliefs, natural disasters can be seen as manifestations of the earth's attempt to restore balance.

In this way, natural disasters are a wake-up call, a reminder of the interconnectedness with the natural world and the consequences of exploiting it. Like the cycle of life and death, natural disasters represent a process of destruction leading to rebirth and regeneration.

But while some disasters are part of natural processes, human activity has amplified their frequency and intensity. In this case, natural disasters may not be the earth "balancing itself" but a response to human-induced imbalances. This had led to collective *climate anxiety*, a sense of distress and powerlessness about the impacts of climate change.

FUN FACT

Well, this is more like a not-so-fun fact. I live in Florida, where the hurricanes have become stronger and more destructive in recent years. As I was writing this book, Hurricanes Helene and Milton devastated my local area and many other places across the southern United States. Shortly after, across the country, fires ravaged California. Natural disasters are becoming more frequent and more intense.

In the aftermath of such storms, imbalances in power and resources are laid bare. Then comes the task of rebalancing energies. That entails turning to the elements, putting out fires (often literally), making sure the water is safe to drink, the air is clear to breathe, and the land is steady enough to hold those who occupy it. It involves helping those who don't have those things and trying to restore balance through long-established indigenous practices for sustainability, like controlled burns in forests.

I make a point to plant native vegetation to offset what's been killed off, to nourish the soil, and call birds and bugs back in. I think of ways society collectively needs to change to regain long-term balance, and I contribute to them any way I can. Although this is the work of mundane reality, I find magic in the way storms can reset priorities and encourage focus on what's important. This kind of magic is a hard calling, but it's magical all the same.

Clearing energy online

Artificial intelligence (AI) has the potential to benefit humanity in countless ways, but as it advances, misinformation is a growing threat. AI systems can create, spread, and amplify false or misleading information at a scale and speed never seen before. Some of the key concerns include:

- **Fielding deepfakes:** AI-powered tools can create *deepfakes*, highly convincing audio, video, and images that make it appear as though someone said or did something they never did.
- **Deciphering fake news:** AI systems like text generators (for example, GPT models) can produce false articles, posts, or propaganda that appear authentic and credible.
- **Identifying misinformation:** AI algorithms that social media platforms use often prioritize engaging or sensational content, which can disproportionately propagate misinformation.

- **Fighting bots:** Bots can flood platforms with false narratives, manipulate trending topics, or attack dissenting voices. AI bots can create the illusion of consensus or popularity for misinformation, making it appear credible.

Although AI poses problems for all sectors of life, it could have serious consequences for online witchcraft communities. AI tools trained on unverified sources may perpetuate witchcraft myths, inaccuracies, or stereotypes. Over-reliance on AI may dilute the personal intent and energy that are central to magic, making the practice feel mechanical or detached.

WARNING

And although this is an extreme scenario, online witch hunts could take place in the future. AI algorithms have the capacity to identify witches or spiritual practitioners based on their online behavior, leading to unwanted attention or harassment. A key threat is *doxxing*, the act of publicly revealing personal, sensitive, or identifying information about an individual without their consent, often with malicious intent.

Because of this threat, *gatekeeping* — the act of imposing arbitrary standards or barriers to entry in witchcraft — may surge, as witches seek to preserve authenticity and limit dilution of practices. Although it's important to protect traditions, ironically, doing so might undermine the accessibility and inclusivity that new technologies could potentially afford.

To avoid these dangers, I'm offering some tips to clear the energy while practicing your magic online:

- **Balance tech with intuition:** Use apps and tools as aids, but prioritize personal intuition when crafting spells, interpreting divinations, or connecting with energies. Create space for offline practice, such as meditating in nature or journaling by hand.
- **Set boundaries:** Limit screen time during rituals or magical workings to avoid distraction. Allocate dedicated time for unplugged activities, like foraging, creating tools, or simply observing nature's cycles.
- **Verify and deepen learning:** Cross-reference online information with reputable sources, such as historical texts or experienced practitioners. Treat social media trends as inspiration rather than dogma, adapting them to your personal craft with care and research.
- **Use tech to enhance, not replace:** Incorporate digital tools to streamline your practice, such as using digital sigils or a digital grimoire, but keep physical rituals and tools in your routine for a tactile connection.

» **Ground in nature:** Combine technology with physical experiences, such as using a stargazing app to locate constellations and then meditating under the night sky. Allow nature to inspire your craft directly, integrating natural materials and settings into your rituals.

Creating New Traditions

Being aware of challenges can help you avoid fear and empower you to work your magic bravely. You are, after all, an ancestor-in-the-making that "baby witches" of the future will one day turn to!

Modern witchcraft is in a constant state of evolution, reflecting the diverse identities, values, and circumstances of those practicing it. This adaptability is one of witchcraft's greatest strengths, allowing it to remain relevant across generations and cultures. As you create new traditions, you can honor the wisdom of the past while forging innovative practices that align with the realities of the modern world.

TIP

Innovation in witchcraft isn't about discarding the old, but about expanding its possibilities.

Witches today are finding ways to adapt ancient practices to new tools, technologies, and philosophies, reflecting unique identities and modern contexts. Honoring the past ensures the preservation of valuable wisdom, while evolving practices make them applicable to current and future generations.

Revolutionizing mind, body, and spirit

Revolution literally means "turning." It refers to a transformative shift that challenges existing systems of power, societal norms, and individual or collective limitations. Historically and in modern practice, witchcraft has often been intertwined with revolutionary movements because it's rooted in resistance, autonomy, and the reclamation of power — particularly for marginalized communities. This is a revolution of the mind, the body, and the spirit.

Following are some tips for revolutionizing your relationship to the mind:

» **Reclaiming autonomy:** Practicing witchcraft often means rejecting societal norms that devalue individual intuition, creativity, and spirituality. It means embracing your power to influence your life and surroundings through intention, energy, and ritual.

- **Challenging internalized oppression:** Witchcraft encourages you to confront fears, traumas, and societal conditioning that limit your growth. By working with tools like divination, rituals, and energy work, you gain the confidence to rewrite your own narrative.
- **Celebrating the sacred self:** Practice radical self-acceptance that challenges systems that thrive on shame, disconnection, and insecurity.
- **Championing accessibility:** Ensure that teachings, books, and resources are written and presented in ways that are accessible to all literacy levels, languages, and backgrounds.

You can revolutionize your relationship to your body by doing these things:

- **Reclaiming power from the patriarchy:** Witches have long been symbols of rebellion against patriarchal systems. Witches of all genders can reclaim their power by unapologetically embracing their identity as witches and by complicating *gender essentialism*, the belief that gender traits are innate, fixed, and biologically determined.
- **Honoring spectrums:** Encourage practices that honor a spectrum of gender experiences, moving beyond binary concepts like "masculine" and "feminine" energies. Avoid suggesting that divinity is gendered.
- **Making accommodations:** Create accommodations for witches with disabilities or neurodivergent experiences by offering visual aids, accessible meeting spaces, or sensory-friendly rituals. Normalize discussions of energy work and spellcraft in ways that account for varied physical or mental abilities.
- **Creating safe havens:** Witchcraft is a revolutionary act for marginalized groups who have been excluded from mainstream religious or cultural spaces. You can offer a path of healing, empowerment, and community for LGBTQ+ individuals, people of color, and people of all body types and abilities.

Following are some tips to revolutionize your relation to the spirit:

- **Connecting to ancestors:** Witchcraft often honors ancestors, spirits, and practices that were historically suppressed or erased. By revitalizing these traditions, you can reclaim cultural and spiritual legacies.
- **Centering spirit in ritual:** Emphasize the spiritual and energetic aspects of the craft over material tools, making it clear that magic resides in intention and connection, not in expensive items.
- **Breaking cycles of oppression:** Shadow work, healing rituals, and magical practices allow you to confront and break generational patterns of trauma, inequality, and harm. (Chapter 4 has more on shadow work.)

Becoming environmental stewards

Eco-magic focuses on sustainability, such as rituals aimed at environmental healing or creating magical tools from reclaimed and recycled materials. To align witchcraft with ecological integrity, you can adopt sustainable approaches that minimize harm and foster a reciprocal relationship with the earth. These practices include ethically sourcing materials, reducing waste, reusing and reducing materials, and crafting in harmony with the seasons.

Some ideas for other eco-magic practices include these:

- **Creating charms from found objects:** Instead of buying new products for each spell, make your own tools and ingredients from abundant and safe resources around your home, like a common weed, for instance.
- **Rewilding rituals:** Make offerings for land healing, such as planting native plants and trees to restore ecosystems.
- **Facing fear of insects:** Face the common cultural fears surrounding bugs like wasps and spiders and advocate for the smallest inhabitants of the planet, setting off a chain reaction of healing up the food chain.

TIP

You're a witch, not a miracle worker. Focus on what you can control and let it fuel your magic.

Although witchcraft doesn't replace scientific solutions or disaster preparedness, it does offer tools for protection, healing, and resilience while fostering a deeper connection to nature. Here's how you can infuse your disaster response with magic:

- **Protective magic:** Cast protective spells and wards to safeguard your home, your family, and your community. I cast a warding spell on my house just before each storm, for instance.
- **Weather rituals:** You can use rituals to influence weather patterns, such as asking for rain during a drought or seeking calm during storms. This work focuses on harmonizing energy, not "controlling" nature, and is often done in alignment with respectful intentions.
- **Elemental magic:** During droughts, you can perform water-focused rituals to honor rain, such as collecting water to pour back into the earth.

Finding the spirit in the machine

Technopaganism refers to the blending of technological tools and digital spaces with spiritual or magical practices, viewing technology as an extension of the sacred rather than separate from it. It aligns with broader ideas about finding spirituality within modern, tech-driven environments.

FUN FACT

Although the origin of the term is debated, the term *technopagan* was popularized by cultural critics in the 1990s. I first heard the term as a teen watching *Buffy the Vampire Slayer*. The computer teacher, Jenny Calendar, called herself a techno-pagan and saved her spells on floppy disks.

Many people have used the term in a tongue-in-cheek way, but as technology advances, technopaganism is becoming less of a joke and more of a reality. A rapidly growing number of witches practice primarily in online spaces. They mix the ancient with the modern, reflecting the adaptability and creativity that lies at the heart of witchcraft.

REMEMBER

Technopaganism honors the interconnectedness of all things — both the analog and the digital realms — embracing tools of the modern age as extensions of magic, intention, and energy.

Technopagans view technology not as a barrier to spirituality but as a tool for connection. The same energy that flows through the earth and sky, they argue, also flows through the wires of the internet and the circuits of today's devices. This perspective reimagines technology as part of the ever-expanding web of life.

The possibilities of technopaganism are endless. Just as ancient witches cast spells with herbs and spoken words, modern witches can type affirmations, code digital symbols, or share their magic exclusively in online spaces. You can even join an online-only coven these days.

The tools of technopaganism reflect both the spiritual and the digital, including these:

- **Virtual sacred spaces:** Technopagans use apps, social media groups, or video calls to create sacred spaces. Online rituals and group ceremonies allow you to come together with other witches across continents to share energy and intention.
- **Digital altars:** You can create an altar on your computer or smartphone that features images of deities, nature, or personal symbols as a focus for meditation and spellwork.
- **Online divination:** Use tarot apps, online rune generators, and astrology software to make traditional tools of divination accessible anywhere. They offer convenience without compromising meaning.

- **Sigil creation:** Use graphic design software or apps to craft intricate digital *sigils*, which you can share, display on your screen, or print for use in spell work.
- **Energy work through technology:** Technopagans recognize the energetic impact of digital interaction. Intentional words shared online, virtual healing sessions, or carefully crafted emails can carry the same focused energy as spoken spells.

The new technopaganism isn't about abandoning the natural world; it's about finding balance. Although digital tools offer accessibility and innovation, techno-pagans remain grounded in the importance of honoring the physical earth. They may forage for herbs while using an app to identify plants or track moon phases through software while performing rituals under the open sky. For technopagans, technology is an extension of the craft, not a replacement for the deep, personal connection to nature, spirit, and community.

WARNING

As with all new developments, technopaganism comes with its challenges. Over-reliance on digital tools can disconnect practitioners from the tangible, sensory experience of magic. Constant access to information can overwhelm or dilute intention.

Yet, it also offers unprecedented opportunities to build global connections, share knowledge, and make witchcraft more inclusive and accessible. I've personally started to share my practices and create witchy community on *Discord*, a communication app designed for creating communities where users can connect via text, voice, and video. Initially developed for gamers to communicate while playing, it has grown into a versatile platform used by people from all walks of life, including students, hobbyists, and online communities like witches and spiritual groups.

The new technopaganism proves that witchcraft, as it always has, can adapt, grow, and thrive — through the flames of a candle or the glow of a screen.

Empowering the next generation

The future of witchcraft is based in sharing resources and helping each other navigate the rapidly shifting world. Witchcraft may have been relegated to the shadows for most of history, but many modern witches and spiritualists today dedicate themselves to publicly researching, organizing, and guiding others through the wealth of information out there. Among my favorites are Bri Luna, a Black and Mexican witch who offers accessible everyday magic through her platform, The Hoodwitch; Alice Sparkly Kat, a queer Chinese astrologer who offers sharp philosophical insights and poetry for making modern magic; and

Lida Pavlova, a Slavic witch who shares information about folk witchcraft in beautiful and highly digestible tidbits.

You'll find a wealth of books on witchcraft on hundreds of special topics, and it can be hard to know which ones to choose. You will probably hear a lot about Doreen Valiente's *Witchcraft for Tomorrow*, Margot Adler's *Drawing Down the Moon*, and Starhawk's *The Spiral Dance*, witchcraft books from the '70s; while outdated, they're still considered seminal works on the Craft. A recent book that does a great job of orienting the reader to modern witchcraft and providing diverse resources is *Witches Among Us: Understanding Contemporary Witchcraft and Wicca* by Thorn Mooney.

In lieu of listing all the wonderful books out there, here are some writers I recommend looking up: Temperance Alden, Mat Auryn, Rebecca Beyer, Amy Blackthorn, Erika Buenaflor, J. Allen Cross, Laura Davila, Juliet Diaz, Lilith Dorsey, Clarissa Pinkola Estés, Daniel Foor, Claire Goodchild, Sarah Faith Gottesdiener, Gabriela Herstik, Arin Hiscock-Murphy, Judika Illes, Coby Michael, Chani Nicholas, Nicholas Pearson, Thomas Prower, and Laura Tempest Zakroff. This is not an exhaustive list, but the works of these modern witches and spiritualists will lead you to endless troves of wisdom.

If you prefer to listen to your content, check out one of the many fantastic podcasts by modern witches. Some of my favorites are Missing Witches by Risa Dickens and Amy Torok; Between the Worlds by Amanda Yates Garcia; The Witch Wave by Pam Grossman; Demystify Magic by Molly Donlan and Madison Lillian; and How to Survive the End of the World, by Autumn Brown and adrienne maree brown, featuring "Witch School" episodes.

Through your creative powers as a modern witch, you can transform challenges and direct your mind, body, and spirit toward enchanting your future with other witches. As the Craft evolves, it's essential to inspire the next generation of witches, passing down not only knowledge but also the values and ethics that define modern witchcraft.

You can set yourself up to be an honored ancestor of the future in several ways:

- **Mentoring and guiding:** You can take on a mentorship role, sharing your wisdom while encouraging creativity and personal exploration. Workshops, podcasts, and books are excellent ways to make knowledge accessible to younger or new practitioners.
- **Encouraging critical thinking:** Teach new witches to question trends, research deeply, and cultivate discernment in their practice.

- **Adapting to new perspectives:** Younger witches bring fresh ideas, including new approaches to technology, activism, and spirituality. If you're an experienced witch, remain open to learning from younger witches, creating a reciprocal relationship.
- **Preserving and innovating:** Pass down core principles, such as respect for nature, inclusivity, and ethical practice while encouraging the creation of new rituals and traditions that reflect contemporary issues and personal creativity.
- **Remembering that it's supposed to be fun:** What's all this for if you're not enjoying yourself? Make room for play and imagination in your craft!

As I get older, I think more and more about how I want to be remembered as a witch. I've been delighted to start mentoring younger witches. As I walk my own crooked path, I'm beginning to look forward to my crone years. I hope I get to someday be an old village witch like the one depicted in Figure 20-1, with my cauldron and my broom and my familiars, turning stereotypes on their heads.

FIGURE 20-1: A crone peacefully crafts by the hearth.

Eleanor Vere Boyle/University of Illinois Board of Trustees/Public domain

6

The Part of Tens

IN THIS PART . . .

Learn ten foundational spells to kick off your own practice, accessible to witches of all levels.

Discover the ten days of ritual observance in modern witchcraft, including the *sabbats* and the *esbats*.

Chapter 21

Ten Foundational Spells

This chapter provides a selection of simple, foundational spells suited for beginners and more advanced practitioners alike. Although these spells are straightforward, they can serve as building blocks for more elaborate rituals and spellwork as your practice grows. Spells direct energy in some way. Before diving in, I assume you've already acquainted yourself with the concept of energy, prepared your sacred space (see Chapter 10), and consecrated and cleansed your tools and ingredients (see Chapter 11).

Grounding: Earth Stones Spell

Grounding spells are used in two ways: to move extra energy that you're carrying down as an offering to the earth, and to call up the power of the earth's energy to stabilize you. Perform grounding spells to manage and center yourself before or after magical work. For this spell, you'll need two small stones. Good grounding crystals include obsidian, garnet, black tourmaline, tiger's eye, and hematite.

1. Sit comfortably with your bare feet flat on the ground. Place a stone on the top of each foot.
2. Close your eyes and take deep breaths. On your out breaths, visualize a white light flowing from the crown of your head down to the stones at your feet.

On your in breaths, imagine a green light reaching up from the earth like roots, moving from the stones on your feet up to your heart.

3. Continue this for a few minutes, until you feel that your energy is balanced in your body.
4. Thank the earth for its support, and then place the stones somewhere meaningful to you. When you need grounding, hold the stones in your palms, close your eyes, take deep breaths, and speak a simple mantra, like, "I am rooted. I am safe." Repeat the larger spell every so often to rebalance the energies of the stones.

Cleansing: Egg "Limpia" Spell

Cleansing spells remove negative, stagnant, or unwanted energies from a person, object, or space, restoring balance and creating a fresh, harmonious environment. I cover basic cleansing techniques in Chapter 10 and a Florida Water recipe in Chapter 14. Cleansing spells vary greatly and can be personalized to your routines and cultures. This common cleansing spell from my culture is open to anyone and is called an egg cleanse or *limpia*. (See Chapter 10.) You need an egg and a clear glass of water.

1. Hold the egg in your hands and take a moment to focus on your intention. Visualize the egg as a magnet, ready to draw out and absorb any negativity, blockages, or heavy energy.
2. Starting at the crown of your head, gently roll or hover the egg over your body in slow, downward motions, making sure not to crack the egg. Move from your head to your feet, paying attention to areas where you feel tension or discomfort. Visualize the egg pulling away all negativity as you work.
3. Once you're finished, you can crack the egg into the glass of water to inspect it. It's said that bubbles, discoloration, or irregularities in the egg can indicate absorbed energy, and over time, you'll learn to intuitively read your egg.
4. Safely dispose of the egg by burying it in the ground or flushing it away, symbolizing the removal of negativity. You might speak a simple incantation, such as, "I release all that holds me back or harms me."
5. Wash your hands with cool water to complete the process. Take a few deep breaths, feeling lighter and refreshed.

TIP

Set the glass outside for the next cleanse. Don't use it for drinking!

Protecting: Psychic Warding Spell

Like cleansing spells, protection spells are necessary prerequisites to other kinds of spell work because practicing magic opens you up and makes you vulnerable to negative energies. This one is a simple warding spell against *psychic attack*, which is a projection of negative energy that can disrupt your well-being. You'll need a white or black candle and a small mirror.

1. Sit quietly and state your purpose, such as, "I create a shield of protection around me."
2. Light the candle. Place the mirror behind the candle so it reflects the flame outward.
3. Visualize the shield. Imagine a glowing barrier of light forming around you, deflecting all harm or negativity away.
4. Say, "This ward protects me, strong and true, reflecting harm away in all I do," and then extinguish the candle.

Making a Boundary: The Circle

Casting a circle is often the first spell in more involved spellwork, after any necessary cleansing. It can be considered a type of protective spell, but it also sets the boundaries of your practice. This is important for safety, so energy is contained, and for your focus. You need a ritual tool of choice like a wand or athame.

1. State your purpose, such as, "This circle protects and contains the energy of my work."
2. (Optional) You can draw the outline of your circle with chalk, put down a salt barrier, or place candles in the shape of a circle or pentagram. This isn't required, but it might add an extra layer of protection for more complex spells — and it looks nice!
3. Holding up your tool of choice, walk clockwise around your space, visualizing a glowing boundary of light forming a protective sphere.
4. Seal the circle. Say, "The circle is cast, my space is sacred and secure," and begin your work.

Enchanting: Magical Objects Spell

To *enchant* something means to imbue or charge it with magical energy and intention. For this, you need an object that you want to make magical, like a ring or book. It can be anything, really. You also need a candle in a color associated with your intention. (See Chapter 12.)

1. Set your intention. Hold the object and focus on your desired purpose, such as protection, luck, or confidence. Visualize the energy flowing from your hands into the object.
2. Charge the object by speaking an incantation such as, "I charge you with *[intention]*, a beacon of *[energy or purpose]*. Serve me well, as I will you. So it shall be."
3. Seal the spell by placing the object next to the candle. Let the candle burn safely for a few minutes, reinforcing your intention. You can carry or use the object as needed, occasionally re-enchanting it.

Attracting: Self-Love Bath Spell

In Chapter 14, I offer a recipe for an herbal bath *sachet*, or bundle. You need something like this or loose dried herbs, such as rose and lavender, along with a pink candle, honey, sea salt, and a crystal that symbolizes love, like rose quartz or emerald.

1. Light the pink candle(s) around your bathtub and cleanse the space with a few deep breaths or a soft chant, such as, "I welcome love and light into this space."
2. Prepare the bath with warm water. Add a handful of sea salt, dried herbs or herbal sachet, and a bit of honey, stirring gently with your hand while thinking about what you love most about yourself.
3. Set your intention. Hold the crystal or place it nearby as you hover your hands over the water and say, "I attract love and kindness to myself. My heart is open to receive joy."
4. Soak in the love. Relax in the bath, visualizing yourself surrounded by a radiant pink light.
5. Seal the spell with these words: "I am love, I am light, I am whole." Drain the water and carry the loving energy with you. You may bury or ritually dispose of the herbs as you see fit.

Manifesting: The Knot Spell

Manifestation is the process of making a wish into material reality. I see it as a form of creativity. This is a fun old folk magic spell, alternately known as the witch's ladder. The opposite spell is cord cutting, which releases something. (See Chapter 16.) You need a piece of cord, ribbon, or string that can be easily knotted, in a color that represents your wish.

1. Hold the cord and focus on your wish, visualizing it as if it has already come true.
2. Tie nine knots, evenly spaced along your cord. For each one, say its special incantation. Feel free to adjust these words to your liking:
   - "By knot of one, the spell's begun."
   - "By knot of two, it will come true."
   - "By knot of three, so mote it be."
   - "By knot of four, my wish grows more."
   - "By knot of five, desire thrives."
   - "By knot of six, the magic sticks."
   - "By knot of seven, the spell is leavened."
   - "By knot of eight, I seal its fate."
   - "By knot of nine, this wish is mine."
3. Keep the cord as a reminder, or bury it somewhere safe.

Dreaming: Lucidity Spell

Lucid dreaming is the act of remembering and controlling your dreams. This spell is simple. Dream control is a delicate act, so you don't want to be too elaborate and scare away your dreams. For this, you need a journal, a pen, and an herb sachet of mugwort or lavender. (See Chapter 14 to make your own.) Don't be discouraged if the dreams don't come quickly. If you need a little extra help, practice good sleep hygiene, like not eating or drinking right before bed and going to sleep at the same time every night.

1. When you're ready for bed, write, "I will remember" at the top of a fresh journal page, and place it on your nightstand.

2. Slip the herb sachet under your pillow. Go to sleep (and hopefully, dream).
3. When you wake, even if it's just for a moment in the middle of the night, jot down a few words about your dream. You'll get better at remembering if you keep practicing this step.

Healing: Laying Hands Spell

Laying hands is a spiritual practice whereby a person places their hands on or near someone (or themselves) to channel energy for healing, protection, or blessing. You'll need a white or green candle and your hands.

1. Light the candle and say, "I call on the light to heal and renew me."
2. Focusing on your breath, place your hands over your heart or the area needing healing, visualizing a warm, glowing light spreading through your body.
3. Seal the spell by saying something like, "Healing flows through me, strong and true," and extinguish the candle safely.

Binding: The Freezer Spell

Binding is a spell to restrict the actions, energy, or influence of a person, situation, or entity. The goal of binding is to prevent harm and negativity from affecting you or others. It's a kind of protection spell, so your focus should be on strengthening your boundaries rather than controlling another. You need a small piece of paper, a pen, a freezer-safe container, and water.

1. Write the name of the person, situation, or behavior you want to bind on the paper. Be clear and concise.
2. Freeze the spell. Fold the paper, place it in the container, fill it with water, and seal it. As you put it in the freezer, say, "Be still, be bound, your harm is undone."
3. Leave it frozen. Keep your spell in the freezer as long as you need to, but bindings should not be kept forever; I recommend thawing them after a few months. When you're ready to release the binding, thaw the container, dispose of the paper, and cleanse your space.

Chapter 22

Ten Days of Ritual Observance

The *sabbats* are festivals celebrated in neopagan traditions to mark important points of the solar cycle, like the solstices and equinoxes, and the turn of the seasons. They form the Wheel of the Year and consist of eight major celebrations described here. The other two are *esbats*, or lunar celebrations. Although the sabbats are influenced by Celtic, Germanic, Norse, and Roman festivals, I've included associated observances from other cultures that modern witches and folk practitioners have increasingly integrated into their rituals. The Wheel of the Year can lend structure to your practices, grounding them in nature and the seasons.

The Sabbats

Samhain

Samhain, pronounced *SAH-win* or *SOW-in*, means "summer's end" in Gaelic. It takes place from October 31 to November 1 in the Northern Hemisphere and from April 30 to May 1 in the Southern Hemisphere. It was traditionally a harvest festival, and fires were lit to guide the dead. Samhain is a time to honor ancestors, connect with spirits, and reflect on transformation. It's sometimes considered the witches' new year, and conversely, it's sometimes seen as the end of the Wheel of the Year. Samhain coincides with Halloween (October 31), All Saints' Day (November 1), and Dia de los Muertos or Day of the Dead (November 1–2). Day of the Dead is a Mexican holiday observed throughout Latin America that shares many rituals with the modern observance of Samhain, including making offerings, or *ofrendas*, to the dead. Modern rituals around this time include creating ancestor altars, donning spooky costumes, and embracing the darkness within through "shadow work" practices.

Yule

Yule, observed around December 20 to 23 in the Northern Hemisphere and June 20 to 23 in the Southern Hemisphere, marks the rebirth of the sun at the winter solstice, the longest night of the year. Based in Norse and Germanic traditions, it honors the return of light and warmth as days begin to grow longer. Yule is sometimes considered the first festival of the Wheel of the Year, instead of Samhain. Traditional symbols include the yule log and the yule goat. Modern practices include lighting candles or fires, decorating with fir and evergreens, and honoring dark deities. Both Christmas and Hanukkah incorporate many pre-Christian Yule traditions, including exchanging gifts and lighting candles to symbolize the return of light. Other solstice celebrations around the world include Dong Zhi in China, Inti Raymi in Peru, Koliada in the Slavic tradition, Mother's Night in Germanic traditions, and Soyal in the Hopi tradition of North America.

Imbolc

Imbolc, the midpoint between the winter solstice and the spring equinox, takes place on February 1 and 2 in the Northern Hemisphere and August 1 and 2 in the Southern Hemisphere. The word *Imbolc* is derived from Old Irish, meaning "in the belly," referring to the time of year that lambs give birth. It's sometimes called *Oimelc*, an old Gaelic word for "ewe's milk." Traditionally associated with Brigid, the Celtic goddess of fertility, poetry, and healing, many practitioners still create altars with symbols of Brigid, such as crosses or flames, and petition her with their greatest hopes. Modern rituals include lighting candles to honor the returning light, and setting intentions for the spring season to come. It's a good time for taking stock and visualizing. Imbolc coincides with *Candlemas*, a Christian feast.

Ostara

Ostara is celebrated on the spring equinox, which takes place between March 20 and 23 in the Northern Hemisphere and between September 20 and 23 in the Southern Hemisphere. The day is said to be named for Eostre, an Anglo-Saxon goddess of spring and fertility, though historical evidence for her worship is sparse and her connection to Ostara is debated. The equinox marks equal day and night, symbolizing balance and renewal. Modern rituals include planting seeds to symbolize new beginnings, decorating eggs, and creating altars with flowers and symbols of fertility. Ostara coincides with Easter, with its themes of resurrection and egg-decorating traditions. Nowruz, the Persian New Year, celebrates rebirth and the arrival of spring with family feasts and rituals. This time of year is also considered the astrological new year among western astrologers.

Beltane

Beltane, meaning "bright fire" in Gaelic, is celebrated on May 1 in the Northern Hemisphere and November 1 in the Southern Hemisphere. It's a fire festival celebrating fertility, and it was traditionally observed by lighting bonfires. Rituals that have survived into modern times include dancing around maypoles, weaving flower crowns, and lighting fires to celebrate vitality, creativity, and passion. Many use this time to honor relationships and sensuality. Beltane coincides with May Day in Europe, featuring similar customs, and Walpurgis Night in Germanic cultures, involving bonfires and warding off spirits.

Litha

Litha or Midsummer is observed on the summer solstice, around June 20 to 23 in the Northern Hemisphere and December 20 to 23 in the Southern Hemisphere. The term *Litha* comes from Old English, referring to the summer months. Celebrations of the sun at its peak power were common in many ancient cultures, including Norse, Celtic, Slavic, and Germanic traditions. Litha is associated with the fairy realm, and this is the time when fairies were said to interact most with humans, leaving tricks and treats. It's a time of great light, but also the point when the light starts to wane. Modern rituals include lighting bonfires, foraging herbs, enjoying hobbies, and celebrating the ephemeral. Midsummer traditions are strongly celebrated in Scandinavian cultures, and countless solstice traditions take place around the world, like Simmer Dim in Scotland, Ivan Kupala in Russia, Rasa in Lithuania, and Kronia in Greece.

Lughnasadh

Lughnasadh, or Lughnasa, pronounced *LOO-nah-sah*, takes place on August 1 in the Northern Hemisphere and February 1 in the Southern Hemisphere. The word *Lughnasadh* honors Lugh, the Celtic god of craftsmanship and skill. Traditionally, it was observed as a festival of labor and competition. Modern rituals include baking bread, sharing feasts, performing feats of strength, and giving thanks for the bounty of the harvest. Ritual themes center on gratitude, abundance, triumph, and the fruits of labor. Symbols of Lughnasadh include prosperity talismans and anything that can be considered a currency. Harvest festivals worldwide, such as the English Lammas, celebrate the first reaping. In Christianity, *Lammas* means "loaf mass," referring to bread made from the first harvest. Obon in Japan honors ancestors with offerings of food and dance.

Mabon

Mabon is celebrated on the autumnal or vernal equinox, which takes place around September 20 to 23 in the Northern Hemisphere and March 20 to 23 in the Southern Hemisphere. The name *Mabon* comes from an obscure figure in Welsh mythology associated with balance. The equinox marks a time of equal day and night. In modern practice, Mabon is celebrated with autumnal symbols like apples, leaves, and gourds. Rituals include giving thanks for the harvest and preparing for the darker half of the year. Across Asia, observances on the autumn equinox involve celebrating family and ancestors and visiting gravesites, including Chuseok in Korea, Higan in Japan, and the Moon Festival in China. In the U.S., Mabon's symbolism is most commonly tied to Thanksgiving, although that's celebrated in November instead of September. In India, the equinox is observed with a nine-day festival called Sharada Navaratri, and in Slavic traditions, Dożynki festivals balance solemnity and celebration.

The Esbats

New Moons

The New Moon Esbat is a monthly lunar ritual observed during the new moon phase, when the moon isn't visible in the sky. This phase symbolizes new beginnings, introspection, and planting seeds for the future. It's a time for turning inward, focusing on intentions, and setting the groundwork for personal or magical growth.

Full Moons

The Full Moon Esbat is a lunar ritual celebrated during the full moon phase, when the moon is at its brightest and fullest in the sky. This phase represents culmination, illumination, and the peak of lunar energy, making it an ideal time for magic, manifestation, and spiritual work. The full moon is the perfect time to bring intentions set during the new moon to fruition.

Appendix

The material in this appendix is supplementary to the chapters in Part 4. Each section here corresponds to a specific chapter, providing symbolic correspondences and properties of different mediums you may use to enhance your practice, including tarot, herbs, planets, and crystals. These aren't exhaustive lists of properties; feel free to use them as a starting point, and over time, log your own associations in your grimoire.

Parts of the Tarot Deck

In Chapter 13, I introduce cartomancy as a medium of divination. The symbolism of the Waite-Smith deck (divided into the Minor Arcana and the Major Arcana) is the default that a majority of tarot readers use today.

The Minor Arcana is a subset of the typical tarot deck that includes 56 cards. It focuses on the everyday experiences, challenges, and triumphs of life. The Minor Arcana closely mirrors a traditional playing deck of cards, divided into four suits, including these:

- **Pentacles (Earth):** Represents materiality, stability, health, and abundance. Focuses on the physical world, resources, career, and practical matters.
- **Cups (Water):** Represents emotions, intuition, relationships, and love. Reflects inner feelings and the flow of emotional experiences.
- **Wands (Fire):** Represents passion, creativity, energy, performance, and ambition. Symbolizes the drive to take action and achieve goals.
- **Swords (Air):** Represents intellect, communication, conflict, and truth. Highlights the power of the mind and the challenges of logic.

When you interpret the suit of a card, you can combine its meaning with that of its number to understand the message of each unique card. The pips, or numbered cards from ace to ten in each suit, represent specific stages of growth, emotions, and actions. The court cards represent archetypal personalities, roles, or energies within the suits. Following are a few correspondences for each to get you started:

- **Ace:** Beginnings, potential, inspiration, opportunity
- **Two:** Duality, partnership, choices, decisions, crossroads

- **Three:** Growth, collaboration, community, expansion, creativity
- **Four:** Stability, foundation, home, structure, pause, reflection
- **Five:** Conflict, change, struggle, challenge, movement, passion
- **Six:** Harmony, balance, progress, healing, service
- **Seven:** Reflection, assessment, options, perseverance, patience
- **Eight:** Movement, mastery, action, power, boundaries, cycles of life
- **Nine:** Transitions, resilience, near-completion, lessons, sharing
- **Ten:** Completion, culmination, manifestation, legacy, start of new cycle
- **Page:** Curiosity, learning, messages, beginnings, exploration
- **Knight:** Action, pursuit, focus, determination, change, force of nature
- **Queen:** Nurturing, wisdom, intuition, mastery, embodiment
- **King:** Leadership, institutions, authority, control, figurehead

As you might notice, the progression of the cards' meanings in order reflects the typical hero's journey. Whereas the Minor Arcana provides personal or mundane details along this journey, the Major Arcana offers bigger themes and archetypes that offer deep spiritual insights. It contains 22 cards, each with its own archetypal themes:

- **The Fool:** Beginnings, spontaneity, risk, potential
- **The Magician:** Manifestation, skill, resourcefulness, power
- **The High Priestess:** Intuition, mystery, inner knowledge, subconscious
- **The Empress:** Abundance, nurturing, creation, fertility
- **The Emperor:** Authority, structure, stability, leadership
- **The Hierophant:** Tradition, spirituality, guidance, conformity
- **The Lovers:** Relationships, choices, harmony, union
- **The Chariot:** Willpower, determination, triumph, direction
- **Strength:** Courage, inner strength, compassion, resilience
- **The Hermit:** Introspection, wisdom, solitude, inner guidance
- **Wheel of Fortune:** Change, cycles, fate, opportunity
- **Justice:** Fairness, truth, balance, accountability
- **The Hanged Man:** Surrender, perspective, letting go, suspension

- **Death:** Transformation, endings, renewal, release
- **Temperance:** Balance, moderation, harmony, patience
- **The Devil:** Restriction, temptation, shadow self, materialism
- **The Tower:** Upheaval, sudden change, revelation, chaos
- **The Star:** Hope, inspiration, renewal, guidance
- **The Moon:** Illusion, intuition, fear, subconscious
- **The Sun:** Joy, success, vitality, enlightenment
- **Judgment:** Awakening, evaluation, rebirth, reckoning
- **The World:** Completion, wholeness, achievement, fulfillment

Magical Properties of Common Herbs

In Chapter 14, I explore green witchcraft, which commonly employs herbs for magical purposes in spells, kitchen witchery, and candle dressing. This section is a nonexhaustive list of common herbs and their properties. Make sure to consult a field expert for your area's native plants and their associations, and be careful to avoid overharvesting of endangered species.

You can find these herbs in a variety of forms, like dried and crushed or extracted into oils. Witches usually burn or sprinkle herbs as part of their workings. Only ingest with guidance from an herbalist or other plant expert because many herbs are toxic or even deadly in high concentrations. The following are common witching herbs:

- **Aloe vera:** Healing, protection, luck. Place in home for luck, use in spells for health, apply gel for magical and physical healing. Revered in many traditions for its soothing and protective properties.
- **Basil:** Protection, prosperity, love. Add to protection spells, sprinkle in corners for abundance, use in love potions. Associated with St. Basil in Christian tradition, often used to ward off evil.
- **Bay leaf:** Protection, strength, wish fulfillment. Write wishes on leaves and burn, include in charm bags, use in protective spells. Sacred to Apollo; used in ancient Greek oracles for prophetic visions.
- **Belladonna:** Visions, death, banishing. Use with extreme caution in rituals to sever toxic ties and enhance trance states. Featured in witch lore for its hallucinogenic use.

- **Black pepper:** Banishing, protection, strength. Use in banishing spells, sprinkle around property for protection, add to rituals for personal power. Associated with fire and strength in folk traditions.
- **Calendula:** Protection, legal success, prophetic dreams. Place petals in charms for protection, use in spells for justice, brew tea for dreamwork. Associated with the sun and used in rituals for its golden hue and protective energies.
- **Cedarwood:** Balancing, calming, grounding. Burn to cleanse spaces, include in grounding rituals, or place in sachets for peace. Sacred to the Native Americans and used for ceremonial fires.
- **Chamomile:** Calm, luck, sleep. Brew for peace rituals, sprinkle in bath for relaxation, carry in sachets for luck. Symbol of the sun in Egyptian mythology, associated with Ra.
- **Cinnamon:** Power, success, love, passion. Add to candles for success, sprinkle on money charms, burn for energy and passion. Mentioned in ancient texts like the Bible and sacred to the Egyptians for embalming.
- **Dandelion:** Divination, wishes, growth. Use seeds in wish spells, drink tea for spiritual insight, include in spells for new opportunities. Associated with the sun and its energy, revered in folk magic for wishes.
- **Datura:** Visions, banishing, transformation. Use sparingly for visionary work, meditative states, and crossing spiritual thresholds. Revered in Indian mythology, sacred to Shiva.
- **Eucalyptus:** Healing, protection, purification. Hang in showers for healing, burn to cleanse spaces, use in health rituals. Revered in Australian Aboriginal spiritual traditions.
- **Foxglove:** Protection, ward against evil, traveling through liminal spaces. Use as a boundary spell ingredient. Associated with the *Fae* in Celtic lore; considered a plant of both protection and peril.
- **Frankincense:** Banishing, justice, spiritual connection. Burn as incense for meditation, use in rituals for spiritual elevation, or carry for protective energy. Mentioned in the Bible as a gift to Jesus and widely used in ancient temple rituals.
- **Ginger:** Passion, power, prosperity. Add to spells for courage, use in rituals for financial gain, include in love spells. Associated with warmth and fire in folk traditions, boosting vitality.
- **Juniper:** Warding, healing, clearing. Burn for space clearing, use berries in healing rituals, or carry sprigs for protective energy. Revered in Celtic traditions for warding off evil spirits and clearing negativity.

- **Lavender:** Calm, love, sleep, healing. Add to sleep sachets, use in rituals for peace, burn for relaxation. Associated with Hecate in Greek mythology for its protective and purifying properties.
- **Lemon balm:** Love, happiness, healing. Use in love potions, brew for emotional healing, add to spells for joy and renewal. Revered in ancient Greek medicine as a plant of joy and healing.
- **Mandrake:** Protection, fertility, prosperity. Use as a talisman for protection, fertility rituals, or enhancement of spells. Linked to numerous myths, including the Bible's Jacob and Leah for fertility magic.
- **Mint:** Prosperity, healing, energy. Add to abundance rituals, use in baths for rejuvenation, place in wallet for luck. Associated with the nymph Minthe, turned into the plant by Persephone in Greek myth.
- **Mugwort:** Dreams, psychic protection, divination, purification. Burn to clear negative energies or place under pillow in a sachet to enhance dreams. Associated with Artemis, the Greek goddess of the hunt and the moon. Revered in European folklore and used in midsummer festivals.
- **Myrrh:** Divinity, meditation, sacred connection. Burn for cleansing sacred spaces, add to rituals for healing or spiritual growth, or use in incense blends for promoting peace and luck. Associated with Egyptian mythology. Used in embalming rituals and as an offering to deities.
- **Nightshade:** Transformation, invisibility, shadow work. Use in shadow spells or exploring the unknown, always with care. Sacred to Hecate and often connected to witchcraft in European folklore.
- **Pine:** Purification, protection, vitality. Burn needles or cones to cleanse a space, place in wreaths for protection, or use in rituals for strength and endurance. Sacred to the Druids and associated with eternal life in many traditions.
- **Rose:** Love, beauty, healing. Use petals in love spells, make rose water for self-love, scatter petals in baths. Sacred to Aphrodite; represents love and desire in many myths.
- **Rosemary:** Purification, protection, memory. Burn for cleansing, use in rituals for clarity, place under pillows for dream recall. Sacred to Aphrodite; symbolized remembrance in Greek and Roman mythology.
- **Sage:** Cleansing, wisdom, protection. Burn for space clearing, carry for wisdom, include in rituals for purification. White sage is revered by Native American traditions as a sacred plant for purification ceremonies.
- **Salt:** Purification, protection, banishing. Sprinkle in corners for protection, use in baths for cleansing, or draw a protective circle in rituals. Universally regarded as a purifier and barrier against negative energy across cultures.

- **Sandalwood:** Grief, justice, well-being. Burn for meditation and spiritual connection, use in healing rituals, or carry for grounding energy. Sacred in Hindu tradition, often used in offerings and purification ceremonies.
- **Thyme:** Courage, health, psychic enhancement. Carry for bravery, burn for healing energy, include in rituals for clarity. Sacred to the Greeks, often burned in temples for courage and strength.
- **Vetiver:** Grounding, stability, tranquility. Add to grounding rituals, use in sachets for financial stability, or carry for protective energy. Known as *khus* in India, it's revered for its stabilizing and calming properties.
- **Wormwood:** Divination, banishing, spirit work. Burn as incense for spirit communication or protection. Featured in Greek mythology; said to have sprung from the tears of Artemis.
- **Yarrow:** Courage, love, protection. Carry for bravery, use in spells for lasting love, place around home for shielding energy. Revered by warriors in ancient Greece for courage in battle.

Planetary Rulerships and Domiciles

In Chapter 15, I introduce the planets and their associations. Each planet is said to "rule" particular zodiac signs, which in turn correspond to certain houses of astrology. The following table shows the *domiciles*, or home signs, of each planet, along with their corresponding houses, which represent areas of life and are numbered 1 to 12. ***Note:*** In astrology, the Sun and Moon are referred to as planets.

Planet	Sign	House Number and Themes
Sun	Leo	5: Creativity, pleasure, self-expression
Moon	Cancer	4: Home, family, emotional foundations
Mercury	Gemini and Virgo	3: Health, service, daily routines
Venus	Taurus and Libra	2: Wealth, values, skills, self-worth; 7: Partnerships, balance, relationships
Mars	Aries and Scorpio (traditional)	1: Self, identity, action; 8: Transformation, shared resources, intimacy
Jupiter	Sagittarius and Pisces (traditional)	9: Philosophy, travel, higher learning; 12: Spirituality, dreams, the subconscious
Saturn	Capricorn and Aquarius (traditional)	10: Career, achievement, public life; 11: Networks, innovation, humanitarian goals

Planet	Sign	House Number and Themes
Uranus	Aquarius (modern)	11: Networks, innovation, humanitarian goals
Neptune	Pisces (modern)	12: Spirituality, dreams, the subconscious
Pluto	Scorpio (modern)	8: Transformation, shared resources, intimacy

Energetic Associations of Crystals

Chapter 16 mentions that crystals and gemstones have energetic properties. Here I list commonly used stones in witchcraft, along with the energies they can help direct. This is nowhere near an exhaustive list; because there are countless crystals, it's helpful to categorize them by their primary elemental associations, although most crystals can fall under multiple elemental categories. Be sure to ethically source your stones. Crystals that help direct earth (material) energy include these:

- **Black tourmaline:** Protection, grounding, banishing negativity
- **Jade:** Prosperity, harmony, health, abundance
- **Malachite:** Transformation, protection, grounding, emotional healing
- **Moss agate:** Growth, stability, connection to nature, prosperity
- **Pyrite:** Abundance, protection, confidence, grounding
- **Obsidian:** Protection, shadow work, clarity
- **Tiger's eye:** Courage, strength, grounding, protection
- **Smoky quartz:** Grounding, detoxification, transformation, release

Crystals that help direct water (emotional) energy include these:

- **Amazonite:** Communication, harmony, truth, emotional balance
- **Aquamarine:** Calm, communication, courage, emotional clarity
- **Emerald:** Love, emotional balance, compassion, renewal
- **Green aventurine:** Luck, prosperity, emotional healing, growth
- **Moonstone:** Intuition, femininity, emotional balance, cycles
- **Rose quartz:** Love, compassion, self-care, emotional healing
- **Unakite:** Emotional healing, balance, grounding, growth

Crystals that help direct fire (creative action) energy include these:

- **Amber:** Motivation, vitality, confidence, creativity
- **Carnelian:** Motivation, vitality, confidence, creativity
- **Citrine:** Abundance, positivity, creativity
- **Dragon Bloodstone:** Strength, courage, grounding, vitality
- **Fire Opal:** Passion, creativity, vitality, transformation
- **Garnet:** Passion, sex, courage, regeneration
- **Red Jasper:** Strength, endurance, passion, grounding
- **Sunstone:** Joy, confidence, empowerment, vitality

Crystals that help direct air (intellectual) energy include the following:

- **Amethyst:** Intuition, protection, peace, spiritual awareness
- **Celestite:** Peace, clarity, spiritual communication, insight
- **Clear quartz:** Amplification, clarity, purification, healing
- **Fluorite:** Focus, clarity, decision-making, spiritual detoxification
- **Labradorite:** Intuition, transformation, protection, magic
- **Selenite:** Cleansing, clarity, connection to the divine

Index

A

B

C

D

E

H

I

L

M

N

Q

R

S

V

W

Y

Z

About the Author

Lorraine Monteagut, PhD, is a queer Latine witch, astrologer, and author. Lorraine studies the diverse backgrounds and traditions of contemporary magical practices. She is the author of *Brujas: The Magic and Power of Witches of Color*, and the creator of Witchy Heights (@witchyheights on Instagram or `witchyheights.com`), where she teaches folk magic, ritual astrology, and spiritual activism.

Dedication

To my parents, Rudy and Gloria, for letting me read whatever I wanted, and to my brothers, Rudy Jr. and Michael, for playing "school" with me.

Author's Acknowledgments

I'm eternally grateful for my fearless agent Kara Rota, who always has an eye out for me. Thanks for sending this wonderful project my way — I never would have imagined a *For Dummies* title like this! Thanks to all the people on the Wiley team who made this possible: to Alicia Sparrow, Lindsay Berg, Kristie Pyles, and Sofia Malik for ushering this project into existence, and especially to my editor, Nicole Sholly, for your constant care and kindness. Thanks to Karen Davis for polishing my writing and to Elana Seplow-Jolley for providing a rigorous technical review. And to the many other people who worked on this book who I didn't have occasion to meet — I appreciate all your efforts to produce great content for the world!

I couldn't have done this without my strong community of friends and family — you know who you are — but I'm especially indebted to my book club for offering much-needed breaks and nurturing creative time between deadlines. Special thanks to the members of Witchy Heights for keeping me afloat while I took on far too much, as usual. And finally, none of this would be possible without the support of my loving partner, Dan Xie — thanks for keeping me, Ava, and Tux alive with constant snuggles and snacks.

Publisher's Acknowledgments

Associate Acquisitions Editor: Alicia Sparrow

Project Manager/Development Editor: Nicole Sholly

Copy Editor: Karen Davis

Technical Editor: Elana Seplow-Jolley

Managing Editor: Sofia Malik

Production Editor: Tamilmani Varadharaj

Cover Image: © samiramay/Adobe Stock